D0288835

Discover
Thailand

Experience the best
of Thailand

This edition written and researched by

China Williams,
Mark Beales, Tim Bewer, Celeste Brash,
Austin Bush, David Eimer, Adam Skolnick

Contents

Contents

Discover Thailand

In Focus

Survival Guide

This Is Thailand

Thailand is blessed: exotic and mysterious yet approachable and hospitable, it has the looks and personality to entice the world to its shores.

Bangkok, the kingdom's capital, is an adrenalin rush. The pace is fast, the spaces cramped and the sights and smells dizzying. It is a bit disorienting at first but addictive for urban junkies.

In contrast, the tranquil southern coast will soothe modern worries. The waters are clear, the diving is spectacular and the pace is akin to an afternoon nap. Thailand's famous islands and beaches specialise in having fun, from beach parties to casual dining. Along the Andaman Coast dramatic limestone mountains cluster like prehistoric monuments.

Beyond the beach scene, Thailand's culture trail educates and enlightens. Witness intense displays of religious devotion and tangible fragments of historic eras. Bangkok, the centre of the Thai universe and the seat of religion and monarchy, boasts flamboyant and revered temples. Further north, the ancient capitals of Ayuthaya and Sukhothai are peppered with gravity-ravaged monuments and serene Buddha figures.

Northern Thailand is all lush mountains, historic cities and border intrigue. The gateway to the region, Chiang Mai, has a well-preserved old city and university atmosphere. In higher altitudes, minority hill tribes preserve a cultural identity that defies modern borders.

In every corner of the kingdom, Thais concoct flavourful feasts from simple ingredients. Travelling from region to region becomes an edible buffet, from fresh coconut curries in southern Thailand to steamy bowls of noodles in Bangkok and hearty stews in Chiang Mai.

> ❝
> In every corner of the kingdom, Thais concoct flavourful feasts
> ❞

Long-tail boat, Hat Phra Nang, Railay (p315)
PHOTOGRAPHER: ANDREW WATSON/GETTY IMAGES ©

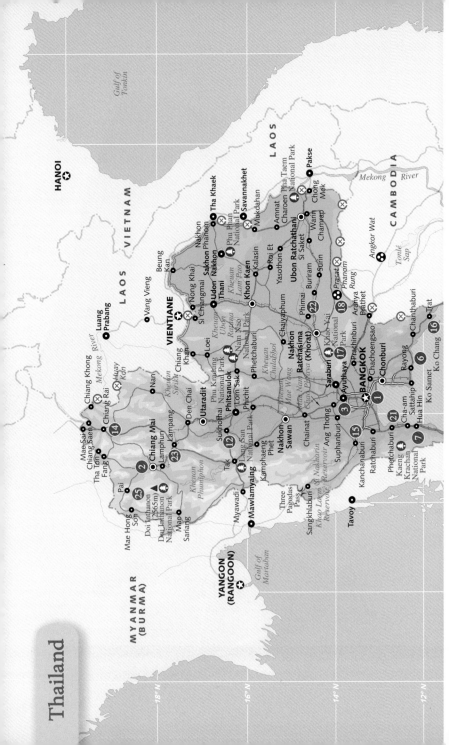

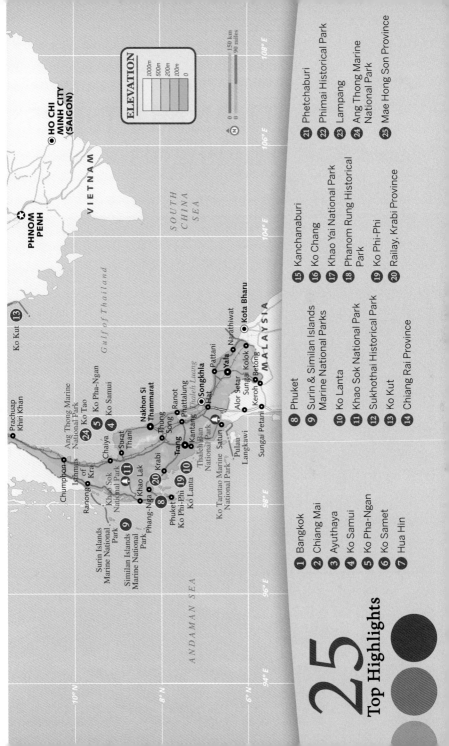

25 Top Highlights

1. Bangkok
2. Chiang Mai
3. Ayuthaya
4. Ko Samui
5. Ko Pha-Ngan
6. Ko Samet
7. Hua Hin
8. Phuket
9. Surin & Similan Islands Marine National Parks
10. Ko Lanta
11. Khao Sok National Park
12. Sukhothai Historical Park
13. Ko Kut
14. Chiang Rai Province
15. Kanchanaburi
16. Ko Chang
17. Khao Yai National Park
18. Phanom Rung Historical Park
19. Ko Phi-Phi
20. Railay, Krabi Province
21. Phetchaburi
22. Phimai Historical Park
23. Lampang
24. Ang Thong Marine National Park
25. Mae Hong Son Province

25
Thailand's Top 25 Highlights

Bangkok

Temples, palaces, malls, restaurants, nightclubs...Bangkok (p51) has it all in super-sized portions. The Bangkok of today is tidier and easier to navigate than ever before, and will pull you in with Chatuchak Weekend Market (p92), one of the world's biggest markets, happening bars, sublime eats and endless opportunities for urban exploration. Supplement your fun with more scholarly pursuits, such as a cooking or Thai massage course, and we're certain you'll see Bangkok as much more than just a transit point.

NIKADA/GETTY IMAGES ©

JOHN ELK/GETTY IMAGES ©

② Chiang Mai

The cultural capital of the north, Chiang Mai (p139) is beloved by temple-spotters and adventure-loving families. The old city is packed with temples built during the Lanna kingdom, while the countryside boasts jungle treks, elephant encounters and minority villages. This laid-back city enjoys fantastic dining thanks to expat imports from Japan and Burma, as well as local specialities including vegetarian fare that will convert carnivores. Above: Wat Chiang Man (p149)

Ayuthaya

Ayuthaya (p106) was once Siam's vibrant, glittering capital packed with hundreds of temples. This emerging regional power hosted seafaring merchants from the east and west and defined the boundaries of much of the modern-day country. Today the splendour of Ayuthaya has been ravaged by war and gravity but the brick-and-stucco ruins, which form a Unesco World Heritage Site, can easily be visited on a cycling tour that evokes their history and artistic legacy. Ayuthaya is an easy day trip north of Bangkok or an alternative landing pad for city phobics. Below: Wat Yai Chai Mongkhon (p107)

STID/GETTY IMAGES ©

The Best...
Beaches

KO PHA-NGAN
Master the art of hammock-hanging. (p268)

KO SAMUI
Devote yourself to sandy beaches, seaside yoga and loads of people-watching. (p257)

KO SAMET
Ditch the chaotic capital for a beach-island fling. (p119)

PHUKET
Bulls-eye high-energy international resort. (p294)

HUA HIN
Mainland surf-and-turf destination for beach frolicking and market noshing. (p250)

KO PHI-PHI
Behold the prettiest (and booziest) tropical island you've ever seen. (p319)

The Best...
Diving &
Snorkelling

**SIMILAN & SURIN ISLANDS
MARINE NATIONAL PARKS**
Snorkel and dive the ac-
claimed reefs of these two
marine preserves; best
visited on live-aboards.
(p293 and p294)

KO TAO
Get dive certified on this
reef-fringed island. (p279)

KO LANTA
Fish big and small flock to
Lanta's coral reefs. (p325)

KO CHANG
Coral-encrusted
seamounts attract turtles
and schools of fish. (p128)

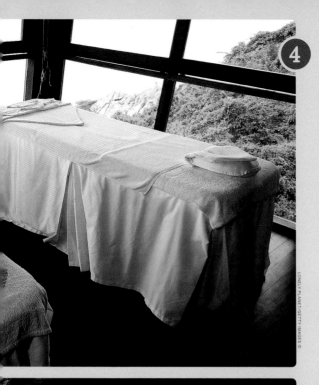

Ko Samui

Eager to please, Ko Samui (p257) is a civilised resort island for the vacationing masses, many of whom fly in and out without having to make much contact with the local culture. Chaweng is a luxurious stretch of sand where sun-worshippers come to see and be seen; but beyond the brassy beach scene are reminders of Samui's old moniker, 'Coconut Island', and a few gentle coves for families. Samui also boasts great amenities and a thriving health scene with yoga, massage, detoxing and other yins to the island's partying yang.

LONELY PLANET/GETTY IMAGES ©

Ko Pha-Ngan

Famous for its sloppy Full Moon parties, Ko Pha-Ngan (p268) has graduated from a sleepy bohemian island to a full-on attraction for migrating party-people. In between the lunar festivities, it still excels in laid-back island life accessible to all, from no-frills backpackers to comfort seekers looking for a less-civilised alternative to Ko Samui. Just offshore is Sail Rock, one of the gulf's best dive sites. Left: Hat Rin (p270)

PETER UNGER/GETTY IMAGES ©

Ko Samet

So close to Bangkok and, oh, so pretty, Ko Samet (p119) is a perfect beach for those pinched for time. The jungle eclipses developments, the sand and sea are tropically proportioned and a wooded coastal trail skirts between rocky headlands and a string of beautiful coves. People-watch by day and party by night on the popular northern beaches or hide away on the southern beaches for a well-earned nap. Right: Roti vendor, Hat Sai Kaew (p119)

KYLIE MCLAUGHLIN/GETTY IMAGES ©

MONTHON WA/GETTY IMAGES ©

Hua Hin

The king's choice, Hua Hin (p250) is a fine fit for city and sea creatures within striking distance of Bangkok. The beaches are long and wide, the market meals are fantastic and there's even Thai culture. Explore the quiet beaches south of the city for a more secluded feel, hike to the top of a headland shrine or master the sea and wind with a kiteboarding lesson. In between seaside frolicking you can feast like Thai royalty from morning to night.

Phuket

An international-strength beach resort, Phuket (p294) is an easy-peasy destination for all ages. You can fly in from Bangkok, cutting out the long land journey, and retreat into a five-star resort or arty boutique hotel for a trouble-free tropical vacation. There are slinky stretches of sand, hedonistic party pits and all the mod cons needed for 21st-century rest and recreation. Add to this day trips to mangrove forests, monkey-rescue centres and a tonne of watersports, from diving to surfing (when the weather is right).

❽

The Best...
Karst Scenery

RAILAY, KRABI PROVINCE
Defy gravity with a rock-climbing scramble up a limestone peak overlooking sparkly seas. (p315)

AO PHANG-NGA
Paddle through a karst canyon into echo-chamber caves at this preserve near Phuket. (p306)

ANG THONG
Discover this deep-ocean collection of limestone islands in the Gulf of Thailand. (p269)

KO PHI-PHI LEH
Snorkel the crags and coves of the Andaman's rocky towers. (p322)

PETE ATKINSON/GETTY IMAGES ©

Surin & Similan Islands Marine National Parks

These world-renowned parks have anchored Thailand as a global diving destination. Live-aboard trips set out from Khao Lak, allowing for more time at the famous sites, where you can meet manta rays and whale sharks. And there is the thrill of being far from land as the sun sinks into the sea and the night shows off its twinkling lights. Back on land, the islands (p293 and p294) are an attraction in their own right, with jungle-filled interiors and smooth beaches surrounded by decent coral reefs.

The Best...
Historic Sites

SUKHOTHAI
Cycle among the ruins of an early Thai kingdom for a meditative journey into the past. (p213)

AYUTHAYA
Tumbledown temples of a former ancient capital now surrounded by a busy provincial town. (p106)

PHIMAI
The closest Khmer ruin to Bangkok for history buffs short on time. (p135)

PHANOM RUNG
An ornate sanctuary of Khmer art overlooking a hardscrabble bucolic landscape. (p136)

PHETCHABURI
A royal hilltop retreat just a skip and a hop south of Bangkok. (p248)

IMAGE SOURCE/GETTY IMAGES ©

Ko Lanta

Far-flung Ko Lanta (p324) sports a mellow island vibe even though it has migrated on to the package-tour circuit. The flat island has a parade of peachy sand beaches that are scenic but not stunning. Social butterflies alight on the northern beaches for a same-same-but-different party scene. Solitude seekers migrate southward to low-key bungalows and a sleepy village ambiance. Activities abound, from hiking through a landscape of limestone caves and crevices to diving in underwater hang-outs for sharks and rays.

Khao Sok National Park

A deep, dark jungle hugs the midsection of southern Thailand. This ancient rainforest (p290) is filled with long sweaty hiking routes up dramatic limestone formations with postcard views. Just remember to wear leechproof gear to prevent an involuntary blood donation. Birds and bats call this forest home as does the rare *Rafflesia kerrii,* one of the stinkiest flowers on the planet. Reward your outdoor work with a relaxing stay at one of the lakeside lodges and listen to the symphony of the jungle.

Sukhothai Historical Park

Step back in time about 800 years at Thailand's most impressive historical park (p213). Exploring the ruins by bicycle is the classic Thailand experience and is a leisurely way to wind past the crumbling temples, graceful Buddha statues and fish-filled ponds. Worthwhile museums and good-value accommodation round out the package. Despite its popularity, Sukhothai rarely feels crowded, but for something off the beaten track head to nearby Si Satchanalai-Chaliang Historical Park, where you might be the only one scaling an ancient stairway.

Ko Kut

Bangkok Thais, families and middle-aged couples move beyond busy Ko Chang to this semi-developed island best known for seclusion and scenery. There's no shopping, dining or nightlife, which suits everyone just fine. This island (p132) excels in layabout living: wake up, wander the beach, snack on tropical fruit, swim, nap under a coconut tree and wait for sunset. Active types scoot between the west coast beaches on a motorcycle, hike the jungle tracks to waterfalls and kayak through mangroves.

Chiang Rai Province

Thailand, Laos and Myanmar converge in what was once a lawless area known as the Golden Triangle, formerly the centre of opium poppy cultivation. Chiang Rai (p195) still packs intrigue in the form of fresh-air fun and country scenery. Chiang Rai town is known for its trekking tours while further flung explorations lead to the Chinese ridget-op hamlet of Mae Salong, the border town of Mae Sai and the river town of Chiang Khong. Below: Wat Rong Khun (p199)

The Best...
Temples

BANGKOK
Glittering and ornate temples protect the faith and attract the faithful. (p60)

CHIANG MAI
A hilltop temple crowns the city's guardian mountain, while teak temples fill the atmospheric old quarter. (p152 and p161)

SUKHOTHAI
Majestic ruins set in a peaceful historic park that's perfect for meditative meanderings. (p213)

PHITSANULOK
Revered bronze Buddha conveniently located along the culture trail. (p210)

The Best...
Shopping

BANGKOK
From markets to malls, you can practically shop anywhere for just about anything. (p93)

CHIANG MAI
Specialises in homespun and chic handicrafts sold at popular pedestrian street fairs. (p174)

LAMPANG
The weekend bazaar turns this city's historic shophouse district into a night on the town. (p193)

CHIANG RAI
The night markets and weekend bazaar peddle hilltribe and northern crafts. (p201)

15

Kanchanaburi

Walks on the wild side are the main reason to visit Kanchanaburi (p111), where dragon-scaled limestone mountains gaze down upon dense jungle. Trek past silvery waterfalls and rushing rivers in search of elusive tigers and gibbons, then spend the night at a homestay organised through an ethnic group. Once you've explored this western province's wartime past – the infamous Death Railway Bridge (p114) is here – hold on tightly to experience the area's adventure activities, which include ziplining, kayaking, elephant rides and hiking to the top of Erawan waterfalls (p121).

Above: Death Railway Bridge; Left: Erawan waterfalls

(ABOVE) WALTER BIBIKOW/GETTY IMAGES © (LEFT) KIMBERLEY COOLE/GETTY IMAGES ©

Ko Chang

Steep mountains rise out of the blue seas of Thailand's far-eastern territorial waters. This jungle-clad island (p125) has a bustling resort atmosphere with plenty of party places, belying its distance from civilisation. It is an athletic island with a variety of adventure sports: diving, snorkelling, hiking and kayaking. In the evenings the tide recedes and the narrow beaches become wide swaths of rippled sand dotted with elegant spiral-shelled molluscs. The west coast is very busy but the east coast is barely developed. Right: Hat Sai Khao (p126)

Khao Yai National Park

Here you'll find elephants, monkeys, gibbons, hornbills, pythons, bears, a million bats and a few wily tigers. Wildlife sightings, of course, are at the mercy of chance, but your odds are excellent at this vast Unesco World Heritage–listed reserve (p112) just a few hours outside Bangkok. Even if you don't meet many big animals, the orchids, birds and waterfalls guarantee a good day.

Phanom Rung Historical Park

Perched high atop an extinct volcano, the biggest Khmer ruin (p136) in Thailand is something special. As you amble along the promenade, up the stairs and over the *naga*-flanked bridges, the sense of anticipation builds. When you enter the temple, completely restored and rich with Hindu sculpture, you will experience a moment of timelessness. It's not as awe-inspiring as Cambodia's Angkor Wat, but impressive and different enough to require a visit.

18

JOHN ELK/GETTY IMAGES ©

The Best...
Jungle Trekking

KHAO YAI NATIONAL PARK
Monkeys, elephants, wilderness – just around the corner from Bangkok. (p112)

KHAO SOK NATIONAL PARK
Trek and paddle through this southern tropical rainforest. (p290)

KANCHANABURI
Elephant riding, river rafting and waterfall spotting close to Bangkok. (p111)

CHIANG RAI PROVINCE
Visit high-altitude hilltribe villages for physical exertion and cultural immersion. (p195)

MAE HONG SON PROVINCE
A remote, mountainous corner overlooking Myanmar (Burma). (p227)

KO CHANG
Reward a sweaty hike with a sea view. (p125)

Ko Phi-Phi

Quite possibly the prettiest island in all of Thailand, Ko Phi-Phi (p319) has gorgeous blonde-sand beaches, scenic limestone cliffs and jewel-toned waters. It's a carless and carefree island where the parties last all night and sound systems serenade the stars. Don't come looking for serenity. Its sister island Ko Phi-Phi Leh (p322) is an uninhabited park where snorkelling tours explore offshore coral reefs and interior lagoons. And, of late, party boats sail among the scenery, tipple in hand. Right: Ko Phi-Phi Leh

GLENN VAN DER KNIJFF/GETTY IMAGES ©

The Best...
Thai Food

BANGKOK
A culinary superstar covering all the bases: humble noodles, haute cuisine and immigrant comfort food. (p79)

CHIANG MAI
This northern town excels in vegetarian cuisine and Thai cooking courses. (p164)

HUA HIN
The always reliable night market serves sensational seafood with a street-fair atmosphere. (p252)

PHUKET
Sample simple southern fare, beachside seafood and high-end fusion. (p299)

Railay, Krabi Province

You'd never know that you were still on the mainland when you wade from a long-tail boat to the shore of this limestone-studded peninsula (p315). Towering karst peaks hem in all sides, creating the illusion of a sandy fortress. Rock climbers have transformed the onshore sea cliffs into vertical challenges, scrambling high enough for a view of the karst-filled bay. Kayakers and snorkellers take to the sea to explore low-tide caves and peek at the marine life sheltered by these hulking missile-shaped islands.

ALEX HARE/GETTY IMAGES ©

Phetchaburi

A delightful mix of culture lies within this provincial capital (p248). Explore a former royal hilltop palace frequented by mischievous monkeys. Head out of town to dramatically lit caves boasting Buddhist shrines and naturally occurring calcified sculptures. Then wander the shophouse neighbourhood filled with old-fashioned businesses. The town is an easy escape from Bangkok and an under-appreciated detour en route to the southern beaches.

Right: Tham Khao Luang (p248)

Phimai Historical Park

Southeast Asia's once great superpower, the Khmer empire, was a dedicated monument builder, adorning trade routes with elaborate temple complexes that stretched from the empire's capital of Angkor into its vast frontier in present-day Thailand. Of its surviving monuments, Phimai (p135) is Thailand's best restored Khmer-era temple. This mini-Angkor poses near the town of Phimai; it's an easy day trip from Khorat, or go overnight from Bangkok.

Lampang

A classic northern Thai town, Lampang (p192) boasts a well-preserved old city where lumber barons built teak manses and Burmese-style temples dominate the skyline. Often described as a mini-Chiang Mai, Lampang is more popular with domestic tourists than foreigners; they are carted around town in horse-drawn carriages, a tradition believed to have been inherited from Yunnanese traders who rode horses along their long-distance trade routes. Outside of town is a government-run elephant conservation centre and a veterinary hospital for pachyderms. Below: Wat Phra Kaew Don Tao (p193)

23

The Best...
Elephant Encounters

CHIANG MAI
The centre of elephant tourism, ranging from camps to sanctuaries and offering jungle treks and conservation education. (p154)

LAMPANG
Learn about the mahout tradition at an elephant education centre. (p195)

AYUTHAYA
Visit the temple ruins like the kings of yore, astride a regally clad elephant. (p114)

KANCHANABURI
Get a canopy view of the forest on an elephant ride. (p115)

JOHN ELK/GETTY IMAGES ©

Ang Thong Marine National Park

Accessible on a boat tour from Ko Samui, this collection of limestone mountain islands (p269) appears on the distant horizon like a lost city. Peach-coloured sand rings the hump-backed peaks, and interior lagoons glow an otherworldly blue. Kayaking, snorkelling and hiking tours on various islands give you a close-up of the pockmarked formations inhabited by barnacles and other tidal creatures. Development is limited to basic park infrastructure, preserving the wild and remote ambience.

24

MICHELE FALZONE/GETTY IMAGES ©

The Best...
Scenic Journeys

MAE SA VALLEY
Climb from the sweaty plains to the cool conifer zone on this mountain loop from Chiang Mai. (p178)

MAE HONG SON
Cascading mountain vistas are the reward for enduring dizzying switchback roads. (p234)

BANGKOK CANALS
Take a long-tail boat through the 'Venice of the East'. (p89)

MAE SALONG
Ride up the ridge to this mountain-top village known for tea cultivation and its Chinese heritage. (p202)

25

Mae Hong Son Province

Tucked in the country's northwest corner, this province (p234) has a lot more in common with neighbouring Myanmar (Burma) than Bangkok, and the provincial capital of Mae Hong Son can seem like a different country altogether. The town excels in hilltribe treks that strike the right balance between being accessible but not overrun by tourists. And in the mountain retreat of Pai, you can soak up the scenery by day and party in cosy blues clubs all night.

Thailand's Top Itineraries

Bangkok to Chiang Dao Jet-Setters' Game Plan

5 DAYS

Thailand makes an easy 'pop-in' for anyone passing through the eastern half of the globe. Touch down in Bangkok, jet to Chiang Mai and escape the urban grind in Chiang Dao.

CHIANG DAO **3**
CHIANG MAI **2**
LAOS
BURMA (MYANMAR)
ANDAMAN SEA
BANGKOK **1**
Gulf of Thailand

1 Bangkok (p51)

Introduce yourself to one of Asia's most dynamic capitals with a two-day crash course. Be dazzled by Wat Phra Kaew, get lost in the cluttered but peaceful temple grounds of Wat Pho and hop across the river to Wat Arun. Cruise back to your hotel aboard the Chao Phraya Express, soaking up the river scenery. Catch dinner at an upscale Thai restaurant and then drink to the stars from a rooftop bar. The next day, shop till you drop at MBK Center then admire the pretty Thai antiques at Jim Thompson House. Stay out late at the rollicking bars and clubs and then grab a noodle nightcap at Soi 38 Night Market.

BANGKOK ◯ CHIANG MAI
✈ **One hour** Fly from Bangkok's Don Muang and Suvarnabhumi airports

2 Chiang Mai (p139)

In this laid-back university town, explore the old quarter, filled with the distinctive temple architecture of northern Thailand. Slurp down a bowl of *kôw soy*, the north's signature noodle dish, and hang out at

Riverside Bar & Restaurant. The next day, make a morning pilgrimage to the cool environs of Doi Suthep and its sacred temple. If you're here on a weekend, visit the Saturday or Sunday Walking Street. Book a cooking course or outdoor activity, like elephant trekking, kayaking or ziplining.

CHIANG MAI ◯ CHIANG DAO
🚗 **One hour** Via Hwy 107

3 Chiang Dao (p179)

After the big-city buzz you'll need a country escape and this small hamlet is just the place. Guesthouses stretch out along the base of the town's namesake mountain surrounded by fruit orchards and jungle-landscaped gardens. It is an instant elixir to city fatigue. Cruise around the back roads through hilltribe villages and small-scale farms, explore Tham Chiang Dao, or visit the Elephant Training Centre in a lush forested setting. Trekking here is ultra low-key with smaller groups and more self-exploration options. And everyone dines at Chiang Dao Nest's exceptional restaurant. To save yourself from backtracking through Bangkok, book your return flight from Chiang Mai.

Wat Phra Kaew (p60), Bangkok

5 DAYS

Bangkok to Hua Hin Travellers' Buffet

Sample a little of everything – culture, nature and beaches – on this quick and convenient tour of sites within a half-day's journey from Bangkok.

② KANCHANABURI

① BANGKOK

Gulf of Thailand

HUA HIN ③

BURMA (MYANMAR)

① Bangkok (p51)

If you're a small-town kid, you might find Thailand's hip and happening city to be as enjoyable as a slap in the face. To avoid the urban mayhem, focus your sightseeing on historic temples along the river and then head out on a canal tour aboard a long-tail boat. Catch the Chao Phraya Express to Ko Kret, an island north of Bangkok known for pottery and its kick-back village lifestyle. If you don't have the time to tour all of Thailand's historic sites, then see them in facsimile at the Ancient City in Samut Prakan. This attraction sounds cheesy but is actually an impressive example of architectural curatorship and makes for a quirky day trip from Bangkok. After two days, you've dodged enough traffic to justify plotting an escape to the nearby towns for a slower pace.

BANGKOK ○ KANCHANABURI

🚌 **Two hours** Departing Bangkok's Victory Monument

② Kanchanaburi (p111)

This western town enjoys a scenic riverside setting with enough traveller amenities to feel comfortable without being conspicuous. Spend a day touring the town's unusual role in WWII at the Thailand-Burma Railway Centre Museum, Death Railway Bridge and Allied War Cemetery. All of these sites can be visited by bicycle. The next day book a tour for one of Thailand's quintessential nature escapes complete with elephant trekking and bamboo rafting. Kanchanaburi's countryside is a delightful mixture of sugar cane fields and thick forests. If you would rather do it yourself, head out of town to visit Erawan National Park (get there early to avoid the tour groups) and Hellfire Pass Memorial. Don't forget to grab dinner at the night market, a well-loved provincial pastime.

KANCHANABURI ○ HUA HIN

🚌 **Three hours** Transfer at Ratchaburi

③ Hua Hin (p250)

Enjoy the ocean without leaving civilisation at this seaside town. Middle-class Thais are Hua Hin's bread and butter and they prefer ocean scenery over ocean frolicking. That means that the city is one big culinary excursion with lively seafood markets, sweaty but revered stir-fry shacks and pier restaurants. There's a long and lovely beach for strolls in between meals. And the seasonal winds make this beach a destination for kiteboarding. Just beyond the city are lush hills where the Hua Hin Hill Vineyard is reinventing winemaking for the tropics. If you have time, nature escapes can be made to Khao Sam Roi Yot National Park, a coastal collection of limestone mountains and inland marshes visited by migratory bird species.

Erawan waterfalls, Erawan National Park (p121)
ANDREW JOHN WELLS/GETTY IMAGES ©

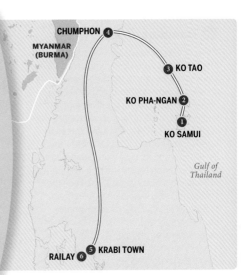

Ko Samui to Railay
Going Bi-Coastal

Soak up the tropical scenery by surveying the beaches and islands of Thailand's famed coasts. Flights from Bangkok to Ko Samui shorten the journey and minibuses burn rubber across the peninsula.

CHUMPHON 4

MYANMAR (BURMA)

3 KO TAO

KO PHA-NGAN 2

1

KO SAMUI

Gulf of Thailand

5 KRABI TOWN

RAILAY 6

❶ Ko Samui (p257)

Make a beeline to the quiet northern beaches of Choeng Mon, Bo Phut and Mae Nam. Dine at one of Fisherman's Village's trendy restaurants. Sunbathe with the masses on Chaweng, Samui's stunning stretch of sand. Just offshore are a handful of toothy limestone islands that make up the Ang Thong Marine National Park, most easily visited on a day tour: visitors kayak and snorkel amongst curious rock formations, semi-submerged tunnels and hidden lagoons.

KO SAMUI ⟩ KO PHA-NGAN

⚓ **20 minutes to one hour** Depart from various piers on Ko Samui

❷ Ko Pha-Ngan (p268)

The boho of the bunch, Ko Pha-Ngan excels in taking it easy, especially on the barely developed east coast. But when the moon is full, the island transforms into a party werewolf with tens of thousands of revellers crowding onto the day-glo-lit beach of Hat Rin; it's a serious scene, not suitable for mere spectators. Solitude seekers and families should visit during different lunar phases when the island returns to its full-time profession of hammock-hanging.

KO PHA-NGAN ⟩ KO TAO

⚓ **One hour** Depart from Ko Pha-Ngan's Thong Sala pier

❸ Ko Tao (p275)

This little island garners international attention not for its beaches but for its many near-shore coral gardens and dive sites. Strap on your snorkelling gear and do an island swimming tour with the fishes, or dive to greater depths to explore underwater landscapes and spot mysterious ocean dwellers.

KO TAO ⟩ CHUMPHON

⚓ **1½ to three hours**

❹ Chumphon (p255)

A ho-hum southern town, Chumphon is the mainland way-station for beach-bound transport. Ko Tao ferries dock just in time for minivans to vacuum up the sun-soaked faces bound for the opposite coast.

CHUMPHON ⟩ KRABI TOWN

🚌 **Five to six hours** Minibus

❺ Krabi Town (p313)

Krabi Town is a transit link for travellers sliding through to the Andaman's stunning karst scenery, which is even prettier than the very pretty gulf coast. Krabi has an airport for a quick return to Bangkok.

KRABI TOWN ⟩ RAILAY

⚓ **45 minutes** Leave from Krabi's Khong Kha pier

❻ Railay (p315)

Stunning karst mountains jutting out of jewel-coloured seas define Railay's pinched bit of sand. If the view from the ground isn't good enough, strap on a harness for a climb up the cliffs to find the horizon. A kayak trip skimming through the towers might offer a better perspective. If not, a sunset cocktail might just do the trick.

Ang Thong Marine National Park (p269)
WATERFALL WILLIAM /GETTY IMAGES ©

Ayuthaya to Chiang Rai Province
The Culture Trail

Follow the culture trail from the ancient capital of Ayuthaya to the Lanna headquarters of Chiang Mai and on to Chiang Rai province, a mix of cultures informed by the border setting.

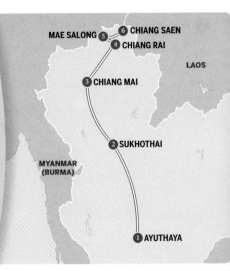

MAE SALONG ⑤ ⑥ CHIANG SAEN
④ CHIANG RAI
LAOS
③ CHIANG MAI
MYANMAR (BURMA)
② SUKHOTHAI
① AYUTHAYA

① Ayuthaya (p106)

Balance out Bangkok's conspicuous consumption with culture in the ancient capital of Ayuthaya. Hire a bicycle, an elephant taxi or a knowledgeable guide for a tour of the Unesco World Heritage–listed ruins, built when this powerful city-state was a stop on the Asian trade-winds route. Ayuthaya is an easy train, bus or minivan ride from Bangkok.

AYUTHAYA ◗ SUKHOTHAI

🚌 **Seven hours** From Ayuthaya's long-distance bus station

② Sukhothai (p212)

The ruins of one of Thailand's first kingdoms reside in a peaceful parklike setting far enough from the modern city of Sukhothai to feel like a lost treasure. Hire a bicycle and spend the day cycling among the eternally meditating Buddha figures and gravity-worn temples. For ruins among the countryside, do a day trip to Si Satchanalai-Chaliang Historical Park, where the surrounding rice paddies and dusty villages are part of the attraction.

SUKHOTHAI ◗ CHIANG MAI

🚌 **Six hours** From Sukhothai's bus station

③ Chiang Mai (p139)

The north's cultural capital, Chiang Mai can easily monopolise three days while you wander around the old city, admiring temples and poking around the handicraft shops for gifts and souvenirs. Spend an evening with the carefree university students along the fashionable avenue of Th Nimmanhaemin.

CHIANG MAI ◗ CHIANG RAI

🚌 **Three to four hours** From Chiang Mai's Arcade bus station

④ Chiang Rai (p195)

Bordering Myanmar and Laos, this northern province is known for its idyllic mountain scenery and ethnic cultures. The provincial capital is a delightful place to sip locally grown coffee and admire northern-style temples before heading off on a trekking tour led by philanthropic NGOs. Don't forget to visit Wat Rong Khun, outside of town.

CHIANG RAI ◗ MAE SALONG

🚌 **30 minutes** Transfer at Ban Pasang, then it's **one hour** by sorng·taa·ou

⑤ Mae Salong (p202)

Leave Thailand without crossing any borders with a day trip to this ethnic Chinese community perched on the spine of a mountain. The slopes are cultivated by tea plantations and the surrounding countryside populated by hilltribe villages. It is an easy day trip or you can stay overnight if you fall in love with the view.

MAE SALONG ◗ CHIANG SAEN

🚌 **30 minutes** Ban Pasang to Chiang Rai; 🚌 **1½ hours** Chiang Rai to Chiang Saen

⑥ Chiang Saen (p207)

An early Lanna kingdom called this sleepy riverside town home. Several tumbledown ruins attest to the era while the modern town hosts Chinese river barges and Mekong River trips.

Wat Si Sawai (p214), Sukhothai Historical Park
JEAN-PIERRE LESCOURRET/GETTY IMAGES ©

Phuket to Mae Hong Son Province
From Sea to Summit

In two weeks, you can slide down the Andaman Coast and hit some of the hot spots: party beaches, dive sites and scenic bays. Then swing north for an altitude adjustment.

① Phuket (p294)

An easy island to reach if transiting by air from Bangkok, Phuket dominates the comfort class for international beach retreats. Spend a day or two downshifting into the island way of life. Take a beach break with a visit to Ao Phang-Nga for its unforgettable scenery and Phuket Town for a historic perspective on this former port town. If Phuket is too urban, stay overnight in Ko Yao, a pair of sleepy Thai-Muslim fishing islands with an unforgettable karst landscape.

PHUKET ⬤ KO PHI-PHI

⚓ **Two hours** Depart from Phuket's Tha Rasada

② Ko Phi-Phi (p319)

An island with perfect proportions, Ko Phi-Phi is decidedly less civilised than Phuket and a bit wilder (in the partying sense). But for quiet types, there are some secluded corners and close proximity to well-known dive sites to the south, snorkelling around Phi-Phi's uninhabited sister island and even rock climbing vertical karst cliffs. After all these outings, reserve some night-time stamina, as this is a devout party beach.

KO PHI-PHI ⬤ KO LANTA

⚓ **1½ hours**

③ Ko Lanta (p324)

If Phi-Phi is too popular for you, then defect to Ko Lanta, which is deliciously low-key though not as heart-achingly pretty. Lanta's personality charms its fans with a friendly, kick-back attitude and none of the brash beach resort distractions. It also goes to bed at a respectable hour unlike some other beaches. Families typically opt for Lanta over rowdy Phi-Phi. Lanta is also admired by divers because of its proximity to the famed Hin Daeng and Hin Muang dive sites.

KO LANTA ⬤ CHIANG MAI

🚌 **1½ hours** Ko Lanta to Krabi; ✈ **1¾ hours** Krabi to Chiang Mai

④ Chiang Mai (p139)

Meet the 'rose of the north', a charming northern city filled with culture, outdoor escapes and down-to-earth but delicious food. Join a cooking class to master the market and turn a handful of ingredients into

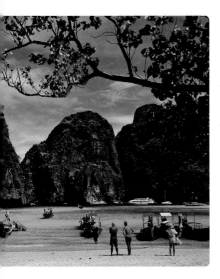

Ao Maya, Ko Phi-Phi Leh (p322)
GLENN VAN DER KNIJFF/GETTY IMAGES ©

like you earned the right to be in a Pai state of mind.

PAI ◯ MAE HONG SON
🚌 Four hours

⑥ Mae Hong Son (p234)

The next stop on the northwest mountain circuit is this provincial capital that attracts cultural enthusiasts turned off by Pai's party scene. Mae Hong Son displays its Burmese heritage with distinctive temple architecture and signature market meals. It is also a gateway to remote jungle landscapes and offers a less popular trekking scene than Chiang Mai. There are daily flights back to Chiang Mai to speed up your return to the lowlands.

a complex curry. Wander the temples, admiring northern-style art and architecture, chatting with the monks about Buddhism and becoming a connoisseur of the temple massage. Head out of town for an ascension of Doi Inthanon, one of Thailand's highest peaks, for a glimpse into the Thai pastime of sampling winter.

CHIANG MAI ◯ PAI
🚌 Three hours From Chiang Mai's Arcade bus station; ✈ 1½ hours From Chiang Mai International Airport

⑤ Pai (p227)

From Chiang Mai, climb into the forested frontier that Thailand shares with Myanmar (Burma). Stop for a while in Pai, a mountain retreat for artists, backpackers and urban Thais. Pai does a little bit of everything: partying, mainly; trekking, some; and a lot of hanging out. Remember to bring some cool-weather clothes as the mountains get chilly after dark. Air travel is faster but you'll miss out on the twisty-turny mountain roads that make you feel

Thailand Month by Month

January

The weather is cool and dry, ushering in the peak tourist season.

⚡ **Chinese New Year**

Thais with Chinese ancestry celebrate the Chinese lunar new year (*drùt jeen*) with a week of house-cleaning and fireworks.

February

Still in the high season, snowbirds flock to Thailand for sun and fun.

⚡ **Makha Bucha**

One of three holy days marking important moments of Buddha's life, Makha Bucha (*mah·ká boo·chah*) falls on the full moon of the third lunar month. It is a public holiday.

⚡ **Flower Festival**

Chiang Mai displays its floral beauty during a three-day period. The festival highlight is the flower-decorated floats that parade through town.

March

Hot and dry season approaches and the beaches start to empty out. This is also Thailand's semester break, and students head out on sightseeing trips.

⭐ **Pattaya International Music Festival**

Pattaya showcases pop and rock bands from across Asia at this free music event, attracting bus loads of Bangkok university students.

🪁 **Kite-Flying Festivals**

During the windy season, colourful kites battle it out over the skies of Sanam Luang in Bangkok and elsewhere in the country.

(Left) April Songkran, Chiang Mai
PETER UNGER/GETTY IMAGES ©

Golden Mango Season

Luscious ripe mangoes come into season from March to June and are sliced before your eyes, packed in a container with sticky rice and accompanied with a sweet sauce.

April

Hot, dry weather sweeps across the land. Though the tourist season is winding down, make reservations well in advance as the whole country is on the move for Songkran.

Songkran

Thailand's traditional new year (13–15 April) starts out as a respectful affair then degenerates into a water war. Morning visits to the temple involve colourful processions and water-sprinkling ceremonies of sacred Buddha images. Afterwards, Thais load up their water guns and head out to the streets for battle. Chiang Mai and Bangkok are the epicentres.

May

Leading up to the rainy season, festivals encourage plentiful rains and bountiful harvests. Prices are low and tourists are few but it is still incredibly hot.

Royal Ploughing Ceremony

This royal ceremony employs astrology and ancient Brahman rituals to kick off the rice-planting season. Sacred oxen are hitched to a wooden plough and part the ground of Sanam Luang in Bangkok.

Rocket Festival

In the northeast, where rain can be scarce, villagers craft bamboo rockets (bâng fai) that are fired into the sky to encourage precipitation. This festival is celebrated in Yasothon, Ubon Ratchathani and Nong Khai.

Visakha Bucha

The holy day of Visakha Bucha (wí·săh·kà boo·chah) falls on the 15th day of the waxing moon in the sixth lunar month and commemorates the date of the Buddha's birth, enlightenment and parinibbana (passing away).

June

In some parts of the country, the rainy season is merely an afternoon shower, leaving the rest of the day for music and merriment. This month is a shoulder season.

Hua Hin Jazz Festival

Jazz groups descend on this royal retreat for a musical homage to the king, an accomplished jazz saxophonist and composer.

Phi Ta Khon

The Buddhist holy day of Bun Phra Wet is given a Carnival makeover in Dan Sai village in northeast Thailand. Revellers disguise themselves in garish 'spirit' costumes and parade through the streets wielding wooden phalluses and downing rice whisky. Dates vary between June and July.

July

The start of the rainy season ushers in Buddhist Lent, a period of reflection and meditation. Summer holidays bring an upsurge in tourists.

Asanha Bucha

The full moon of the eighth lunar month commemorates Buddha's first sermon, in which he described the religion's four noble truths. It is considered one of Buddhism's holiest days.

October

Religious preparations for the end of the rainy season and the end of Buddhist Lent begin. The monsoons are reaching the finish line (in most of the country).

🍴 Vegetarian Festival

A holiday from meat is taken for nine days in adherence with Chinese beliefs of mind and body purification. In Phuket the festival gets extreme, with entranced marchers turning themselves into human shish kebabs.

✹ Ork Phansaa

The end of the Buddhist lent (three lunar months after Khao Phansaa) is followed by the *gà·tǐn* ceremony, in which new robes are given to the monks by merit-makers.

✹ King Chulalongkorn Day

Rama V is honoured on the anniversary of his death at the Royal Plaza in Dusit. Held on 23 October.

November

The cool, dry season has arrived and if you get here early enough, you'll beat the tourist crowds. The beaches are inviting and the landscape is lush.

✹ Surin Elephant Round-Up

Held on the third weekend of November, Thailand's biggest elephant show celebrates this province's most famous residents.

✹ Loi Krathong

One of Thailand's most beloved festivals, Loi Krathong

✹ Khao Phansaa

The day after Asanha Bucha marks the beginning of Buddhist Lent (the first day of the waning moon in the eighth lunar month), the traditional time for men to enter the monastery. In Ubon Ratchathani, traditional candle offerings have grown into a festival of elaborately carved wax sculptures.

August

Overcast skies and daily showers mark the middle of the rainy season.

✹ HM the Queen's Birthday

The Thai Queen's Birthday (12 August) is a public holiday and national mother's day.

is celebrated on the first full moon of the 12th lunar month. Small origami-like boats (called *krathong* or *grà·tong*) festooned with flowers and candles are sent adrift in the waterways. Northern Thais call this festival Yi Peng, which is traditionally celebrated by launching illuminated lanterns into the night sky.

🎇 Lopburi Monkey Festival

During the last week of November, the town's troublesome macaques get pampered with their very own banquet, while merit-makers watch merrily.

December

The peak of the tourist season has returned with fair skies, busy beach resorts and a holiday mood.

🎇 HM the King's Birthday

Honouring the King's birthday on 5 December, this public holiday hosts parades and merit-making events. Everyone wears pink shirts, pink being the colour associated with the monarchy.

Far left: October Vegetarian Festival, Phuket Town **Below: November** Yi Peng, Chiang Mai

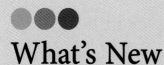

What's New

For this new edition of Discover Thailand, our authors hunted down the fresh, the transformed, the hot and the happening. Here are a few of our favourite things. For up-to-the-minute recommendations, see lonelyplanet.com/thailand

1 FLY EVERYWHERE
Air routes now link every provincial capital to Bangkok so that you can skip those frigid overnight bus journeys. You can also fly from Phuket and Chiang Mai to major Chinese cities. And Ko Pha-Ngan's drunken Full Moon raves just got easier to get to; a privately owned airport served by Kan Air's turboprop planes is scheduled to open in 2014.

2 ASIA DISCOVERS ITSELF
Chinese, Indians, Koreans, Singaporeans and more – Asia's emerging middle class is backpacking, package touring and weekending in Thailand. Russians are on board too, especially for the Gulf of Thailand beaches.

3 OVERLAND TO/FROM MYANMAR
The cloistered country of Myanmar (Burma) is now 'open' and foreigners can enter and exit from one of four land borders with Thailand. Well, sort of. The most open crossing is Mae Sot to Myawaddy.

4 TAKE ME TO ANGKOR
There is a new government bus from Bangkok direct to Siem Reap that cuts out some of the hassles of the infamous Aranya Prathet–Poipet border. However, scams are rampant and there's still the line at immigration.

5 HIP HOSTELS
Bangkok and Chiang Mai have sprouted hip hostels, where sleeping with the pack means saving baht and scoring style points. Now solo travellers have an alternative to single occupancy.

6 THE CORAL BLEACH JOB
In recent years, rising sea temperatures have caused coral bleaching and even coral death. Snorkelling sites in shallow waters have been hit the worst.

7 WHAT A WRECK
Ko Chang and Ko Tao both have new wreck dives created by decommissioned Thai navy ships. In Tao the wreck dive is accessible to novice divers with regular scuba gear. Meanwhile, Ko Pha-Ngan has cheap scuba schools and Ranong now has live-aboards.

8 BRIDGING BORDERS
The fourth Mekong River Bridge now links Laos and Thailand via Huay Xai–Chiang Khong, making the crossing faster and easier for shipping and passenger travel to Laos and Yunnan, China.

9 CAFFEINATED & CULTURED CHIANG MAI
New and professional culture museums have replaced the government offices that once occupied Chiang Mai's old city, and cafes and fruit shake stands outnumber 7-Elevens.

10 THE LOCAL PRESS KNOWS BEST
Protests have been in full swing in Bangkok of late and there is seemingly no good solution ahead. Stay informed about rally sights (and avoid them) through the local press. Follow Richard Barrow on Twitter for on-the-ground coverage.

Get Inspired

📖 Books

o **Very Thai: Everyday Popular Culture** (Philip Cornwel-Smith) Colourful compendium of the kingdom's whys and whats, from dashboard shrines to uniform obsessions.

o **Fieldwork** (Mischa Berlinski) A story about a fictional hill-tribe village in northern Thailand.

o **Sightseeing** (Rattawut Lapcharoensap) Short stories that provide a 'sightseeing' tour of Thai life.

o **The Beach** (Alex Garland) Follows a backpacker's discovery of a secluded island utopia.

o **King Bhumibol Adulyadej: A Life's Work** (Nicholas Grossman et al) Official biography of the king.

o **The Judgement** (Chart Korbjitti) A SEA Write award-winning novel about a young village man wrongly accused of a crime.

🎞 Films

o **Paradoxocracy** (Pen-ek Ratanaruang; 2013) Traces the country's political history from the 1932 revolution to today.

o **36** (Nawapol Thamrongrattanarit; 2012) Indie love affair remembered through 36 static camera set-ups.

o **Pee Mak Phra Khanong** (Banjong Pisanthanakun; 2013) Perennial ghost story gets a comedy makeover.

o **Fah Talai Jone** (Tears of the Black Tiger; 2000) Wisit Sasanatieng pays tribute to Thai action flicks.

🎵 Music

o **That Song** (Modern Dog) Anthemic alt-rock.

o **Best** (Pumpuang Duangjan) The best from the late country diva.

o **Boomerang** (Bird Thongchai) Beloved album from the king of Thai pop.

o **Romantic Comedy** (Apartment Khunpa) Leading post alt-rock.

o **The Sound of Siam: Leftfield Luk Thung, Jazz & Molam in Thailand 1964–1975** Compilation of vintage tunes.

🌐 Websites

o **Lonely Planet** (www.lonelyplanet.com) Country-specific information and Thorn Tree user-exchange.

o **Bangkok Post** (www.bangkokpost.com) English-language daily.

o **One Stop Thailand** (www.onestopthailand.com) One-stop travel site.

Short on time?

This list will give you instant insight into the country.

Read *Bangkok 8* (John Burdett) is about a hardboiled Thai-Western cop.

Watch *Last Life in the Universe* (Ruang Rak Noi Nid Mahasan; 2003), directed by Pen-Ek Ratanaruang; unfurls a dark tale of two lost souls.

Listen *Made in Thailand* (Carabao) is Thailand's classic classic-rock album.

Log On Richard Barrow on Twitter, the go-to blogger for breaking news.

Ao Maya (p322), Ko Phi-Phi Leh
MATTEO COLOMBO/GETTY IMAGES ©

Need to Know

Currency
Thai baht (B)

Language
Thai

Money
ATMs are widespread and charge a 150B foreign-account fee; Visa and MasterCard accepted at most hotels and high-end restaurants but not at small family-owned businesses

Visas
International air arrivals receive a 30-day visa

Mobile Phones
Thailand is on a GSM network through inexpensive prepaid SIM cards; 3G is in urban areas

Wi-Fi
Widespread and access is cheap

Internet Access
Internet cafes common in tourist centres

Tipping
In high-end hotels and restaurants: 10% gratuity, 7% tax

When to Go

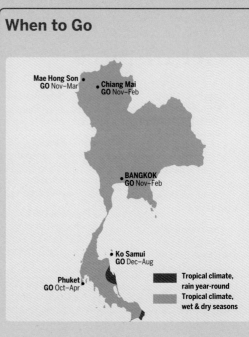

Mae Hong Son
GO Nov–Mar

Chiang Mai
GO Nov–Feb

BANGKOK
GO Nov–Feb

Ko Samui
GO Dec–Aug

Phuket
GO Oct–Apr

Tropical climate, rain year-round

Tropical climate, wet & dry seasons

High Season (Nov–Mar)
- A cool, dry season follows the monsoons, meaning the landscape is lush and temperatures are comfortable.
- Christmas and New Year holidays bring crowds and inflated rates to the beaches.

Shoulder Season (Apr–Jun, Sept & Oct)
- Hot and dry (April to June), but less so in the northern mountains.
- Tail end of rainy season (September and October) is ideal for visiting the north and the Gulf Coast.

Low Season (Jul–Oct)
- Monsoon season can range from afternoon showers to multiday soakers.
- Some islands shut down and boat service is limited during stormy weather.
- Be flexible with travel plans.

Advance Planning

- **One month before** Start shopping for airfares, planning an itinerary, booking accommodation for resort islands like Ko Samui and Phuket, and arranging Bangkok–Chiang Mai overnight train tickets.

- **One week before** Book your arrival hotel in Bangkok, Thai cooking course and dive trip. Start watching the web for Thailand news.

- **One day before** Confirm your flight, choose a hearty book for your holiday and bid adieu to ho-hum home life.

Daily Costs

Budget Less than 1000B
- Basic guesthouse room 300–800B
- Excellent market/street food 40–60B
- One or two evening drinks 200B
- Public transport 20–100B

Midrange 1000–3000B
- Flashpacker guesthouse or midrange hotel 800–1500B
- Western meals/seafood 150–350B
- Motorbike hire 300–500B
- Organised tour or activity 1000–1500B

Top End Over 3000B
- Boutique hotel room 3000B
- Fine dining 350–500B
- Private tours 1500B
- Car hire 1500B

Exchange Rates

Australia	A$1	29B
Canada	C$1	29B
China	Y1	5B
Euro zone	€1	45B
Japan	¥100	32B
New Zealand	NZ$1	28B
Russia	R10	9B
UK	£1	53B
USA	US$1	32B

For current exchange rates see www.xe.com

What to Bring

- **Pack light** Laundry is cheap. Take one jacket for excessive air-con and mountain mornings.
- **Slip-on shoes** Easily removed at temples.
- **Handy items** Waterproof money/passport container (for swimming outings), earplugs and high SPF sunscreen (it's expensive). You can buy most toiletries everywhere.

Arriving in Thailand

Suvarnabhumi International Airport (Bangkok)

Airport Rail Link Local service (30 minutes, 45B) to Phaya Thai station; express service (15 minutes, 90B) to Makkasan station (Bangkok City Air Terminal).

Taxi Metered taxis 200B to 300B plus 50B tolls.

Don Muang International Airport (Bangkok)

Airport bus A1 to BTS Mo Chit; A2 to BTS Mo Chit & BTS Victory Monument (hourly, 9am to midnight, 30B).

Taxis Metered taxis cost 300B to 400B, plus 50B tolls.

Getting Around

- **Air** Domestic routes from Bangkok are plentiful.
- **Bus** Intercity buses are convenient, affordable and comfortable; purchase tickets at bus stations to avoid unscrupulous agents.
- **Hired transport** Bangkok has metered taxis; elsewhere túk-túk and motorcycle taxis have negotiated fares. Motorcycles and cars are easily rented.
- **Public transport** Bangkok has public buses, an elevated train system (BTS) and a subway (MRT). Most Thai cities have sŏrng·tăa·ou (converted pick-up trucks) on fixed routes.
- **Train** Slow but scenic; popular overnight between Bangkok and Chiang Mai or the southern islands.

Accommodation

- **Guesthouses** Thailand's most common option; tend to have a common lobby, a restaurant for socialising and tons of tourist information.
- **Hotels** Hip options in Bangkok, Chiang Mai and the resort islands; the impersonal Thai-Chinese hotels in the provinces often feel a little lonely.

Be Forewarned

- **Travel warnings** Check advisory warnings online.
- **Health** Dengue fever is a concern.
- **Dress** Cover up when visiting temples.
- **Rainy season** Some island resorts close; boat service is limited.

Bangkok

Formerly the epitome of the steamy Asian metropolis, in recent years Bangkok has gone under the knife and emerged as a rejuvenated starlet. Her wrinkles haven't been totally erased, but you might not notice them in the expanding and efficient public transport system, air-conditioned megamalls and international-standard restaurants. A diverse expat community, a burgeoning art scene and a brand-new airport complete the new look, making even frequent visitors wonder what happened to the woman they once knew.

But don't take this to mean that there's no 'real' Bangkok left. The traditional framework that made this city unique is still very much alive and kicking, and can be found a short walk from any BTS station – or probably just around the corner from your hotel.

Along the way we're sure you'll find that the old personality and the new face culminate in one sexy broad.

Wat Phra Kaew (p60)

Traditional dancers at Erawan Shrine (p71)
KIMBERLEY COOLE /GETTY IMAGES ©

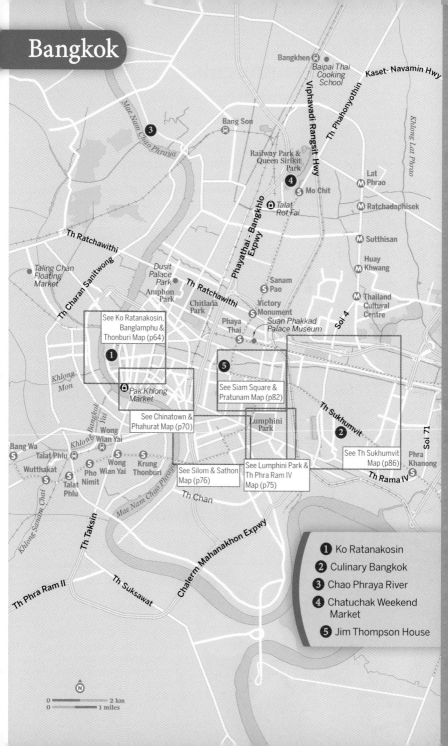

Bangkok

Bangkhen

Baipai Thai
Cooking
School

Kaset- Navamin Hwy

Bang Son

Railway Park &
Queen Sirikit
Park

Lat
Phrao

Ⓜ Ratchadaphisek

Ⓜ Mo Chit

Talat
Rot Fai

Ⓜ Sutthisan

Th Ratchawithi

Huay
Khwang

Taling Chan
Floating
Market

Th Charan Sanitwong

Dusit
Palace
Park

Sanam
Ⓢ Pao

Ⓜ Thailand
Cultural
Centre

Amphon
Park

Th Ratchawithi

Chitlada
Park

Victory
Monument

Phaya
Thai

Suan Phakkad
Palace Museum

See Ko Ratanakosin,
Banglamphu &
Thonburi Map (p64)

❶

Khlong
Mon

Ⓐ Pak Khlong
Market

See Siam Square &
Pratunam Map (p82)

❺

See Chinatown &
Phahurat Map (p70)

Lumphini
Park

Th Sukhumvit

Wong
Wian Yai

See Th Sukhumvit
Map (p86)

Bang Wa
Ⓢ

Talat Phlu Ⓡ

Wong
Wian Yai

Krung
Thonburi

See Silom & Sathon
Map (p76)

See Lumphini Park &
Th Phra Ram IV
Map (p75)

❷

Phra
Khanong

Wutthakat
Ⓢ

Pho
Nimit

Talat
Phlu

Th Chan

Th Rama IV

Th Taksin

Mae Nam Chao Phraya

Th Phra Ram II

Th Suksawat

Chalerm Mahanakhon Expwy

❶ Ko Ratanakosin

❷ Culinary Bangkok

❸ Chao Phraya River

❹ Chatuchak Weekend
   Market

❺ Jim Thompson House

Ⓝ

0 ———— 2 km
0 ———— 1 miles

Bangkok's Highlights

Ko Ratanakosin

The country's most famous and sacred sites are in Ko Ratanakosin, the old royal district. Here you'll find Wat Phra Kaew (p60), a glittering and ornate temple that typifies Thai temple architecture and shelters the revered Emerald Buddha. More subdued Wat Pho (p60) is home to the gigantic reclining Buddha and is the national school for traditional Thai massage. Elsewhere, the entire neighbourhood is packed with colourful religious displays. Below: Wat Phra Kaew

GREG ELMS/GETTY IMAGES ©

Culinary Bangkok

Bangkok is a veritable food buffet, from the streetside carts serving Thai-style fast food to high-end restaurants reinventing royal recipes. You can forage by day, wandering from cart to humble shophouse, becoming a noodle expert and serial snacker, and then dine like an aristocrat by night at the likes of Bo.lan (p85). As an international city, Bangkok provides a global menu of Indian, French and Italian (to name a few) if you tire of Thai curries.

GREG ELMS/GETTY IMAGES ©

Chao Phraya River

③

The Chao Phraya River (p89; River of Kings) is the symbolic bloodline of the Thai people, connecting the capital with the Gulf of Thailand. Long-tail boats ricochet between its riverbanks, cargo-laden barges plod along, and commuter ferries hustle between piers. Despite the constant activity, it is a peaceful place to watch this throbbing metropolis and offers a glimpse into an old-fashioned life along its minor tributaries and canals. Right: Wat Arun (p60)

④

Chatuchak Weekend Market

Bangkok's malls and markets make their overseas counterparts look like country-bumpkin garage sales. Chatuchak Weekend Market (p92) is the mother of all markets, selling everything and the kitchen sink. Its excess of merchandise crammed into claustrophobic lanes turns shopping into an extreme sport. If you're heat- and crowd-averse, head for one of the city's happening (and air-conditioned) malls.

⑤

Jim Thompson House

Jim Thompson was one of Thailand's most famous expats; he introduced the Western world to Thai-style silks through his export business inspired by his silk-weaving neighbours. But locally he is most famous for his appreciation of Thai art and architecture. He rescued antique wooden houses and collected stunning traditional art that is now on display at the Jim Thompson House (p72), his former residence.

Bangkok's Best...

Spas & Massage

○ **Wat Pho Thai Traditional Medical and Massage School** The original training centre located within the temple grounds. (p71)

○ **Spa 1930** A spa oasis smack dab in the centre of Bangkok. (p74)

○ **Ruen-Nuad Massage Studio** An old-fashioned setting for a good old-fashioned massage. (p71)

○ **Thann Sanctuary** Mall spa for post-shopping therapy. (p74)

Places to Wander

○ **Chinatown** Ramble through a maze of old-world commerce. (p61)

○ **Amulet Market** Pick your way through the vendors selling protective talismans. (p61)

○ **Dusit Palace Park** Take a stroll through a pretty park filled with even prettier palaces. (p67)

○ **Wat Pho** This rambling temple has plenty of curious corners, shady nooks and loads of people-watching. (p60)

Dining

○ **nahm** High-end Thai for educated palates. (p81)

○ **MBK Food Island** Delicious market-style meals served in air-con comfort. (p84)

○ **Krua Apsorn** A homey kitchen beloved by the Thai royalty for shellfish delicacies. (p80)

○ **Bo.lan** Haute Thai cuisine combining five-star flavour and flourish. (p85)

Drinking & Clubbing

o **Moon Bar** Raise a glass to the stars and the twinkling city below at this rooftop bar. (p89)

o **Amorosa** Toast the sunset from this picture-perfect riverside perch. (p88)

o **Iron Fairies** High-concept wine bar for Gothic imbibers. (p90)

o **WTF** Get cosy with cocktails at this art-house pub. (p90)

Need to Know

VITAL STATISTICS

o **Population** 10 million

o **Elevation** 1.50m

ADVANCE PLANNING

o **Two weeks before** Book accommodation and a Thai cooking course.

o **One day before** Pack your hippest outfits.

RESOURCES

o **Thai Food Blog** (www. austinbushphotography. com/blog) Meals and food tales from a Lonely Planet writer.

o **Coconuts Bangkok** (bangkok.coconuts.co) Snippets of news and lifestyle trends.

o **Bangkok Information Center** (www. bangkoktourist.com) City tourism office.

GETTING AROUND

o **Bus** Plentiful and cheap; get a bus map for handy routes. Frequent service.

o **MRT** Underground train (metro) from Sukhumvit and Silom to the train station. Frequent service.

o **River ferry** Hop between riverside temples and neighbourhoods. Frequent daytime service.

o **BTS** Elevated skytrain from Sukhumvit, Siam Square, Silom and Chatuchak. Frequent service.

o **Taxi** Plentiful and comfortable; insist on the meter.

o **Túk-túk** Cute but a rip-off.

BE FOREWARNED

o **Dress** Cover past your shoulders and knees in important temples.

o **Smoking** Banned indoors at bars and restaurants.

o **Street stalls** Don't set up on Monday.

o **Touts** Ignore friendly locals with touring/ shopping advice.

o **Gems** Don't buy unset gems; it is an expensive con game.

o **Tailor-made clothes** Set aside a week to get clothes tailored; most reliable tailors ask for at least two fittings.

Left: nahm (p81); **Above:** Chinese New Year celebrations, Chinatown (p61)

Bangkok Walking Tour

Stroll between Bangkok's must-see temples and attractions in the former royal district of Ko Ratanakosin. Start early to beat the heat, dress modestly for the temples, and ignore shopping advice from well-dressed touts.

WALK FACTS

- **Start** Wat Phra Kaew & Grand Palace
- **Finish** Sanam Luang
- **Distance** 5km
- **Duration** Three hours

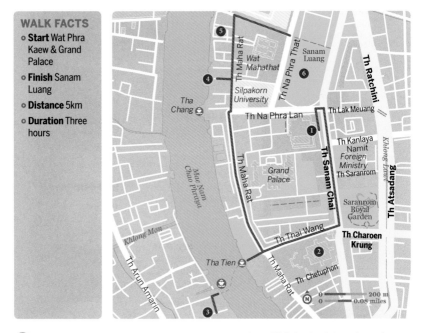

① Wat Phra Kaew & Grand Palace

Architecturally flamboyant and domestically revered, this formerly cloistered royal complex (p60) now rules as the city's most famous attraction. It is best appreciated with a hired or an audio guide, both of which will explain the ins and outs of Thai Buddhism and the religious symbolism of the temple architecture. Don't miss the temple's beautiful Ramakian murals.

② Wat Pho

Head to the temple (p60) with the most superlatives, including the biggest reclining Buddha. This is a shady and subdued attraction with lots of quiet nooks and crannies. There are also on-site traditional Thai massage pavilions carrying on the temple's primary purpose as a repository for traditional healing. Where else can you tend to your soul and your soles?

③ Wat Arun

Catch the cross-river ferry from Tha Tien to this military-looking temple (p60) boasting a Khmer-style *chedi* (stupa). This temple served as the precursor to Bangkok after the fall of Ayuthaya. A closer look reveals that the granite-looking spire is really covered in ornate porcelain mosaic.

④ Trok Tha Wang

Return to the east bank and turn left on Th Maha Rat and then left again to explore this narrow alleyway containing classic Bangkok architecture and riverside accoutrements.

⑤ Amulet Market

Head back to Th Maha Rat and then left into Trok Mahathat to discover this cramped market (p61) where amulets are bought, sold and seriously inspected. Follow the alley all the way towards the river to appreciate how extensive the amulet trade is. As you continue north alongside the river, amulets are replaced by food vendors and amulet shoppers get crowded out by uniformed university students.

⑥ Sanam Luang

Exiting at Th Phra Chan, cross Th Maha Rat and continue east, passing even more traditional Thai medicine shops and amulet vendors until you reach the 'Royal Field'. The park is the site for the annual Ploughing Ceremony, in which the crown prince officially initiates the rice-growing season. A large kite competition is also held here during the kite-flying season (mid-February to April). The southern end of the park affords a photographic view of Wat Phra Kaew. Taxis and buses circle this shadeless expanse, offering a quick getaway for tuckered-out tourists.

Bangkok in...

ONE DAY

Take the Chao Phraya Express Boat (p95) to Tha Chang to explore the museums and temples of Ko Ratanakosin, followed by lunch in Banglamphu. Then turn shopping into imbibing on Th Khao San (p88).

TWO DAYS

Take the BTS to a shopping mall or Jim Thompson House (p72), and wrap up the daylight hours with a Thai massage. Visit a rooftop bar for cocktails, followed by an upscale Thai dinner at nahm (p81).

THREE DAYS

Spend a day at Chatuchak Weekend Market (p92), enrol in a cooking class, or jump aboard a long-tail boat to explore Thonburi's canals. Hit Chinatown for a street-food dinner.

FOUR DAYS

Escape Bangkok's chaos with a visit to Dusit Palace Park (p67). Splash out at one of Sukhumvit's international restaurants (p85) and then hang out with Bangkok's hipsters at Iron Fairies (p90).

Thai cooking course

Discover Bangkok

Reclining Buddha, Wat Pho
PETER UNGER/GETTY IMAGES ©

⊙ Sights

KO RATANAKOSIN, BANGLAMPHU & THONBURI
เกาะรัตนโกสินทร์/บางลำพู/ธนบุรี

Welcome to Bangkok's birthplace.

Wat Phra Kaew & Grand Palace
Buddhist Temple, Historical Site
(วัดพระแก้ว, พระบรมมหาราชวัง; Map p64; Th Na Phra Lan; admission 500B; ☺8.30am-4pm; 🚤Tha Chang) Also known as the Temple of the Emerald Buddha, **Wat Phra Kaew** is the colloquial name of the vast, fairy-tale compound that also includes the former residence of the Thai monarch, the Grand Palace. Guides can be hired at the ticket kiosk; ignore offers from anyone outside. An audio guide can be rented for 200B for two hours. For an illustrated guide to these sights, see p62.

Wat Pho
Buddhist Temple
(วัดโพธิ์ (วัดพระเชตุพน), Wat Phra Chetuphon; Map p64; Th Sanam Chai; admission 100B; ☺8.30am-6.30pm; 🚤Tha Tien) You'll find (slightly) fewer tourists here than at Wat Phra Kaew, but Wat Pho is our personal fave among Bangkok's biggest sights. In fact, the compound incorporates a host of superlatives: the city's largest reclining Buddha, the largest collection of Buddha images in Thailand and the country's earliest centre for public education (including a massage school; see p71). For an illustrated guide to Wat Pho, see p68.

Wat Arun
Buddhist Temple
(วัดอรุณฯ; Map p64; www.watarun.net; off Th Arun Amarin; admission 50B; ☺8am-6pm; 🚤cross-river ferry from Tha Tien) The striking Wat Arun

commands a martial pose as the third point in the holy trinity (along with Wat Phra Kaew and Wat Pho) of Bangkok's early history. After the fall of Ayuthaya, King Taksin ceremoniously clinched control here on the site of a local shrine (formerly known as Wat Jaeng) and established a royal palace and a temple to house the Emerald Buddha. The temple was renamed after the Indian god of dawn (Aruna) and in honour of the literal and symbolic founding of a new Ayuthaya.

Amulet Market
Market

(ตลาดพระเครื่องวัดมหาธาตุ; Map p64; Th Maha Rat; ☉7am-5pm; ⛴Tha Chang) This arcane and fascinating market claims both the footpaths along Th Maha Rat and Th Phra Chan, as well as a dense network of covered market stalls near Tha Phra Chan. The trade is based around small talismans prized by collectors, monks, taxi drivers and people in dangerous professions.

Museum of Siam
Museum

(สถาบันพิพิธภัณฑ์การเรียนรู้แห่งชาติ; Map p64; www.museumsiam.com; Th Maha Rat; admission 300B; ☉10am-6pm Tue-Sun; ⛴Tha Tien) This fun museum employs a variety of media to explore the origins of the Thai people and their culture. Housed in a European-style 19th-century building that was once the Ministry of Commerce, the exhibits are presented in an engaging, interactive fashion not often found in Thailand. They are also refreshingly balanced and entertaining, with galleries dealing with a range of questions about the origins of the nation and its people.

National Museum
Museum

(พิพิธภัณฑสถานแห่งชาติ; Map p64; 4 Th Na Phra That; admission 200B; ☉9am-4pm Wed-Sun; ⛴Tha Chang) Often touted as Southeast Asia's biggest museum, Thailand's National Museum is home to an impressive collection of religious sculpture, best appreciated on one of the museum's twice-weekly guided **tours** (free with museum admission; ☉9.30am Wed & Thu).

CHINATOWN & PHAHURAT
เยาวราช/พาหุรัด

Bangkok's Chinatown (called Yaowarat after its main thoroughfare, Th Yaowarat) is the urban explorer's equivalent of the Amazon Basin. The highlights here aren't necessarily tidy temples or museums, but rather a complicated web of tiny alleyways, crowded markets and delicious street stalls.

At the western edge of Chinatown is a small but thriving Indian district, generally called Phahurat.

Wat Phra Kaew & Grand Palace

EXPLORE BANGKOK'S PREMIER MONUMENTS TO RELIGION AND REGENCY

This tour can be covered in a couple of hours. The first area tourists enter is the Buddhist temple compound generally referred to as Wat Phra Kaew. A covered walkway surrounds the area, the inner walls of which are decorated with the **murals of the *Ramakian* ❶** and **❷**. Originally painted during the reign of Rama I (r 1782–1809), the murals, which depict the Hindu epic the *Ramayana*, span 178 panels that describe the struggles of Rama to rescue his kidnapped wife, Sita.

After taking in the story, pass through one of the gateways guarded by *yaksha* ❸ to the inner compound. The most important structure here is the *bòht*, or ordination hall ❹, which houses the eponymous **Emerald Buddha ❺**.

Kinaree
These graceful half-swan, half-women creatures from Hindu-Buddhist mythology stand outside Prasat Phra Thep Bidon.

Borombhiman Hall

Prasat Phra Thep Bidon

Phra Si Ratana

The Murals of the *Ramakian*
These wall paintings, which begin at the eastern side of the Wat Phra Kaew, often depict scenes more reminiscent of 19th-century Thailand than of ancient India.

Hanuman
Rows of these mischievous monkey deities from Hindu mythology appear to support the lower levels of two small *chedi* near Prasat Phra Thep Bidon.

Head east to the so-called Upper Terrace, an elevated area home to the **spires of the three primary chedi 6**. The middle structure, Phra Mondop, is used to house Buddhist manuscripts. This area is also home to several of Wat Phra Kaew's noteworthy mythical beings, including beckoning **kinaree 7** and several grimacing **Hanuman 8**.

Proceed through the western gate to the compound known as the Grand Palace. Few of the buildings here are open to the public. The most noteworthy structure is **Chakri Mahaprasat 9**. Built in 1882, the exterior of the hall is a unique blend of western and traditional Thai architecture.

The Three Spires
The elaborate seven-tiered roof of Phra Mondop, the Khmer-style peak of the Prasat Phra Thep Bidon, and the gilded Phra Si Ratana chedi are the tallest structures in the compound.

Emerald Buddha
Despite the name, this diminutive statue (it's only 66cm tall) is actually carved from nephrite, a type of jade.

Amarindra Hall

The Death of Thotsakan
The panels progress clockwise, culminating at the western edge of the compound with the death of Thotsakan, Sita's kidnapper, and his elaborate funeral procession.

Chakri Mahaprasat
This structure is sometimes referred to as fa•ràng sài chá•dah (Westerner in a Thai crown) because each wing is topped by a mon•dòp: a spire representing a Thai adaptation of a Hindu shrine.

Dusit Hall

Yaksha
Each entrance to the Wat Phra Kaew compound is watched over by a pair of vigilant and enormous yaksha, ogres or giants from Hindu mythology.

Bòht (Ordination Hall)
This structure is an early example of the Ratanakosin school of architecture, which combines traditional stylistic holdovers from Ayuthaya along with more modern touches from China and the West.

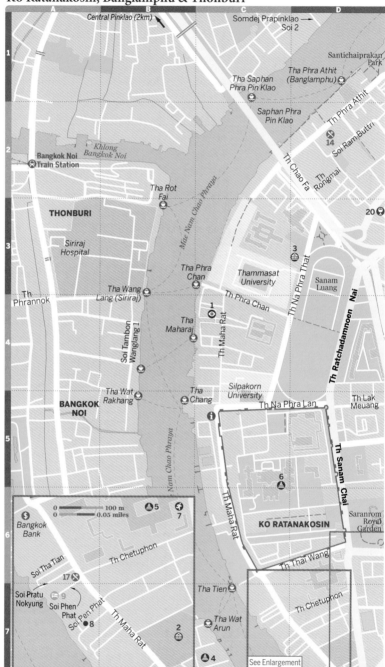

Central Pinklao (2km)

Somdej Prapinklao — Soi 2

Santichaiprakan Park

Tha Saphan Phra Pin Klao

Tha Phra Athit (Banglamphu)

Th Phra Athit

Saphan Phra Pin Klao

Th Chao Fa

Th Rongmai

Soi Ram Buttri

14

Khlong Bangkok Noi

Bangkok Noi Train Station

Mae Nam Chao Phraya

Tha Rot Fai

20

THONBURI

Siriraj Hospital

Tha Phra Chan

Thammasat University

Th Na Phra That

3

Sanam Luang

Th Ratchadamnoen Nai

Th Phrannok

Tha Wang Lang (Siriraj)

Th Phra Chan

Soi Tambon Wanglang 1

Tha Maharaj

1

Th Maha Rat

BANGKOK NOI

Tha Wat Rakhang

Tha Chang

Silpakorn University

Th Na Phra Lan

Th Lak Meuang

Th Sanam Chai

Nam Chao Phraya

6

Saranrom Royal Garden

KO RATANAKOSIN

Th Thai Wang

Bangkok Bank

0 —— 100 m
0 —— 0.05 miles

5

7

Th Chetuphon

Soi Tha Tian

Soi Pratu Nokyung

17

9

Soi Phen Phat

Soi Pen Phat

8

Th Maha Rat

Tha Tien

2

Th Chetuphon

Tha Wat Arun

4

See Enlargement

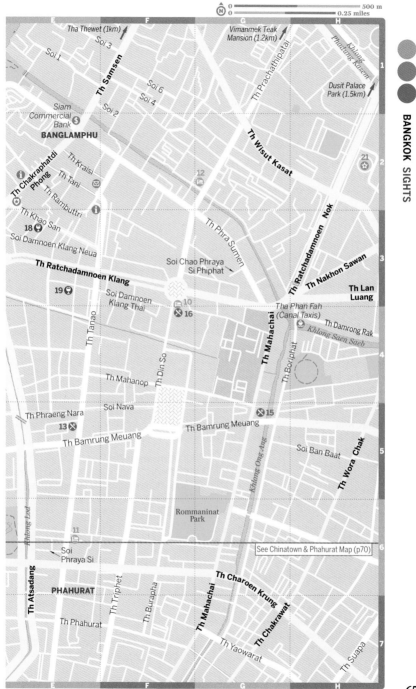

0
0

500 m
0.25 miles

Tha Thewet (1km)

Soi 3

Vimanmek Teak
Mansion (1.2km)

Klong Phadung Kasem

Soi 1

Th Samsen

Soi 6

Th Prachathipatai

Dusit Palace
Park (1.5km)

Soi 4

Siam
Commercial
Bank

Soi 2

BANGLAMPHU

Th Wisut Kasat

Th Chakraphatdi Phong

Th Kraisi

Th Tani

Th Rambuttri

12

21

Th Khao San

18

Soi Damnoen Klang Neua

Th Phra Sumen

Th Ratchadamnoen Nok

Th Ratchadamnoen Klang

Soi Chao Phraya
Si Phiphat

19

Soi Damnoen
Klang Thai

10

Tha Phan Fah
(Canal Taxis)

Th Nakhon Sawan

Th Lan
Luang

16

Th Damrong Rak

Th Tanao

Th Mahanop

Th Din So

Th Mahachai

Th Boriphat

Khlong Saen Saeb

Soi Nava

15

Th Phraeng Nara

13

Th Bamrung Meuang

Th Bamrung Meuang

Soi Ban Baat

Th Wora Chak

Khlong Ong Ang

Rommaninat
Park

11

See Chinatown & Phahurat Map (p70)

Khlong Lot

Soi
Phraya Si

Th Atsadang

PHAHURAT

Th Triphet

Th Burapha

Th Charoen Krung

Th Phahurat

Th Mahachai

Th Yaowarat

Th Chakrawat

Th Suapa

Ko Ratanakosin, Banglamphu & Thonburi

Wat Traimit   Buddhist Temple
(วัดไตรมิตร, Temple of the Golden Buddha; Map p70; Th Mitthaphap (Th Traimit); admission 40B; ⊙8am-5pm; 🚤Tha Ratchawong, Ⓜ Hua Lamphong exit 1) The attraction at Wat Traimit is undoubtedly the impressive 3m-tall, 5.5-tonne, solid-gold Buddha image, which gleams like, well, gold. Sculpted in the graceful Sukhothai style, the image was 'discovered' some 40 years ago beneath a stucco or plaster exterior when it fell from a crane while being moved to a new building within the temple compound.

Talat Mai   Market
(ตลาดใหม่; Map p70; Soi Charoen Krung 16 (Trok Itsaranuphap), Soi 6, Th Yaowarat; ⊙6am-6pm; 🚤Tha Ratchawong, Ⓜ Hua Lamphong exit 1 & taxi) While much of the market centres on Chinese cooking ingredients, the section north of Th Charoen Krung (equivalent to Soi 21, Th Charoen Krung) is known for selling incense, paper effigies and ceremonial sweets – the essential elements of a traditional Chinese funeral.

SILOM & SATHON สีลม/สาธร

The business district of Th Silom has only a handful of tourist attractions scattered among the corporate hotels, office towers and wining-and-dining restaurants. As you get closer to the river, the area becomes spiced with the sights and smells of its Indian and Muslim residents. Moving north along Th Charoen Krung, the area adjacent to the river was the international mercantile district during Bangkok's shipping heyday.

Sri Mariamman Temple   Temple
(วัดพระศรีมหาอุมาเทวี (วัดแขก), Wat Phra Si Maha Umathewi; Map p76; cnr Th Silom & Th Pan; ⊙6am-8pm; Ⓢ Surasak exit 3) FREE Standing out, even among Bangkok's golden wát, this Hindu temple virtually leaps off the block. Built in the 1860s by Tamil immigrants in the centre of a still thriving ethnic enclave, the structure is a stacked facade of intertwined, full-colour Hindu deities.

Kathmandu Photo Gallery   Art Gallery
(Map p76; www.kathmandu-bkk.com; 87 Th Pan; ⊙11am-7pm Tue-Sun; Ⓢ Surasak exit 3) FREE Bangkok's only gallery wholly dedicated to photography is housed in an attractively restored Sino-Portuguese shophouse. The owner, photographer Manit Sriwanichpoom, wanted Kathmandu to resemble photographers' shops of old, where customers could flip through photographs for sale. Manit's own work is on display on the ground floor, and the small but airy upstairs gallery plays host to changing exhibitions by local and international artists and photographers.

Silom Galleria
Art Gallery

(Map p76; 919/1 Th Silom; ⏱6am-10pm; 🚇Surasak exit 3) Not a gallery per se, but the top floors of this abandoned-feeling mall are home to some of Bangkok's best commercial galleries: **Number 1 Gallery** (Map p76; www.number1gallery.com; 4th fl, Silom Galleria; ⏱10am-7pm Mon-Sat) **FREE** features edgy contemporary Thai art; **Tang Gallery** (Map p76; 5th fl, Silom Galleria; ⏱11am-7pm Mon-Sat) **FREE** showcases the work of contemporary Chinese artists, and **Thavibu Gallery** (Map p76; www.thavibu.com; 4th fl, Silom Galleria; ⏱11am-7pm Tue-Sat) **FREE** focuses on the work of Vietnamese and Burmese artists.

SIAM SQUARE & PRATUNAM
สยามสแควร์/ประตูน้ำ

Dusit Palace Park
Museum, Historical Site

(วังสวนดุสิต; ☎0 2628 6300; bounded by Th Ratchawithi, Th U Thong Nai & Th Ratchasima; ticket for all Dusit Palace Park sights adult/child 100/20B, or free same-day entry with Wat Phra Kaew & Grand Palace ticket; ⏱9.30am-4pm Tue-Sun; 🚤Tha Thewet, 🚇Phaya Thai exit 2 & taxi) Following Rama V's first European tour in 1897, he returned home with visions of European castles swimming in his head and set about transforming these styles into a uniquely Thai expression, today's Dusit Palace Park.

Originally constructed on Ko Si Chang in 1868 and moved to the present site in 1910, **Vimanmek Teak Mansion** (⏱9.30am-4pm Tue-Sun, last entry 3.15pm) contains 81 rooms, halls and anterooms, and is said to be the world's largest golden-teak building, allegedly built without the use of a single nail. The mansion was the first permanent building on the Dusit Palace grounds, and served as

Dress for the Occasion

Many of Bangkok's biggest tourist attractions are sacred places, and visitors should dress and behave appropriately. In particular, you won't be allowed to enter Wat Phra Kaew & Grand Palace and Dusit Park unless you're well covered. Shorts, sleeveless shirts or spaghetti-strap tops, short skirts, capri pants – basically anything that reveals more than your arms (certainly don't show your shoulders) knees and head – are not allowed. Violators can expect to be shown into a dressing room and loaned a sarong before being allowed to go in.

Rama V's residence in the early 1900s. Compulsory tours (in English) leave every half-hour between 9.45am and 3.15pm, and last about an hour.

Siam Square
JEAN-PIERRE LESCOURRET/GETTY IMAGES ©

Wat Pho

A WALK THROUGH THE BIG BUDDHAS OF WAT PHO

The logical starting place is the main *wí•hăhn* (sanctuary), home to Wat Pho's centrepiece, the immense **Reclining Buddha ❶**. Apart from its huge size, note the **mother-of-pearl inlays ❷** on the soles of the statue's feet. The interior walls of the *wí•hăhn* are covered with murals depicting previous lives of the Buddha, and along the south side of the structure are 108 bronze monk bowls; for 20B you can buy 108 coins, each of which is dropped in a bowl for good luck.

Exit the *wí•hăhn* and head east via the two **stone giants ❸** who guard the gateway to the rest of the compound. Directly south of these are the four towering **royal *chedi* ❹**.

Continue east, passing through two consecutive **galleries of Buddha**

Southern *Wí•hăhn*

Phra Ubosot
Built during the reign of Rama I, the imposing *bòht* (ordination hall) as it stands today is the result of renovations dating back to the reign of Rama III (r 1824–51).

Buddha Galleries
The two series of covered hallways that surround the Phra Ubosot feature no fewer than 394 gilded Buddha images, many of which display classic Ayuthaya or Sukhothai features.

Eastern *Wí•hăhn*

Massage Pavilions
If you're hot and footsore, the two air-conditioned massage pavilions are a welcome way to cool down while experiencing high-quality and relatively inexpensive Thai massage.

❻

❼

❽

Phra Buddha Deva Patimakorn
On an impressive three-tiered pedestal that also holds the ashes of Rama I is this Ayuthaya-era Buddha statue originally brought to the temple by the monarch.

Northern *Wí•hăhn*

Western *Wí•hăhn*

AUSTIN BUSH ©

statues ⑤ linking four *wí•hăhn*, two of which contain notable Sukhothai-era Buddha statues; these comprise the exterior of **Phra Ubosot** ⑥, the immense ordination hall that is Wat Pho's second-most noteworthy structure. The base of the building is surrounded by bas-relief inscriptions, and inside is the notable Buddha statue, **Phra Buddha Deva Patimakorn** ⑦.

Wat Pho is often referred to as Thailand's first university, a tradition that continues today in an associated traditional Thai medicine school and, at the compound's eastern extent, two **massage pavilions** ⑧.

Interspersed throughout the eastern half of the compound are several additional minor *chedi* and rock gardens.

Royal Chedi
Decorated in coloured tiles in a classic example of Ratanakosin style, these four *chedi* are meant to represent the first four kings of the Chakri dynasty.

Reclining Buddha
Modelled around a brick core 46m long and 15m high and finished in plaster and gold leaf, Wat Pho's Reclining Buddha is an imposing reminder of the Buddha's passing into nirvana (the Buddha's death).

Crocodile Pond

Phra Mondop

Thai Massage Inscriptions

④

⑤

③

①

②

Main *Wí•hăhn*

Stone Giants
These huge granite figures – depictions range from Chinese opera characters to Marco Polo – originally arrived in Thailand in the 19th century as ballast aboard Chinese junks.

Mother-Of-Pearl Inlay
The 108 auspicious *lák•sà•nà*, physical characteristics of the Buddha, are depicted on the soles of the feet of the Reclining Buddha.

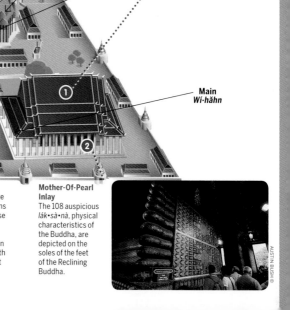

Chinatown & Phahurat

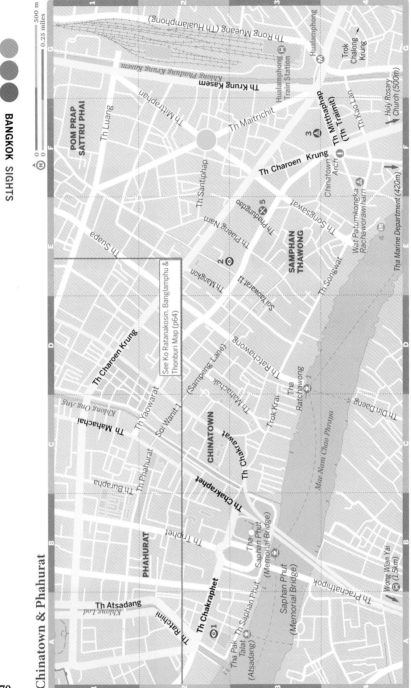

See Ko Ratanakosin, Banglamphu & Thonburi Map (p64)

Because Dusit Palace Park is royal property, visitors should wear long pants (no capri pants) or long skirts and shirts with sleeves.

Erawan Shrine   Monument

(ศาลพระพรหม; Map p82; cnr Th Ratchadamri & Th Ploenchit; ⊙6am-11pm; Ⓢ Chit Lom exit 8) FREE The Erawan Shrine was originally built in 1956 as something of a last-ditch effort to end a string of misfortunes that occurred during the construction of a hotel, at that time known as the Erawan Hotel. Following the suggestion of a Brahmin priest, a statue of Lord Brahma was built, and lo and behold, the misfortunes miraculously ended.

Bangkok Art & Culture Centre   Art Gallery

(BACC; Map p82; www.bacc.or.th; cnr Th Phayathai & Th Phra Ram I; ⊙10am-9pm Tue-Sat; Ⓢ National Stadium exit 3) FREE This large, modern building in the centre of Bangkok is the most recent and promising addition to the city's arts scene. In addition to three floors and 3000 sq metres of gallery space used for revolving exhibitions, the centre also contains shops, private galleries and cafes.

🟢 Activities

THAI MASSAGE

Ruen-Nuad Massage Studio   Massage

(Map p76; 🕿 0 2632 2662; 42 Th Convent; massage per hr 350B; ⊙10am-9pm; Ⓜ Si Lom exit 2, Ⓢ Sala Daeng exit 2) Set in a refurbished wooden house, this charming place successfully avoids both the tackiness and New Agedness that characterise most Bangkok massage joints. Prices are approachable, too.

Wat Pho Thai Traditional Medical and Massage School   Thai Massage

(Map p64; 🕿 0 2622 3551; www.watpomassage .com; 392/25-28 Soi Phen Phat; lessons from 2500B; ⊙lessons 9am-4pm; 🚢 Tha Tien) This, the primary training ground for the masseuses who are deployed across the country, also offers massage. There are associated **massage pavilions** (Map p64; Thai massage per hr 420B; ⊙8.30am-6.30pm; 🚢 Tha Tien) inside the Wat Pho temple complex.

Thai massage at Wat Pho
LONELY PLANET/GETTY IMAGES ©

Jim Thompson House

This is the former home of an American silk entrepreneur and art collector with a keen sense of beauty and appreciation of Thai arts and craft. Though adapted into a Western-style residence, the home preserves traditional Thai craftwork, and features a fine collection of Buddhist sculpture, historic textiles and other collectibles.

Map p82

www.jimthompsonhouse.com

Soi Kasem San 2

adult/child 100/50B

⊙9am-5pm, compulsory tours in English & French every 20 min

🚤klorng boat to Tha Saphan Hua Chang, Ⓢ National Stadium exit 1

The House

Thompson collected parts of various derelict Thai homes and had them reassembled in their current location in 1959. Some of the homes were brought from the old royal capital of Ayuthaya; others were pulled down and floated across the *klorng* from Baan Krua, including the first building you enter on the tour. One striking departure from tradition is the way each wall has its exterior side facing the house's interior, thus exposing the wall's bracing system. Thompson's small but splendid Asian art collection and personal belongings are on display in the main house.

The Man

Part of the appeal of the museum is the charismatic owner. Thompson was born in Delaware in 1906 and briefly served in the Office of Strategic Services (the forerunner of the CIA) in Thailand during WWII. Settling in Bangkok after the war, he became interested in Thai silk thanks to his neighbours' traditional livelihood of silk-weaving. His business sense detected an opportunity and he sent samples to fashion houses in Milan, London and Paris, gradually building a steady worldwide clientele and the surviving business that bears his name.

Thompson's story doesn't end with his informal reign as Bangkok's best-adapted foreigner. While out for an afternoon walk in the Cameron Highlands of western Malaysia in 1967, Thompson mysteriously disappeared. That same year his sister was murdered in the USA, fuelling various conspiracy theories. Although the mystery has never been solved, evidence revealed by journalist Joshua Kurlantzick in his profile of Thompson, *The Ideal Man,* suggests that the vocal anti-American stance Thompson took later in his life may have made him a potential target of suppression by the CIA. (Other theories are less spectacular.)

Local Knowledge

Jim Thompson House

NATTEERA YUMONGKOL, CO-SENIOR MANAGER, JIM THOMPSON HOUSE

1 **ARCHITECTURE**
Jim Thompson was an architect, eclectic antique collector and socialite. While his Thai contemporaries were choosing to live in modern (Western-style) houses and bungalows, he envisioned a landscaped jungle residence. Though the buildings – six teak houses collected from different regions – are of traditional Thai construction, the house is organised like a Western residence with a lofty entrance hall, an interior mezzanine staircase, and all rooms arranged on the same level overlooking the terrace and the canal.

2 **ARTS**
A collector with a penchant for Southeast Asian antiques, Thompson bought from travelling merchants and neighbouring countries. He collected objects that were not well known at the time, including from the Dvaravati period. These objects became, with other works in the collection, renowned among art historians and archaeologists.

3 **DESIGN**
His collection is eclectic and includes Ayuthaya, Lopburi and Khmer sculptures as well as Buddhist and rare paintings, Burmese sculptures and tapestries, a large collection of ceramics (especially blue and white china) and an extensive collection of *benjarong* (five-coloured Thai ceramic). He had an acute sense of taste: his collection is beautifully displayed within the house and accented by ambience and natural light.

4 **HISTORY & HERITAGE**
Thompson became a legend. In November 1959 he opened his house to the public for twice-weekly viewings. He intended to leave his house and collection to the Thai people with the aim of preserving Thai arts and crafts that were unknown or vanishing.

If You Like…
House Museums

If you like Jim Thompson House (p72), you'll like these other monuments to traditional local life.

1 BAN KAMTHIENG
(บ้านคำเที่ยง; Map p86; Siam Society, 131 Soi 21 (Asoke), Th Sukhumvit; adult/child 100B/free; ⊙9am-5pm Tue-Sat; Ⓜ Sukhumvit exit 1, Ⓢ Asok exit 3 or 6) Preserves a northern Thai-style house with engaging and informative cultural displays of daily rituals and folk beliefs.

2 SUAN PAKKAD PALACE MUSEUM
(วังสวนผักกาด; Th Si Ayuthaya; admission 100B; ⊙9am-4pm; Ⓢ Phaya Thai exit 4) This collection of eight traditional houses was once a royal residence and is now a museum of traditional Thai arts and crafts.

3 BANGKOKIAN MUSEUM
(พิพิธภัณฑ์ชาวบางกอก; Map p76; 273 Soi 43, Th Charoen Krung; ⊙10am-4pm Wed-Sun; 🚢 Tha Si Phraya) Consisting of three wooden houses, this family-run museum offers a window into Bangkok life during the 1950s and 1960s.

SPAS

Thann Sanctuary   Spa
(Map p82; ☏ 0 2658 0550; www.thann.info; 4th fl, Gaysorn Plaza, cnr Th Ploenchit & Th Ratchadamri; Thai massage from 1500B, spa treatments from 2800B; ⊙10am-9pm; Ⓢ Chit Lom exit 9) This local brand of herbal-based cosmetics also has a series of mall-based spas – perfect for post-shopping therapy. Also at **CentralWorld** (Map p82; ☏ 0 2658 6557; www.thann.info/thann_sanctuary.php; 2nd fl, CentralWorld, Th Ratchadamri; Thai massage from 1500B, spa treatments from 2800B; ⊙10am-7.30pm; Ⓢ Chit Lom exit 9 to Sky Walk, Siam exit 6 to Sky Walk).

Spa 1930   Spa
(Map p82; ☏ 0 2254 8606; www.spa1930.com; 42 Soi Tonson; Thai massage from 1200B, spa packages from 3800B; ⊙9.30am-9.30pm;

Ⓢ Chit Lom exit 4) The menu here is simple (face, body care and body massage), and all scrubs and massage oils are based on traditional Thai herbal remedies.

🎓 Courses

Helping Hands   Cooking
(☏ 08 4901 8717; www.cookingwithpoo.com; 1200B; ⊙lessons 8.30am-1pm) This popular cookery course was started by a native of Khlong Toey's slums and is held in her neighbourhood. Courses, which must be booked in advance, span four dishes and include a visit to Khlong Toey Market and transport to and from **Emporium** (Map p86; www.emporiumthailand.com; cnr Soi 24 & Th Sukhumvit; ⊙10am-10pm; Ⓢ Phrom Phong exit 2).

Amita Thai
Cooking Class   Cooking Course
(☏ 0 2466 8966; www.amitathaicooking.com; 162/17 Soi 14, Th Wutthakat, Thonburi; 3000B; ⊙lessons 9.30am-1pm Thu-Tue) In a canalside house in Thonburi, a course here includes a romp in a herb garden and instruction in four dishes. The fee covers transportation, including boat transfer from Tha Maharaj.

👉 Tours

If you would like someone to guide you through Bangkok, recommended outfits include **Tour with Tong** (☏ 08 1835 0240; www.tourwithtong.com; day tour from 1500B), whose team conducts tours in and around Bangkok, and **Thai Private Tour Guide** (☏ 08 9661 6706, 08 9822 1798; www.thaitourguide.com; day tour from 2000B), where Ms Pu and TJ get good reviews.

RIVER & CANAL TRIPS

Glimpses of Bangkok's past as the 'Venice of the East' are still possible today, even though the motor vehicle has become the city's conveyance of choice. Along the river and the canals is a motley fleet of watercraft from paddled canoes to rice barges. In these areas many homes, trading houses and temples remain oriented towards life on the water, providing a

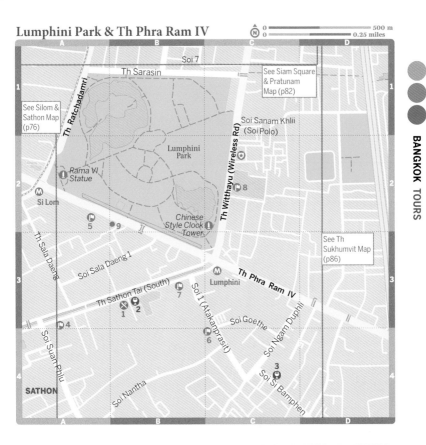

BANGKOK TOURS

Lumphini Park & Th Phra Ram IV

fascinating glimpse into the past when
Thais considered themselves *jôw nám*
(water lords).

The most obvious way to commute
between riverside attractions is on the
public ferries run by Chao Phraya Express
Boat (p95). The terminus for most
northbound boats is Tha Nonthaburi
and for most southbound boats it's Tha
Sathon (also called Central Pier), near
the Saphan Taksin BTS station, although
some boats run as far south as Wat
Ratchasingkhon.

For a more customised view, you might
consider chartering a long-tail boat along
the city's canals.

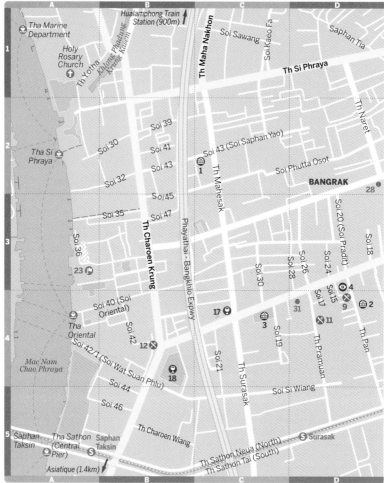

🛏 Sleeping

KO RATANAKOSIN, BANGLAMPHU & THONBURI

Lamphu Treehouse   Hotel **$$**
(Map p64; ☑0 2282 0991; www.lamphutreehotel.
com; 155 Wanchat Bridge, off Th Prachathipatai;
r incl breakfast 1450-2500B; ste incl breakfast
3600-4900B; ❄ @ 🛜 🏊; 🚤Tha Phan Fah)
The rooms, panelled in wood and decorat-
ed with subtle Thai accents, are attractive
and inviting, and the rooftop bar, pool,
internet, restaurant and quiet canal-side
location ensure that you may never feel
the need to leave.

Feung Nakorn Balcony   Hotel **$$**
(Map p64; ☑0 2622 1100; www.feungnakorn.
com; 125 Th Fuang Nakhon; dm incl breakfast
600B; r incl breakfast 1650B; ste incl breakfast
2000-3000B; ❄ @ 🛜; 🚤klorng boat to Tha
Phan Fah) Located in a former school,
the 42 rooms here surround an inviting
garden courtyard and are generally large,
bright and cheery. A charming and invit-

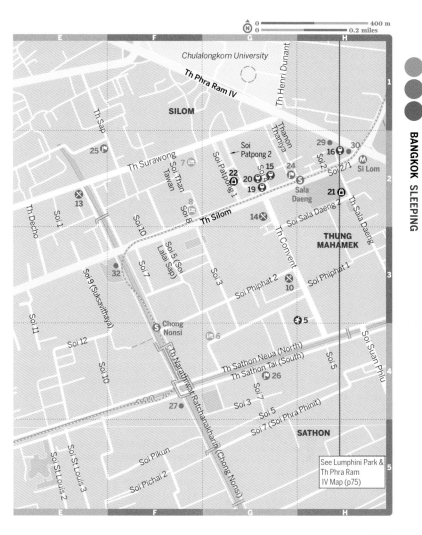

ing, if not extremely great-value, place to stay.

Baan Dinso @ Ratchadamnoen
Hotel $$

(Map p64; ☏ 08 6815 3300; www.baandinso.com; 78/3 Th Ratchadamnoen Klang; r incl breakfast 800-3100B; ✳ 🛜; 🚤 klorng boat to Tha Phan Fah) This antique wooden villa may not represent the best deal in Bangkok, but for accommodation with a nostalgic feel and palpable sense of place, it's almost impossible to beat.

Arun Residence
Hotel $$$

(Map p64; ☏ 0 2221 9158; www.arunresidence.com; 36-38 Soi Pratu Nokyung; r incl breakfast 4000-4200B; ste incl breakfast 5800B; ✳ @ 🛜; 🚤 Tha Tien) Although strategically located across from Wat Arun, this multilevel wooden house on the river boasts much more than just brilliant views. The six rooms here manage to feel both homey and stylish, some being tall and loftlike, while others join two rooms (the best is the top-floor Arun Suite, with its own balcony). There are also inviting communal

Silom & Sathon

areas, including a library, rooftop bar and restaurant. Reservations essential.

CHINATOWN

Loy La Long Hotel $$
(Map p70; ☎0 2639 1390; www.loylalong.com; 1620/2 Th Songwat; dm incl breakfast 1300B, r incl breakfast 2100-4000B; ❄@🛜; 🚤Tha Ratchawong, Ⓜ Hua Lamphong exit 1 & taxi) Rustic, retro, charming: the six rooms in this 100-year-old wooden house can claim heaps of personality. And united by breezy, inviting nooks and crannies and a unique location elevated over Mae Nam Chao Phraya, the whole place boasts a hidden, almost secret feel. The only downside is finding it; to get there, proceed to Th Songwat and cut directly through Wat Patumkongka Rachaworawiharn to the river.

SILOM & SATHON

Smile Society Hotel $$
(Map p76; ☎08 1343 1754, 08 1442 5800; www.smilesocietyhostel.com; 30/3-4 Soi 6, Th Silom; dm incl breakfast 420B, r incl breakfast 900-1880B; ❄@🛜; Ⓜ Si Lom exit 2, Ⓢ Sala Daeng exit 1) Part boutique, part hostel, this four-storey shophouse combines small but comfortable and well-equipped rooms and dorms with spotless shared bathrooms. A central location, a communal area with TV and free computers, and helpful, English-speaking staff are additional perks.

Café Ice Residence Guesthouse $$
(Map p76; ☎0 2636 7831; cafeiceresidences@gmail.com; 44/4 Soi Phiphat 2; r incl breakfast 1900-3300B; ❄@🛜; Ⓢ Chong Nonsi exit 2) More home than hotel, the nine rooms in this spotless, classy villa are inviting, spacious and comfortable.

Siam Heritage Hotel $$$
(Map p76; ☎0 2353 6101; www.thesiamheritage. com; 115/1 Th Surawong; incl breakfast r 2900B, ste 4000-9300B; ❄@🛜🏊; Ⓜ Si Lom exit 2, Ⓢ Sala Daeng exit 1) Tucked off busy Th Surawong, this classy boutique hotel oozes with homey Thai charm – probably because the owners also live in the same building. The 73 rooms are decked out in silk and dark woods with classy design touches and thoughtful amenities.

SIAM SQUARE & PRATUNAM

Wendy House
Hostel **$$**

(Map p82; ✆0 2214 1149; www.wendyguest house.com; 36/2 Soi Kasem San 1; r incl breakfast 1100-1490B; ✷ @ ⏾; S National Stadium exit 1) The rooms here are small and basic, but exceedingly clean and relatively well stocked (TV, fridge) for this price range.

Golden House
Hotel **$$**

(Map p82; ✆0 2252 9535; www.goldenhouses. net; 1025/5-9 Th Ploenchit; r incl breakfast 1800-2000B; ✷ ⏾; S Chit Lom exit 1) With parquet flooring and built-in wooden furniture, the 27 rooms here are more like modern Thai condos than hotel rooms. The beds are huge, but just like those of Thai condos, they have a tendency to sag.

SUKHUMVIT

Fusion Suites
Hotel **$$**

(Map p86; ✆0 2665 2644; www.fusionbangkok. com; 143/61-62 Soi 21 (Asoke), Th Sukhumvit; r incl breakfast 2600-5200B; ✷ @ ⏾; M Sukhumvit exit 1, S Asok exit 1) A disproportionately funky hotel for this price range, unconventional furnishings provide the rooms here with heaps of style, although the cheapest can feel a bit dark.

Seven
Hotel **$$$**

(Map p86; ✆0 2662 0951; www.sleepatseven. com; 3/15 Soi 31, Th Sukhumvit; r incl breakfast 4708-7062B; ✷ ⏾; S Phrom Phong exit 5) This tiny hotel somehow manages to be chic and homey, stylish and comfortable, Thai and international all at the same time. Each of the five rooms is decked out in a different colour that corresponds to Thai astrology, and thoughtful amenities and friendly service abound.

 Eating

Fans of street food be forewarned that all of Bangkok's stalls close on Monday for compulsory street cleaning (the results of which are never entirely evident come Tuesday morning).

During the annual **Vegetarian Festival** (◷**Sep or Oct**) in September/October, Bangkok's Chinatown becomes a virtual orgy of nonmeat cuisine. The festivities centre on Chinatown's main street, Th Yaowarat, and the Talat Noi area, but food shops and stalls all over the city post yellow flags to announce their meat-free status.

Chinatown

KO RATANAKOSIN & BANGLAMPHU

Pa Aew
Thai $

(Map p64; Th Maha Rat, no Roman-script sign; mains 20-60B; ⏰10am-5pm; 🚤Tha Tien) Yes, it's a bare-bones, open-air curry stall, but if we're talking taste, Pa Aew is our favourite place to eat in this corner of town. Pa Aew is in front of the Krung Thai Bank near Soi Pratu Nokyung.

Krua Apsorn
Thai $$

(Map p64; www.kruaapsorn.com; Th Din So; mains 65-350B; ⏰10.30am-8pm Mon-Sat; 🚤klorng boat to Tha Phan Fah) Must-eat dishes include mussels fried with fresh herbs, the decadent crab fried in yellow chilli oil and the *tortilla Española*-like crab omelette.

Hemlock
Thai $$

(Map p64; 56 Th Phra Athit; mains 75-280B; ⏰4pm-midnight Mon-Sat; 🌱; 🚤Tha Phra Athit (Banglamphu)) This white-tablecloth, shophouse-bound local is an appropriately 'safe' intro to Thai food.

Jay Fai
Thai $$$

(Map p64; 327 Th Mahachai; mains from 400B; ⏰3pm-2am Tue-Sun; 🚤klorng boat to Tha Phan Fah) You wouldn't think so by looking at her bare-bones dining room, but Jay Fai is known far and wide for serving Bangkok's most expensive – and arguably most delicious – *pàt kêe mow* ('drunkard's noodles').

CHINATOWN & PHAHURAT

Thanon Phadungdao Seafood Stalls
Thai $$

(Map p70; cnr Th Phadungdao & Th Yaowarat; mains 100-600B; ⏰4pm-midnight Tue-Sun; 🚤Tha Ratchawong, Ⓜ Hua Lamphong exit 1 & taxi) After sunset, these two opposing open-air restaurants – each of which claims to be the original – become a culinary train wreck of outdoor barbecues, screaming staff, iced seafood trays and messy sidewalk seating.

SILOM & SATHON

Chennai Kitchen
Indian $

(Map p76; 10 Th Pan; mains 70-150B; ⏰10am-3pm & 6-9pm; 🌱; Ⓢ Surasak exit 3) The arm-length *dosai* (a crispy southern Indian bread) here is always a wise choice, but if you're feeling indecisive, go for the vegetarian *thali* set that seems to incorporate just about everything in the kitchen.

Kalapapruek
Thai $

(Map p76; 27 Th Pramuan; mains 80-150B; ⏰8am-6pm Mon-Sat, to 3pm Sun; Ⓢ Surasak exit 3) This venerable Thai eatery has numerous branches and mall spin-offs around town, but we always go back to this, the free-standing original branch. The diverse menu spans regional Thai specialities from just about every region,

Street food stall
DESIGN PICS/RAY LASKOWITZ/GETTY IMAGES ©

A Taste of Bangkok

You can't say you've tried Bangkok-style Thai food unless you've tasted at least a couple of the following:

○ *Gŏo·ay dĕe·o reu·a* – Known as boat noodles because they were previously served from small boats along the canals of central Thailand, these intense pork- or beef-based bowls are among the most full-flavoured of Thai noodle dishes. Try a bowl at **Bharani** (Sansab Boat Noodle; Map p86; 96/14 Soi 23, Th Sukhumvit; mains 50-200B; ⊙11am-10pm; M̄Sukhumvit exit 2, S̄Asok exit 3).

○ *Gŏo·ay dĕe·o kôo·a gài* – Wide rice noodles fried with little more than egg, chicken, preserved squid and garlic oil is a humble but delicious Thai-Chinese dish sold from numerous stalls in Bangkok's Chinatown.

○ *Kôw mòk* – Biryani, a dish found across the Muslim world, also has a foothold in Bangkok. We love the old-school version served at decades-old **Muslim Restaurant** (Map p76; 1354-6 Th Charoen Krung; mains 40-140B; ⊙6.30am-5.30pm; 🚣Tha Oriental, S̄Saphan Taksin exit 1).

○ *Mèe gròrp* – Crispy noodles made the traditional way, with a sweet/sour flavour (a former palace recipe), are a dying breed. Longstanding Banglamphu restaurant **Chote Chitr** (Map p64; 146 Th Phraeng Phuthon; mains 30-200B; ⊙11am-10pm; 🚣klorng boat to Tha Phan Fah) serves an excellent version of the dish.

daily specials and, occasionally, seasonal treats as well.

Somtam Convent
Northeastern Thai **$**

('Hai'; Map p76; 2/4-5 Th Convent; mains 30-100B; ⊙11am-9pm Mon-Fri, to 5pm Sat; M̄Si Lom exit 2, S̄Sala Daeng exit 2) An unintimidating introduction to the wonders of *lâhp* (a minced meat 'salad'), *sôm·đam* (spicy green papaya salad) and other Isan delights can be had at this noisy shophouse restaurant.

nahm
Thai **$$$**

(Map p75; ✆0 2625 3388; www.comohotels. com/metropolitanbangkok/dining/nahm; ground fl, Metropolitan Hotel, 27 Th Sathon Tai (South); set lunch 1100B, set dinner 2000B, mains 180-700B; ⊙noon-2pm Mon-Fri, 7-10.30pm daily; M̄Lumphini exit 2) Australian chef/author David Thompson is behind what is quite possibly the best Thai restaurant in Bangkok. Using ancient cookbooks as his inspiration, Thompson has given new life to previously extinct and exotic-sounding dishes such as 'smoked fish curry with prawns, chicken livers, cockles and black pepper'.

Eat Me
International **$$$**

(Map p76; ✆0 2238 0931; www.eatmerestaurant. com; Soi Phiphat 2; mains 340-1350B; ⊙3pm-1am; ✐; M̄Si Lom exit 2, S̄Sala Daeng exit 2) The dishes at this longstanding restaurant, with descriptions like 'fig & blue cheese ravioli w/ walnuts, rosemary and brown butter', or 'beef cheek tagine w/ saffron and dates', may sound all over the map or perhaps even somewhat pretentious, but they're actually just plain tasty.

Somboon Seafood
Thai **$$$**

(Map p76; ✆0 2233 3104; www.somboonsea food.com; cnr Th Surawong & Th Narathiwat Ratchanakharin (Chong Nonsi); mains 120-900B; ⊙4-11.30pm; S̄Chong Nonsi exit 3) Holy seafood factory: ascending the many staircases to a free table might make you nervous about the quality of so much quantity. But Somboon's legendary 'fried curry crab' will make you messy and full.

Siam Square & Pratunam

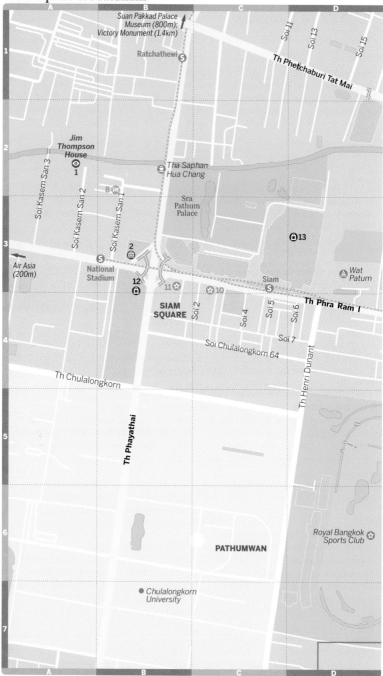

Suan Pakkad Palace
Museum (800m);
Victory Monument (1.4km)

Ratchathewi Ⓢ

Th Phetchaburi Tat Mai

Soi 11
Soi 13
Soi 15

Jim
Thompson
House
◎ 1

Soi Kasem San 3

Soi Kasem San 2

Soi Kasem San 1

8 ▣

Tha Saphan
Hua Chang

Sra
Pathum
Palace

🔒 13

Air Asia
(200m)

Ⓢ
National
Stadium

2
🏛

12
🔒

11 ☆

Siam Ⓢ

Wat
Patum

☆ 10

Th Phra Ram I

SIAM
SQUARE

Soi 2

Soi 4

Soi 5

Soi 6

Soi 7

Soi Chulalongkorn 64

Th Henri Dunant

Th Chulalongkorn

Th Phayathai

PATHUMWAN

Royal Bangkok
Sports Club ☆

Chulalongkorn
University

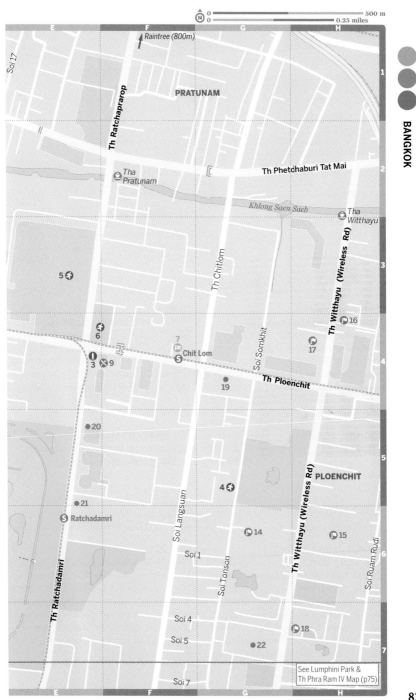

Raintree (800m)

PRATUNAM

Th Ratchaprarop

Th Phetchaburi Tat Mai

Tha Pratunam

Khlong Saen Saeb

Tha Witthayu

Th Chitlom

5

6

7

Chit Lom

3 9

Soi Somkhit

16

17

Th Witthayu (Wireless Rd)

Th Ploenchit

19

20

21

Ratchadamri

4

Th Ratchadamri

Soi Langsuan

Soi 1

Soi Tonson

PLOENCHIT

14

Th Witthayu (Wireless Rd)

15

Soi Ruam Rudi

Soi 4

Soi 5

18

22

Soi 7

See Lumphini Park &
Th Phra Ram IV Map (p75)

Siam Square & Pratunam

SIAM SQUARE & PRATUNAM

MBK Food Island   Thai $

(Map p82; 6th fl, MBK Center, cnr Th Phra Ram I & Th Phayathai; mains 35-150B; ⊙10am-10pm; ☝; ⑤National Stadium exit 4) The granddaddy of food courts offers tens of vendors selling dishes from virtually every corner of Thailand and beyond. Standouts include a good vegetarian food stall (stall C8) and a very decent Isan food vendor (C22).

Gourmet Paradise   Thai $

(Map p82; ground fl, Siam Paragon, 991/1 Th Phra Ram I; ⊙10am-10pm; ⑤ Siam exits 3 & 5) The perpetually busy Gourmet Paradise unites international fast-food chains, domestic restaurants and food court–style stalls, with a particular emphasis on the sweet stuff.

Crystal Jade La Mian Xiao Long Bao   Chinese $$

(Map p82; basement, Erawan Bangkok, 494 Th Ploenchit; mains 115-450B; ⊙11am-10pm; ☝; ⑤Chit Lom exit 8) The tongue-twistingly long name refers to the restaurant's signature wheat noodles (la mian) and the famous Shanghainese steamed dumplings (xiao long pao).

SUKHUMVIT

Imoya   Japanese $

(Map p86; 3rd fl, Terminal Shop Cabin, 2/17-19 Soi 24, Th Sukhumvit; mains 40-400B; ⊙6pm-midnight; ⑤Phrom Phong exit 4) A visit to this well-hidden Japanese restaurant, with its antique advertisements, wood panelling, wall of sake bottles and stuck-in-time prices is like taking a trip in a time machine.

Soi 38 Night Market   Thai $

(Map p86; cnr Soi 38 & Th Sukhumvit; mains 30-60B; ⊙8pm-3am; ⑤Thong Lo exit 4) After a hard night of clubbing, this strip of basic Thai-Chinese stalls will look like a shimmering oasis. If you're going sober, stick to the knot of 'famous' vendors on the right-hand side as you enter the street.

Pier 21   Thai $

(Map p86; 5th fl, Terminal 21, cnr Th Sukhumvit & Soi 21 (Asoke); mains 39-200B; ⊙10am-10pm; ☝; ⓂSukhumvit exit 3, ⑤Asok exit 3) Ascend a seemingly endless number of escalators to arrive at this noisy food court made up of vendors from across the city. The selection is vast and the dishes are exceedingly cheap, even by Thai standards.

Supanniga Eating Room   Thai $$
(Map p86; www.supannigaeatingroom.com; 160/11 Soi 55 (Thong Lor), Th Sukhumvit; mains 120-350B; ⏱11.30am-2.30pm & 5.30-11.30pm; 🔧; S Thong Lo exit 3 & taxi) Thais are finally starting to take a serious interest in their own cuisine, and over the past few years Bangkok has seen an explosion of sophisticated-feeling places serving regional Thai dishes. The best of the lot is probably Supanniga, which focuses on the typically seafood-based, herb-forward dishes of Chanthaburi and Trat in western Thailand.

Nasir Al-Masri   Middle Eastern $$$
(Map p86; 4/6 Soi 3/1, Th Sukhumvit; mains 160-370B; ⏱24hr; 🔧; S Nana exit 1) One of several Middle Eastern restaurants on Soi 3/1, Nasir Al-Masri is easily recognisable by its thoroughly impressive floor-to-ceiling stainless steel 'theme'.

Bo.lan   Thai $$$
(Map p86; 🕿0 2260 2962; www.bolan.co.th; 42 Soi Rongnarong Phichai Songkhram, Soi 26, Th Sukhumvit; set dinner 1980B; ⏱6pm-midnight Tue-Sun; S Phrom Phong exit 4) Chefs Bo and Dylan (Bo.lan is a play on words that also means 'ancient') take a scholarly approach to Thai cuisine, and generous set meals featuring full flavoured Thai dishes are the results of this tuition. Reservations recommended.

Opposite Mess Hall   International $$$
(Map p86; www.oppositebangkok.com; 2nd fl, 27/2 Soi 51, Th Sukhumvit; mains 220-650B; ⏱6-11pm Tue-Sun; 🔧; S Thong Lo exit 1) Much like the dishes it serves (example: 'savoury duck waffle, leg confit, pate, crispy skin & pically relish'), Opposite can be a bit hard to pin down. But how can you go wrong with a cosy space, friendly service and really excellent cocktails?

Soul Food Mahanakorn   Thai $$$
(Map p86; 🕿0 2714 7708; www.soulfoodmahanakorn.com; 56/10 Soi 55 (Thong Lor), Th Sukhumvit; mains 220-300B; ⏱5.30pm-midnight; 🔧; S Thong Lo exit 3) Soul Food gets its interminable buzz from its dual nature as both an inviting restaurant – the menu spans tasty interpretations of rustic Thai dishes – and a bar serving deliciously boozy, Thai-influenced cocktails. Reservations recommended.

Barbecue stall, Th Sukhumvit

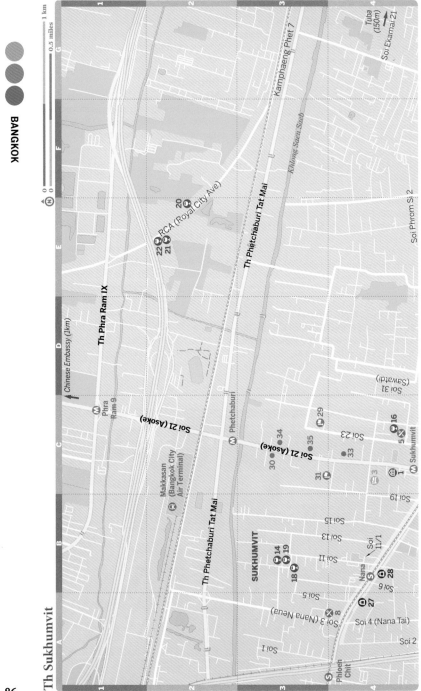

Th Sukhumvit

BANGKOK

0   0.5 miles
0   1 km

Chinese Embassy (1km)

Th Phra Ram IX

RCA (Royal City Ave)

Th Phetchaburi Tat Mai

Th Phetchaburi Tat Mai

Phra Ram 9

Soi 21 (Asoke)

Makkasan
(Bangkok City
Air Terminal)

M Phetchaburi

Soi 21 (Asoke)

Khlong Saen Saeb

Kamphaeng Phet 7

Tuba
(150m)

Soi Ekamai 21

Soi Phrom Si 2

Soi 31
(Sawatdi)

Soi 23

M Sukhumvit

Soi 19

SUKHUMVIT

Soi 15

Soi 13

Soi 11

Soi
11/1

Nana

Soi 9

Soi 6

Soi 5

Soi 3 (Nana Neua)

Soi 4 (Nana Tai)

Soi 2

Soi 1

Phloen
Chit

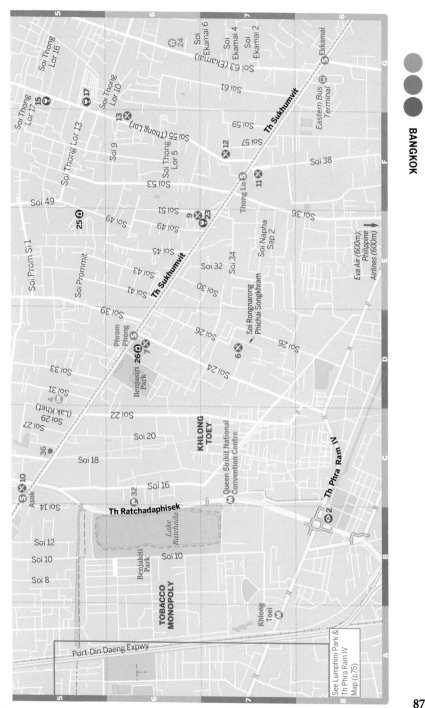

Th Sukhumvit

🍷 Drinking & Nightlife

KO RATANAKOSIN, BANGLAMPHU & THONBURI

Rolling Bar   Bar
(Map p64; Th Prachathipatai; ⏰5pm-midnight; 🚤klorng boat to Tha Phan Fah) An escape from hectic Th Khao San is a good enough excuse to schlep to this quiet canal-side boozer. Tasty bar snacks and live music are excuses to stay.

Center Khao Sarn   Bar
(Map p64; Th Khao San; ⏰24hr; 🚤Tha Phra Athit (Banglamphu)) Come here for centre-court, front-row views of the human parade on Th Khao San. The upstairs bar hosts late-night bands.

Phra Nakorn Bar & Gallery   Bar
(Map p64; 58/2 Soi Damnoen Klang Tai; ⏰5pm-1am; 🚤klorng boat to Tha Phan Fah) Located an arm's length from the hype of Th Khao San, Phranakorn Bar is a home away from hovel for students and arty types, with eclectic decor and changing gallery exhibits. Our tip: head directly for the breezy rooftop and order some of the bar's cheap 'n' tasty Thai food.

Amorosa   Bar
(Map p64; www.arunresidence.com; rooftop, Arun Residence, 36-38 Soi Pratu Nokyung; ⏰5pm-midnight Mon-Thu, to 1am Fri-Sun; 🚤Tha Tien) This is the original venue for a riverside sundowner in Ko Ratanakosin. The views of Wat Arun are a lot more impressive than the quality of the drinks.

Triple-d   Bar
(Map p64; 3rd fl, 44 Th Chakraphong; ⏰6pm-late; 🚤Tha Phra Athit (Banglamphu)) This vaguely Middle Eastern–themed bar represents the posh alter ego of Th Khao San. There's live music, lounges for sucking down a sheesha, and a dark club. And the bar's elevated setting appears to lend it some leniency with the city's strict closing times.

SILOM & SATHON

Tapas Room   Nightclub
(Map p76; 114/17-18 Soi 4, Th Silom; admission 100B; ⏰9pm-2am; Ⓜ Si Lom exit 2, Ⓢ Sala Daeng exit 1) You won't find gazpacho here, but the name is an accurate indicator of

the Spanish/Moroccan-inspired vibe of this multilevel den. Come from Wednesday to Saturday when the combination of DJs and live percussion brings the body count to critical level.

Maggie Choo's
Bar

(Map p76; www.facebook.com/maggiechoos; basement, Novotel Bangkok Fenix Silom, 320 Th Silom; ☺6.30pm-1.30am; ⑤Surasak exit 1) A former bank vault with a Chinatown opium den vibe; secret passageways; lounging women in silk dresses; with all this going on, it's easy to forget that the new Maggie Choo's is actually a bar.

Moon Bar
Bar

(Map p75; www.banyantree.com; 61st fl, Banyan Tree Hotel, 21/100 Th Sathon (South) Tai; ☺5pm-1am; ⓂLumphini exit 2) The Banyan Tree Hotel's Moon Bar kick-started the rooftop trend and, as Bangkok continues to grow at a mad pace, the view from 61 floors up only gets better. Arrive well before sunset (and be well dressed) and grab a coveted seat to the right of the bar for the most impressive views.

Sky Bar
Bar

(Map p76; www.lebua.com/sky-bar; 63rd fl, State Tower, 1055 Th Silom; ☺6pm-1am; ⑤Saphan Taksin exit 3) Allegedly one of the highest alfresco bars in the world, Sky Bar, located on the 63rd floor of this upmarket restaurant compound, provides heart-stopping views over Chao Phraya River. Note that the dress code doesn't allow access to those wearing shorts and sandals.

DJ Station
Nightclub

(Map p76; www.dj-station.com; 8/6-8 Soi 2, Th Silom; admission from 100B; ☺10.30pm-3am; ⓂSi Lom exit 2, ⑤Sala Daeng exit 1) Lower Th Silom is Bangkok's unofficial gaybourhood, and highlights include tiny Soi 2, which is lined with dance clubs including this place, one of Bangkok's and indeed Asia's most legendary gay dance clubs. The crowd is a mix of Thai guppies (gay professionals), money boys and a few Westerners.

Local Knowledge

River & Canal Life

PYLIN (JANE) SANGUANPIYAPAND, OWNER OF SEVEN (P79)

1 KHLONG BANGKOK NOI
This Thonburi canal has a wonderful simplicity to it. Kids play in the water, granddads check out the scene from a humble wooden porch, monks clean the temple grounds. There are also vendors selling all kinds of things from their boats. You can charter a long-tail boat to tour the canals from any of the riverside piers, including Tha Chang and Tha Phra Athit.

2 WAT ARUN
This fantastic riverside temple commands a powerful view of the river and holds an important place in Bangkok's history. It was founded after the fall of Ayuthaya as a sign that the country could be reborn. Though Wat Arun (p60) looks very good from the water, it is even better looking from land. Be sure to tour the grounds to discover that the imposing structure is actually covered with delicate pieces of porcelain mosaic.

3 DINING & DRINKING
I live in a condo beside the river so I often toast it from my own balcony but tourists can enjoy the view from Amorosa (p88). This is one of the best places to photograph Wat Arun, directly across the river. There are many riverfront restaurants but lately I've migrated inland to Ruan Urai (Rose Hotel, 118 Th Surawong). Prices are high but the standards and the authenticity of the food are amazing.

4 KO KRET
Ko Kret is a car-free island in the middle of Mae Nam Chao Phraya and home to one of Thailand's oldest settlements of Mon people. The Mon are skilled potters, and Ko Kret continues the ancient tradition of hand-thrown earthenware made from local clay. You can get there by cross-river ferry from Pak Kret, north of Bangkok and accessible by Chao Phraya Express Boat.

Reputable Tailors

One night in Bangkok...is not enough to get a suit made. Especially at recommended tailors such as these:

July (Map p76; 📞 0 2233 0171; www.julytailor.com; 30/6 Th Sala Daeng; 🕙9am-7pm; Ⓜ Si Lom exit 2, Ⓢ Sala Daeng exit 4) Tailor to Thailand's royalty and elite alike, the suits here don't come cheap and the cuts can be somewhat conservative, but the quality is unsurpassed.

Duly (Map p86; 📞 0 2662 6647; www.laladuly.co.th; Soi 49, Th Sukhumvit; 🕙10am-7pm; Ⓢ Phrom Phong exit 1) High-quality Italian fabrics and experienced tailors make Duly one of the best places in Bangkok to commission a sharp shirt.

Raja's Fashions (Map p86; 📞 0 2253 8379; www.rajasfashions.com; 160/1 Th Sukhumvit; 🕙6.30am-10.30pm Mon-Sat; Ⓢ Nana exit 4) One of Bangkok's more famous tailors, Raja's gets a mixed bag of reviews, but the majority swear by the service and quality.

Nickermann's (Map p86; 📞 0 2252 6682; www.nickermanns.net; basement, Landmark Hotel, 138 Th Sukhumvit; 🕙10am-8.30pm Mon-Sat, noon-6pm Sun; Ⓢ Nana exit 2) Corporate women rave about Nickermann's tailor-made power suits: pants and jackets that suit curves and busts.

Telephone Pub   Bar
(Map p76; www.telephonepub.com; 114/11-13 Soi 4, Th Silom; 🕙6pm-1am; 🛜; Ⓜ Si Lom exit 2, Ⓢ Sala Daeng exit 1) Soi 4 is home to a more casual gay scene than that on Soi 2.

Balcony   Bar
(Map p76; www.balconypub.com; 86-88 Soi 4, Th Silom; 🕙5.30pm-1am; 🛜; Ⓜ Si Lom exit 2, Ⓢ Sala Daeng exit 1) Located directly across from Telephone, this is yet another long-standing cafelike pub that features the occasional drag-queen performance.

SUKHUMVIT

WTF   Bar
(Map p86; www.wtfbangkok.com; 7 Soi 51, Th Sukhumvit; 🕙6pm-1am Tue-Sun; Ⓢ Thong Lo exit 3) No, not that WTF; Wonderful Thai Friendship combines a bar and an art gallery in one attractive package. Throw in some of Bangkok's best cocktails, delicious Spanish-influenced bar snacks and a friendly, artsy clientele and as far as we're concerned, you've got Bangkok's best bar.

Badmotel   Bar
(Map p86; www.facebook.com/badmotel; Soi 55 (Thong Lor), Th Sukhumvit; 🕙5pm-1.30am; Ⓢ Thong Lo exit 3 & taxi) The new Badmotel blends the modern and the kitschy, the cosmopolitan and the Thai, in a way that has struck a (admittedly detached) nerve among Bangkok hipsters.

Glow   Nightclub
(Map p86; www.glowbkk.com; 96/415 Soi Prasanmit, Th Sukhumvit; admission from 400B; 🕙7pm-2am; Ⓜ Sukhumvit exit 2, Ⓢ Asok exit 3) Glow is a small venue with a big reputation. Boasting a huge variety of vodkas and a recently upgraded sound system, the tunes range from hip-hop to electronica and just about everything in between.

Iron Fairies   Bar
(Map p86; www.theironfairies.com; 394 Soi 55 (Thong Lor), Th Sukhumvit; 🕙6pm-2am; Ⓢ Thong Lo exit 3 & taxi) Imagine, if you can, an abandoned fairy factory in Paris c 1912, and you'll get an idea of the design theme at this popular wine bar. If you manage to wrangle one of a handful of seats, the staff claim to serve Bangkok's

best burgers and there's live music after 9.30pm.

Q Bar
Nightclub

(Map p86; www.qbarbangkok.com; 34 Soi 11, Th Sukhumvit; admission from 600B; ⊗8pm-2am; Ⓢ Nana exit 3) In club years, Q Bar is fast approaching retirement age, but big-name guest DJs and a recent renovation have ensured that it still maintains a place in Bangkok's club scene. For something a bit more low-key, consider the attached Parsian-themed absinthe speakeasy, **Le Derrière** (Map p86; Q Bar, 34 Soi 11, Th Sukhumvit; ⊗9pm-3am; Ⓢ Nana exit 3).

Above 11
Bar

(Map p86; ☑08 3542 1111; www.aboveeleven. com; 33rd fl, Fraser Suites Sukhumvit, Soi 11, Th Sukhumvit; ⊗6pm-2am; Ⓢ Nana exit 3) Couple downward glances of Bangkok's most cosmopolitan neighbourhood with the Peruvian/Japanese bar snacks at this sophisticated rooftopper.

Wong's Place
Bar

(Map p75; 27/3 Soi Si Bamphen; ⊗9pm-late Tue-Sun; Ⓜ Lumphini exit 1) This dusty den is a time warp into the backpacker world of the early 1980s. The namesake owner died several years ago, but a relative removed the padlock and picked up where Wong left off. Wong's works equally well as a destination or a last resort, but don't bother knocking until midnight, keeping in mind that it stays open until the last person crawls out.

RCA
Nightclub

(Royal City Avenue; Map p86; Royal City Ave, off Th Phra Ram IX; Ⓜ Phra Ram 9 exit 3 & taxi) Formerly a bastion of the teen scene, this Vegas-like strip has finally graduated from high school to become Bangkok's premier clubbing zone, although it must be said

that its Top 40 roots still show. **Slim/Flix** (Map p86; www.facebook.com/slimbkk; Royal City Ave, off Th Phra Ram IX; ⊗8pm-2am; Ⓜ Phra Ram 9 exit 3 & taxi) and **Route 66** (Map p86; www.route66club.com; 29/33-48 Royal City Ave (RCA), off Th Phra Ram IX; ⊗8pm-2am; Ⓜ Phra Ram 9 exit 3 & taxi) are the big hitters here, and foreigners must pay a 300B entry fee on Fridays and Saturdays.

⭐ Entertainment

LIVE MUSIC

Parking Toys
Live Music

(☑0 2907 2228; 17/22 Soi Mayalap, off Kaset-Navamin Hwy; ⊗6pm-2am; Ⓢ Mo Chit exit 3 & taxi) One of Bangkok's best venues for live music, Parking Toys hosts an eclectic revolving cast of fun bands ranging from acoustic/classical ensembles to electro-funk jam acts. Take a taxi heading north from BTS Mo Chit and ask the driver to go to Kaset-Navamin Hwy. Upon passing the second stop light on this road, look for the small Heineken sign on your left.

Sky Bar (p89)
VISIONS OF OUR LAND /GETTY IMAGES ©

OLIVER STREWE/GETTY IMAGES ©

⭐ Don't Miss
Chatuchak Weekend Market

Among the largest markets in the world, Chatuchak seems to unite everything buyable, from used vintage sneakers to baby squirrels. Plan to spend a full day, as there's plenty to see, do and buy. But come early, ideally around 9am to 10am, to beat the crowds and the heat.

Once you're deep in the bowels of Chatuchak, it will seem like there is no order and no escape, but the market is arranged into relatively coherent sections. Use the clock tower as a handy landmark.

NEED TO KNOW

ตลาดนัดจตุจักร, Talat Nat Jatujak; www.chatuchak.org; Th Phahonyothin; ⊙9am-6pm Sat & Sun; Ⓜ Chatuchak Park exit 1, Kamphaeng Phet exits 1 & 2, Ⓢ Mo Chit exit 1

Raintree   Live Music
(116/63-64 Th Rang Nam; ⊙8pm-2am; Ⓢ Victory Monument exit 2) This rustic pub is one of the few remaining places in town to hear 'songs for life', Thai folk music with roots in the communist insurgency of the 1960s and 1970s.

Sonic   Live Music
(Map p86; www.facebook.com/SonicBangkok; 90 Soi 63 (Ekamai), Th Sukhumvit; ⊙6pm-2am; Ⓢ Ekkamai exit 4 & taxi) Drawing a mixture of Thai bands, touring indie acts, big-name DJs and a painfully hip crowd, the new Sonic has emerged as Bangkok's hottest venue for live music.

THAI BOXING (MOO·AY TAI)

Thai boxing's best of the best fight it out at Bangkok's two boxing stadiums: **Ratchadamnoen Stadium** (Map p64; off Th Ratchadamnoen Nok; tickets 3rd-class/2nd-class/ringside 1000/1500/2000B; 🚣 klorng boat to Tha Phan Fah, Ⓢ Phaya Thai exit 3 & taxi) and **Lumpinee Boxing Stadium**

(www.muaythailumpinee.net/en/index.php; Th
Ramintra; tickets 3rd class/2nd class/ringside
1000/2000/3000B; M Chatuchak Park exit 2 &
taxi, S Mo Chit exit 3 & taxi).

Fights are held throughout the week,
alternating between the two stadiums.
Ratchadamnoen hosts the matches at
6pm on Monday, Wednesday, Thursday
and Sunday. Lumpinee hosts matches
at 6.30pm on Tuesday and Friday and
at 4pm and 8.30pm on Saturday.

As a prematch warm-up, grab a
plate of *gài yâhng* (grilled chicken)
and other northeastern dishes
from the restaurants surrounding
Ratchadamnoen Stadium.

CINEMA

Movies are a fantastic deal in Bangkok.

Paragon Cineplex　　Cinema
(Map p82; 📞 0 2129 4635; www.paragon
cineplex.com; 5th fl, Siam Paragon, 991/1 Th
Phra Ram I; S Siam exits 3 & 5) This cinema
offers both quantity (more than a
dozen screens) and quality (several
classes of viewing).

Scala　　Cinema
(Map p82; 📞 0 2251 2861; Soi 1, Siam Sq;
S Siam exit 2) An old-school standalone
theatre.

Lido　　Cinema
(Map p82; 📞 0 2252 6498; www.apexsiam-
square.com; btwn Soi 2 & Soi 3, Siam Sq; S Siam
exit 2) A good option for the retro-inclined
cinema-goer.

🔒 Shopping

MBK Center　　Shopping Centre
(Map p82; www.mbk-center.com; cnr Th Phra Ram
I & Th Phayathai; ⏰10am-10pm; S National Stadium exit 4) This colossal mall has become
a tourist destination in its own right.
Swedish and other languages can be
heard as much as Thai, and on any given
weekend half of Bangkok can be found
combing through its inexhaustible range
of small stalls and shops.

❤ If You Like...
Markets

If you like Chatuchak Weekend Market,
check these out for more shopping heaven.

1 PAK KHLONG TALAT
(ปากคลองตลาด, Flower Market; Map p70; Th
Chakraphet; ⏰24hr; 🚢Tha Saphan Phut (Memorial
Bridge)) The city's largest depot for wholesale
flowers; deliveries arrive after dark.

2 ASIATIQUE
(www.thaiasiatique.com; Soi 72-76, Th Charoen
Krung; ⏰4-11pm; 🚢shuttle boat from Tha Sathon
(Central Pier)) An upscale version of Chatuchak
Market along Mae Nam Chao Phraya.

3 PATPONG NIGHT MARKET
(Map p76; Soi Patpong 1 & 2, Th Silom; ⏰6pm-
midnight; M Si Lom exit 2, S Sala Daeng exit 1)
One of many after-dark souvenir markets with the
added pedigree of being amidst one of the city's
most famous red-light districts.

4 KHLONG TOEY MARKET
(ตลาดคลองเตย; Map p86; cnr Th
Ratchadaphisek & Th Phra Ram IV; ⏰5-10am;
M Khlong Toei exit 1) The city's largest fresh
market selling fruit, vegetables, meat, fish and
other foodstuffs.

Siam Paragon　　Shopping Centre
(Map p82; www.siamparagon.co.th; 991/1 Th
Phra Ram I; ⏰10am-10pm; S Siam exits 3 & 5)
The biggest and glitziest of Bangkok's
shopping malls, Siam Paragon is more
of an urban park than a shopping centre.
Astronomically luxe brands occupy most
floors, but there's also **Siam Ocean World**
(สยามโอเชี่ยนเวิร์ล; Map p82; www.siamocean-
world.com; basement, Siam Paragon, 991/1 Th
Phra Ram I; adult/child 900/700B; ⏰10am-9pm;
S Siam exits 3 & 5), Siam Paragon Cineplex,
a huge basement-level food court, and on
the 3rd floor **Kinokuniya**, Thailand's
largest English-language bookstore.

Detour:
Ancient City

Ancient City (เมืองโบราณ, Muang Boran; www.ancientcity.com; 296/1 Th Sukhumvit, Samut Prakan; adult/child 500/250B; ⊙8am-5pm) Claiming to be the largest open-air museum in the world, the site covers more than 80 hectares of peaceful countryside littered with 109 scaled-down facsimiles of many of the kingdom's most famous monuments. Ancient City lies outside Samut Prakan, which is accessible via air-conditioned bus 511 from Bearing BTS station at the east end of Th Sukhumvit. Upon reaching the bus terminal at Pak Nam, board minibus 36, which passes the entrance to Ancient City.

ℹ Getting There & Away

Air

Bangkok has two airports. **Suvarnabhumi International Airport** (☏ 0 2132 1888; www.suvarnabhumiairport.com), 30km east of central Bangkok, began commercial international and domestic service in 2006 after several years of delay.

Bangkok's former international and domestic **Don Muang International Airport** (DMK; ☏ 0 2535 1111; www.donmuangairportonline.com), 25km north of central Bangkok, was retired from commercial service in September 2006, only to reopen later as Bangkok's de-facto budget hub.

Bus

Eastern Bus Terminal (Ekamai; Map p86; ☏ 0 2391 2504; Soi 40, Th Sukhumvit; Ⓢ Ekkamai exit 2) The departure point for buses to Pattaya, Rayong, Chanthaburi and other points east.

Northern & Northeastern Bus Terminal (Mo Chit; ☏ northeastern routes 0 2936 2852, ext 602/605, northern routes 0 2936 2841, ext 325/614; Th Kamphaeng Phet; Ⓜ Kamphaeng Phet exit 1 & taxi, Ⓢ Mo Chit exit 3 & taxi) Buses depart from here for all northern and northeastern destinations.

Southern Bus Terminal (Sai Tai Mai; ☏ 0 2894 6122; Th Boromaratchachonanee) Besides serving as the departure point for all buses south of Bangkok, it also has departures to Kanchanaburi and western Thailand.

Suvarnabhumi Public Transport Centre (☏ 0 2132 1888; Suvarnabhumi Airport) Located 3km from Suvarnabhumi International Airport, this terminal has relatively frequent departures to points east and northeast including Aranya Prathet (for the Cambodian border), Chanthaburi, Ko Chang, Nong Khai (for the Lao border), Pattaya, Rayong, Trat and Udon Thani.

Minivan

Minivans bound for a number of destinations wait at various points around the Victory Monument.

Train

Hualamphong Train Station (☏ 0 2220 4334, call centre 1690; www.railway.co.th; off Th Phra Ram IV; Ⓜ Hua Lamphong exit 2) Hualamphong is the terminus for the main rail services to the south, north, northeast and east.

ℹ Getting Around

To/from the Airport

Suvarnabhumi International Airport

Airport Rail Link The elevated train service linking central Bangkok and Suvarnabhumi International Airport is comprised of a local service, which makes six stops before terminating at Phaya Thai station (45B, 30 minutes, every 15 minutes from 6am to midnight), connected by a walkway to BTS at Phaya Thai station, and an express service that runs, without stops, between Phaya Thai and Makkasan stations and the airport (90B, 15 to 17 minutes, hourly from 6am to midnight).

Bus & Minivan The public-transport centre is 3km from Suvarnabhumi and includes a public bus terminal, metered taxi stand and long-term parking.

Relatively frequent minivans to Don Muang International Airport wait on floor 1, outside door 8 (50B, 40 minutes, from 5.30am to 5pm).

Taxi Typical metered fares from the airport are as follows: 200B to 250B to Th Sukhumvit; 250B to 300B to Th Khao San; 500B to Mo Chit. Toll charges (paid by the passengers) vary between 25B and 45B. Note also that there's an additional 50B surcharge added to all fares departing from the airport, payable directly to the driver.

Don Muang International Airport

Bus & Minivan From outside the arrivals hall, there are two airport bus lines from Don Muang: A1 makes stops at BTS Mo Chit and the Northern and Northeastern Bus Terminal (30B, hourly from 9am to midnight); A2 makes stops at BTS Mo Chit and BTS Victory Monument (30B, hourly from 9am to midnight).

Taxi A trip to Banglamphu, including airport change and tollway fees, will set you back about 400B.

Boat

Chao Phraya Express Boat (☎0 2623 6001; www.chaophrayaexpressboat.com) provides one of the city's most scenic (and efficient) transport options, running passenger boats along Mae Nam Chao Phraya to destinations both south and north of Bangkok.

Tickets range from 10B to 40B and are generally purchased on board the boat, although some larger stations have ticket booths.

The company operates express (indicated by an orange, yellow or green flag), local (without a flag) and tourist boat (blue flag) services.

BTS & MRT

The elevated **BTS** (☎0 2617 7300; www.bts.co.th), also known as the Skytrain, spans two lines that whisk you through 'new' Bangkok (Th Silom, Th Sukhumvit and Siam Sq). Fares range from 15B to 40B, or 120B for a one-day pass. Most ticket machines only accept coins, but change is available at the information booths.

Bangkok's **MRT** (www.bangkokmetro.co.th) or metro is helpful for people staying in the Th Sukhumvit or Th Silom area to reach the train

station at Hualamphong. Fares cost 15B to 40B, or 120B for a one-day pass.

Bus

The city's public bus system is operated by **Bangkok Mass Transit Authority** (☎0 2246 0973; www.bmta.co.th); the website is a great source of information on all bus routes, but this doesn't really help the fact that Bangkok's bus system is confusing and generally lacks English.

Taxi

Fares to most places within central Bangkok cost 60B to 80B, and freeway tolls – 20B to 45B depending where you start – must be paid by the passenger.

Túk-Túk

A short trip on a túk-túk will cost at least 60B.

Bangkok Getaways

You don't have to travel far from the capital to sample the best of Thailand. Within a day's journey from Bangkok are beautiful beaches, ancient temple ruins, historical towns and jungle excursions.

North of Bangkok is the ancient royal capital of Ayuthaya and its once-golden temple ruins. Northwest is Kanchanaburi, which played a minor role in WWII as the site of the Death Railway. Just beyond the town are rugged mountains and outdoor adventures.

Due east of Bangkok is a long and pretty coastline dotted with islands, such as pint-sized Ko Samet and jungle-clad Ko Chang. In the northeast is Thailand's first national park, Khao Yai, an easy and rewarding jungle escape for elephant- and monkey-spotting. Scattered throughout the northeast's rice fields are Khmer temple ruins built by Southeast Asia's ancient superpower.

Wat Yai Chai Mongkhon (p107), Ayuthaya
LIGHTKEY/GETTY IMAGES ©

Ko Samet (p119)

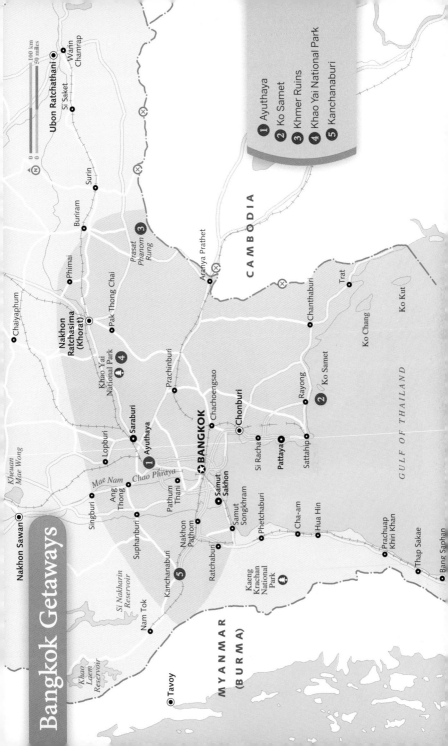

Bangkok Getaways Highlights

Ayuthaya

An easy day trip north of Bangkok, the former Siamese capital of Ayuthaya (p106) contains a collection of crumbling temples, designated a Unesco World Heritage Site, and surrounded by a bustling provincial capital. The ruins can be visited on foot or aboard an elephant, the ancient royals' preferred mode of transport. The city's museums offer informative perspectives on Ayuthaya's history and dominance of the region.

1

Ko Samet

2

Just a few hours west of Bangkok, Ko Samet (p119) is a blissful break from the urban tangle, with nary a túk-túk or skyscraper in sight. Float in the warm water or follow the footpaths over rocky headlands to the next picturesque cove. Dine under the stars at one of the numerous beach-side barbecues and drink a selection of beverages that will keep you blathering into the night.

Khmer Ruins

Smaller versions of Angkor Wat dot the rural northeast. Temples, including Phimai (p135) and Phanom Rung (p136), linked the distant empire's capital with its far-flung frontier outposts. In addition to ornate and ancient architecture, the surrounding countryside is a fascinating look at rural Thailand: rice paddies, sarong-clad grannies and long-suffering water buffalo resting in muddy ponds. Right: Phanom Rung

Khao Yai National Park

Khao Yai (p112) is Thailand's oldest national park and internationally recognised for its biodiversity as a monsoon forest. Despite its well-protected wilderness, the park is well within the reach of civilisation. It has well-developed infrastructure, making watching wildlife, including gibbons and elephants, easier than your average walk in the woods.

Kanchanaburi

The foothills northwest of Bangkok hosted a dramatic WWII subplot. The town of Kanchanaburi (p111) was the site of a brutal Japanese-run prisoner-of-war labour camp that constructed a rail route through the treacherous terrain with rudimentary supplies. Today, two lovingly maintained war cemeteries shelter the Allied dead and several interesting museums document the wartime conquest of the jungle. Above: Death Railway Bridge (p114)

Bangkok Getaways Best...

Beaches

○ **Hat Sai Khao** Ko Chang's widest beach is perfect for bar-hopping and people-watching. (p126)

○ **Ao Phutsa** Ko Samet's subdued bay offers tropical scenery without a lot of hubbub. (p120)

○ **Hat Khlong Chao** Ko Kut's picture-perfect beach with looking-glass-clear water. (p132)

○ **Hat Kaibae** A kid-friendly beach with smooth waves, soft sand to sculpt, and family-size villas. (p126)

Museums

○ **Thailand–Burma Railway Centre Museum** Learn more about Kanchanaburi's role in WWII. (p114)

○ **Hellfire Pass Memorial** Visit the infamous Death Railway. (p120)

○ **Ayuthaya Historical Study Centre** Imagine when the temples were capped with gold. (p107)

Temple Ruins

○ **Wat Phra Si Sanphet** Ayuthaya's premier example of its architecturally stylish heyday. (p110)

○ **Wat Chai Wattanaram** Ayuthaya's photogenic temple. (p107)

○ **Phimai Historical Park** Khmer temple with easy access to Bangkok. (p135)

○ **Phanom Rung Historical Park** Sublime Khmer temple. (p136)

Need to Know

Outdoor Activities

○ **Ko Chang** Dive the deep, kayak through mangroves or trudge through the forest on this athletic island. (p127)

○ **Khao Yai National Park** Spot birds, butterflies and bats in Thailand's first national park. (p112)

○ **Kanchanaburi** Waterfall spotting, river rafting and elephant riding. (p115)

○ **Ko Wai** Snorkel with the fishes in gin clear waters on this rustic island near Ko Chang. (p133)

ADVANCE PLANNING

○ **One month before** Watch the movie *Bridge On the River Kwai*.

○ **One week before** Book your accommodation if you're visiting the beaches during high season (December to March).

○ **One day before** Buy train or bus tickets directly from the station.

RESOURCES

○ **Tourist Authority of Thailand** (TAT; Map p108; ☎0 3524 6076; 108/22 Th Si Sanphet; ⊘8.30am-4.30pm Mon-Fri) Ayuthaya

○ **Tourist Authority of Thailand** (TAT; Map p116; ☎0 3451 1200; Th Saengchuto; ⊘8.30am-4.30pm) Kanchanaburi

○ **Tourist Authority of Thailand** (TAT; ☎0 4421 3666; tatsima@tat.or.th; Th Mittaphap; ⊘8.30am-4.30pm) Nakhon Ratchasima/Khorat

GETTING AROUND

○ **Boats** Travel between the islands and mainland.

○ **Bus & minivan** Best way to get to/from Bangkok.

○ **Bicycle & motorcycle** Self-touring option in the cities.

○ **Sŏrng·tǎa·ou** Handy shared or chartered taxis in the cities.

○ **Train** Bypasses Bangkok traffic to Ayuthaya; also links Ayuthaya to Khao Yai.

○ **Sǎhm·lór & túk-túk** Chartered vehicles for in-town trips; negotiate the price beforehand.

BE FOREWARNED

○ **Avoid** Sightseeing is not best during the hot season (February to June); Ko Kut closes and Ko Chang slows down during the rainy season (June to October).

○ **Dress** Cover to the elbows and ankles when visiting Ayuthaya's temples and don't pose for pictures in front of Buddha images.

○ **Motorcycle safety** Wear a helmet and protective clothing, especially on Ko Chang and Ko Samet.

○ **Waterfalls** At their peak from June to December.

○ **Weekends & holidays** High rates and low vacancies on Ko Chang and Ko Samet.

Left: Wat Yai Chai Mongkhon (p107), Ayuthaya;
Above: Ko Chang (p125)
(LEFT) PHILIP GAME/GETTY IMAGES ©; (ABOVE) ELENA ERMAKOVA (LUNARLYNX)/GETTY IMAGES ©

Bangkok Getaways
Itineraries

By sticking close to Bangkok, you can pack a whole lot of history, jungle trekking and ruin-spotting into less than a week. You'll also enjoy the slower rhythms of these provincial towns, best navigated on a bicycle.

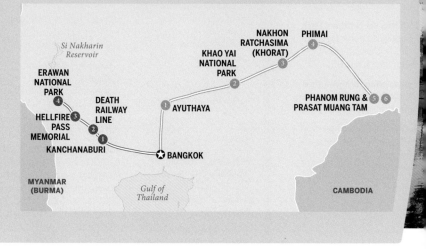

KANCHANABURI TO ERAWAN NATIONAL PARK
Railroads & Rivers
3 DAYS

A half-day journey from Bangkok, **❶ Kanchanaburi** (p111) offers a quick jungle escape and attractions for WWII history buffs. The town was a base for a Japanese-run POW camp and today provides a respectful commemoration of fallen Allied soldiers through several cemeteries and museums.

During WWII, the Japanese military used the labour of captives to build a rail line to Burma, a task that resulted in thousands of deaths. Today trains travel over surviving portions of the **❷ Death Railway** (p114), crossing the Mae Nam Khwae (made famous by the book and film *Bridge on the River Kwai*). The **❸ Hellfire Pass Memorial** (p120) is located at one of the railway's most difficult cuttings. The pass earned its forbidding moniker during night-time construction when burning torches eerily illuminated the labourers.

A more uplifting attraction is **❹ Erawan National Park** (p121), best known for its seven-tiered waterfall said to resemble Erawan, the three-headed elephant of Hindu mythology. Walking to the first three tiers is simple, but the entire 1.5km hike is tough. Most tours stop here in the morning, but you can make a day of it with your own transport.

 5 DAYS

AYUTHAYA TO PRASAT MUANG TAM
Monuments & Mountains

In the fertile central plains is the powerful city-state of Ayuthaya, which ruled for 400 years. In the more arid northeast, the Khmer empire built temple fortresses. Sandwiched in between is Thailand's first national park.

1 Ayuthaya (p106) is a must-see stop on the culture trail and is easily accessible from Bangkok via train or bus. Though many of the great monuments and treasures have been destroyed or stolen, Ayuthaya remains historically important. You can visit the most important ruins within a day.

Nature enthusiasts detour to **2 Khao Yai National Park** (p112) via train or bus. The park includes a 1351m summit,

herds of elephants, troops of monkeys and splendid waterfalls. Spend a few days trekking through the woods and socialising with vacationing Thais.

3 Nakhon Ratchasima (Khorat, p133) provides transit access to the region's Angkor ruins. **4 Phimai** (p135) is easy to reach and has the best tourist infrastructure. Far-flung **5 Phanom Rung** (p136) is considered the apex of Thailand's Khmer architecture, while nearby **6 Prasat Muang Tam** (p137) provides a time-worn counterpoint.

Bang Pa In Palace (p123)

Discover Bangkok Getaways

CENTRAL THAILAND

Ayuthaya   พระนครศรีอยุธยา

POP 137,553

Between 1350 and 1767 Ayuthaya was the capital of Siam. As a major trading port during the time of the trade winds, international merchants visited and were left in awe by the temples and treasure-laden palaces. At one point the empire ruled over an area larger than England and France combined. Ayuthaya had 33 kings who engaged in more than 70 wars during its 417-year period; however, fine diplomatic skills also ensured no Western power ever ruled Siam.

The last of the empire's battles was in 1767, when an invading Burmese army sacked the city, looting most of its treasures. What was left continued to crumble until major restoration work began. In 1991 Ayuthaya's ruins were designated a Unesco World Heritage Site.

◎ Sights

Most temples are open from 8am to 4pm; the more famous sites charge an entrance fee. A one-day pass for most sites on the island is available for 220B and can be bought at the museums or ruins.

The ruins are symbols of royalty and religion, two fundamental elements of Thai society, so please show respect.

ON THE ISLAND

Ayutthaya Tourist Center   Museum
(☏ 0 3524 6076; www.tourismthailand.org/ayut-thaya; ◷ 8.30am-4.30pm) FREE This should be your first stop in Ayuthaya, as the excellent upstairs exhibition hall puts everything in

Khao Yai National Park (p112)
ANDREW WATSON/GETTY IMAGES ©

context and describes the city's erstwhile glories. Also upstairs is the tiny but interesting Ayutthaya National Art Museum. Downstairs, the TAT office has lots of maps and good advice.

Chao Sam Phraya National Museum
Museum

(พิพิธภัณฑสถานแห่งชาติเจ้าสามพระยา; cnr Th Rotchana & Th Si Sanphet; adult/child 150B/free; ⊙9am-4pm Wed-Sun; P) The largest museum in the city has 2400 items on show, ranging from a 2m-high bronze-cast Buddha head to glistening treasures found in the crypts of Wat Phra Mahathat and Wat Ratburana.

Wat Phra Mongkhon Bophit
Buddhist Temple

(วัดพระมงคลบพิตร; ⊙8.30am-4.30pm) FREE Next to Wat Phra Si Sanphet (p110) is this sanctuary hall, which houses one of the largest bronze Buddha images in Thailand. This 17m-high figure has undergone several facelifts due to lightning strikes and fire.

Wat Phra Mahathat
Ruin

(วัดพระมหาธาตุ; cnr Th Chee Kun & Th Naresuan; admission 50B; ⊙8am-6pm) The most photographed image in Ayutthaya is here: a sandstone Buddha head that lies mysteriously tangled within a tree's entwined roots. Built in 1374 during the reign of King Borom Rachathirat I, Wat Phra Mahathat also has a central *prang* (Khmer-style *chedi*) and rows of headless Buddha images.

Wat Ratburana
Ruin

(วัดราชบูรณะ; admission 50B; ⊙8am-6pm) The *prang* in this temple is one of the best extant versions in the city, with detailed carvings of lotus and mythical creatures. The temple, just north of Wat Phra Mahathat, was built in the 15th century by King Borom Rachathirat II on the cremation site for his two brothers who died while fighting each other for the throne.

Ayutthaya Historical Study Centre
Museum

(ศูนย์ศึกษาประวัติศาสตร์อยุธยา; Th Rotchana; adult/child 100/50B; ⊙9am-4.30pm ; P) This well-

If You Like…
Temple Ruins

If you like Wat Phra Mahathat, check out these ruins.

1 **WAT SUWANNARAM**
(วัดสุวรรณาราม; off Th U Thong; ⊙8am-7pm) An infrequently visited temple in the southeast of the island displaying a late-Ayuthaya architectural style.

2 **WAT YAI CHAI MONGKHON**
(วัดใหญ่ชัยมงคล; admission 20B) A 7m-long reclining Buddha is the highlight at this temple. King U Thong built the monastery in 1357 to house monks from Sri Lanka. The bell-shaped *chedi* was built later to honour King Naresuan's victory over Burma.

3 **PHU KHAO THONG**
(เจดีย์ภูเขาทอง; P) Northwest of the island, this *chedi* was originally built by the Burmese during a 15-year occupation and has splendid views of the city. The top section and the memorials to the liberator King Naresuan were added later by Thais.

designed, open-plan museum features a diorama of the city's former glories, replica vessels and an exhibition on how traditional villagers used to survive.

OFF THE ISLAND

Wat Chai Wattanaram
Buddhist Temple

(วัดไชยวัฒนาราม; admission 50B; ⊙8am-6pm) Just 40 years ago this temple and one-time garrison was immersed in thick jungle. Today it is one of Ayutthaya's most-photographed sites thanks to its impressive 35m-high Khmer-style central *prang*. Built in 1673 by King Prasat Thong, the temple is a great place to watch sunsets. The site is west of the island and can be reached by bicycle via a nearby bridge.

Wat Phanan Choeng
Buddhist Temple

(วัดพนัญเชิง; 20B; ⊙8am-7pm) Merit-making ceremonies, firecrackers and ritualistic

Ayuthaya

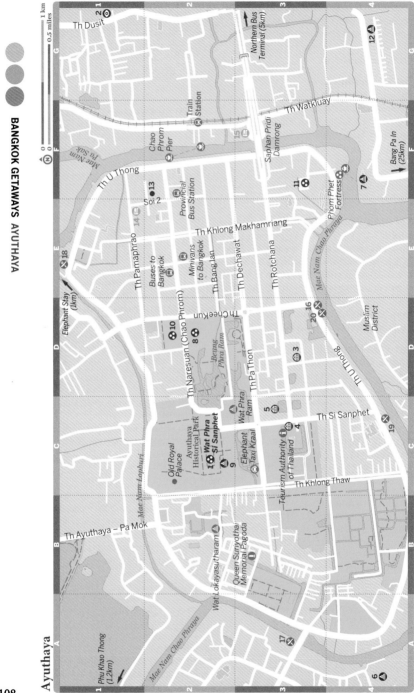

Phu Khao Thong (1.2km)

Mae Nam Chao Phraya

Th Ayuthaya – Pa Mok

Mae Nam Lopburi

Old Royal Palace

Ayuthaya Historical Park

Wat Phra Si Sanphet

Wat Lokayasutharam

Queen Suriyothai Memorial Pagoda

Wat Phra Ram

Th Khlong Thaw

Tourism Authority of Thailand

Elephant Taxi Kraal

Th Si Sanphet

Th Pa Thon

Th Cheekun

Bueng Phra Ram

Th Naresuan (Chao Phrom)

Th Pamaphrao

Th Pamaprao

Elephant Stay (1km)

Soi 2

Th U Thong

Mae Nam Pa Sak

Chao Phrom Pier

Train Station

Th Dusit

Th Watkluay

Northern Bus Terminal (5km)

Saphan Pridi Damrong

Th Khlong Makhamriang

Provincial Bus Station

Minivans to Bangkok

Buses to Bangkok

Th Bang Ian

Th Dechawat

Th Rotchana

Mae Nam Chao Phraya

Phom Phet Fortress

Muslim District

Th U Thong

Bang Pa In (25km)

Ayuthaya

fish feeding make this a hectic temple. The signature attraction is the 19m-high Phra Phanan Choeng, which was created in 1324 and sits in the *wí·hǎhn,* surrounded by 84,000 Buddha images that line the walls. The statue's broad shape is typical of the U Thong period.

Wat Phanan Choeng, southeast of the old city, can be reached by ferry (5B) from the pier near Phom Phet Fortress.

Ayuthaya Floating Market Market

(ตลาดน้ำอโยธยา; www.ayutthayafloatingmarket. com; ⊙9am-7pm; P) FREE A touch kitsch, but popular with locals and visitors, the floating market sells snacks, artwork and clothes. It's set on wooden platforms above the water; long-tail boats (20B) offer rides through the waterways. Traditional performances take place throughout the day. Avoid the neighbouring Ayodia Inter Market as it has some dubious animal attractions.

The market is to the east of the old city off Th Dusit, near Wat Kudi Dao.

⊘ Tours

You can take brief rides around the historical park by **elephant** (☏0 8066 87727; www.elephantstay.com; rides 200-500B). The elephants stay at a kraal on Th Pa Thon.

To see more of the surrounding countryside, guides are available and two-day trips are possible. Try **Tour With Thai** (☏0 3523 1084; www.tourwiththai.com; Th Naresuan).

Guesthouses offer two-hour sunset tours of the ruins (180B), though these can be cancelled if numbers are too low.

🛏 Sleeping

Baan Lotus
Guest House   Guesthouse $

(☏0 3525 1988; 20 Th Pamaphrao; s 200B, d 450-600B; P❄🛜♿) The gorgeous, green grounds surrounding this converted teak schoolhouse make staying here a treat. Staff are as charmingly old-school as the building itself.

Krungsri River Hotel   Hotel $$$

(☏0 3524 4333; www.krungsririver.com; 27/2 Th Rotchana; d/ste 1800/5738B; P❄@🛜⚓) Splendid river views and more than 200 stylish rooms make this four-star hotel the best spot in town.

Audio Guides

Audio guides (150B) can be hired at Wat Phra Si Sanphet, Wat Phra Mahathat and Wat Chai Wattanaram. The English-language guides provide excellent background information and vivid detail that help visitors imagine exactly what once stood on these sites.

PAOLO CORDELLI/GETTY IMAGES ©

Don't Miss
Wat Phra Si Sanphet

The three magnificent *chedi* (stupas) at Wat Phra Si Sanphet are the most iconic image in Ayuthaya. Built in the late 15th century, it was the city's largest temple and was used by several kings. It once contained a 16m-high standing Buddha (Phra Si Sanphet) covered with 250kg of gold, which was melted down by Burmese conquerors.

NEED TO KNOW
วัดพระศรีสรรเพชญ์; admission 50B; ⊗8am-6pm; P

🍴 Eating

Centuries of mingling with foreign traders has resulted in a rich tapestry of food options. Muslim snacks, fresh seafood and Dutch coffee can all be found here.

Sai Thong
Thai $
(Th U Thong; dishes 90-150B; ⊗9.30am-10pm;) The number of cars vying for parking spaces each night is testament to how much locals love Sai Thong. The 180 menu items include classics as well as some slight variations, so browse before picking.

Hua Raw Night Market
Market $
(Th U Thong) This evening market offers simple riverside seating and a range of Thai and Muslim dishes; for the latter look for the green star and crescent.

Roti Sai Mai Stalls
Thai Sweets $
(Th U Thong; ⊗10am-8pm) The Muslim dessert of *roh-đee săi măi* is famous in these parts. Buy a bag then make your own by rolling together thin strands of melted palm sugar and wrapping them inside the roti. Stalls can be found opposite Ayuthaya Hospital.

Baan Mai Rim Nam
Seafood $

(☎ 0 3521 1516; Th U Thong; dishes 150-250B; ☺10am-10pm; 🖊) One of the livelier restaurants along Th U Thong, this riverfront restaurant specialises in fried and steamed fish.

Baan Watcharachai
Thai $$

(off Th Worachate; dishes 120-250B; 🚲) Not only do you get to dine on this wooden boat while gazing at the temples across the water, you can also sample great *yam ƀlah dùk ƀòo* (crispy catfish salad). Head to Wat Kasatthirat and look for the restaurant to the rear.

❶ Getting There & Away

Bus

Ayuthaya's provincial bus stop is on Th Naresuan, a short walk from the guesthouse area. Minivans and air-con buses depart from down the road. The northern bus terminal is 5km east of the old city, off Th Rotchana. A túk-túk from the terminal to the old city will cost 100B. For Kanchanaburi, transfer at Suphanburi. Buses to Mo Chit can stop at Don Muang Airport.

Train

The train station is east of central Ayuthaya and is accessible by a quick cross-river ferry from the centre of town (4B) or *sŏrng·tăa·ou* (50B). Pak Chong is the nearest station to Khao Yai National Park. For Bangkok's Th Khao San area, get off at Bang Sue.

❶ Getting Around

Sǎhm·lór (three-wheeled pedicabs; also spelt *sǎamláw*) or túk-túk are readily available. Always agree on a price before you get on. For trips on the island, the rate is 30B to 40B.

As most of the ruins are close together, the most environmentally friendly way to see them is by bicycle or elephant. Guesthouses rent bicycles (30B) and motorcycles (200B).

Kanchanaburi
กาญจนบุรี

POP 47,147

Today the town is busy and alive but the WWII memorials and museums are a reminder of darker times.

Being just 130km from Bangkok, many city folk come here for the weekend,

Transport to/from Ayuthaya

BUS

DESTINATION	FARE (B)	DURATION (HR)	FREQUENCY
Bang Pa In	20	45min	every 20min (*sŏrng·tăa·ou*)
Bangkok (Victory Monument)	60	1½hr	every 25min (minivan)
Bangkok's Northern (Mo Chit) station	56-60	1½hr	every 25min
Chiang Mai	438-876	8hr	frequent
Sukhothai	279-387	7hr	frequent
Suphanburi	80	1½hr	every 20min (minivan)

TRAIN

DESTINATION	FARE (B)	DURATION (HR)	FREQUENCY
Bang Pa In	3-20	15min	frequent
Bangkok's Bang Sue station	14-345	1½hr	frequent
Bangkok's Hua Lamphong station	15-345	1½hr	frequent
Chiang Mai	586-1198	8hr	6 departures a day
Pak Chong	23-173	4hr	7 departures a day

Don't Miss
Khao Yai National Park

Up there on the podium with some of the world's greatest parks, Khao Yai is Thailand's oldest and most visited reserve. Covering 2168 sq km, it incorporates one of the largest intact monsoon forests remaining in mainland Asia, which is why it was named a Unesco World Heritage site (as part of the Dong Phayayen-Khao Yai Forest Complex).

อุทยานแห่งชาติเขาใหญ่

📞 08 6092 6529

adult/child 400/200B, car 50B

Tours

The typical day tour costs 1300B to 1900B per person. Greenleaf Guesthouse and **Khaoyai Garden Lodge** (☏0 4436 5178; www. khaoyaigardenlodgekm7.com; Th Thanarat, Km 7; r 250-2500B, f 2800B; 🅿🍴❄@🛜🏊) have earned praise, as has **Bobby's Apartments & Jungle Tours** (☏08 6262 7006; www.bobbys jungletourkhaoyai.com) in Pak Chong. Noted birdwatching guides are Tony at **Khao Yai Nature Life Resort** (☏08 1827 8391; www. khaoyainaturelifetours.com), and **Nang** (☏08 9427 1823; www.thailandyourway.com).

Sleeping & Eating

There are plenty of options near Th Thanarat (Rte 2090) or in the not-so-pleasant gateway city of Pak Chong but the best setting is the park. Choose from **campsites** (per person with own tent 30B, 3-person tent 225B) and **lodgings** (☏0 2562 0760; www.dnp.go.th/parkreserve; tents 150-400B, r & bungalows 800-3500B, 30% discount Mon-Thu), or from good-value **Greenleaf Guest-house** (☏0 4436 5073; www.greenleaftour. com; Th Thanarat, Km 7.5; r 200-300B; 🅿🛜) (note that it'll probably be 'full' if you don't book a tour), tasteful French-colonial chic **Hotel des Artists** (☏0 4429 7444; www. hotelartists.com; Th Thanarat, Km 22; r/bungalow incl breakfast 5000/6000B; 🅿🍴❄@🛜🏊), and the (remodelled) original luxury lodge **Balios** (☏0 4436 5971; www.balioskhaoyai.com; Th Thanarat, Km 17; r incl breakfast 3600-4400B; 🅿🍴❄@🛜🏊).

There are restaurants at campsites and some waterfalls throughout the park.

Getting There

Sŏrng·tăa·ou regularly travel the 30km from Pak Chong (40B, 45 minutes). Motorcycle shops in Pak Chong do rentals for 300B per day; try **Petch Motor** (☏08 1718 2400; Th Mittaphap, at Th Tesabarn 13). Frequent 2nd-class buses and minivans run from Khorat (60B, 1½ hours), and minivans (180B, 2½ hours, hourly) and 1st-class buses from Bangkok (150B, 2½ hours) and Khorat (80B, one hour). From Ayuthaya we recommend the train (23B to 363B, two to three hours, nine daily).

Local Knowledge

Visting Khao Yai

RITTICHAI (NINE) KENGSUNGNOEN, OWNER OF GREENLEAF GUESTHOUSE (P113)

1 BIRD WATCHING

Khao Yai has one of Thailand's largest populations of hornbills, including the great hornbill (*nók gòk or nók gah·hang*), wreathed hornbill (*nók grahm cháhng*; literally, 'elephant-jaw bird'), Indian pied hornbill (*nók kàak*) and brown hornbill (*nók ngêuak sĕe nám đahn*). The park's bird list boasts 392 species. On most days we see hornbills, which can be found at fruit-bearing fig trees. There's nothing like hearing the whooshing of a great hornbill flying over your head.

2 ANIMAL WATCHING

We can't guarantee what we will see but we try our best and hope to be lucky. It is common to see snakes, elephants and gibbons. Animals can often be found at different spots in the park depending on the season. For example, at waterfalls and streams you can find snakes and lots of insects, and at fig trees bearing fruit, you can easily spot gibbons. Some 200 elephants tramp the park's boundaries and they are sometimes spotted in the evenings, travelling along the road. The rainy season is a good time for someone who loves to see insects and reptiles.

3 TREKKING

Trekking without a guide isn't recommended because trails in the park aren't well marked and get disturbed during the rainy season. Trekkers sometimes get lost and the rangers have to spend time and resources looking for them. It is better to hire a guide for trekking. A guide will know where the animals are feeding in the forest.

4 NAM TOK HAEW SUWAT

The park's most famous waterfall (pictured left) is very beautiful. Swimming is no longer allowed due to injuries caused by jumping from the top into the shallow pool below.

Helping an Old Friend

The **Elephant Stay** (📞08 0668 7727; www.elephantstay.com) in Ayuthaya does its part by running a hugely successful breeding program and providing brief tourist rides around the ruins (200B to 500B). This nonprofit organisation protects elephants by buying sick or abused animals, including bulls that have killed villagers.

Laithongrien Meepan opened the centre in 1996 after buying his daughter an elephant as a present. Australians Michelle Reedy, a former zoo keeper, and Ewa Nakiewicz run an Elephant Stay program (12,000B for three days, two nights minimum) where visitors learn how to ride, bathe and earn the trust of the animals.

The site is not designed for walk-in tourists, but those who spend time living with the elephants usually come away with a new-found admiration for Thailand's national animal.

though they prefer to board booming karaoke boats than enjoy the serenity.

◉ Sights

Death Railway Bridge
Historical Site

(สะพานข้ามแม่น้ำแคว, **Bridge Over the River Kwai; Th Mae Nam Khwae**) Bypass the tourist scrum by the entrance, and the famous 300m railway bridge still retains its power and symbolism. The centre was destroyed by Allied bombs in 1945 so only the outer curved spans are original. Every 30 minutes a train rolls over the sleepers – stand in one of the safety points along the bridge when one appears.

The mini rainbow-coloured train runs regular trips (20B; 8am to 10am and noon to 2pm) over the bridge from the nearby train station.

Allied War Cemetery
Historical Site

(สุสานทหารพันธมิตรดอนรัก; Th Saengchuto; ⏰24hr) FREE Across the street from the Thailand-Burma Railway Centre is the Allied War Cemetery, which is immaculately maintained by the War Graves Commission. Of the 6982 POWs buried here, nearly half were British; the rest came mainly from Australia and the Netherlands.

Thailand–Burma Railway Centre Museum
Museum

(ศูนย์รถไฟไทย-พม่า; www.tbrconline.com; 73 Th Jaokannun; adult/child 120/60B; ⏰9am-5pm) This informative museum uses video footage, models and detailed displays to explain Kanchanaburi's role in WWII. Nine galleries tell the history of the railway, how prisoners were treated and what happened after the line was completed.

Jeath War Museum
Museum

(พิพิธภัณฑ์สงคราม; Th Wisuttharangsi; admission 30B; ⏰8am-5pm) This small museum contains cuttings, correspondence and artwork from WWII. Located in bamboo-*ata,* similar to the shelters used for POWs, it details the harsh punishments meted out by Japanese troops.

The museum is run by the monks of the adjacent Wat Chaichumphon (Wat Tai).

Heritage Walking Street
Historical Street

Set near the City Gate, this wonderful old street offers a glimpse of a bygone Kanchanaburi. More than 20 yellow signs reveal the history and architecture of this fascinating area. Leave at least an hour to stroll and note the variety of buildings, which include Sino-Portuguese, Thai and

Chinese styles. Coffee and art shops are now also here.

🏃 Activities

Elephant rides, bamboo rafting, jungle trekking and cycling tours can be booked via tour agents.

AS Mixed Travel   Trekking, Cycling
(📞0 3451 2017; www.applenoi-kanchanaburi.com; Apple's Retreat) A well-organised company with knowledgeable staff. Trips can be tailor-made depending on travellers' preferences and pockets.

Good Times Travel   Trekking, Cycling
(📞0 3462 4441; www.good-times-travel.com; 63/1 Tha Mae Nam Khwae) All the normal day trips are available, plus adventure packages to more remote areas.

River Kwai Canoe Travel Services   Kayaking
(📞0 3451 2346; riverkwaicanoe@yahoo.com; Th Mae Nam Khwae) Arranges one- or two-day trips that include visits to the main attractions.

🛏 Sleeping

Blue Star Guest House   Guesthouse $
(📞0 3451 2161; bluestar_guesthouse@yahoo.com; 241 Th Mae Nam Khwae; r 200-850B; 🅿❄📶) Arguably the best of the raft house options, nature wraps itself around Blue Star, creating a feeling of remoteness and tranquility. Cheaper rooms have cold showers.

Bamboo House   Guesthouse $
(📞0 3462 4470; www.bamboohouse.host.sk; 3-5 Soi Vietnam, Th Mae Nam Khwae; r 200-1100B; 🅿❄📶) A new block of smart, airy rooms has breathed fresh life into this place. Set in spacious grounds, the cheaper raft rooms have stunning sunset views.

Sabai@Kan   Hotel $$
(📞0 3462 5544; www.sabaiatkan.com; 317/4 Th Mae Nam Khwae; r 1400-1700B; 🅿❄📶🏊♿) With the kind of king-size beds you just want to jump on, this pretty boutique resort does everything well. Rooms overlook a swimming pool and have heaps of natural light. Service is excellent.

Death Railway Bridge

ANDREW BAIN/GETTY IMAGES ©

Kanchanaburi

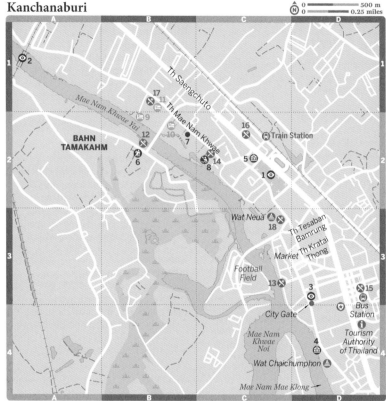

Kanchanaburi

◎ Sights

1 Allied War Cemetery	C2
2 Death Railway Bridge	A1
3 Heritage Walking Street	D3
4 Jeath War Museum	D4
5 Thailand-Burma Railway Centre	
Museum	C2

⊕ Activities, Courses & Tours

6 AS Mixed Travel	B2
7 Good Times Travel	B2
8 River Kwai Canoe Travel Services	C2

🛌 Sleeping

9 Bamboo House	B2
10 Blue Star Guest House	B2
11 Sabai@Kan	B1

✖ Eating

12 Blue Rice	B2
13 Floating Restaurants	C3
14 Mangosteen Cafe	C2
15 Market	D3
16 Night Market	C2
17 Pai Kan	B1
18 Saisowo	C3

Royal River Kwai Resort & Spa   Hotel $$$

(☏ 0 3465 3342; www.royalriverkwairesort.com; 88 Kanchanaburi-Saiyok Rd; r 2450-4650B; P ❄ 🛜 🏊) With vast grounds, a massive pool, a restaurant serving local and international dishes and more than 60 fabulous rooms, this resort is one of the finest places to stay in Kanchanaburi. Its spa is also renowned for its various treatments. The resort is 4km north of town.

🍴 Eating

For more authentic food, visit the **night market** (Th Saengchuto; dishes 30-60B; ⏲6-11pm) near the train station, which is packed with stalls serving fried treats and smoothies. Several good-quality **floating restaurants** (Th Song Khwae; dishes 80-200B; ⏲6-11pm) are often full of Korean or Thai package-company tourists. The **market** (Th Saengchuto) near the bus station is well-known for its *hŏy tôrt* (fried mussels in an egg batter).

Blue Rice
Thai $

(153/4 Mu 4 Ban Tamakahm; dishes 95-150B; 📶✏️🛈) A perfect riverside setting, brilliant menu and fantastic flavours make this a winner. Chef Apple puts a fresh spin on Thai classics, such as the eponymous rice, *yam sôm oh* (pomelo salad) and chicken soup with banana plant.

Mangosteen Cafe
Cafe $

(📞08 1793 5814; www.mangosteencafe.net; 13 Th Mae Nam Khwae; dishes 70-150B; ⏲9.30am-10pm; 📶✏️🛈) Browse the 1000 or so books on offer while munching through the divine pizza toasties and sipping real coffee.

Pai Kan
Thai $

(Th Mae Nam Khwae; dishes 30-50B; ⏲4-10pm) Scribble down your order on scraps of paper, then watch as the cooks go to work in the open kitchen. Thai dishes are simple but flavoursome and authentic; Western dishes are reasonable.

Don't Be a Buffalo

The movie *The Bridge on the River Kwai* made the waterway famous, and also left a generation pronouncing it incorrectly. You should talk about the River Khwae (sounds like 'square' without the 's') and not Kwai (sounds like 'why'). Get it wrong and you'll be referring to the River Buffalo, which the Thais always find amusing.

Thai-style seafood dishes

CARLINA TETERIS/GETTY IMAGES ©

Why Bridge the River Khwae?

The construction of the 'Death Railway' was an astonishing feat of engineering but the prisoners and conscripted workers who toiled to build it paid a terrible price. Around 100,000 labourers died due to the extreme conditions.

The railway was built during the WWII-era Japanese occupation of Thailand (1942–43) and its objective was to link 415km of rugged terrain between Thailand and Burma (Myanmar) to secure an alternative supply route for the Japanese conquest of other west Asian countries. Some considered the project impossible but the track was completed despite a lack of equipment and in appalling conditions.

The bridge that spans the River Khwae near Kanchanaburi (dubbed the 'Death Railway Bridge') was used for just 20 months before the Allies bombed it in 1945. Rather than being a supply line, the route quickly became an escape path for Japanese troops. After the war the British took control of the railway on the Burmese side and ripped up 4km of the tracks leading to Three Pagodas Pass for fear of the route being used by Karen separatists.

On the Thai side, the State Railway of Thailand (SRT) assumed control and continues to operate trains on 130km of the original route between Nong Pladuk, south of Kanchanaburi, to Nam Tok.

Saisowo   Noodles **$**
(Th Chaokunen; dishes 20-30B; ⊘8am-4pm)
When a place is this popular with locals, it must be doing something right. This long-established noodle spot has a few surprise options, such as the excellent *gŏoay ḏĕeo ḏôm yam kài kem* (noodle soup with salted eggs).

❶ Getting There & Away

Bus

Kanchanaburi's bus and minivan station is to the south of the town on Th Saengchuto. If heading south, transfer at Ratchaburi. If aiming for Ayuthaya, go to Suphanburi first. Minivans run to Victory Monument and Mo Chit in Bangkok.

Train

Kanchanaburi's train station is walking distance from the guesthouse area and 2km northwest of the bus station. Kanchanaburi is on the Bangkok Noi-Nam Tok rail line, which includes a portion of the historic Death Railway built by WWII POWs during the Japanese occupation of Thailand. The SRT promotes this as a historic route, and so charges foreigners 100B for any one-way journey along the line, regardless of the distance.

Buses to/from Kanchanaburi

DESTINATION	FARE (B)	DURATION (HR)	FREQUENCY
Bangkok's Northern (Mo Chit) bus terminal	105-135	2hr	every 90min 6am to 6pm
Bangkok's Southern (Sai Tai Mai) bus terminal	95-110	2hr	frequent 4am to 8pm
Bangkok's Victory Monument	120	2hr	hourly until 8pm
Suphanburi	50	2hr	frequent

Destinations from Kanchanaburi include:

Nam Tok (100B, two hours, 6.07am, 10.35am, 4.26pm)

Thonburi's Bangkok Noi station (100B, three hours, 7.19am and 2.48pm, 5.41pm)

ℹ️ Getting Around

Trips from the bus station to the guesthouse area will cost 50B on a *săhm·lór* and 30B on a motorcycle taxi. Public *sŏrng·tǎa·ou* run up and down Th Saengchuto for 10B per passenger (get off at the cemetery if you want the guesthouse area).

KO CHANG & THE EASTERN SEABOARD

Rayong & Ban Phe

ระยอง/บ้านเพ

POP 106,737/16,717

You're most likely to transit through these towns en route to Ko Samet. Rayong has frequent bus connections to elsewhere and the little port of Ban Phe has ferry services to Ko Samet. Blue *sŏrng·tǎa·ou* link the two towns (25B, 45 minutes, every 15 minutes).

ℹ️ Getting There & Away

Minivans from Rayong's bus station go to Bangkok's eastern (Ekamai) and northern (Mo Chit) bus terminals, as well as Suvarnabhumi Airport (160B, 3½ hours, frequently 5am to 8pm).

Buses from Ban Phe's bus station (near Th Thetsaban) go to/from Bangkok's Eastern (Ekamai) station (173B, four hours, hourly 6am to 6pm).

Ban Phe also has minivan services to Laem Ngop for boats to Ko Chang (300B, four hours, three daily), Pattaya (230B,

two hours, three daily) and Bangkok's Victory Monument (250B, four hours, hourly 7am to 6pm).

Ko Samet   เกาะเสม็ด

An island idyll, Ko Samet bobs in the sea with a whole lot of scenery: small sandy bays bathed by clear aquamarine water. You'll have to share all this prettiness with other beach lovers as it's an easy weekend escape from Bangkok, as well as a major package-tour destination.

◎ Sights & Activities

Hat Sai Kaew   Beach

(หาดทรายแก้ว) Starting in the island's northeastern corner, Hat Sai Kaew, or 'Diamond Sand', is the island's widest and whitest stretch of sand, as well as its busiest beach. With sunbathers, sarong-sellers, speedboats, jet-skis, resorts and restaurants galore, the people-watching here is part of the appeal. At night, the scene is equally rambunctious with late-night parties and karaoke sessions.

Statues (p120), Hat Sai Kaew, Ko Samet
PENG WU/GETTY IMAGES ©

Detour:
Hellfire Pass Memorial

The poignant **Hellfire Pass Memorial** (ช่องเขาขาด; Rte 323; museum admission by donation; ⏰ grounds 9am-4.30pm, museum to 4pm) **FREE** is a beautifully maintained tribute to those who died while building the Burma-Thailand Railway in WWII.

Start your visit to the memorial at the **museum** on the top level and hire the free audio guide, which has detailed descriptions of the area and fascinating anecdotes from survivors. Gaze out over the contemplation deck, then walk the trail that runs alongside the original rail bed.

The museum is 80km northwest of Kanchanaburi on Hwy 323 and can be reached by the Sangkhlaburi–Kanchanaburi bus (80B, 1½ hours, frequent departures). The last bus back to Kanchanaburi passes here at 4.45pm.

At the southern end of Hat Sai Kaew are the **prince and mermaid statues** that memorialise Samet's literary role in *Phra Aphaimani*, the great Thai epic by Sunthorn Phu.

Ao Hin Khok & Ao Phai   Beach
(อ่าวหินโคก/อ่าวไผ่) Less frenetic than their northern neighbour, Ao Hin Khok and Ao Phai are two gorgeous bays separated by rocky headlands. The crowd here tends to be younger and more stylish than the tour groups who gather in Hat Sai Kaew; these two beaches are the traditional backpacker party centres of the island.

Beach Admission Fee

Ko Samet is part of the Mu Ko Samet National Park and charges all visitors an entrance fee (adult/child 200/100B) upon arrival. The fee is collected at the **national parks office** (btwn Na Dan & Hat Sai Kaew; ⏰ sunrise-sunset) in Hat Sai Kaew; *sŏrng·tǎa·ou* from the pier will stop at the gates for payment. Hold on to your ticket for later inspections.

Ao Phutsa (Ao Tub Tim)   Beach
(อ่าวพุทรา (อ่าวทับทิม)) Further still is wide and sandy Ao Phutsa (Ao Tub Tim), a favourite for solitude seekers, families and couples who need access to 'civilisation' but not a lot of other stimulation.

Ao Wong Deuan   Beach
(อ่าววงเดือน) A smaller sister to Hat Sai Kaew, Ao Wong Deuan is a lovely crescent-shaped bay. Busy at the weekends, it's much more relaxed during the week.

Ao Thian   Beach
(อ่าวเทียน; Candlelight Beach) Ao Thian is punctuated by big boulders that shelter small sandy spots creating a castaway ambience. More developed than it once was, it's still one of Samet's most easy-going beaches and is deliciously lonely on weekdays. On weekends, Bangkok university students serenade the stars with all-night guitar sessions.

Ao Wai   Beach
(อ่าวหวาย) The cove 'caboose' is Ao Wai, a lovely beach far removed from everything else (in reality it is 1km from Ao Thian).

🛏 Sleeping

Weekday rates remain good value (fan rooms start at 600B). Prices increase at weekends and public holidays, when it is advisable to book ahead.

KIMBERLEY COOLE/GETTY IMAGES ©

⭐ Don't Miss
Erawan National Park

Famed for its impressive seven-tiered waterfall, Erawan National Park is an extremely popular weekend spot for locals. The Erawan waterfall gets its name as the top level is said to resemble Erawan, the three-headed elephant of Hindu mythology. Walking to the first three tiers is easy, but after that good walking shoes and some endurance are needed to complete the 1.5km hike. Bring a bathing costume as you will appreciate the cool water after reaching the top. Levels 2 and 4 are impressive, but be wary of monkeys who may snatch belongings while you're taking a dip.

Buses from Kanchanaburi stop by the entrance of the Erawan waterfall (50B, 1½ hours, every 90 minutes from 8am to 5.20pm). The last bus back to Kanchanaburi is at 4pm. Within the park you can rent bicycles for 20B to 40B per day.

NEED TO KNOW

อุทยานแห่งชาติเอราวัณ; 200B; ⊗8am-4pm

HAT SAI KAEW

Laem Yai Hut Resort
Guesthouse **$$**

(☎0 3864 4282; Hat Sai Kaew; r 1000-2000B; ❄️📶) A colourful collection of 25 bungalows varying in size and age are camped out in a shady garden on the north end of the beach. The laid-back vibe creates an alternative backpacker universe amid the package tour madness.

Chilli Hotel
Hotel **$$**

(☎0 3864 4039; www.chilli-hotel.com; Hat Sai Kaew; r 1000-1800B; ❄️📶) Evidence of how Samet is changing, this smart new boutique hotel has artfully decorated and swish rooms. It's 200m from the beach, close to the national park ticket office.

121

AO HIN KHOK & AO PHAI

Tok's　　　　　　　Guesthouse $$

(📞 0 3864 4073; www.tok-littlehut.com; Ao Hin Khok; r 1500-2000B; ❄ 🛜) One of the top spots on this part of the island, well-maintained villas climb up a landscaped hillside with plenty of shade and flowering plants. The attached bar is popular.

Jep's Bungalows　　　Guesthouse $$

(📞 0 3864 4112; www.jepbungalow.com; Ao Hin Khok; r 300-1800B; ❄ @ 🛜) If the stars are right, and it's quiet, you can still score a very basic fan hut for a mere 300B. But the 600B ones are a far better deal.

Le Blanc　　　　　Guesthouse $$

(📞 0 3861 1646; www.leblancsamed.com; Ao Hin Khok; r 1500-2500B; ❄ 🛜) Formerly known as Ao Pai, this place has gone upmarket and re-branded itself with smart, all-white bungalows. They're perched amid trees and there's enough space between them for proper privacy.

Ao Prao Oil Spill

In late July 2013, the east coast of Ko Samet was severely affected by the fourth-largest oil spill in Thailand's history. Around 50,000L of crude oil gushed out of a pipeline operated by PTT Global Chemical, a subsidiary of Thailand's largest energy company, into the Gulf of Thailand close to Samet.

Worst hit was the beach of Ao Prao, where an estimated 20% of the oil ended up. After a massive clean-up operation, the beach has been restored to its usual, sandy state. Less certain is the condition of the ocean, with reports in the Thai media stating that the number of fish being caught in the area has plummeted since the spill.

AO PHUTSA & AO NUAN

Tubtim Resort　　　　　Hotel $$

(📞 0 3864 4025; www.tubtimresort.com; Ao Phutsa; r 600-3600B; ❄ @ 🛜) This is a well-organised place with great, nightly barbecues and a range of solid, spacious bungalows of varying quality all close to the same dreamy beach. It's popular with upmarket Thais.

AO WONG DEUAN & AO THIAN (CANDLELIGHT BEACH)

Apache　　　　　Guesthouse $

(📞 08 1452 9472; www.apachesamed.com; Ao Thian; r 800-1300B; ❄) Still one of the most chilled spots on Samet, Apache's bungalows have seen better days but are good enough. The bar/restaurant is popular with people who like to roll their own cigarettes.

Nice & Easy　　　　　Hotel $$

(📞 0 3864 4370; nice.easy_samed.island@ hotmail.com; Ao Wong Deuan; r 1200-2000B; ❄ 🛜) As the name suggests, a very amenable place with comfortable, modern and big bungalows set around a garden behind the beach. A decent deal for this part of Samet.

AO WAI

Ao Wai is about 1km from Ao Thian but can be reached from Ban Phe by chartered speedboat.

Samet Ville Resort　　　Hotel $$$

(📞 0 3865 1682; www.sametvilleresort.com; Ao Wai; r 1080-4500B; ❄ 🛜) Under a forest canopy, it's a case of 'spot the sky' at the only resort at this secluded bay. It is an unpretentious place with a range of rooms and cottages that suit most budgets. And the beach is great.

🍴 Eating

Most hotels and guesthouses have restaurants that moonlight as bars after sunset. The food and the service won't blow you away, but there aren't many alternatives. Nightly beach barbecues are

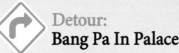

Detour:
Bang Pa In Palace

Built in the 17th century and restored during the reign of Rama V (King Chula-longkorn; r 1868–1910), the European, Chinese and Thai buildings of **Bang Pa In Palace** (บางปะอิน; admission 100B; ☉8am-3.15pm) reflect the wide influences of Rama V.

Highlights include a replica of the Tiber Bridge in Rome, the stunning Chinese-style Wehut Chamrun, the Victorian-influenced observatory Withun Thatsana and a Thai pavilion in the middle of a pond housing a statue of Rama V.

Trains run from Ayuthaya (3B, 15 minutes). The train station is closer to the palace than the bus station, but you'll still need a motorbike taxi (20B) to complete the last leg. Or you can charter a túk-túk for about 400B return.

an island favourite but pick one that looks professionally run and popular.

Red Ginger   International-Thai **$$**
(Na Dan; dishes 125-285B; ☉11am-10pm) Red Ginger serves a small but select menu of the French-Canadian chef's favourite dishes at this atmospheric eatery in between the pier and Hat Saw Kaew. Good salads, great oven-baked ribs. There's Thai food too.

Sea Breeze   Seafood **$$**
(Ao Phai; dishes 80-500B; ☉11am-11pm) This place is appropriately named: you can dine on a wide range of seafood right on Ao Phai's pretty beach here. There's some Western food on the menu as well.

Ploy   Seafood **$$**
(Hat Sai Kaew; dishes 50-400B; ☉11am-11pm) Ploy is a long-established, massive operation that's packed most nights with Thais crunching crabs and lobster. There's a huge array of dishes and a humming bar too.

🍷 Drinking & Nightlife

On weekends, Ko Samet is a boisterous night-owl with provincial tour groups crooning away on karaoke machines or the young ones slurping down beer and buckets to a techno beat. The bar scene changes depending on who is around but there is usually a crowd on Hat Sai

Ko Chang (p125)
WOODS WHEATCROFT/GETTY IMAGES ©

Kaew, Ao Hin Khok, Ao Phai and Ao Wong Deuan.

Ao Prao Resort
Bar

(Ao Prao; drinks from 90B; 🛜) On the sunset-side of the island, there's a lovely sea-view restaurant perfect for an evening sundowner. You'll need private transport to reach it.

ℹ Getting There & Away

Ko Samet is accessed via the mainland piers in Ban Phe. There are dozens of piers each used by different ferry companies, but they all charge the same fares (one way/return 70/100B, 40 minutes, hourly 8am to 5pm) and dock at Na Dan, the main pier on Ko Samet. The last boat back to the mainland leaves at 6pm.

If you're staying at Ao Wong Deuan or further south, catch a ferry from the mainland directly to the beach (one way/return 90/140B, one hour, three daily departures).

Speedboats charge 200B one way and will drop you at the beach of your choice, but they only leave when they have enough passengers.

ℹ Getting Around

Ko Samet's small size makes it a great place to explore on foot. A network of dirt roads connects most of the western side of the island.

Green *sŏrng·tǎa·ou* meet arriving boats at the pier and provide drop-offs at the various beaches (100B to 400B, depending on the beach).

Trat ตราด

POP 21,590

A major transit point for Ko Chang and coastal Cambodia, Trat's provincial charms are underappreciated.

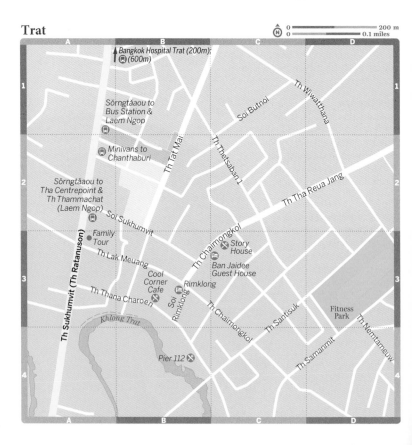

Sleeping

Ban Jaidee Guest House
Guesthouse $

(📞08 3589 0839; banjaideehouse@yahoo.com; 6 Th Chaimongkol; r 200B; 📶) In a charming neighbourhood, this relaxed traditional wooden house has simple rooms with shared bathrooms (hot-water showers). It's very popular and booking ahead is essential.

Rimklong
Hotel $$

(📞0 3952 3388; soirimklong@hotmail.co.th; 194 Th Lak Meuang; r 800-900B; ❄📶) Trat's only boutique hotel occupies both ends of the soi. Rooms are bright and welcoming, if a little small. There's a pleasant, attached cafe.

Eating & Drinking

Trat is all about market eating: head to the day market on Th Tat Mai for *gah·faa bohrahn* ('old-style' coffee), the indoor market for lunchtime noodles, or the night market for a stir-fried dinner. Food stalls line Th Sukhumvit come nightfall.

Cool Corner Cafe
International-Thai $

(📞08 4159 2030; 49-51 Th Thana Charoen; dishes 60-160B; ⊙8am-10pm) Run by Khun Morn, a modern Renaissance woman (writer, artist and traveller) from Bangkok, Cool Corner is an anchor for Trat's expats.

Story House
International-Thai $

(61-65 Th Chaimongkol; dishes 50-150B; ⊙9.30am-9.30pm) Bright and cheerful restaurant serving up Thai and Western classics, as well as sandwiches. It makes for a good coffee/smoothie stop as well.

Pier 112
Thai $$

(132/1 Th Thana Charoen; dishes 80-250B; ⊙10.30am-10.30pm; 🍴) Large selection of vegetarian dishes here, as well as reliable curries, and you can eat outside in a plant-festooned garden.

Getting There & Around

Trat's bus station is 2km out of town.

Minivans leave from various points along Th Sukhumvit. **Family Tour** (📞08 1940 7380; Th Sukhumvit cnr Th Lak Meuang) has minivans to Bangkok's Victory Monument and northern (Mo Chit) bus terminal.

The three piers that handle boat traffic to Ko Chang, Ko Kut, Ko Mak and Ko Wai are located in Laem Ngop, about 30km southwest of Trat.

Sŏrng·tăa·ou to Laem Ngop and the piers (50B per person for six passengers, 200B for the whole vehicle, 35 to 50 minutes) leave from Th Sukhumvit just past the market.

Bangkok Airways (📞Trat airport 0 3955 1654, 0 3955 1655, in Bangkok 0 2265 5555; www.bangkokair.com) operates flights from the airport, which is 40km from town. Taxis to Trat cost a ridiculous 600B.

Motorbike taxis charge 20B to 30B for local hops.

Ko Chang
เกาะช้าง

POP 7033

With steep, jungle-covered peaks, picturesque Ko Chang (Elephant Island) retains its remote and rugged spirit despite its current status as a package-tour resort akin to Phuket. The island's swathes of sand are girl-next-door pretty but not beauty-queen gorgeous. What it lacks in sand, it makes up for in an unlikely combination: accessible wilderness with a thriving party scene.

Trat Transport Connections

DESTINATION	BUS	AIR
Bangkok Suvarnabhumi International Airport	272B; 5-6hr; 5 daily	from 2550B; 1hr; 3 daily
Bangkok Eastern (Ekamai) Bus Terminal	265B; 5hr; 17 daily	NA
Bangkok Northern (Mo Chit) Bus Terminal	272B; 5-6hr; 5 daily	NA

Sights

WEST COAST

The west coast has the island's widest and sandiest beaches and the greatest amount of development. Frequent public *sŏrng·tăa·ou* make beach-hopping easy and affordable. It is a good idea to bring swim shoes, especially for children, as many of the beaches are rocky in spots. These shallow, gentle seas are great for inexperienced swimmers, but be careful of riptides during storms and the rainy season (May to September).

Hat Sai Khao
Beach

(หาดทรายขาว, White Sand Beach) The longest, most luxurious stretch of sand on the island is packed with package-tour hotels and serious sunbathers. Along the main road, the village is busy and brash – but comes with all the necessary amenities.

Ao Khlong Prao
Beach

(อ่าวคลองพร้าว) Khlong Prao's beach is a pretty sweep of sand pinned between hulking mountainous headlands and bisected by two estuaries. Sprawling luxury resorts dominate here and the primary pastime is sunbathing by the pool, as high tide gobbles up much of the beach.

Hat Kaibae
Beach

(หาดไก่แบ้) A companion beach to Khlong Prao, Hat Kaibae is a good spot for families and 30-something couples.

Lonely Beach
Beach

Ko Chang's backpacker enclave is the most social place on the island come nightfall, when the music is loud, the drinks are strong and the young crowd have shaken off the previous night's hangovers. The beach itself is a bit scruffy, but still a decent strip of sand.

Ban Bang Bao
Village

(บ้านบางเบ้า) This former fishing community is built in the traditional fashion of

Left: Ko Samet (p119); **Below:** A resort on Ko Chang (p125)

(LEFT) SANTI SUKARNJANAPRAI/GETTY IMAGES ©; (BELOW) JOAKIM LEROY/GETTY IMAGES ©

interconnected piers. The villagers of Bang Bao have swapped their nets for renting out portions of their homes to souvenir shops and restaurants.

Hat Khlong Kloi   Beach

At the eastern end of Ao Bang Bao, Khlong Kloi is a sandy beach that feels a lot like a secret though there are other people here and all the requisite amenities (beer, fruit, food, massage) and a few guesthouses if you want the place to yourself. You'll need private transport to get out here.

NORTHERN INTERIOR

Ban Kwan Chang   Elephant Camp

(บ้านควาญช้าง; ☏08 1919 3995; changtone@ yahoo.com; ⏰8am-5pm) In a beautiful forested setting, this is the best of the three elephant camps on the island; deeper in the jungle and you get more time riding the beasts. Tours range from 1½ to three hours (500/900B) and involve feeding, bathing and riding a pachyderm. Trans-

port is included in the price. Be sure to apply mozzie spray.

🏃 Activities

KAYAKING

KayakChang   Kayaking

(☏0 3955 2000; www.kayakchang.com; Amari Emerald Cove Resort, Khlong Prao) For more serious paddlers, KayakChang rents high-end, closed-top kayaks (from 1000B per day) that handle better and travel faster. They also lead one-day and multiday trips (from 2200B) to other islands in the archipelago.

Salak Kok Kayak Station   Kayaking

(☏08 1919 3995; kayak rentals per hr 100B) On the east side of the island, explore the mangrove swamps of Ao Salak Kok, while supporting an award-winning eco-tour program. Salak Kok Kayak Station rents self-guided kayaks and is a village-work project designed to promote

127

DAVID GREEDY/GETTY IMAGES ©

⭐ Don't Miss
Diving & Snorkelling

The dive sites near Ko Chang offer a variety of coral, fish and beginner-friendly shallow waters on par with other Gulf of Thailand dive sites.

The following are recommended dive operators:

BB Divers (0 3955 8040; www.bbdivers.com) Based at Bang Bao with branches in Lonely Beach, Khlong Prao and Hat Sai Khao, as well as outposts on Ko Kut and Ko Wai (high season only).

Lonely Beach Divers (📞08 0619 0704; www.lonelybeachdivers.com) Operating out of Lonely Beach, this place offers multilingual instructors.

tourism without affecting the traditional way of life.

HIKING

Ko Chang is unusual for a Thai island in having a well-developed trekking scene. Mr Tan from **Evolution Tour** (📞0 3955 7078; www.evolutiontour.com) or Lek from **Jungle Way** (📞08 9247 3161; www.jungleway.com) lead one-day treks (700B to 1400B) through Khlong Son Valley.

🛏 Sleeping

On the west coast, Lonely Beach is still the best budget option, Hat Kai Bae is the best-value option and Hat Sai Khao is the most overpriced. You will also find accommodation on the east coast at Ao Salak Kok and Ao Dan Kao.

HAT SAI KHAO

Independent Bo's Guesthouse **$**
(📞08 5283 5581; Hat Sai Khao; r 400-850B; ❄️🛜) Despite the eccentric Scottish owner (no reservations here) this place

on the jungle hillside exudes a creative, hippy-ish vibe that Ko Chang used to be famous for. All bungalows are funky and different.

Koh Chang Hut Hotel   Hotel $$

(☏08 9831 4851; www.kohchanghut.com; r 450-1800B; ❄️🛜) At the southern end of the beach, this cliff-side hotel was being extensively refurbished at the time of writing. A pleasant, breezy spot, you're within walking distance of the beach without spending a lot of baht. The cheaper street-side rooms are noisier.

AO KHLONG PRAO

Lin Bungalow   Guesthouse $$

(☏08 4120 1483; lin.bungalow@gmail.com; r 1300B; ❄️🛜) Ten sturdy and sizeable bungalows right on the beach. A good midrange choice.

Baan Rim Nam   Guesthouse $$

(☏08 7005 8575; www.iamkohchang.com; r from 1200-1600B; ❄️🛜) Converted fisher's-house-turned-guesthouse teeters over a mangrove-lined river; kayaks and dialled-in advice free of charge.

Keereeta Resort   Guesthouse $$$

(☏0 3955 1304; www.keereeta.com; Khlong Prao; r 3500B; ❄️🛜) Only five very special rooms here; all individually colour-themed, huge, secluded and oh-so-stylish. There are free kayaks for guests to paddle to the beach or the restaurants opposite. Book ahead.

HAT KAIBAE

Porn's Bungalows   Guesthouse $

(☏08 0613 9266; www.pornsbungalows-kohchang.com; Hat Kaibae; r 550-1500B) Very chilled spot at the far western end of the beach. All bungalows are fan-only. The 900B beachfront bungalows are a great deal.

KB Resort   Hotel $$

(☏0 3955 7125; www.kbresort.com; r 1250-5000B; ❄️@🛜🏊) Lemon yellow bungalows have cheery bathrooms and pose peacefully beside the sea. Listen to the gentle lapping surf while the kids

construct mega-cities in the sand. The fan bungalows are overpriced. Sleepy staff.

GajaPuri Resort & Spa   Hotel $$$

(☏0 3969 6918; www.gajapuri.com; r 4350-19,000B; ❄️🛜🏊) Polished wooden cottages gleam with quintessential Thai touches so that you have a sense of place and pampering. Oversized beds with crisp linens, sun-drenched reading decks and a pretty beach are even more luxurious if you score an online discount.

LONELY BEACH

Paradise Cottages   Hotel $

(☏08 1773 9337; www.paradisecottage kochang.com; Lonely Beach; r 400-1000B; ❄️🛜) Stylishly minimalist rooms and a mellow atmosphere with hammocks for guests to swing their worries away. It's oceanfront, but the beach is too rocky for swimming.

Warapura Resort   Hotel $$

(☏0 3955 8123; www.warapuraresort.com; r 1400-3300B; ❄️@🛜🏊) Chic for relatively cheap prices, Warapura has a collection of adorable cottages tucked in between

National Park Status

Some areas of Ko Chang are protected and maintained as part of the Mu Ko Chang National Marine Park. Conservation efforts are a bit haphazard, but you will be required to pay a 200B park entrance fee when visiting some of the waterfalls (entrance fees are stated in the reviews and payable at the site). **National Park headquarters** (☏0 3955 5080; Ban Than Mayom; ⏰8am-5pm) is on the eastern side of the island near Nam Tok Than Mayom.

Be aware also that nudity and topless sunbathing are forbidden by law in Mu Ko Chang National Marine Park; this includes all beaches on Ko Chang, Ko Kut, Ko Mak and Ko Wai.

Below: Ko Chang (p125); **Right:** Aerial view of Ko Chang

(BELOW) PENG WU/GETTY IMAGES ©; (RIGHT) ATHIT PERAWONGMETHA/GETTY IMAGES ©

the village and a mangrove beach. The oceanfront pool is perfect for people who would rather gaze at the ocean than frolic in it.

BAN BANG BAO

Bang Bao Paradise Guesthouse **$**
(☎08 8838 0040; r 500-700B; ❄) Six mini-huts perched over the water, all in bright, fresh colours and all sharing bathrooms.

Koh Chang Sea Hut Hotel **$$**
(☎08 1285 0570; www.kohchang-seahut.com; Ban Bang Bao; r 2500B; ❄ 🛜) With seven luxurious bungalows built on the edge of Bang Bao's pier, this is one of Ko Chang's most unusual places to stay, offering near panoramic views of the bay. Each bungalow is surrounded by a private deck where breakfast is served. There are five rooms here too.

 ## Eating & Drinking

Virtually all of the island's accommodation has attached restaurants with adequate but not outstanding fare. Parties abound on the beaches and range from the older, more restrained scene on Hat Sai Khao, to the younger and sloppier on Lonely Beach.

WEST COAST

Porn's Bungalows Restaurant Thai **$**
(Hat Kaibae; dishes 80-180B; ⏱11am-11pm) This laid-back, dark-wood restaurant is the quintessential beachside lounge. Great barbecue. Feel free to have your drinks out-size your meal and don't worry about dressing for dinner.

Norng Bua Thai **$$**
(Hat Sai Khao; dishes 40-300B; ⏱8am-11pm) Once a stir-fry hut, now a fully fledged restaurant that makes everything fast

and fresh and with chillies and fish sauce (praise the culinary gods). Always crowded with visiting Thais, a good sign indeed.

Phu-Talay   Seafood $$
(Khlong Prao; 100-320B; ☺10am-10pm) There's a cute, homey feel at this wooden-floored, blue-and-white decorated place perched over the lagoon. Check out the sensible menu of Ko Chang classics (lots of fish), which is far more reasonably priced than many other seafood places.

Ton Sai   Thai $$
(Khlong Prao; dishes 80-350B; ☺11am-10pm) A favourite of locals, visiting Thais and for-eigners, paintings adorn this much-tipped hut of a restaurant. A mix of well-prepared, creative Thai and Western dish-es are on the menu. Closed low season.

Chowlay   Seafood $$
(Ban Bang Bao; dishes 100-450B; ☺10am-10pm) Fine bay views at this pier restaurant and enough fresh fish to start your own aquarium.

❶ Getting There & Away

Ferries from the mainland leave from either Tha Thammachat, operated by **Koh Chang Ferry** (☏0 3955 5188), or Tha Centrepoint (Laem Ngop) with **Centrepoint Ferry** (☏0 3953 8196). Boats

Transport to/from Ko Chang

ORIGIN	DESTINATION	BOAT	BUS
Bangkok Eastern Bus Terminal	Tha Thammachat	–	275B; 7hr; 3 daily
Ko Chang	Ko Kut	900B; 5hr; 1 daily	–
Ko Chang	Bangkok Airport	–	550B; 6-7hr; 3 daily

131

from Tha Thammachat arrive at Tha Sapparot; Centrepoint ferries at a pier down the road.

The inter-island ferry **Bang Bao Boats** (www. bangbaoboat.com) connects Ko Chang with Ko Mak, Ko Kut and Ko Wai during the high season. The boats leave from Bang Bao in the southwest of the island.

Speedboats travel between the islands during high season.

It's possible to go direct to and from Ko Chang from both Bangkok's Eastern (Ekamai) bus terminal and Bangkok's Suvarnabhumi International Airport, via Chanthaburi and Trat. It is not recommended to drive between Ban Khlong Son south to Hat Sai Khao, as the road is steep and treacherous with several hairpin turns. There are mud slides and poor conditions during storms.

🛈 Getting Around

Shared *sŏrng·tăa·ou* meet arriving boats to shuttle passengers to the various beaches (Hat Sai Khao 100B, Khlong Prao 150B and Lonely Beach 200B). Hops between neighbouring beaches range from 50B to 200B but prices rise dramatically after dark, when it can cost 500B to travel from Bang Bao to Hat Sai Khao.

Motorbikes can be hired from 200B per day. Ko Chang's hilly and winding roads are quite

dangerous; make sure the bike is in good working order.

....

Ko Kut   เกาะกูด

All the paradise descriptions apply to Ko Kut: the beaches are graceful arcs of sand, the water clear, coconut palms outnumber buildings, and a secluded, unhurried atmosphere embraces you upon arrival. Far less busy than Ko Chang, there's nothing in the form of nightlife, or even dining really, but those are the reasons for visiting.

◉ Sights & Activities

White sand beaches with gorgeous aquamarine water are strewn along the western side of the island. **Hat Khlong Chao** is the island's best and could easily compete with Samui's Hat Chaweng in a beach beauty contest. **Ao Noi** is a pretty boulder-strewn beach with a steep drop-off and steady waves for strong swimmers. **Ao Prao** is another lovely sweep of sand.

There is no public transport on Ko Kut but you can rent motorbikes for exploring

Ko Kut

the west coast beaches. Traffic is minimal and the road is mostly paved from Khlong Hin in the southwest to Ao Noi in the northeast.

Sleeping & Eating

During low season (May to September) many boats stop running and bungalow operations wind down. Call ahead during busy periods so you can be dropped off at the appropriate pier by the speedboat operators.

Cozy House Guesthouse $
(☏08 5101 4838; www.kohkoodcozy.com; Khlong Yai; r 250-600B; ❄ ☎) The go-to place for backpackers, Cozy is just a 10-minute walk from delightful Hat Khlong Yai.

Koh Kood Ngamkho Resort Guesthouse $
(☏08 1825 7076; www.kohkood-ngamkho.com; Ao Ngam Kho; r 750B; @ ☎) One of the best budget options around. Agreeably rustic huts perch on a forested hillside over a reasonable beach. Some are bigger than others.

Koh Kood Boutique House Hotel $$
(☏08 4524 4321; www.kohkoodboutiquehouse. com; Ao Prao; r 1200-2800B; ❄ ☎) Almost at the southernmost point of the island is this secluded, very peaceful hotel that was converted from two traditional houses on stilts. Reservations are required.

Bann Makok Hotel $$$
(☏08 1643 9488; www.bannmakok.com; Khlong Yai Ki; r 2800-4000B; ❄ @ ☎) Be the envy of the speedboat patrons when you get dropped off at this boutique hotel tucked into the mangroves. Recycled timbers painted in vintage colours have been constructed into a maze of eight rooms designed to look like a traditional pier fishing village.

❶ Information

There are no banks or ATMs, though major resorts can exchange money.

Detour:
Ko Wai เกาะหวาย

Stunning Ko Wai is teensy and primitive, but endowed with gin-clear waters, excellent coral reefs for snorkelling and a handsome view across to Ko Chang. Expect to share the bulk of your afternoons with day-trippers but have the remainder of your time in peace.

Most bungalows close during the May-to-September low season when seas are rough and flooding is common.

❶ Getting There & Around

Ko Kut is accessible from the mainland pier of Laem Sok, 22km southeast of Trat, the nearest bus transfer point.

Koh Kood Princess (☏08 6126 7860; www.kohkoodprincess.com; 350B) runs an air-con boat (one way 350B, one daily, one hour 40 minutes) that docks at Ao Salad, in the northeastern corner of the island. There's free land transfer on your arrival.

Speedboats also make the crossing to/from Laem Sok (one way 600B, 1½ hours) during high season and will drop you off at your hotel's pier.

Bang Bao Boat (www.bangbaoboat.com) is the archipelago's inter-island ferry running a daily loop from Ko Chang, departing at 9am, to Ko Kut (one way 900B, five to six hours).

Motorbikes can be rented for 250B per day.

NORTHEASTERN THAILAND

Nakhon Ratchasima (Khorat) นครราชสีมา (โคราช)
POP 209,881

Khorat is a city that grows on you. It has a strong sense of regional identity (people

Pàt Mèe Koh·râht

One speciality you must try once is *pàt mèe koh·râht*. It's similar to *pàt tai*, but boasts more flavour and is made with a local style of rice noodle, *mèe koh·râht*.

call themselves *kon koh·râht* instead of *kon ee·sǎhn*) and is at its best in its quieter nooks, such as inside the east side of the historic moat, where local life goes on in a fairly traditional way.

This urban centre provides transit links to the Angkor ruins of Phimai.

🛏 Sleeping

Sansabai House
Hotel $
(🕿 0 4425 5144; www.sansabai-korat.com; Th Suranaree; r 300-550B; P 🐕 ❄ 🛜) Walk into the welcoming lobby of Sansabai House and you half expect the posted prices to be a bait-and-switch ploy. But no, all rooms are bright and cheerful and come with good mattresses, mini-fridges and little balconies.

Thai Inter Hotel
Hotel $$
(🕿 0 4424 7700; www.thaiinterhotel.com; Th Yommarat; r incl breakfast 750-850B; P ❄ @ 🛜) This little hotel tries to be hip by patching together an odd mix of styles, and it pretty much pulls it off. The lobby is homey and the rooms are comfy.

🍴 Eating

Gai Yang
Saang Thai
Northeastern Thai $
(Th Rajadamnern; whole free-range chicken 150B; 🕑7.30am-8pm) Has served some of the best *gài yâhng* (grilled chicken) in Khorat for half a century.

Rabieng Kaew
Thai $$
(Th Yommarat; dishes 80-300B; 🕑11am-5pm) This lovely spot has an antique-filled dining room and a leafy garden in back. The food, all big dishes meant to be shared, is simply excellent.

ℹ Getting There & Away

Bus
Khorat has two bus terminals. Terminal 1 (🕿 0 4424 2899; Th Burin), in the city centre, serves Bangkok (1st-class only) and most towns within Khorat Province, including Pak Chong (60B, 1½ hours, every 20 minutes). Buses to other destinations, plus more Bangkok buses and minivans, use Terminal 2 (bor kor sor sŏrng; 🕿 0 4429 5271; Hwy 2) north of downtown.

Train
Many trains pass through Khorat Railway Station (🕿 0 4424 2044), but buses are much faster.

ℹ Getting Around
Túk-túk cost between 40B and 70B to most places in town.

Korat Car Rental (🕿 08 1877 3198; www.koratcarrental.com) is a local firm with a stellar reputation. The Sima Thani Hotel (🕿 0 4421 3100; Th Mittaphap) also arranges cars with drivers, some of whom speak English.

Buses from Nakhon Ratchasima's Terminal 2

DESTINATION	DURATION (HR)	PRICE (B)	DEPARTURES
Ayuthaya (minivan)	4	132	6am-7pm (frequent)
Chiang Mai	12-13	473-710	3am-8.30pm (11 daily)
Nang Rong	2	75-95	all day (frequent)
Nang Rong (minivan)	1½	75	5am-8pm (every 30 minutes)
Trat	8	324	1am, 11.15am, 9pm

Phimai พิมาย

Reminiscent of Cambodia's Angkor Wat, Prasat Phimai once stood on an important trade route linking the Khmer capital of Angkor with the northern reaches of the realm. Phimai is an easy day trip out of Khorat, but if you prefer the quiet life, you could always make Khorat a day trip out of Phimai instead.

Sights

Phimai Historical Park — Historical Site

(อุทยานประวัติศาสตร์พิมาย; ☎0 4447 1568; Th Anantajinda; admission 100B; ⏰7.30am-6pm) Started by Khmer King Jayavarman V (AD 968–1001) during the late 10th century and finished by his successor King Suriyavarman I (1002–49), Phimai is one of the most impressive and beautiful Khmer ruins in Thailand. Though built as a Mahayana Buddhist temple, the carvings also feature many Hindu deities and, as explained in the **visitor center (⏰8.30am-4.30pm)**, design elements at Prasat Phimai influenced Angkor Wat.

You enter over a cruciform **naga bridge**, which symbolically represents the passage from earth to heaven, and then through the **southern gate** (which is unusual since most Khmer temples face east) of the outer wall, which stretches 565m by 1030m. A raised passageway, formerly covered by a tiled roof, leads to the inner sanctum and the 28m-tall **main shrine** built of white sandstone and covered in superb carvings. At the centre of the **Prang Brahmathat**, in front of the main shrine, is a replica stone sculpture of Angkor King Jayavarman VII sitting cross-legged and looking very much like a sitting Buddha.

Sleeping

Khru Pom — Guesthouse $

(☎08 6648 9383; Th Anantajinda; s without bathroom 150B, r 350-450B; P ⊖ ❄ @ ≋) This quiet and immaculate little place in the centre of the block won't excite you, but it won't let you down either. The friendly owners speak English.

Prasat Phimai, Phimai Historical Park

IGOR PRAHIN/GETTY IMAGES ©

Moon River Homestay

Guesthouse $

(☎08 5633 7097; www.moon-river-phimai. com; Ban Sai Ngam Patana Soi 2; r 400-600B, f 1200B; P⊖✳️🛜) This German-Thai run guesthouse is in an almost rural location on the north bank of the river (you can swim here) and features mostly simple but good wooden cabins, some with air-con and some with fan.

ℹ Getting There & Away

Buses and minivans for Phimai leave Khorat's Bus Terminal 2 (50B, 1½ hours) about every 20 minutes throughout the day.

Phanom Rung Historical Park อุทยานประวัติศาสตร์เขาพนมรุ้ง

The largest and best restored Khmer monument in Thailand, **Phanom Rung** (☎0 4466 6251; admission 100B, combined ticket with Prasat Muang Tam 150B; ⏰6am-6pm) has a knock-me-dead location. Crowning the summit of a spent volcano (the name is derived from the Khmer words for 'big mountain'), this sanctuary sits 200m above the paddy fields.

The temple was erected as a Hindu monument to Shiva between the 10th and 13th centuries, the bulk of it during the reign of King Suriyavarman II (r AD 1113–50), which was the peak time of Angkor architecture. The complex faces east, and four times a year the sun shines through all 15 sanctuary doorways. The correct solar alignment happens during sunrise from 3 to 5 April and 8 to 10 September and sunset from 5 to 7 March and 5 to 7 October (some years are one day earlier).

◎ Sights

One of the most remarkable aspects of Phanom Rung is the **promenade** leading to the main gate. It begins on a slope 400m east of the main tower with three earthen **terraces**. Next comes a cruciform base for what may have been a wooden pavilion. To the right of this is the **changing pavilion** (Phlab Phla) where royalty bathed and changed clothes before entering the temple complex. You then step down to a 160m-long **processional walkway** flanked by sandstone pillars with early Angkor style (AD 1100–80) lotus-bud tops. This walkway ends at the first and largest of three **naga bridges**, flanked by 16 five-headed *naga* (mythical serpents) in the classic Angkor style. As at all Khmer temple, these represent

Vishnu & the King of Pop

Phanom Rung's most famous carving is the **Narai Bandhomsindhu lintel**, which depicts a reclining Vishnu ('Phra Narai' in Thai) in the Hindu creation myth. Growing from his navel is a lotus that branches into several blossoms, on one of which sits the creator god, Brahma. Vishnu is asleep on the milky sea of eternity, here represented by a *naga,* and alongside him are heads of Kala, the god of time and death. This lintel sits above the eastern gate (the main entrance) beneath the impressive dancing Shiva relief.

Its fame stems not from its beauty, but from its role in a quarter-century-long whodunit-cum-David-versus-Goliath tale that began in 1965 when it was discovered to have been stolen. In 1972 it was found on display at the Art Institute of Chicago and Thailand pressed for its return. Superstars Carabao helped the cause with their song 'Thaplang' (Lintel) featuring the line 'Take back Michael Jackson, Give us Phra Narai'. Phra Narai finally came home in 1988, the year the Phanom Rung restoration was finished.

the passing from the earthly realm to the heavenly.

After crossing this bridge and climbing the stairs you come to the magnificent **east gallery** leading into the main sanctuary. The **main tower** has a gallery on each of its four sides and the entrance to each gallery is itself a smaller version of the main tower.

ⓘ Getting There & Away

P California Inter Hostel in Nang Rong has a standard one-day tour (2736B for four people), which is a good choice.

Nang Rong นางรอง

POP 23,778

This workaday city is even more forget-table than the provincial capital city, 45km to the north, but it's the most convenient base for visiting Phanom Rung, and a full range of services and a good selection of hotels make it a friendly and comfortable one.

🛏 Sleeping & Eating

P California Inter Hostel Guesthouse $

(☎08 1808 3347; www.pcalifornianangrong. webs.com; Th Sangkakrit; s 250-500B; d 300-600B; P⊜✳️📶) This great place, which isn't actually a hostel, on the east side of town offers bright, nicely decorated rooms with good value in all price ranges, including the cheapest, which have fans and cold-water showers. English-speaking owner Khun Wicha is a wealth of knowledge about the area and leads tours.

Cabbages & Condoms Hotel $$

(☎0 4465 7145; Hwy 24; r 240-1500B; P⊜✳️@📶) The cheapest (shared bathroom) rooms at this Population & Community Development Association–

♥ If You Like…
Khmer Ruins

Lovers of tumbledown temples won't want to miss these ruins near Phanom Rung.

1 PRASAT MUANG TAM
(admission 100B; ⊙6am-6pm) This restored temple, 8km from Phanom Rung, is an ideal bolt-on. Sponsored by King Jayavarman V, it dates to the late 10th or early 11th century and was once a shrine to Shiva; it is surrounded by laterite walls, within which are four lotus-filled reservoirs, each guarded by whimsical five-headed naga.

2 PRASAT TA MEUAN
(⊙dawn-dusk) This is a collection of three sites, 55km from Phanom Rung and sitting along the Cambodian border. The ruins include a 12th-century rest stop used by ancient pilgrims, a healing station and a Shiva shrine.

run resort, set in a garden, are pretty limp. But move up the price scale (where you get large rooms with stone floors) and this is a pleasant place to stay. It's 6.5km west of town.

Phob Suk Thai $$

(Hwy 24; dishes 40-360B; ⊙9am-9.30pm; 📶) The picture menu at this well-known restaurant near the bus station presents the typical mix of Thai, Isan and Chinese, but we recommend the city's famous *kăh mŏo* (pork-rump roast).

ⓘ Getting There & Around

Nang Rong's **bus station** (☎0 4463 1517) is on the west side of town. Most buses running to the Phanom Rung Historical Park stop in Nang Rong.

P California hires motorcycles, starting at 250B per day, and also has mountain bikes for 100B per day.

Chiang Mai

Snuggled into the foothills of northern Thailand, Chiang Mai is a sanctuary of sorts, with a refreshing combination of city accoutrements and country sensibilities. It is a city of artisans and craftspeople, of university professors and students, of idealists and culture hounds – creating a disposition that is laid-back, creative and reverential.

The city is lauded for its enduring northern Thai (also known as Lanna) characteristics, for the quaint walled quarter filled with temples, and its guardian temple-crowned mountain endowed with mystical attributes.

Outside the urban sphere, you'll find scenic countryside and two of Thailand's highest mountain peaks: Doi Inthanon (2565m) and Doi Chiang Dao (2195m). Boasting more natural forest cover than any other northern province, Chiang Mai offers activities such as cycling, hiking, bird-watching, elephant trekking and river rafting.

Yi Peng festival, Chiang Mai

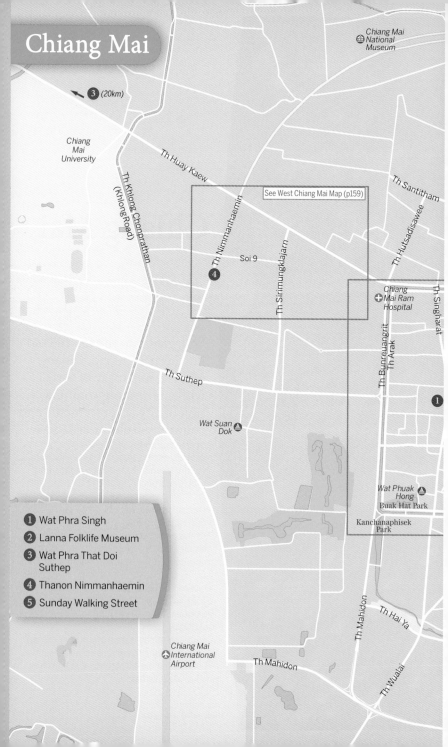

Chiang Mai

Chiang Mai National Museum

3 (20km)

Chiang Mai University

Th Huay Kaew

Th Khlong Chonprathan (Khlong Road)

Th Santitham

Th Nimmanhaemin

See West Chiang Mai Map (p159)

Soi 9

Th Sirimungklajarn

Th Hutsadisawee

4

Chiang Mai Ram Hospital

Th Singharat

Th Bunreuangrit

Th Arak

Th Suthep

1

Wat Suan Dok

Wat Phuak Hong

Buak Hat Park

Kanchanaphisek Park

1. Wat Phra Singh
2. Lanna Folklife Museum
3. Wat Phra That Doi Suthep
4. Thanon Nimmanhaemin
5. Sunday Walking Street

Th Mahidon

Th Hai Ya

Chiang Mai International Airport

Th Mahidon

Th Wualai

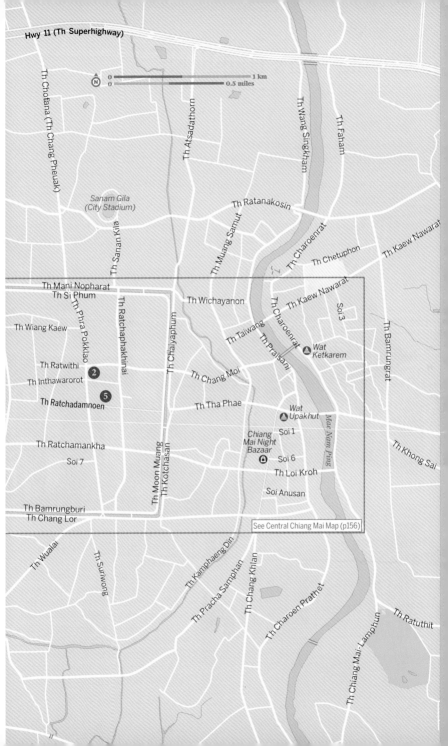

Chiang Mai's Highlights

Wat Phra Singh

Chiang Mai's temples showcase traditional Lanna art and architecture, using teak harvested in the once-dense frontiers and demonstrating traditions inherited from Burma and China. The old city is a veritable temple orchard with many royal temples built by the Lanna Mengrai dynasty. The most revered is Wat Phra Singh (p161), which sits regally at the terminus of Th Ratchadamnoen.

Lanna Folklife Museum

Chiang Mai was the capital of the Lanna kingdom, a culturally and ethnically distinct region far removed from the dominating influence of Bangkok and the central plains. Lanna Folklife Museum (p164) provides an atmospheric stroll through northern Thailand's unique religious customs. Rare for Thai museums, the displays are artful and informative with well-written English signage.

AUSTIN BUSH ©

Wat Phra That Doi Suthep

Chiang Mai's guardian mountain ascends from the humid plains into a cool cloud belt where moss and ferns flourish. Nestled on the mountain ridge is Wat Phra That Doi Suthep (p152), an important religious pilgrimage site for Thai Buddhists. The architecture and views are splendidly photogenic and the temple lore is fittingly mystical. The forested mountain is also a national park criss-crossed by hiking and mountain-biking trails.

Thanon Nimmanhaemin

The epicentre of 'new' Chiang Mai, Th Nimmanhaemin (p173) is *the* place to wine, dine and stay up all night (or at least until closing time). The main road and its tributary soi are a hive of energy fuelled by the latest trends in dining and imbibing. In between the bars and restaurants are funky boutiques, hip uni students and NGO expats.

Sunday Walking Street

Chiang Mai is Thailand's handicraft centre, producing unique and creative gifts infused with the spirit of old-fashioned traditions. The Sunday Walking Street (p167) transforms the old city's main thoroughfare into a crowded but artistic commercial enterprise. Souvenirs and snacks fill the vendors' tables while musicians serenade the parade and footpath massage centres take the stress out of retail therapy.

Chiang Mai's Best...

Culture Spots

○ **Chiang Mai City Arts & Cultural Centre** Get educated about the city's history. (p148)

○ **Wat Suan Dok** Do a two-day meditation retreat or chat with a monk about Buddhism. (p151)

○ **Cooking courses** Master the mortar and pestle in a Thai cooking class. (p160)

○ **Cafes** Do as the locals do and court a local cafe for morning eye-openers and afternoon refreshers. (p172)

Outdoor Activities

○ **Trekking** Chiang Mai is Thailand's base for mountain voyages, elephant rides and visits to high-altitude hill-tribe villages.(p153)

○ **Elephant sanctuaries** Become a pachyderm devotee at Chiang Mai's sanctuaries and mahout-training camps. (p154)

○ **Cycling** Explore the town or hit the mountain-biking trails in Doi Suthep-Pui National Park. (p158)

○ **White-water rafting** Brave the rapids of Mae Taeng River from July to March. (p155)

Shopping

○ **Sunday Walking Street** Stroll, eat, shop and repeat at this weekend market. (p167)

○ **Saturday Walking Street** Tour the old silver-smithing village during this weekend bazaar. (p151)

○ **Chiang Mai Night Bazaar** Stock up on souvenirs at this behemoth. (p174)

○ **Adorn with Studio Naenna** Shop for a cause at this village weaving cooperative. (p176)

Need to Know

Places to Relax

○ **Vocational Training Center of the Chiang Mai Women's Correctional Institution** Professional massage by female prisoners. (p158)

○ **Pun Pun** Wholesome and creative vegetarian fare served in the grounds of a contemplative temple. (p169)

○ **Scorpion Tailed River Cruise** Rustic scenery on a river journey aboard a traditional vessel. (p177)

○ **Riverside Bar & Restaurant** Long-standing purveyor of suds, grub, good-time tunes and river views. (p173)

ADVANCE PLANNING

○ **One month before** Book accommodation and overnight train tickets from Bangkok.

○ **One week before** Book air tickets from Bangkok.

○ **One day before** Book your cooking course and outdoor activity tour.

RESOURCES

○ **1 Stop Chiang Mai** (www.1stopchiangmai. com) Online city guide.

○ **Citylife** (www. chiangmainews.com) Lifestyle magazine with restaurant recommendations.

○ **Chiangmai Mail** (www. chiangmai-mail.com) English-language news weekly.

○ **Guidelines Living** (www.guidelines chiangmai.com) Monthly bilingual lifestyle magazine.

○ **Tourism Authority of Thailand** (TAT; Map p156; ✆0 5327 6140; www.tourismthailand.org; Th Chiang Mai-Lamphun; ☺8.30am-4.30pm) Chiang Mai's tourism information centre.

GETTING AROUND

○ **Bicycle** Easy and 'green' travel for central Chiang Mai.

○ **Motorcycle** Good self-touring option for outside central Chiang Mai.

○ **Sǒrng·tǎa·ou** Shared taxis go just about everywhere (20B to 40B).

○ **Túk-túk** Chartered vehicles (60B to 80B); remember to bargain.

BE FOREWARNED

○ **In temples** Dress and act respectfully. Sit in the 'mermaid' position (legs tucked behind you) in front of Buddha figures.

○ **Women travellers** Should not touch monks and should step off the footpath if passing by one.

○ **Guides** Hire a guide through the Tourism Authority of Thailand to learn more about northern Thai temples.

Left: Elephant Nature Park (p154);
Above: Trekking in Mae Taeng (p153)

Chiang Mai Walking Tour

Chiang Mai's famous temples reside in the historic old city. Start in the cooler morning hours, dress modestly (covering shoulders and knees) and when inside remove your shoes and sit in the 'mermaid' position.

WALK FACTS

- **Start** Wat Phra Singh
- **Finish** Vocational Training Center of the Chiang Mai Women's Correctional Institution
- **Distance** 2.5km
- **Duration** Two to three hours

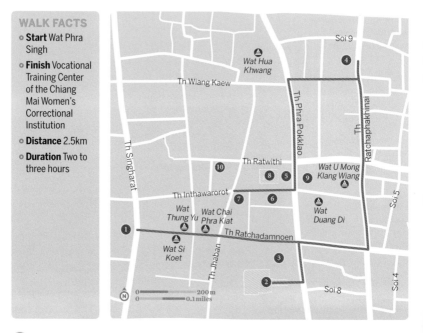

① Wat Phra Singh

Chiang Mai's most revered Buddha image is sheltered in regal style at this beautiful temple (p161), a textbook example of Lanna architecture. During Songkran, Phra Singh is paraded about in religious festivities.

② Wat Chedi Luang

Before condo towers, this now-ruined chedi (p148) was Chiang Mai's tallest structure. It once sheltered the famed Emerald Buddha (Phra Kaew), now in Bangkok.

③ Wat Phan Tao

Next door is this tiny teak temple (p148) that is more photogenic than venerated.

Chiang Mai has a tradition of woodcarving, inherited from Burmese craftspeople, and the surrounding forests supplied durable teak for residences and temples. Once you've seen this temple and its delicate ornamentation, you'll instinctively understand what is meant by 'classic Lanna style'.

④ Wat Chiang Man

If it isn't too hot, squeeze in a visit to one more temple. Wat Chiang Man (p149) is the city's oldest and features all of Lanna's signature architectural elements. It was renovated in the 1920s by a famous northern monk, who was dedicated to resuscitating dilapidated temples.

5 Anusawari Sam Kasat

Nod reverentially to the Three King's Monument (p164), a spiritual focal point of the city. It depicts the northern Thai kings who formed an alliance during the Lanna era.

6 Wat Inthakhin Saduemuang

This pretty, pint-size temple has recently been refurbished and is a popular specimen among the camera-phone tourists.

7 Kow Soy Siri Soy

Sitting at the end of a lunch row, this humble noodle house (p164) does northern Thailand's signature dish of *kôw soy*, a spicy and flavourful stamina builder for more sightseeing.

8 Chiang Mai City Arts & Cultural Centre

Synthesise the morning's tour of art, architecture and history into a cohesive narrative at this informative and blissfully air-conditioned museum (p148). The building is recognised as an architectural stand-out.

9 Lanna Folklife Museum

Just across the street, this newly opened museum (p164) is professionally run and provides a beautiful stroll through a well-restored historic building filled with informative and artistic displays.

10 Vocational Training Center of the Chiang Mai Women's Correctional Institution

After a long day, reward yourself with a visit to the Women's Prison. Wait, not that entrance (unless you have something to confess!). Continue to the building on the south side of the road with the 'Prison Shop' sign, where massages (p158) are given by well-behaved inmates. This is a public outreach program to provide job skills for soon-to-be-released prisoners.

Chiang Mai in...

TWO DAYS

Visit the temples highlighted in the Walking Tour, then explore Wat Phra That Doi Suthep (p152). Finish the day at a riverside restaurant. The next day do a Thai cooking course (p160), then check out the Saturday Walking Street (p151) or Sunday Walking Street (p167) if you're in town on a weekend.

FOUR DAYS

On day three, organise a full-day outdoor activity, such as trekking, ziplining, rock-climbing or white-water rafting. The next day, tour the shops and restaurants of Th Nimmanhaemin (p173). Return later for its nightlife.

SEVEN DAYS

With an extra few days, you'll have time to retreat into the surrounding countryside for mountain scenery. Hire a motorcycle and follow the ridges through Mae Sa Valley (p178), or make an escape to Chiang Dao (p180) for bird-watching, hiking and caving.

Ziplining at Flight of the Gibbon (p154)

Discover
Chiang Mai

Monks praying at Wat Chedi Luang
STUART DEE/GETTY IMAGES ©

◉ Sights

OLD CITY เมืองเก่า

Chiang Mai's historic quarter is hemmed in by a brick rampart and a moat, old-fashioned defences that now repulse the traffic and urban chaos of modern Thai life.

Wat Chedi Luang   Buddhist Temple
(วัดเจดีย์หลวง; Map p156; Th Phra Pokklao; donations appreciated; ⊙6am-6pm) An historic and venerable temple, Wat Chedi Luang is built around a crumbling Lanna-style *chedi* (built in 1441) that was one of the tallest structures in ancient Chiang Mai.

The famed Phra Kaew (Emerald Buddha), now held in Bangkok's Wat Phra Kaew, resided in the eastern niche in 1475. Today there is a jade replica, given as a gift from the Thai king in 1995 to celebrate the 600th anniversary of the *chedi* and the 700th anniversary of the city.

Wat Phan Tao   Buddhist Temple
(วัดพันเถา; Map p156; Th Phra Pokklao; donations appreciated; ⊙6am-6pm) This pretty little temple evokes mist-shrouded forests and the largess of the teak trade. The main *wí·hǎhn* is constructed entirely of moulded teak panels supported by 28 gargantuan teak pillars. Coloured mirror mosaics decorate *naga* bargeboards, and the facade's primary ornamentation of a peacock over a dog represents the astrological year of the former royal resident's birth.

Chiang Mai City Arts & Cultural Centre   Museum
(หอศิลปวัฒนธรรมเชียงใหม่; Map p156; ☏0 5321 7793; Th Phra Pokklao; adult/child 90/40B; ⊙8.30am-5pm Tue-Sun) This museum offers a

fine primer on Chiang Mai history. The 1st floor has engaging and informative historical and cultural displays. The 2nd-floor rooms have life-sized exhibits of bygone eras, including an early Lanna village.

Nearby are two sister museums: Chiang Mai Historical Centre and Lanna Folklife Museum (p164). A combination ticket for all three costs 180B.

The Arts & Culture Centre is housed in a lovely 1920s building that used to be Chiang Mai's former Provincial Hall.

Wat Chiang Man   Buddhist Temple
(วัดเชียงมั่น; Map p156; Th Ratchaphakhinai; donations appreciated; ◷6am–6pm) Chiang Mai's oldest temple, Wat Chiang Man, was established by the city's founder, Phaya Mengrai, some time around 1296. The temple contains two famous Buddhas, which reside in the small sanctuary to the right of the main chapel. **Phra Sila** is a marble bas-relief Buddha that stands about 30cm high and reportedly came from Sri Lanka or India. **Phra Sae Tang Khamani**, a 10cm-high, crystal image, is thought to have come from Lavo (Lopburi) 1800 years ago.

In front of the *bòht* (ordination hall), a stone slab, engraved in 1581, bears the earliest known reference to the city's founding.

EAST OF THE OLD CITY

Passing through Pratu Tha Phae leads to a standard-issue commercial neighbourhood of concrete shophouses and busy multilaned roads. Amid the clutter are old heritage houses built by British and Burmese teak merchants. Shopping and dining are the primary pastimes in this part of town. Further east, Mae Ping (Ping River) carves out a meandering path once populated on the eastern bank by foreign missionaries.

Talat Warorot   Market
(ตลาดวโรรส; Map p156; cnr Th Chang Moi & Th Praisani; ◷6am–5pm) Chiang Mai's oldest and most famous market, Talat Warorot, excels in every category: day market, souvenir shopping, people-watching

> **Local Knowledge**

Chiang Mai's Temples

DR RATANAPORN SETHAKUL, ASSOCIATE PROFESSOR OF HISTORY, PAYAP UNIVERSITY

1 WAT PHRA SINGH
Wat Phra Singh (p161) houses a well-known Buddha image (Phra Singh), which Thai people regularly come to pay respect to. During important festivals the image is moved outside for public merit-making. Inside the sanctuary where Phra Singh resides are mural paintings depicting the traditional life of ordinary people. As a royal temple, it holds many state ceremonies.

2 WAT CHEDI LUANG
Wat Chedi Luang (p148) is well known for the city pillar (*làk meu·ang* or *sŏw in·tá·kĭn*) where an annual merit-making festival takes place prior to the planting season. This pillar shows the historical relationship between the Mon-Khmer people, the indigenous people of Lanna, and the Tai people who came to conquer this area in the 13th century. The temple was a centre of Buddhist education from the 15th to the 16th century.

3 WAT BUAK KHROK LUANG
This temple (Th Charoen Muang) is outside town on the way to San Kampheng district. The murals are a distinctive example of Lanna folk paintings. They depict Lanna's multiracial society and wonderful historical evidence of Burmese artistic and architectural influences.

4 WAT KETKARAM
Wat Ketkaram (Wat Ket; Th Charoenrat) is located on the Mae Ping (Ping River) in a community of Chinese traders. In the 19th century Chiang Mai became more multiracial with the arrival of Chinese, Hindu and Western merchants and missionaries. There is Chinese art in the ordination hall since Chinese traders were major donors to the temple. The temple museum is worth visiting too.

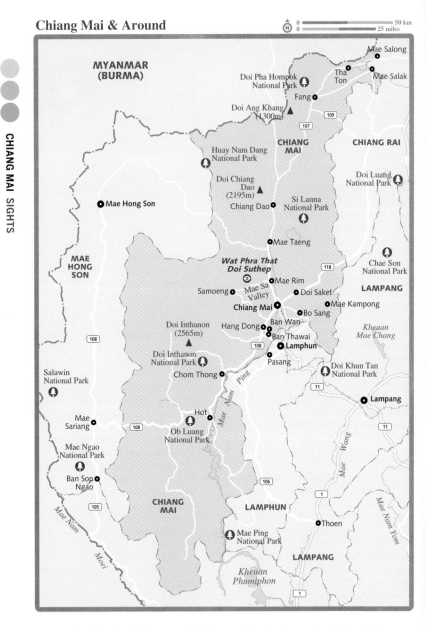

and snacking. It is locally known as 'gàht lŏo·ang', which is northern Thai for 'great market'. There are two multistorey buildings, a beehive of outdoor vendors and several disorienting lanes filled with additional commerce. It is a smaller and less hectic version of Bangkok's Chatuchak Weekend Market.

Talat Tonlamyai
Market

(Map p156; Th Praisani; ⊗24hr; 🕾) Facing the river, the city's main fresh **flower**

The Story of Chiang Mai

Chiang Mai and Thailand's other northern provinces share more of their early development with the Shan state of present-day Myanmar (Burma), neighbouring parts of Laos and even the southern mountains of China than with Bangkok and Thailand's central plains.

King Phaya Mengrai (also spelt Mangrai) is credited with founding the Lanna kingdom in Chiang Saen and expanding it into the Mae Ping (Ping River) valley. Around 1296, King Mengrai relocated the Lanna capital to a more picturesque spot between Doi Suthep and Mae Ping and named the city Nopburi Si Nakhon Ping Chiang Mai (shortened to Chiang Mai, meaning the 'New Walled City').

The Lanna kingdom was soon confronted by challenges from Ayuthaya, but it was the Burmese who would overtake the city and the kingdom in 1556, an occupation that lasted 200 years.

Chao Kavila, a chieftain from nearby Lampang principality, helped 'liberate' northern Thailand from Burmese control. Under Kavila, Chiang Mai became an important regional trade centre. In 1800 Kavila built the monumental brick walls around Chiang Mai's inner city and expanded the city in southerly and easterly directions, establishing a river port at the end of what is today Th Tha Phae. Many of the later Shan- and Burmese-style temples were built by wealthy teak merchants who emigrated from Burma during this period.

There were many political and technological factors that ultimately led to the demise of an independent Lanna state. In 1933, Chiang Mai officially became a province of Siam.

market (*gàht dòrk mái*) offers a bouquet of tropical and temperate flowers that are brought to market at night to avoid the wilting daytime heat. Cool-weather varieties, including daisies and roses, are grown in the nearby highlands. Catch the flower market during citywide festivals, such as Loi Krathong and the Flower Festival.

SOUTH OF THE OLD CITY

Th Wualai is renowned for its **silver shops** and is often filled with the tapping sound of a decorative pattern being imprinted onto a plate of silver (or, more often, aluminium).

Saturday Walking Street Market

(ถนนเดินวันเสาร์; Th Wualai; ⏰4pm-midnight Sat) On Saturdays, Th Wualai is closed to traffic and mobbed by pedestrians parading past food and souvenir vendors. Come early to have enough room to shop as it does get crowded. There are additional food stalls across the street near Talat Pratu Chiang Mai.

Wat Sisuphan Buddhist Temple

(วัดศรีสุพรรณ; Soi 2, Th Wualai; donations appreciated; ⏰6am-6pm) The district's silver craftsmanship is given a spectacular setting at this neighbourhood temple. The prime attraction is the 'silver' *ubosot* (ordination hall), covered entirely with silver, nickel and aluminium embossed panels. The temple also hosts local silver artisans, monk chat, meditation courses and Poy Luang Festival (a Shan ordination in March).

WEST OF THE OLD CITY

Wat Suan Dok Buddhist Temple

(วัดสวนดอก; Th Suthep; donations appreciated; ⏰6am-6pm) Built on a former flower garden in 1373, this plain-jane temple has a photogenic collection of whitewashed *chedi* that pose in front of the blue peaks of Doi Suthep and Doi Pui.

According to legend, a relic was brought to Wat Suan Dok, miraculously duplicated itself and was then used as

151

JOHN AND TINA REID/GETTY IMAGES ©

Don't Miss
Wat Phra That Doi Suthep

Overlooking the city from its mountain throne, Wat Suthep is one of the north's most sacred temples.

The temple was established in 1383 under King Keu Naone and enjoys a mystical birth story. A visiting Sukhothai monk instructed the Lanna king to establish a temple with the twin of a miraculous Buddha relic (enshrined at Wat Suan Dok). The relic was mounted on a white elephant, which wandered the mountain until it died at this spot, interpreted as the 'chosen' location.

The temple is reached by a strenuous, 306-step staircase, intended as an act of meditation. (For the less fit, there's a tram for 20B.)

The 1st-floor terrace documents this history of the temple with a shrine to Sudeva, the hermit who lived on the mountain, and a statue of the white elephant who carried the Buddha relic up the mountain. On the 2nd-floor terrace is the picturesque golden *chedi* that enshrines the relic; it is topped by a five-tiered umbrella in honour of the city's independence from Burma and its union with Thailand.

Within the monastery compound, the International Buddhism Center conducts a variety of religious outreach programs for visitors.

NEED TO KNOW
วัดพระธาตุดอยสุเทพ; Th Huay Kaew, Doi Suthep; admission 30B; ⏰6am-6pm

a 'guide' for the founding of Wat Doi Suthep. The relic is enshrined in the temple's central *chedi*.

Wat U Mong　Buddhist Temple
(วัดอุโมงค์; Soi Wat U Mong, Th Khlong Chon-prathan; donations appreciated; ⏰6am-6pm)

This **forest wát** is best known for its secluded sylvan setting and a series of interconnecting brick **tunnels** built around 1380 for the clairvoyant monk Thera Jan. A marvellously grisly fasting Buddha sits on top of the tunnel hill, along with a large and venerated *chedi*.

Wat U Mong is off Th Suthep near Chiang Mai University. Note that there is another Wat U Mong in town, so to clearly instruct a driver ask for 'Wat U Mong Thera Jan'.

Doi Suthep-Pui National Park   Park
(อุทยานแห่งชาติดอยสุเทพ – ปุย; ☎ 0 5321 0244; Th Huay Kaew; adult/child 100/50B, car 30B; ⏰8am-sunset) Often bearing a crown of clouds, **Doi Suthep** (1676m) and **Doi Pui** (1685m) are Chiang Mai's sacred peaks. The mountains ascend from the humid lowlands into the cool (and even cold) cloud belt where moss and ferns thrive. Portions of the mountains form a 265-sq-km **national park** that is home to famous Wat Doi Suthep and other attractions.

The park is 16km northwest of central Chiang Mai. Shared *rót daang* leave from Chiang Mai University (Th Huay Kaew entrance) to various points within the national park. One-way fares start at 40B to Wat Doi Suthep and 70B to Phra Tamnak Bhu Bhing. You can also charter a *sŏrng·tăa·ou* for about 600B.

Phra Tamnak Bhu Bhing   Gardens
(พระตำหนักภูพิงค์ | Bhu Bhing Palace; Th Huay Kaew, Doi Suthep; admission 50B; ⏰8.30-11.30am & 1-3.30pm) The grounds of the royal family's winter palace are open to the public (when the royals aren't visiting). Thanks to Doi Suthep's cool climate, the gardens specialise in 'exotic' species such as roses. More interesting is the **water reservoir** brought to life by dancing fountains and the king's musical compositions. Though not a must, 'nature sightseers' might like the paved footpaths.

Hmong Villages   Village
(Doi Suthep; museum 10B) Near the summit of Doi Pui are two Hmong villages. **Ban Doi Pui** is off the main road and is

Monk Chat

Many Chiang Mai temples offer 'monk chat', in which monks get to practise their English by fielding questions from visitors about religion, rituals and life in the monastery. Remember that it is respectful to dress modestly: cover your shoulders and knees. Women should take care not to touch the monks or their belongings, or to pass anything directly to them.

Wat Suan Dok (p151) has a dedicated room just beyond the main sanctuary hall and holds its chats from 5pm to 7pm, Monday, Wednesday and Friday. Wat Sisuphan (p151) holds its sessions from 5.30pm to 7pm just before its meditation course. Wat Chedi Luang (p148) has a table under a shady tree where monks chat from 9am to 6pm daily.

basically a tourist market at altitude. A more interesting stop is **Ban Kun Chang Kian**, 500m down a dirt track just past the Doi Pui campground. It is best to park at the campground's visitor centre and walk from there. The village runs a coffee house surrounded by coffee plants that are harvested in January.

🜚 Activities
OUTDOOR ACTIVITIES

Outdoor escapes are easy in Chiang Mai: scenic countryside and lush forests are within an hour's drive or less of the city, and a variety of outfitters tackle the byways, waterways and jungle tracks. Book directly with tour providers, either at their offices (listed here) or online, to avoid agent commissions.

Chiang Mai is not the only base for hill-tribe treks but it is the most accessible and one of the cheapest. Most companies operating out of Chiang

Mai offer the same type of tour: a one-hour minibus ride to Mae Taeng or Mae Wang (depending on the duration of the trip), a brief hike to an elephant camp, a one-hour elephant ride to a waterfall, another hour rafting down a river and, for multiday tours, an overnight stay in or near a hill-tribe village. The day goes by pretty quickly and is perfectly suited for travellers who want a little bit of everything at an affordable price; day tours typically start at 1000B, which is shockingly cheap and is only sustainable if the trips are sold in great quantities and a lot of corners are cut. Most guesthouses in Chiang Mai act as booking agents in exchange for a commission, which in turn subsidises the cheap room rates.

Flight of the Gibbon   Ziplining
(Map p156; ☎ 0 5301 0660; www.treetopasia. com; 29/4-5 Th Kotchasan; 3hr tour 3400B) 🖉 This adventure outfit in Chiang Mai started the zipline craze a few years ago. Nearly 5km of wire with 33 staging platforms are strung up through the for-

est canopy some 1300m above sea level. Multiday, multi-activity tours include a night at a homestay in Mae Kampong, a high-altitude village an hour's drive east from Chiang Mai.

Elephant Nature Park   Elephant Encounter
(Map p156; ☎ 0 5381 8754; www.elephant naturepark.org; 1 Th Ratchamankha; 1-/2-day tour 2500/5800B) 🖉 A pioneer in the new wave of elephant tourism, Khun Lek (Sangduen Chailert) runs this sanctuary for injured and rescued elephants. Visitors help wash the elephants and watch the herd, but there is no show or riding.

Patara Elephant Farm   Elephant Encounter
(☎ 08 1992 2551; www.pataraelephantfarm. com; day tour 5800B) Khun Pat is a passionate and thoughtful player in Chiang Mai's elephant-conservation tourism industry. His primary focus is to support the mother-baby bond, and combat Thailand's declining domesticated elephant

Left: Elephant trek; **Below:** Flight of the Gibbon
(LEFT) BUENA VISTA IMAGES/GETTY IMAGES ©; (BELOW) MATTHEW MICAH WRIGHT/GETTY IMAGES ©

population through tourism. His elephant farm is in a beautiful forested setting and offers an intimate and educational elephant encounter.

Baan Chang Elephant Park
Elephant Encounter
(Map p156; ☎ 0 5381 4174; www.baanchang elephantpark.com; 147/1 Th Ratchadamnoen; tours 2400-4200B) Educating visitors about elephants and their preservation, Baan Chang is a solid choice in the conservation tourism model. Tours involve a day of mahout training, including guiding, riding and bathing. Less expensive tours are for two people to one elephant. It is in Mae Taeng, 50 minutes north of Chiang Mai.

Chiang Mai Rock Climbing Adventures
Rock Climbing
(CMRCA; Map p156; ☎ 08 6911 1470; www. thailandclimbing.com; 55/3 Th Ratchaphakhi-nai; climbing course 3000-4000B) CMRCA maintains many of the climbing routes at Crazy Horse Buttress (also known as 'The Crack'). Tours teach introductory and fundamental rock climbing, bouldering and caving.

Peak Adventure Tour
Adventure Sports
(Map p156; ☎ 0 5380 0567; www.thepeak adventure.com; tours 1800-2500B) The Peak offers a variety of adventure trips, including quad biking, abseiling, trekking, white-water rafting and rock climbing.

Siam River Adventures
White-water Rafting
(Map p156; ☎ 08 9515 1917; www.siamrivers.com; 17 Th Ratwithi; tours from 1800B) With more than a decade of experience, this white-water rafting outfit has a well-regarded safety reputation. The guides have swift-water rescue training and additional staff are located at dangerous parts of the river with throw ropes. Trips can be combined with elephant trekking and village overnight stays. It also operates kayak trips.

Central Chiang Mai

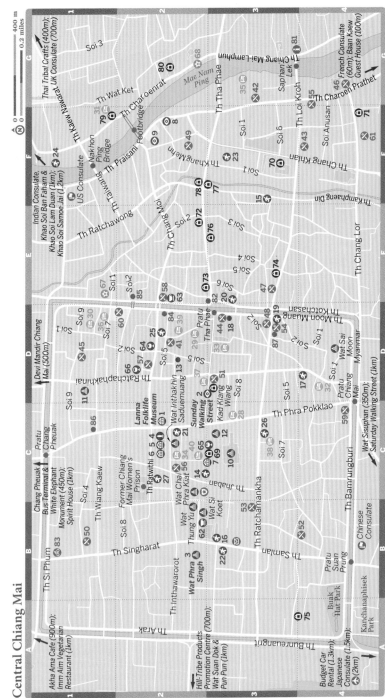

Central Chiang Mai

CHIANG MAI

Get Around Like a Pro

A copy of Nancy Chandler's *Map of Chiang Mai,* available in bookshops, is a worthwhile investment. It shows the city's main points of interest, shopping venues and oddities that you will be pleased to stumble upon. This schematic map will help you wander with confidence.

Chiang Mai Mountain Biking & Kayaking
Mountain Biking

(Map p156; ☎ 0 5381 4207, 08 1024 7046; www.chiangmaikayaking.com; 1 Th Samlan; tours 1550-2000B) A variety of guided mountain biking and kayaking trips head into the jungles and rivers, respectively, for fresh air, a good workout and mountain scenery. Tours are suited for all levels and adjusted for the seasons. There is a **second branch** (Map p156; 28 Th Kamphaeng Din) near the night market.

MASSAGE

Vocational Training Center of the Chiang Mai Women's Correctional Institution
Massage

(Map p156; 100 Th Ratwithi; foot/traditional massage 150/180B; ☺8am-4.30pm Mon-Fri, 9am-4.30pm Sat & Sun) Fantastic massages performed by female inmates participating in the prison's job-training rehabilitation program. **Lila Thai Massage** (Map p156; Th Phra Pokklao; massage 200-600B; ☺10am-10pm) was established by the director of the prison and offers post-release employment to the inmates who participated in the training program.

Ban Hom Samunphrai
Massage

(☎ 0 5381 7362; www.homprang.com; Saraphi; steam bath 200B, massage 600-1300B) A unique time capsule of old folk ways, 9km from Chiang Mai near the McKean Institute. Maw Hom ('Herbal Doctor') is a licensed herb practitioner and massage therapist. She runs a traditional herbal steam bath, re-creating what was once a common feature of rural villages.

Herbal compresses used in traditional Thai massage

West Chiang Mai

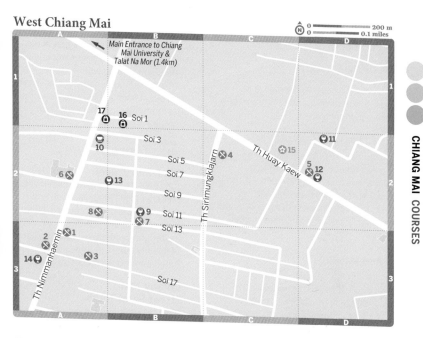

West Chiang Mai

Thai Massage Conservation Club   Massage

(Map p156; 99 Th Ratchamankha; massages 150-250B) This place employs only blind masseuses, who are considered to be expert practitioners because of their heightened sense of touch.

Oasis Spa   Massage

(Map p156; ☏ 0 5392 0111; www.oasisspa.net; 4 Th Samlan; treatments from 1700B) Oasis has a tranquil garden setting navigated by elevated walkways that lead to private villas for singles' or couples' treatments.

🎓 Courses

Dozens of cooking schools offer classes, typically costing around 900B to 1100B a day, either in town, such as at an atmospheric old house, or out of town in a garden or farm setting. When booking your course, ask about the student-to-teacher ratio as this will affect the quality of the experience.

If You Like...
Kids' Stuff

Chiang Mai is popular with families, especially with kids who enjoy outdoor activities and animal encounters.

1 CHIANG MAI NIGHT SAFARI
(เชียงใหม่ไนท์ซาฟารี; ☏0 5399 9000; www.chiangmainightsafari.com; Rte 121/Th Klorng Chonprathan; tours adult/child 800/400B; ⏰11am-10pm) After-dark tram tours travel through this open-air zoo that includes up-close interactions with savannah animals and safe-distance spottings of predators.

2 CHIANG MAI ZOO
(สวนสัตว์เชียงใหม่; ☏0 5322 1179; www.chiangmaizoo.com; 100 Th Huay Kaew; adult/child 100/50B; ⏰8am-5pm) This mediocre municipal zoo with a pretty woodland setting gives kids a traffic-free zone to roam.

3 MUSEUM OF WORLD INSECTS & NATURAL WONDERS
(Map p156; Th Ratchadamnoen; admission 100B; ⏰9am-5pm) Bugs, butterflies and creepy crawlies are showcased at this quirky museum.

Asia Scenic Thai Cooking   Cooking
(Map p156; ☏0 5341 8657; www.asiascenic.com; 31 Soi 5, Th Ratchadamnoen; courses 900-1000B) Khun Gayray's cooking school has expanded to include an out-of-town farm location as well as its original in-town spot for those with less time. The city classroom has a kitchen garden so you'll still see the food source.

Chiang Mai Thai Cookery School   Cooking
(Map p156; ☏0 5320 6388; www.thaicookeryschool.com; 47/2 Th Moon Muang; course 1450B) One of Chiang Mai's first cooking schools holds classes in a rural setting outside of Chiang Mai. The school also has a master-class with a northern Thai menu and it is run by TV chef Sompon Nabnian.

Gap's Thai Culinary Art School   Cooking
(Map p156; ☏0 5327 8140; www.gaps-house.com; 3 Soi 4, Th Ratchadamnoen; course 900B; ⏰Mon-Sat) Affiliated with the guesthouse Gap's House, cooking classes are held out of town at the owner's house. The student-to-teacher ratio is an intimate 6:1.

Tours

Click and Travel   Cycling
(☏0 5328 1553; www.clickandtravelonline.com; tours 1050-1200B; 🚲) Click and Travel offers a pedal-powered, cultural trip with full- and half-day tours, visiting temples and attractions outside of the city centre. Routes and bikes suited for children are also available.

Chiang Mai Street Food Tours   Food
(☏08 5033 8161; www.chiangmaistreetfoodtours.com; tours 700B) Cooking schools are all the rage in Chiang Mai but for the rest of us who would rather eat than work, this tour comes to the rescue. Morning and evening tours take curious appetites through the old city to sample hallmark dishes. The evening market tour is a good introduction to this classic Thai dining experience.

Sleeping

OLD CITY

Awanahouse   Guesthouse $
(Map p156; ☏0 5341 9005; www.awanahouse.com; 7 Soi 1, Th Ratchadamnoen; r 375-1000B; ❄🛜♨🚲) Popular with families, this multistorey building has bright and well-decorated rooms, ranging from basic to just right. The ground-level pool and the rooftop chill-out area are added bonuses.

Gap's House   Guesthouse $
(Map p156; ☏0 5327 8140; www.gaps-house.com; 3 Soi 4, Th Ratchadamnoen; r 550-850B; ❄🛜) A matron among guesthouses, good old Gap's still has a jungle-like garden and budget rooms in old-fashioned

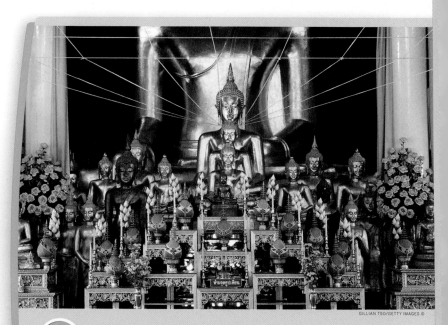

GILLIAN TSO/GETTY IMAGES ©

⭐ Don't Miss
Wat Phra Singh

Chiang Mai's most revered temple, Wat Phra Singh draws pilgrims and sightseers for its resident Buddha and its classic Lanna art and architecture. Visitors should dress modestly (clothing covering shoulders and knees).

Phra Singh, the temple's famous image, is housed in Wihan Lai Kham, a small chapel to the rear of the temple grounds next to the *chedi* (stupa). The building boasts a Lanna-style three-tiered roof and carved gables. Inside are sumptuous *lai·krahm* (gold-pattern stencilling) and murals.

NEED TO KNOW

วัดพระสิงห์; Map p156; Th Singharat; admission 20B; ⊙6am-6pm

---

wooden houses. Bring your mozzie spray. No advance reservations.

Gap's is also famous for its Thai cooking course and nightly vegetarian buffet.

Thong Ran's House   Guesthouse $

(Map p156; ☎0 532 77307; www.thongranhouse. com; 105 Th Ratchamankha; r 600B; ❄ ⑇) This new guesthouse has cosy, stylish rooms in a quiet soi off the main road. The location is slightly removed from the usual tourist hubbub but still central.

Banjai Garden   Guesthouse $

(Map p156; ☎08 5716 1635; 43 Soi 3, Th Phra Pokklao; r 350-450B; ⑇) This pretty wooden house has a homey appeal and a pleasant garden for hanging out. The simple rooms have shared bathrooms and better-than-average beds. There's also a shared mini-kitchen.

Sri Pat
Guest House   Guesthouse $$

(Map p156; ☎0 5321 8716; 16 Soi 7, Th Moon Muang; r 1000-1400B; ❄ ⑇ ⌷) A standout in the flashpacker category, Sri Pat has just

the right dose of personality. Rooms have sunny dispositions, celadon-coloured tiles, folksy cotton drapes and balconies.

Villa Duang Champa
Hotel $$

(Map p156; ☎ 0 5332 7199; http://duangchampa. com; 82 Th Ratchadamnoen; r from 1500B; ❄ ☎) Duang Champa is an excellent small hotel in a heritage-style building. Rooms are pretty enough to be featured in a design magazine, with minimalist modern furnishings. Stick to the hotel as the dark, cramped guesthouse rooms are not a good deal.

TJR Boutique House
Hotel $$

(Map p156; ☎ 0 5332 6525; Soi 1, Th Moon Muang; r 1000-1200B; ❄ @ ☎) A new apartment-style hotel, TJR has huge rooms, huge beds and bathrooms with tubs. Street-facing rooms get views of the mountain. It is often booked as the desk clerk speaks Chinese and English.

3 Sis
Hotel $$

(Map p156; ☎ 0 5327 3243; www.the3sis.com; 1 Soi 8, Th Phra Pokklao; d 1500-1800B; ❄ ☎)

A mini hotel empire occupies this corner spot. Rooms are well proportioned with plenty of flashpacker appeal. The 'vacation lodge' building has more flair than the 'front' building, with lovely wooden floors and additional mod cons. The breezy lobby provides a communal space and rates include breakfast.

Koko Palm Inn
Hotel $$

(Map p156; ☎ 08 6428 0495; www.kokopalminn. com; Soi 6, Th Ratchadamnoen; r 1200-1400B; ❄ ☎) This new boutique has only eight rooms facing a garden filled with ponds and palms. The rooms are compact yet cute, and bathrooms are big enough for serious grooming.

Baan Hanibah
Bed & Breakfast
Hotel $$

(Map p156; ☎ 0 5328 7524; www.baanhanibah. com; 6 Soi 8, Th Moon Muang; r 900-1400B; ❄ ☎) Protected by a garden of fragrant frangipani trees, Baan Hanibah is a relaxed boutique escape in the heart of the old city. The converted teak house

Left: Students take part in a Thai cooking class; **Below:** Taste-testing during a Thai cooking class

retains its traditional ambience while providing small yet stylish rooms.

Tamarind Village   Hotel **$$$**

(Map p156; ☎ 0 5341 8896-9; www.tamarind village.com; 50/1 Th Ratchadamnoen; r from 7000B; ❄ ⓦ ⌕ ♨) One of the first of the 'Lanna revival' hotels in Chiang Mai, Tamarind Village recreates the quiet spaces of a temple on the grounds of an old tamarind orchard. The bamboo-shrouded walkway and whitewashed perimeter wall shut out the distracting modern world, while the garden courtyards create an intimate space for some serious self-indulgence.

EAST OF THE OLD CITY

Baan Kaew Guest House   Guesthouse **$**

(☎ 0 5327 1606; www.baankaew-guesthouse. com; 142 Th Charoen Prathet; r 680-800B; ❄ ⓦ ♨) This two-storey, apartment-style place is a good honest deal in a quiet part of town. Rooms have all the basics plus small balconies to enjoy the spacious garden. The setting, away from the road and slightly removed from the touristy night bazaar, will make you feel like a local instead of a visitor.

Baan Orapin   B&B **$$**

(Map p156; ☎ 0 5324 3677; www.baan orapin.com; 150 Th Charoenrat; r 2400-3600B; ❄ @ ⌕) It's a family affair at Baan Orapin, a pretty garden compound anchored by a stately teak house, which has been in the family since 1914. Luxurious guest residences (a total of 15 rooms) are in separate and modern buildings spread throughout the property.

River View Lodge   Hotel **$$**

(Map p156; ☎ 0 5327 1109; www.riverviewlodgch. com; 25 Soi 4, Th Charoen Prathet; r 1800-2200B; ❄ @ ⌕) This breezy lodge is the perfect antidote to the hustle of the night bazaar area. Its quiet riverside setting is enhanced by a lush garden and pool. The rooms are a tad lacklustre but many don't

AUSTIN BUSH ©

Don't Miss
Lanna Folklife Museum

This new and professional museum is a sister site to the other cultural attractions near Anusawari Sam Kasat (Three Kings Monument). Life-size dioramas explain northern Thai religious beliefs and customs, temple paraphernalia and symbolism, traditional crafts and other features of ordinary life. Combination tickets to nearby museums, including the Chiang Mai City Arts & Cultural Centre (p148), are available.

NEED TO KNOW

พิพิธภัณฑ์พื้นถิ่นล้านนา; Map p156; Th Phra Pokklao; adult/child 90/40B; ⏰8.30am-5pm Tue-Sun

---

mind when a chirping red bul-bul volunteers as a morning alarm clock.

🍴 Eating

OLD CITY

Night markets set up in front of Talat Pratu Chiang Mai and on Th Mani Nopharat near Pratu Chang Pheuak.

Kow Soy Siri Soy
Thai $

(Map p156; Th Inthawarorot; mains 40-50B; ⏰7am-3pm Mon-Fri) Well known among locals, this is an easy and tasty lunch stop for *kôw soy*, a northern speciality; it's a curried noodle dish that's served with pickled vegetables and thick red chilli sauce. Order *kôw man gài* (chicken and rice) for children and the chilli-averse.

Angel's Secrets
International $

(Map p156; Soi 1, Th Ratchadamnoen; mains 90-150B; ⏰Tue-Sun 7am-4pm; 🕸🍴) True to its name, this sweet little restaurant is shielded by a fence of greenery from peeping appetites. Inside you'll find creative and wholesome Western breakfasts, including crusty homemade bread, crepes and omelettes, and made-to-order vegetarian Thai food.

Detour:
Country Escapes

Acclimatising to Chiang Mai's laid-back pace and then finding it too hectic is a common affliction. To escape from your escape, there are many scenic country resorts just beyond the superhighways and the sun-stroked suburbs where you can adore misty mountains, green fields and tropical forests. The following are less than two hours' drive from Chiang Mai.

Kaomai Lanna Resort (✆ 0 5383 4470; www.kaomailanna.com; Th Chiang Mai-Hot/Rte 108, Km29, San Pa Thong; r from 3500B; ❄ ➰) has turned many of the property's abandoned tobacco-curing sheds into comfortable lodgings amid a lush garden. The resort is south of Chiang Mai on the outskirts of San Pa Thong and can be used as a base for exploring Doi Inthanon.

Rabeang Pasak Tree House (✆ 08 7660 1243; ChiangmaiTreehouse@gmail.com; Rd 4031, Baan Pasak Ngam, Doi Saket; r from 2000B) is a kid's fantasy come true: wooden huts are built high among the tree branches. Lodging is simple – open-air bathrooms and basic beds – but far from ordinary. It is 75km north of Chiang Mai in Doi Saket area.

Chai Lai Orchid (✆ 08 6923 0867; www.chailaiorchid.com; 202 Moo 9, Tambon Mae Win, Mae Wang; r 1200-2250B; ❄ ➰) is a nature resort planted in the middle of the forest, across the Mae Wang river via a suspended footbridge, and shares space with an elephant camp. Huts range from rustic to resort-ish. A variety of activities (elephant bathing, bamboo rafting, Thai cooking) are offered. It is 45km southwest of Chiang Mai.

Stonefree House (✆ 08 5031 7332; 7/4 Moo 7, Yuwa, San Pa Thong; r from 400B) redefines easygoing with its backpacker country 'resort'. The price is modest and the vibe is rasta. It is 21km south of Chiang Mai.

Tharnthong Lodge (✆ 08 6420 5354; www.tharnthonglodges.com; r 1200-4000B) is the Thai version of the idyllic alpine chalet tucked into a jungle embrace. A pebble-strewn stream bisects the garden-filled property that backs up against a dense jungle. It is 50km east of Chiang Mai in the Mae Kampong area.

Dada Kafe
Vegetarian $

(Map p156; Th Ratchamankha; mains 60-100B; ⏱8am-10pm; 🛜🖊) Tasty health food is marched from the kitchen to the dining room of this busy restaurant. Cure-all fruit juices, hearty breakfasts and stir fries with tofu and brown rice become daily rituals for many visitors.

AUM
Vegetarian Food
Vegetarian $

(Map p156; 66 Th Moon Muang; mains 75-150B; ⏱8am-5pm; @🛜🖊) One of Chiang Mai's original health-food peddlers, AUM (pronounced 'om') creates a meditative space to enjoy fresh and original vegetarian dishes. There's organic coffee from Laos, refreshing lemon-mint juices, fried tempeh and sushi-style vegie rolls.

Fern Forest Cafe
Desserts $

(Map p156; 2/2 Soi 4, Th Singharat; dishes 70-100B; ⏱8.30am-8.30pm; 🛜) Festooned with ferns and babbling water features, this cafe does delectable desserts, coffees and fruit juices. The lush garden provides a respite from the heat of the day.

Blue Diamond
Vegetarian $

(Map p156; 35/1 Soi 9, Th Moon Muang; mains 70-150B; ⏱7am-9pm Mon-Sat; 🛜🖊) Chock-full of fresh produce and baked goods, this backpacker kitchen is a jack-of-all health trends: big salads, vegie stir-fries, and 'inter' food such as fish-sauce spaghetti.

Good Morning Chiang Mai
International $

(Map p156; 29/5 Soi 6, Th Ratchamankha; mains 75-95B; ⏰8am-4pm; 🛜) A favourite among expats, this hip cafe near Wat Phra Jao Mengrai does breakfasts, standard Thai curries and stir-fries and sandwiches.

The shady garden with shabby-chic bric-a-brac provides a stylish backdrop for chit-chat and hanging out.

Juicy 4U
Vegetarian $

(Map p156; 5 Th Ratchamankha; mains 90-120B; ⏰8.30am-5.30pm; 🛜🍴) This funky cafe does vegan and veg dishes, hangover-fighting juices and make-your-own-vegetarian sandwiches – all to a cool techno soundtrack.

Swan
Burmese $

(Map p156; Th Chaiyaphum; mains 70-150B; ⏰11am-10pm; 🍴) This grubby restaurant east of the old city offers a trip across the border with its Burmese menu. The backyard courtyard provides an escape from the moat traffic.

Girasole
Italian $

(Map p156; 📞0 5327 6388; Kad Klang Wiang, Th Ratchadamnoen; mains 90-150B; ⏰11am-9pm) Kad Klang Wiang, the garden arcade at the corner of Th Ratchadamanoen and Th Ratchaphakhinai, is a hub for dining and people-watching. Adding to its appeal is this small Italian restaurant with fantastic pizzas: crispy crust, tangy sauce and imported cheeses. Pizza Hut can't compete.

New Delhi
Indian $$

(Map p156; Th Ratwithi; mains 150-280B; ⏰11am-10pm) This basic eatery serves up some of Chiang Mai's best Indian food – lots of complex flavours without an oily afterglow. The *handi* dishes, among other northern Indian fare, are the restaurant's specialities.

Heuan Phen
Northern Thai $$

(Map p156; 📞0 5327 7103; 112 Th Ratchamankha; mains 80-200B; ⏰11am-10pm) True northern food is difficult to find in a restaurant setting, but this tourist-friendly place does its best to introduce visitors to regional specialities. During the day, pre-made dishes are set up in a large canteen out front. In the evenings, an antique-cluttered dining room offers more of a culinary experience.

EAST OF THE OLD CITY

Chiang Mai's small Chinatown, along Th Chang Moi, is a tasty quarter to investigate early in the morning for stalls selling *nám đow·hôo* (soy milk) and baton-shaped Chinese-style doughnuts.

Past Saphan Nakhon Ping is Th Faham, known as Chiang Mai's *kôw soy* ghetto. Situated here are **Khao Soi Lam Duan** (Th Faham; dishes 50-70B), which also serves *kà·nŏm rang pêung* (literally beehive

For the Love of Pork

Chiang Mai reveals its Chinese heritage with its devotion to pork products, most obvious in the northern Thai speciality of *sâi òo·a* (pork sausage). Good quality *sâi òo·a* should be zesty and spicy with discernible flavours of lemongrass, ginger and turmeric. Here are a few well-known purveyors.

The sign is in Thai but you'll know **Dom Rong** (Map p156; Talat Warorot; dishes from 80B; ⏰8am-8pm), a famous sausage stall in the Talat Warorot's dried goods section, by the crowd of people gathered around it. Further out of town are **Mengrai Sai Ua** (Th Chiang Mai–Lamphun), near the Holiday Inn on the east bank of the river, and our favourite, **Sai Ua Gao Makham** (Rte 121), a small stall in Talat Mae Huay (Mae Huay market), which is a few kilometres south of the Night Safari on the way to Hang Dong.

OLIVER STREWE/GETTY IMAGES ©

⭐ Don't Miss
Sunday Walking Street

The old city's central avenue is closed to traffic for the weekly Sunday Walking Street, a convergence of provincial culture, commerce and people-watching. It is also a resurrection of the itinerant merchant tradition from the ancient caravan days.

Vendors line the length of Th Ratchadamnoen. The temples host food stalls selling northern Thai cuisine and other shopping-stamina boosts. The market gets very crowded, so come early. There is also a Saturday Walking Street (p151).

NEED TO KNOW

ถนนเดินวันอาทิตย์; Map p156; Th Ratchadamnoen; ⏰4pm-midnight Sun

---

pastry, a coconut-flavoured waffle), **Khao Soi Samoe Jai** (Th Faham; dishes 50-70B) and **Khao Soi Ban Faham** (Th Faham; dishes 45-55B). Foodies sometimes spend the day sampling a bowl at each place to select their favourite.

Anusan Food Centre   Market
(Map p156; Th Chang Khlan, Anusan Night Bazaar; mains 80-350B; ⏰5-10pm) Anusan is a buzzing food market best known for Thai-Chinese seafood. There is a market stall section with communal seating and stand-alone restaurants.

Just Khao Soy   Thai $
(Map p156; 108/2 Th Charoen Prathet; mains 100-150B; ⏰11am-9pm) This restaurant is a confidence builder: it offers a primer on northern Thailand's signature dish of *kôw soy*.

First you order your meat (or vegies), then level of spice, type of noodles and sauce, and a delicious, hearty broth is born. The food is beautifully presented but it's a bit overpriced. Nevertheless, now you can order *kôw soy* wherever you want.

167

Chez Marco Restaurant & Bar
French $$

(Map p156; ☎ 0 5320 7032; 15/7 Th Loi Kroh; mains 150-350B; ☼5.30pm-midnight Mon-Sat) It is quite surprising to find such a beloved restaurant in the middle of Loi Kroh's girlie bar scene. But Chez Marco catapults past the ho-hum tourist joints with top-notch French fare and reasonable prices. Homemade bread, duck dishes and tuna carpaccio are just some of the specialities on offer here, and there's a kids menu too.

Antique House
Thai $$

(Map p156; 71 Th Charoen Prathet; mains 100-250B; ☼11am-10pm) Set in a quaint teak house with a suitably antique-filled garden, this rather touristy restaurant does a much better job with ambience than it does with food. Regardless, it remains a popular place to entertain out-of-towners and the grilled fish dishes won't disappoint.

Whole Earth Restaurant
Thai, Indian $$

(Map p156; 88 Th Si Donchai; mains 150-350B; ☼11am-10pm) This confectionery-coloured teak house wears a garden of hanging vines and orchids growing in the crooks of tree limbs. It is the sort of place Thais take someone special – where the staff will treat you like royalty and the dishes seem exotic (Thai, Indian and vegetarian) without being demanding.

Chedi
International $$$

(Map p156; ☎ 0 5325 3385; 123 Th Charoen Prathet; mains 500-1000B; ☼7am-10pm) Decor and design are the main ingredients at this luxury hotel's restaurant. The property transformed the former British consulate into an experiment in minimalism with geometric grounds and spare common spaces. Come to dine on a gorgeous riverside view with a side order of slightly overpriced Vietnamese, Indian, Thai and international dishes.

Left: A restaurant on the banks of Mae Ping (Ping River);
Below: Parcels of food for sale on the Bangkok–Chiang Mai train
(LEFT) JOHN ELK/GETTY IMAGES ©; (BELOW) OLIVER STREWE/GETTY IMAGES ©

NORTH OF THE OLD CITY

Huan Soontaree
Thai **$**

(☏ 0 5387 2707; 208 Th Paton; mains 160-200B; ⏱4pm-midnight) Visiting Bangkok Thais make the pilgrimage to this rustic restaurant, partly for the food but mainly for the owner, Soontaree Vechanont, a famous northern singer popular in the 1970s. She performs at the restaurant from 8.30pm to 9.30pm Monday to Saturday. The menu is a pleasant blend of northern, northeastern and central Thai specialities. It is 8km north of town beyond the superhighway along the west side of the river.

Spirit House
International **$$**

(Soi Viangbua, Th Chang Pheuak; mains 150-230B; ⏱5-11pm, Mon-Sat) North of the old city, this antique-filled dining room is the creative outlet for the owner, a former chef in New Orleans and self-described 'nut about food'. He builds the daily menu around what looks interesting at the market. The restaurant also hosts concerts and cultural events.

WEST OF THE OLD CITY

Pun Pun
Vegetarian **$**

(Th Suthep, Wat Suan Dok; mains 50-65B; ⏱9am-5pm; ☝) ⦿ This simple spot practises all of the popular health-food trends without any of the marketing. Meatless and vegan meals use little-known herbs and vegetables, whole grains and no refined sugars.

Most ingredients are sourced from the restaurant's farm, a project in sustainable agriculture and seed preservation. The restaurant is behind the 'monk chat' office. There is another branch called **Imm Aim Vegetarian Restaurant** (10 Th Santhitham; ⏱10am-9pm).

Khun Churn
Vegetarian **$**

(Map p159; Soi 17, Th Nimmanhaemin; buffet 129B; ⏱8am-10pm; ☝) The 'professor' of

169

Market Meals

Foodies will love Chiang Mai's markets, which offer everything from morning noodles to daytime snacking and evening supping. To impress a Thai friend, pick up a bag of *man gâa·ou*, a roasted acorn-like nut harvested at the end of the rainy season.

Talat Warorot (p149) is the grandmother of Chiang Mai markets and has northern Thai food stalls tucked in all sorts of corners. Just squeeze in and act like you belong.

North of the Th Ratwithi intersection, **Talat Somphet** (Somphet Market; Map p156; Soi 6, Th Moon Muang; ◷6am-6pm) sells all the fixings for a takeaway feast: fried chicken, fresh juices, sweets and fruit. Many of the cooking schools do their market tours here.

In the early morning, **Talat Pratu Chiang Mai** (Map p156; Th Bamrungburi; ◷4am-noon & 6pm-midnight) is the city's communal larder, selling foodstuffs and ready-made dishes. Things quieten down by lunchtime, but the burners are re-ignited for a large and popular night market that sets up across the road.

Talat Na Mor (Malin Plaza, Th Huay Kaew; dishes from 60B; ◷5-10pm) is a night market filled with food and fashion for the teeny-boppers. Cruise the stalls and restaurants to see what is hip with the new generation – sushi, K-pop, crepes and nerd glasses.

vegetarian, Khun Churn is best known for its all-you-can-eat meatless buffet (11am to 2pm) boasting dozens of dishes, salads, herbal drinks and Thai-style desserts. Dining with the Churn is a Chiang Mai ritual for expats and Thais.

NinjaRamen & Japanese Food
Japanese $
(Map p159; Th Sirimungklajarn; mains 80-160B; ◷11am-3pm & 4-10pm) This cramped Japanese noodle house does ramen every which way, plus soba and udon noodles, sashimi and sushi. The medium size is big enough for non-practising ninjas. Pat yourself on the back when a Japanese family arrives; you're dining among those who know.

Barfry
International $
(Map p159; Soi 15, Th Nimmanhaemin; mains from 60B; ◷5-11pm Mon-Sat) French fries get an attitude adjustment at this upscale fry shack with a menu of toppings, ranging from restrained mayonnaise to the 'pimp my fries' option. Next door is a wine bar

and a sushi restaurant should you want to migrate to another trough.

Lemontree
Thai $
(Map p159; Th Huay Kaew; mains 70-110B; ◷11am-10pm) The well-worn dining room tells you it's been around for a long time and it still garners praise for its cheap, quick and generous portions of Thai standards.

Why Not? Mediterranean Restaurant
Mediterranean $$
(Map p159; 14 Soi 11, Th Nimmanhaemin; mains 180-300B; ◷5-11pm) Why not? 'Of course yes' is the answer at this al fresco restaurant serving authentic pizzas, pastas and imported seafood. Keep an eye out for their weekend wine buffets.

Salsa Kitchen
Mexican $$
(Map p159; Th Huay Kaew; mains 150-220B; ◷11am-11pm) Baja-style Mexican earns high praise for its fresh and zesty dishes served in super-sized portions. It's an expat favourite but Thais dig it too, and it's often busy in the evening.

Sumo Sushi
Japanese $$

(Map p159; 28/7 Soi 11, Th Nimmanhaemin; mains 120-250B; ⊙11am-9pm) Chiang Mai has a serious sushi addiction and everyone claims to know *the* best in town. We ascribe to the 'love the one you're with' theory, meaning that where you are now is good too. If you're in the neighbourhood, Sumo does American-style rolls along with sashimi and sets.

Smoothie Blues
Western $$

(Map p159; 32 Th Nimmanhaemin; mains 100-180B; ⊙7.30am-9pm) This expat favourite is known for its breakfasts, as well as its sandwiches, baguettes and the namesake drink.

Palaad Tawanron
Thai $$

(☏0 5321 6039; Th Suthep; mains 160-320B; ⊙lunch, dinner) Set into a rocky ravine near Doi Suthep, this restaurant inhabits a magical spot overlooking the twinkling city below. Everyone loves the ambience but the food, mainly Thai seafood, receives mediocre reviews. Follow the signs at the end of Th Suthep.

If You Like...
History

If you want to know more about Chiang Mai's history, check out these sites to become a wannabe Lanna scholar.

1 **CHIANG MAI HISTORICAL CENTRE**
(หอประวัติศาสตร์เมืองเชียงใหม่; Map p156; Th Ratwithi; 8.30am-5pm Tue-Sun; ⊙adult/child 90/40B) This new museum covers the founding of the capital, the Burmese occupation and the modern era of trade and unification with Bangkok.

2 **WIANG KUM KAM**
(เวียงกุมกาม; ⊙8am-5pm) The ruins of this predecessor capital to Chiang Mai are located in a bucolic setting 5km southeast of town.

Green Table Restaurant
International $$

(Map p159; 44/12 Th Nimmanhaemin, 2nd fl, Kantary Terrace; mains 160-400B; ⊙11am-midnight) Posh and professional, this Mediterranean restaurant is preferred by

Hawker food

Stimulating Brews

Courting a cafe is a common Chiang Mai pastime and here are a few introductory dates:

Libernard Cafe (Map p156; 36 Th Chaiyaphum; dishes 50-110B; ⊙8am-5pm Tue-Sun) Unassuming Libernard Cafe is run by Pong who roasts her own beans daily, making adjustments based on the day's climate. She brews a smooth latte, hardly needing to be spiked with sugar, and her banana pancakes will make you a fan of this often-derided dish.

Ristr8to (Map p159; Th Nimmanhaemin; coffee 60-120B; ⊙7am-8pm) The complicated menu requires selecting coffee strength (beans to water ratio), bean origin and then coffee type (coffee to cream ratio). Your drink comes with tasting notes (juicy with hints of berries) and is easily the best cup of mud in town.

Akha Ama Cafe (9/1 Soi 3, Th Hutsadisawee, Mata Apartment; coffee drinks from 50B; ⊙9am-9pm) Organic, fair trade coffee is the centrepiece of this cafe, the brainchild of an enterprising Akha who was the first in his village to graduate from college. His personal story adds sweetness to each cup. There is a second **branch** (Map p156; www.akhaama.com; 175/1 Th Ratchadamnoen; ⊙8am-8pm; 🛜) in the old city.

Raming Tea House (Map p156; Th Tha Phae; drinks 50-100B; ⊙9.30am-6pm) The northern mountains also produce Assam tea, served in this Victorian-era cafe within the Siam Celadon shop.

Chiang Mai's sophisticated set for its light lunch fare of grilled fish salads and hearty dinners of high-end steaks.

🍷 Drinking & Nightlife

OLD CITY

Zoe In Yellow   Bar
(Map p156; 40/12 Th Rathwithi; ⊙5pm-2am)
Everybody's party pal, Zoe is a beer garden, club and live music venue. Start off in the garden for sobriety cure-alls then stumble over to the dance floor with your new found confidence.

Writer's Club & Wine Bar   Bar
(Map p156; 141/3 Th Ratchadamnoen;
⊙10am-midnight) Run by a former foreign correspondent, this bar and restaurant is popular with expats, including current and retired writers, and anybody else who wanders by. There's also English pub grub to help anchor a liquid meal.

UN Irish Pub   Pub
(Map p156; 24/1 Th Ratwithi; ⊙10am-midnight)
Chiang Mai's leading pub ambassador, this is *the* place for international sport matches and Thursday quiz nights. There's Guinness on tap, a backyard garden and a bakery.

WEST OF THE OLD CITY

Beer Republic   Bar
(Map p159; Soi 11, Th Nimmanhaemin; ⊙5pm-midnight Tue-Sun) Fifteen draft beers keep the hop-sippers happy at this upscale beer bar in trendy Nimman.

Soho Bar   Bar
(Map p159; www.sohochiangmai.com; 20/3 Th Huay Kaew; ⊙5pm-midnight) Personality is on tap at this cosy shopfront bar. It is gay-friendly but all-inclusive and the affable owners attract a steady supply of regulars and newcomers with cheerful chats and cold drinks.

Small House Kafe
Bar

(Map p159; 18/1 Th Sermsuk; ☺5pm-midnight Tue-Sat) A groovy place to howl at the moon with expats and Thais alike. Hip hop on Friday nights, periodic book swaps and lots of built-in friends.

That's Wine
Bar

(Map p159; Soi 9, Th Nimmanhaemin; ☺5pm-1am) Wine, wine, wine (and water, if you must) is the tipple of choice at this contemporary Nimman bar, owned by a former porn star.

Warm-Up
Nightclub

(Map p159; ☎0 5340 0676; 40 Th Nimmanhaemin; ☺9pm-2am) Still going strong, this hi-so dance club attracts the young and the beautiful. Hip hop is spun in the main room, electronic house reverberates in the lounge, and rock/indie bands jam in the garden.

⭐ Entertainment

Sudsanan
Live Music

(Map p159; Th Huay Kaew; ☺5pm-2am) Down a dark driveway near Kad Suan Kaew, this old wooden house is filled with characters and songs. Mainly acoustic bands jog from samba to *pleng pêu·a chee·wít* (songs for life) and the eclectic crowd bows solemnly during tear-jerking songs.

Riverside Bar & Restaurant
Live Music

(Map p156; 9-11 Th Charoenrat; ☺noon-midnight) Long-running Riverside does dining, drinking and music with a view of the twinkly Mae Ping. Bands range from classic-rock, jazz and even pop and a recent expansion across the road adds more elbow room.

Le Brasserie
Live Music

(Map p156; Th Chaiyaphum; ☺5pm-2am) A popular late-night spot has recently moved from its riverside location to this convenient spot near Pratu Tha Phae. Devotees come to hear local guitarist Took pay homage to all the rock and blues legends.

Local Knowledge

Th Nimmanhaemin

PIM KEMASINGKI, MANAGING EDITOR, CITYLIFE CHIANG MAI

1 DINING
From gourmet noodle and salad houses to quirky bistros, Nimman is the place to be to sample a bewildering number of cuisines, mostly at great prices. Green Table Restaurant's (p171) succulent steaks are to die for. **Café Mini** (12/2 Soi 9, Th Nimmanhaemin) is an adorable venue serving creative little pieces of art for the mouth. Why Not? Mediterranean Restaurant (p170) offers the best-value Italian, and **Mix Restaurant & Bar** (Soi 1, Th Nimmanhaeming) has a tome of a menu that spans the globe, mixing and matching to serve original and creative dishes.

2 CAROUSING
The heart of Chiang Mai's nightlife, where university students, tourists, upwardly mobile locals and expats hang out, offers something for everyone. **Sangdee Gallery** (Soi 5, Th Sirimungklajarn) has open mic nights and art exhibitions, and is a friendly place to meet locals. **House of Wine** (Soi 15, Th Nimmanhaemin) is where wine lovers meet for a night with the city's young trendies, and then head for a night of dancing or live music at Warm-Up (p173).

3 SHOPPING
There are a great number of shops ranging from the cutesy to the sophisticated along the various lanes shooting off Nimman. For all things women head to **Ginger** (6/21 Th Nimmanhaemin) where you can find handbags, fashion, accessories and more. Adorn with Studio Naenna (p176) creates hand-dyed scarves and clothing using ye olde local techniques. **Gallery See Scape** (Soi 17, Th Nimmanhaemin), home to funky artists, always has a conversational piece to take home to wow your friends. Then there is the spanking new **Maya shopping mall** (Th Huay Kaew).

🔒 Shopping

Chiang Mai is Thailand's handicraft centre, or at least it used to be. There are still some small cottage factories and workshops dotting the outskirts of town, though modernisation is taking its toll.

OLD CITY

Mengrai Kilns Ceramics
(Map p156; ✆0 5327 2063; www.mengraikilns. com; 79/2 Th Arak; ◷10am-6pm) In the south-western corner of the old city, Mengrai Kilns keeps the tradition of Thai celadon pottery alive with a showroom full of table settings, decorative items and even Thai- and Western-style nativity scenes.

Chiang Mai Cotton Clothing
(Map p156; Th Ratchadamnoen; ◷10am-6pm) The old city has sprouted several cute boutiques including this clothing shop selling high-quality natural cotton cut for modern tropical living.

EAST OF THE OLD CITY

Wander the soi in between Th Tha Phae and Talat Warorot for a plethora of textile shops selling Thai and imported handicrafts.

Chiang Mai Night Bazaar Market
(Map p156; Th Chang Khlan; ◷7pm-midnight) One of the city's main night-time attractions, especially for families, this is the modern legacy of the original Yunnanese trading caravans that stopped here along the ancient trade route between Simao (in China) and Mawlamyaing (on Myanmar's Gulf of Martaban coast). Today the night bazaar sells the usual tourist souvenirs, like what you'll find at Bangkok's street markets. Vendors set up stalls along the footpath of Th Chang Khlan from Th Tha Phae to Th Loi Kroh; even if you're just out for a stroll, browsing is unavoidable.

The quality and bargains aren't especially impressive, but the allure is the variety and concentration of stuff, and the

Left: A food stall at the Chiang Mai Night Bazaar;
Below: Lanterns light up the Chiang Mai sky

(LEFT) BEN PIPE/GETTY IMAGES ©; (BELOW) SPACES IMAGES/GETTY IMAGES ©

dexterity and patience it takes to trawl through it all.

Elements
Jewellery

(Red Ruby; Map p156; 400-402 Th Tha Phae;
⏰10am-9pm) An eclectic and fun collection of sterling silver and stone jewellery and other trinkets fill this unsigned store near Pratu Tha Phae. Their shop next door sells silks and decorative items.

Nova
Jewellery

(Map p156; www.nova-collection.com; 201 Th Tha Phae; ⏰10am-8pm Mon-Sat, 12.30-8.30pm Sun) For contemporary jewellery, this studio makes high-quality rings, pendants and earrings using silver, gold and precious stones. Pieces can be custom made and are very classy.

Dee Dee Pan Pan
Jewellery

(Map p156; 33 Th Tha Phae; ⏰10am-6pm) Murano-glass beaded necklaces and other handmade jewellery decorate this pleasant shop.

Kesorn
Handicrafts

(Map p156; 154-156 Th Tha Phae) A collector's best friend, this cluttered shop has been trading old stuff for years. It specialises mainly in hill-tribe textiles, beads and crafts.

Siam Celadon
Ceramics

(Map p156; www.siamceladon.com; 158 Th Tha Phae; ⏰8am-6pm) This established company sells its fine collection of cracked-glazed celadon ceramics in a lovely teak building. Enjoy the Victorian-era structure and its dainty fretwork for longer with a proper English tea at the attached Raming Tea House (p172).

Praewphun Thai Silk
Textiles

(Map p156; 83-85 Th Tha Phae; ⏰10am-6pm) This 50-year-old shop sells silks of all ilks, and the octogenerian owner is a spry and dedicated saleswoman.

Shopping for a Cause

Chiang Mai is Thailand's conscience, in part because the city is the de facto caretaker of struggling immigrants from Myanmar and hill-tribe villagers. Both groups lack the proper citizenship to get an education, well-paid jobs and medical care. **Adorn with Studio Naenna** (Map p159; 22 Soi 1, Th Nimmanhaemin; ☺10am-6pm) is the in-town showroom of a village weaving project that gives young women in the Chom Thong district of Chiang Mai a viable economic income without having to leave their families and migrate to the city for work. It also preserves traditional weaving techniques and aims for a softer environmental footprint through the use of natural fibres and dyes. Other handicraft outlets for village-weaving projects include KukWan Gallery (p176), **Sop Moei Arts** (Map p156; ☎0 5330 6123; www.sopmoeiarts.com; 150/10 Th Charoenrat; ☺10am-6pm), **Thai Tribal Crafts** (☎0 5324 1043; www.ttcrafts.co.th; 208 Th Bamrungrat; ☺10am-6pm) and the **Hill-Tribe Products Promotion Centre** (21/17 Th Suthep; ☺10am-6pm).

KukWan Gallery
Textiles
(Map p156; 37 Th Loi Kroh; ☺9am-6pm) Set slightly back from the road, this charming teak building sells natural cotton and silk by the metre. It's a great place to shop for better-than-market quality scarves and bedspreads available in subtle colours.

Chilli Antiques & Arts
Antiques
(Map p156; Th Si Donchai; ☺10am-6pm) A reliable purveyor of antiques and reproductions, Chilli's has this in-town studio and a larger showroom in Hang Dong.

Vila Cini
Textiles
(Map p156; ☎0 5324 6246; www.vilacini.com; 30-34 Th Charoenrat; ☺10am-6pm) Vila Cini sells high-end, handmade silks and cotton textiles that are reminiscent of the Jim Thompson brand. Perhaps the real draw is the store's atmospheric teak house with marble floors and a narrow, rickety staircase that leads to a galleried courtyard. It's on the eastern side of the road about 400m north of Saphan Nawarat.

WEST OF THE OLD CITY

Srisanpanmai
Textiles
(Map p159; 6 Soi 1, Th Nimmanhaemin; ☺10am-6pm) The display cases here show a visual textbook of the textiles of the Lanna people. From the technicolour rainbow patterns of Myanmar to the wide-hem panel style of Chiang Mai, Srisanpanmai specialises in silks made using traditional techniques.

❶ Getting There & Away

Air

Regularly scheduled flights arrive and depart from Chiang Mai International Airport (www.chiangmaiairportonline.com), which is 3km south of the old city. International and domestic routes and frequencies vary with the seasons and tourist demand. Direct flights linking Chiang Mai to Chinese cities are expanding rapidly.

Air Asia (Map p156; ☎0 5323 4645; www.airasia.com; 416 Th Phae; ☺10am-8pm) Flies to Bangkok (Don Muang Airport), Kuala Lumpur, Phuket and Macau.

Air China (☎0 2134 2452; www.airchina.com) Flies to Beijing daily.

Bangkok Airways (☎0 5328 9338; www.bangkokair.com; Room A & B, Kantary Terrace, 44/1 Soi 12, Th Nimmanhaemin; ☺8.30am-noon & 1-6pm Mon-Sat) Flies daily to Bangkok (Suvarnabhumi Airport) and continues to Samui.

Dragon Air (☎0 2263 0606; www.dragonair.com) Flies to Hong Kong four days a week.

Jin Air (☎0 2168 7495; www.jinair.com) Flies to Seoul three days a week.

Nok Air (☎ 0 5392 2183; www.nokair.com; 2nd fl, Chiang Mai International Airport; ◷ 8am-5pm) Flies to Bangkok (Don Muang Airport), Mae Hong Son, Mae Sot and Udon Thani; note that Nok Air is a subsidiary of Thai Airways.

Thai Airways International (THAI; Map p156; ☎ 0 2356 1111, 0 5321 1044; www.thaiair.com; 240 Th Phra Pok Klao; ◷ 8.30am-4.30pm Mon-Fri) Flies to Bangkok (Suvarnabhumi Airport).

Tiger Air (www.tigerair.com; from 2000B) Flies to Singapore four days weekly.

Bus

Chiang Mai has two bus stations (long distance and provincial) as well as several *sŏrng·tăa·ou* stops (for nearby destinations).

Arcade Bus Station (Th Kaew Nawarat) is Chiang Mai's long-distance station and is about 3km from the old city. From the town centre, a túk-túk should cost 80B to 100B; *rót daang,* about 60B.

Do note that from Bangkok, the most reliable companies use Bangkok's Northern and Northeastern bus terminal (Mo Chit). It is not advisable to go north with a bus company that leaves from Bangkok's tourist centres such as Th Khao San. These invariably over-promise and under-deliver.

Chang Pheuak Bus Terminal (Th Chang Pheuak) is just north of the old city and serves destinations within Chiang Mai province, including Chiang Dao, Fang, Tha Ton, Chom Thong and Hot. Minibuses to Chiang Dao leave from Soi Sanam Gila, which is behind the bus terminal.

Train

Chiang Mai's **train station** (Th Charoen Muang) is about 2.5km east of the old city. For information on schedules and fares contact the **State Railway of Thailand** (☎ free hotline 1690; www.railway.co.th) or grab a timetable from the station. Local transport to the train station from the old city should cost 40B to 60B.

All Chiang Mai–bound trains originate from Bangkok's Hua Lamphong station. Sleeping berths are increasingly hard to reserve without booking well in advance.

In 2013, there were 13 derailments along a section of track between Uttaradit and Chiang Mai. As of 13 September, SRT closed this portion of the line for repairs. Repairs have met with delays and at the time of writing it was unclear when the line would be fully operational. In the

Detour:

Superhighway of Yore: Mae Ping

Chiang Mai's exalted river, Mae Ping, connects the forested highlands and fertile agricultural valleys to the commercial centres on its 569km course before it merges with Chao Phraya river. It feeds a vast agricultural system of rice paddies, coffee plantations, *lam yai* orchards, strawberry fields and flower gardens, and was the primary thoroughfare for the teak trade in the 19th century.

For more river history, hop aboard a traditional watercraft affiliated with **Scorpion Tailed River Cruise** (Map p156; ☎ 08 1960 9398; www.scorpiontailedrivercruise.com; Th Charoenrat; ticket 500B). Tours depart from Wat Srikhong pier near Rim Ping Condo.

meantime, SRT has arranged bus transport to cover the closed portion.

ⓘ Getting Around

To/from the Airport

There is only one licensed airport taxi service, charging a flat 120B fare. Many guesthouses and hotels also provide airport transfers.

Bicycle

Cycling is a good way to get around Chiang Mai. Chiang Mai Mountain Biking (p158) rents mountain bikes and city bikes (80B to 150B) for the day. **Cacti Bike** (Map p156; ☎ 0 5321 2979; 94/1 Th Singharat; bike hire 80-350B) also offers reliable bike hire, from simple cruisers to serious mountain bikes with all the accessories.

Car & Truck

One of Chiang Mai's most well-regarded vehicle rental agencies is **North Wheels** (Map p156;

☎ 0 5387 4478; www.northwheels.com; 70/4-8 Th Chaiyaphum), which offers hotel pick-up and delivery, 24-hour emergency road service, and comprehensive insurance. Another good bet is **Thai Rent a Car** (Petchburee Car Rent; ☎ 0 5390 4188; www.thairentacar.com; Chiang Mai International Airport), located at the airport. Other car-rental agencies in town include **Budget Car Rental** (☎ 0 5320 2871; 201/2 Th Mahidol), across from Central Airport Plaza.

Motorcycle

One of the most popular options for getting about on your own is to rent a motorcycle.

If you're renting a motorcycle for touring the countryside around Chiang Mai, check out the tips and routes at **Golden Triangle Rider** (www. gt-rider.com).

Mr Mechanic (Map p156; ☎ 0 5321 4708; www.mr-mechanic1994.com; 4 Soi 5, Th Moon Muang) There are also two other branches in the old city; new, well-maintained fleet and comprehensive insurance.

Tony's Big Bikes (Map p156; ☎ 0 5320 7124; 17 Th Ratchamankha) Rents well-maintained 125cc to 400cc motorbikes that all have license plates.

Also offers riding lessons, gives touring advice and repairs motorcycles.

Public & Chartered Transport

Chiang Mai residents who don't have their own wheels rely on the ubiquitous *rót daang* (literally 'red truck' or *sŏrng·tăa·ou*) or túk-túk.

Rót daang are shared taxis: you can flag them down, tell them your destination and if they are going that way they'll nod (ever so slightly). Short trips should cost 20B per person (eg around the old city) and longer trips from 40B per person (eg from the old city to Th Nimmanhaemin), and more depending on the distance and your negotiation skills.

Túk-túk work only on a charter basis and are more expensive than *rót daang*. Rates start at 60B to 80B for most trips and creep up to 100B at night when people are returning home from the bars.

Taxi

It is very rare to see a metered taxi to flag down in Chiang Mai. Call **Taxi Meter** (☎ 0 5326 2878; www.taxichiangmai.com) for a pick-up if you want one – most fares within greater Chiang Mai are no more than 150B.

AROUND CHIANG MAI

Mae Sa Valley & Samoeng แม่สา/สะเมิง

One of the easiest mountain escapes, the Mae Sa– Samoeng loop travels from the lowlands' concrete expanse into the highlands' forested frontier. The 100km route makes a good day trip with private transport or a country getaway with an overnight in Samoeng.

Head north of Chiang Mai on Rte 107 (Th Chang Pheuak) toward Mae Rim,

Elephant Training Center of Chiang Dao (p180)
FELIX HUG/GETTY IMAGES ©

then left onto Rte 1096. The road becomes more rural but there's a steady supply of tour-bus attractions: orchid farms, butterfly parks, snake farms, you name it.

Only 6km from the Mae Rim turn-off, **Nam Tok Mae Sa (adult/child 100/50B, car 30B)** is part of the Doi Suthep-Pui National Park. The falls are more of a series of pools than a full-blown cascade but it is a picturesque spot to picnic or tramp around in the woods for a bit. It is a favourite weekend getaway for locals so get there early and stake out your waterhole.

The road starts to climb and twist after the waterfall entrance. Catch your breath at **Mae Sa Elephant Camp** (☏ 0 5320 6247; www.maesaelephantcamp.com; Rte 1096; shows adult/child 200/100B, ride for 2 people 800B; ⊙ shows 8am, 9.40am & 1.30pm), one of the north's largest.

Two kilometres past the elephant camp is the **Queen Sirikit Botanic Gardens** (☏ 0 5384 1333; www.qsbg.org; Rte 1096; adult/child 100/50B; ⊙ 8.30am-4.30pm), a shorn mountainside displaying 227 hectares of various exotic and local flora for conservation and research purposes.

After the botanic gardens the road climbs up into the fertile Mae Sa Valley, once a high-altitude basin for growing opium poppies. Now the valley's hill-tribe farmers have re-seeded their terraced fields with sweet peppers, cabbage, flowers and fruits – which are then sold to the royal agriculture projects under the Doi Kham label. The royal project at the Hmong village of **Nong Hoi** sits some 1200m above sea level and is accessible by a turn-off road in the village of Pong Yeang. Continue on this road to **Mon Cham** (Nong Hoi Mai; mains from 60-150B; ⊙ 9am-7pm), a collection of bamboo huts teetering on the ridgeline. The restaurant serves tasty Thai food using the royal project's produce but the food takes second spoon to the panoramic view. The last 100m to the restaurant is a steep gravel climb that is difficult to ascend on a motorbike.

Sitting at the western wedge of the valley, **Proud Phu Fah** (☏ 0 5387 9389; www.proudphufah.com; Rte 1096, Km17; r 2500-

CHIANG MAI CHIANG DAO

Detour:
Dokmai Garden

A great stop for flower enthusiasts and plant geeks who collect floral trivia, **Dokmai Garden** (☏ 08 7187 5787; Hang Dong; admission 300B, tour 1200-1900B; ⊙ Jan-Jun) is a private botanic garden south of Chiang Mai that preserves and propagates native flora and floral knowledge. The garden is run by the Seehamongkol family, a Thai gardening team, and Eric Danell, an academic plant researcher. Call ahead to make an appointment. The garden is about 30 minutes south of Chiang Mai airport and can be reached by chartered transport (about 300B); you may need to contact the garden to provide specific directions to the driver.

4000B; ✳ @ 🛜 ⛱) is a small boutique hotel with creature-comfort villas designed to give the illusion of sleeping amid the great outdoors. The open-air restaurant serves healthy Thai food (dishes 150B to 250B) with a view of the valley.

After Proud Phu Fah, the road swings around the mountain ridge and starts to rise and dip until it reaches the conifer zone. Beyond, the landscape unfolds in a cascade of mountains. Eventually the road spirals down into Samoeng, a pretty village. To return to Chiang Mai, stay on Rte 1269 all the way to the Th Khlong Chonprathan (canal road).

Chiang Dao   เชียงดาว

In a lush, jungle setting in the shadow of a mighty limestone mountain, Chiang Dao is a popular country escape from the steaming urban plains of Chiang Mai.

179

Detour:
Doi Inthanon National Park
อุทยานแห่งชาติดอยอินทนนท์

Thailand's highest peak is Doi Inthanon (often abbreviated to Doi In), which measures 2565m above sea level, an impressive altitude for the kingdom, but a tad diminutive compared to its cousins in the Himalayan range. It is a popular day trip from Chiang Mai for tourists and locals, especially during the New Year holiday when there's the rarely seen phenomenon of frost.

There are eight waterfalls that dive off the mountain. Nam Tok Mae Klang (at Km 8) is the largest and the easiest to get to.

About 3km before the summit of Doi Inthanon, **Phra Mahathat Naphamethanidon and Nophamethanidon** (Km 41-42; admission to both 40B) are two chedi built by the Royal Thai Air Force to commemorate the king's and queen's 60th birthdays in 1989 and 1992, respectively.

The whole point of the park is to get as high as you can to see life in a colder climate, and the coolness is such a relief from the sweltering plains. Thais relish bundling up in hats and jackets and posing for pictures among conifers and rhododendrons. Almost at the exact summit there's a chedi dedicated to one of the last Lanna kings (Inthawichayanon). From there, a lovely boardwalk through the thick, cool forest leads to a cafe, obligatory souvenir shop and the start of the Ang Ka nature trail, a 360m platform walkway through a moss-festooned bog.

The park is one of the top destinations in Southeast Asia for naturalists and birdwatchers. The mist-shrouded upper slopes produce abundant orchids, lichen, moss and epiphytes, while supporting nearly 400 bird species, more than any other habitat in Thailand.

Families and 30-something travellers come to relax and wander, enjoying the area's rural character.

◉ Sights & Activities

Tham Chiang Dao
Cave

(ถ้ำเชียงดาว, Chiang Dao Cave; admission 40B) In the heat of the day, the coolest place in town is the Chiang Dao Cave, a complex said to extend some 10km to 14km into Doi Chiang Dao. There are four interconnected caverns that are open to the public. Tham Phra Non (360m) is the initial segment and is electrically illuminated and can be explored on your own.

Doi Chiang Dao
Mountain

(ดอยเชียงดาว, Doi Luang) Part of the Doi Chiang Dao National Park, Doi Chiang Dao pokes into the heavens at 2195m above sea level. From the summit, reachable by a two-day hike, the views are spectacular. The southern side of the mountain is believed to be one of the most accessible spots in the world to see the giant nuthatch and Hume's pheasant. **Birdwatching** and **overnight treks** can be arranged through local guesthouses.

Elephant Training Center of Chiang Dao
Elephant Encounter

(☎ 0 5329 8553; www.chiangdaoelephantcamp. com; show 100B; ⏱ shows 9am & 10am) In a lovely wooded setting near the highway, this elephant camp enjoys a good reputation. It hosts educational training exhibitions in which visitors are offered a rare insight into how young elephants are taught to obey mahout commands, work with other elephants and accept mahouts on their backs.

Sleeping

Chiang Dao Nest
Guesthouse $$

(📞 08 6017 1985; http://nest.chiangdao.com; r 895-1500B; @ 🛜 🏊) The guesthouse that put Chiang Dao on the travellers' map creates an inviting rural retreat. Simple bungalows get the basics right – comfy beds, privacy and immaculate interiors. Those closest to the restaurant have terrific views from the rickety rear porches.

But the primary reason for the Nest's success is the sensational restaurant known among Chiang Mai expats as a dining destination.

Nature Guest House
Guesthouse $$

(📞 08 9955 9074; r 650-900B; @ 🛜) This quiet place is set in a fruit orchard with mountain views. The fan-cooled wooden huts are well-maintained and have generous porches; modern air-con bungalows are newer and have more 'bells'. Chickens wander the grounds, longan litter the pathways, and all that fresh air makes an irresistible sleep aid.

Malee's Nature Lovers Bungalows
Guesthouse $$

(📞 08 1961 8387; www.maleenature.com; r 350-1500B; @ 🏊) Malee's has a rustic traveller vibe with its collection of variously priced and sized bungalows. The cheapest share bathrooms, while the 'honeymoon bungalows' have privacy, wrap-around porch, and one is set high off the ground for birders to watch the canopy activity. There is also a family cabin, which has an extra sleeping room.

ℹ️ Getting There & Around

Chiang Dao is 72km north of Chiang Mai along Rte 107. Buses to Chiang Dao (40B, 1½ hours, six daily) leave from Chiang Mai's Chang Pheuak terminal. The buses arrive and depart from Chiang Dao's bus station; from there, hire a *sŏrng·tăaou* (100B) to your guesthouse.

Phra Mahathat Naphamethanidon and Nophamethanidon, Doi Inthanon National Park

FELIX HUG/GETTY IMAGES ©

Chiang Rai & Northern Thailand

Northern Thailand ascends from the fertile central plains to a rugged mountain range that belts the border between Southeast Asia and China.
These mountains reach into the conifer zone and unite the kingdom culturally with its neighbours Laos, Myanmar and China. Travelling around the region yields spectacular scenery, unique cuisine and glimpses into life beyond Thailand's borders.

The region is best accessed via the culture trail from the ancient capital of Sukhothai and its time-worn ruins to the diamond ramparts of Kamphaeng Phet and the teak mansions of Lampang. The provinces of Chiang Rai and Mae Hong Son are both known for their natural beauty and are often explored on organised hikes to minority tribal villages. Border lovers should trace the contours of the Mekong River in the once-infamous Golden Triangle or just wander through small towns and morning markets, enjoying makeshift breakfasts and provincial commerce.

Ancient temples, Sukhothai (p212)
JEAN-PIERRE LESCOURRET/GETTY IMAGES ©

Hilltribe girl, Chiang Rai
FELIX HUG/GETTY IMAGES ©

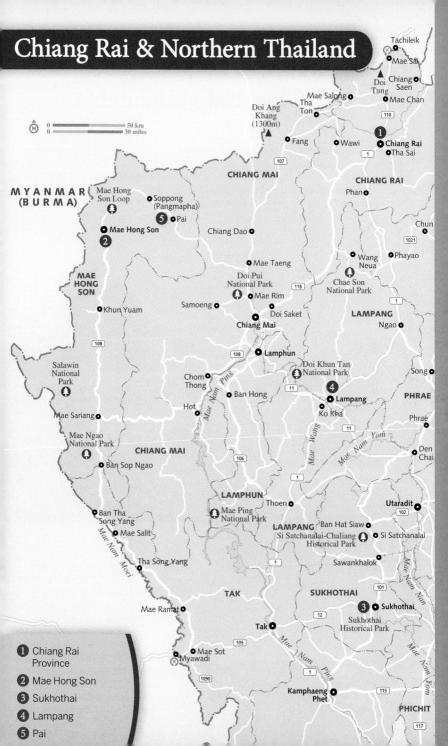

Chiang Rai & Northern Thailand

① Chiang Rai Province
② Mae Hong Son
③ Sukhothai
④ Lampang
⑤ Pai

Chiang Rai & Northern Thailand's Highlights

Chiang Rai Province

Thailand's northernmost province (p195) contains a dynamic collection of scenery and culture. There are fields and forests, mountains and plains, all of which are well photographed as the northern Thai idyll. The shared border with Laos and Myanmar creates the illusion of multicountry journeys, and a variety of hilltribe villages struggling to maintain their cultural identity and traditional lifestyle can be visited on ecotour trekking programs.

1

Mae Hong Son

2

In the mountains overlooking Burma is Mae Hong Son (p234), a provincial capital so far removed from the lowlands that you'll forget that no international borders have been crossed. Peruse the markets for Burmese snacks, wander through temples dolled up in mountain finery, or trek into a wilderness of forested peaks and valleys, home to a variety of hilltribe groups. Left: Hilltribe woman weaving, Mae Hong Son Province

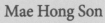

PETE ATKINSON/GETTY IMAGES ©

Sukhothai

3

You may have had your fill of tumbled-down bricks in Ayuthaya but the ancient capital of Sukhothai (p212) is worth the extra effort. The old city is sheltered in a quiet parklike setting that creates a meditative calm, perfect for enjoying the gravity of the gravity-defying monuments. Cycle around the ruins to appreciate the kingdom credited with Thailand's creative awakening.

4

Lampang

Lampang (p192), a smaller, gentler version of Chiang Mai, attracts many domestic tourists (but not as many foreigners), who enjoy wandering the old city. It's filled with stately teak manses and horse-drawn carriages, and there are palpable remnants of old northern ways alongside modern amenities. Outside of town is the government-run elephant conservation centre and a renowned elephant hospital. Above: A temple in Lampang

5

Pai

Peaceful Pai (p227) is in a scenic mountain valley northwest of Chiang Mai and specialises in rest and relaxation (and even recreation in the form of late-night parties). It is a popular mountain getaway for Chiang Mai and Bangkok Thais and expats and is beloved by young island-hoppers looking for a high-altitude party. Little planning is needed to appreciate Pai's attractions, which fall somewhere between spiritual and social. Above: View from top of Pai Canyon (p228)

Chiang Rai & Northern Thailand's Best.

Scenic Journeys

○ **Mae Salong** Slide along the serpentine ridge that bisects this ethnic Chinese village surrounded by tea plantations. (p202)

○ **Mae Hong Son** Climb up the mountain switchbacks to this provincial capital. (p234)

○ **Doi Tung** Tiptoe past Myanmar (Burma) with a visit to this former opium-growing area. (p208)

Eating

○ **Larp Khom Huay Poo** Meat eats in the tofu town of Pai. (p232)

○ **Lung Eed** Northern-style grub that makes Chiang Rai salivate. (p200)

○ **Paa Suk** Famous Chiang Rai noodle house. (p200)

○ **Bamee Chakangrao** Fresh homemade noodles in Kamphaeng Phet. (p226)

Temples

○ **Wat Phra Si Ratana Mahathat** Phitsanulok's famous bronze Buddha. (p210)

○ **Wat Rong Khun** Ultramodern temple near Chiang Rai. (p199)

○ **Wat Jong Kham & Wat Jong Klang** Ornate temples with a scenic Mae Hong Son setting. (p234)

○ **Wat Mahathat** Sukhothai's larger-than-life Buddha statue. (p213)

Markets

○ **Lampang's Walking Street** Admire an atmospheric shophouse neighbourhood. (p193)

○ **Chiang Rai's Walking Street** Traffic is dismissed for shopping and noshing. (p201)

○ **Mae Sai's Gem Market** Sparkly stones are traded on the side streets of this border town. (p206)

○ **Phitsanulok's Night Markets** Provincial life in full swing at various night markets and bazaars. (p210)

Need to Know

ADVANCE PLANNING

○ **One week before** Make hotel reservations in Pai if visiting during the high season (December to January).

○ **One day before** Buy train or bus tickets directly from the station.

RESOURCES

○ **Chiang Rai Tourism Authority of Thailand** (TAT; Map p196; ☎ 0 5374 4674, nationwide 1672; tatchrai@tat.or.th; Th Singhaclai; ◷8.30am-4.30pm)

○ **Lampang Tourism Authority of Thailand** (☎ 0 5423 7229; Th Thakhrao Noi; ◷8.30am-5pm Mon-Fri)

○ **Mae Hong Son Tourism Authority of Thailand** (☎ 0 5361 2982; www.travelmaehongson.org; Th Ni-wet Pi-sarn; ◷8.30am-4.30pm)

○ **Phitsanulok Tourism Authority of Thailand** (☎ 0 5525 2742; tatphlok@tat.or.th; 209/7-8 Th Baromtrilokanart; ◷8.30am-4.30pm)

○ **Sukhothai Tourism Authority of Thailand** (Map p217; ☎ 0 5561 6228, Th Jarot Withithong; ◷8.30am-4.30pm)

GETTING AROUND

○ **Air** Fly to Mae Hong Son from Chiang Mai, or to Chiang Rai from Bangkok

○ **Bus** Extensive regional travel connections through Chiang Mai

○ **Bicycle & motorcycle** Self-touring option

○ **Sŏrng·tăa·ou** Small pick-up trucks that act as shared taxis and public buses

○ **Train** Overnight option for Bangkok to Chiang Mai with detours to Phitsanulok and Lampang

○ **Túk-túk** Chartered vehicles for trips around town; negotiate the price beforehand

BE FOREWARNED

○ **Checkpoints** Have your passport handy as there are military checkpoints around the border.

○ **Clothes** From November to January bring a jacket and socks.

○ **Motorcycle safety** Wear a helmet and protective clothing.

○ **Trekking** Avoid trekking during March to May (hot) and June to October (wet).

○ **Waterfalls** At their peak June to December.

Left: Harvesting rice in Mae Hong Son Province (p227); **Above:** Dishes at Lung Eed (p200)
(LEFT) PETER STUCKINGS/GETTY IMAGES ©; (ABOVE) AUSTIN BUSH ©

Chiang Rai & Northern Thailand's Itineraries

Tour Thailand's ancient capitals and historical parks for a heaping helping of history. Or leapfrog up to the former Golden Triangle border region.

5 DAYS

Map locations:

MYANMAR (BURMA)

SOP RUAK
⑥

MAE SAI
③

LAOS

CHIANG SAEN
⑤

MAE SALONG
②

DOI TUNG
④

CHIANG RAI
①

⑤ LAMPANG

③ SI SATCHANALAI-CHALIANG HISTORICAL PARK

② SUKHOTHAI

① PHITSANULOK

KAMPHAENG PHET ④

PHITSANULOK TO LAMPANG

The Culture Trail

Start in ❶ Phitsanulok – it's an average provincial town with bus access to Sukhothai, an ancient capital known for its signature Buddhist sculpture. Thai tourists stop to make merit at Wat Phra Si Ratana Mahathat (p210), and eat *gŏoay·dĕe·o hôy kăh* (literally, 'legs-hanging' noodles) at a restaurant where bench seating provides the eponymous experience.

Continue to ❷ **Sukhothai** (p212), whose dynasty lasted 200 years and included the reign of King Ramkhamhaeng (1275–1317), credited with developing the first Thai script. Though the town is a ho-hum affair, the ruins are spectacular. Deeper into the countryside is ❸ **Si Satchanalai-Chaliang Historical Park** (p220), a satellite city of the Sukhothai kingdom, where ancient ruins sprawl across the bucolic landscape.

Detour to ❹ **Kamphaeng Phet** (p223), a pleasant provincial town with a handful of Sukhothai-era ruins. Then head north to ❺ **Lampang**, filled with teak temples, horse-drawn carts and the country's leading elephant conservation centre.

Top Left: Wat Phra Kaeo, Kamphaeng Phet;
Top Right: Mountain views, Chiang Rai
(TOP LEFT) / ANDREA PISTOLESI GETTY IMAGES ©;
(TOP RIGHT) EKKACHAI PHOLROJPANYA/GETTY IMAGES ©

7 DAYS

CHIANG RAI TO SOP RUAK

Cruise Around the Countryside

Thailand's northernmost province, Chiang Rai has always been a migration route: for the ancestral Tai people of southern China, the pony caravans during the Silk Road era and the pack mules carrying opium from the Golden Triangle.

Start in **1 Chiang Rai** (p195), where you can enjoy the provincial capital's cafe culture and night bazaar and then head out of town for a multiday trek, the proceeds of which go to aid local hill-tribe villages with infrastructure and education projects.

Day-trip to **2 Mae Salong** (p202), an ethnic Chinese village that balances on a mountain ridge cultivated with tea plantations. Or base yourself in **3 Mae Sai** (p205), a border town convenient for exploring the former Golden Triangle area of Chiang Rai Province. Do a driving tour of **4 Doi Tung** (p208) where coffee now grows instead of opium poppies.

Move on to the Mekong border town of **5 Chiang Saen** (p207), filled with temple ruins and river barges delivering goods from the interior of China. Take a day trip to **6 Sop Ruak** (p208), the Golden Triangle's official 'centre' and home to museums documenting the region's role in the production of the illicit substance.

Discover Chiang Rai & Northern Thailand

Rice paddies, Chiang Saen (p207)
JEAN-CLAUDE SOBOUL/GETTY IMAGES ©

LAMPANG ลำปาง

POP 59,000

Boasting lumbering elephants, the elegant mansions of former lumber barons and impressive (and in many cases, timber-based) Lanna-era temples, Lampang seems to unite every northern Thai cliché – but in a good way. Despite all this, the city sees relatively few visitors, giving it more of an 'undiscovered' feel than some of the more touristed destinations in the north.

History

Although Lampang Province was inhabited as far back as the 7th century in the Dvaravati period, legend has it that Lampang city was founded by the son of Hariphunchai's Queen Chama Thewi, and the city played an important part in the history of the Hariphunchai Kingdom.

Like Chiang Mai, Phrae and other older northern cities, modern Lampang was built as a walled rectangle alongside a river (in this case, Mae Wang). At the end of the 19th and beginning of the 20th century, Lampang, along with nearby Phrae, became an important centre for the domestic and international teak trade. A large British-owned timber company brought in Burmese supervisors familiar with the teak industry in Burma to train Burmese and Thai loggers in the area. These well-paid supervisors, along with independent Burmese teak merchants who plied their trade in Lampang, sponsored the construction of more than a dozen temples in the city, a legacy that lives on in several of Lampang's most impressive wáts and the beautiful antique homes along Th Talad Gao.

Sights & Activities

Wat Phra Kaew Don Tao
Buddhist Temple

(วัดพระแก้วดอนเต้า; off Th Phra Kaew; admission 20B; daylight hrs) From 1436 to 1468, Wat Phra Kaew Don Tao was among four wát in northern Thailand to have housed the Emerald Buddha (now in Bangkok's Wat Phra Kaew).

Th Talad Gao
Neighbourhood

(ถนนตลาดเก่า; Th Talad Gao) Lampang's multi-cultural history can be seen along this riverside street, which is lined with old homes, temples and shophouses showcasing Thai, English, Chinese and Burmese architectural styles. It's also where the town's weekly **Walking Street** (Th Talad Gao; 4-10pm Sat & Sun) market is held.

Baan Sao Nak
Museum

(บ้านเสานัก; 85 Th Radwattana; admission 50B; 10am-5pm) A huge Lanna-style house built in 1895 and supported by 116 square teak pillars, Baan Sao Nak was once owned by a local kun·yĭng (a title equivalent to 'Lady' in England); it now serves as a local museum.

Horse Carts
Guided Tour

(Th Suandawg; 30-/60-minute tour 200/300B; 5am-9pm) Lampang is the only town in Thailand where horse carts are still found. A 30-minute tour goes along Mae Wang while a one-hour tour stops at Wat Phra Kaew Don Tao and Wat Si Rong Meuang.

Horse carts can be found waiting on Th Suandawg, near the Pin Hotel, and just east of the market on Th Boonyawat.

Sleeping

Akhamsiri Home
Hotel $

(0 5422 8791; www.akhamsirihome.com; 54/1 Th Pamaikhet; r 590B;) The tagline here ought to be 'Midrange amenities at a budget price'. The large cool rooms are lo-cated in a tidy residential compound and all have TV, fridge and a garden/balcony.

Riverside Guest House
Guesthouse $$

(0 5422 7005; www.theriversidelampang.com; 286 Th Talad Gao; r 350-900B, ste 1800-2000B;) Although still within budget range, this leafy compound of refurbished wooden houses is one of the more pleasant places to stay in Lampang, if not all of northern Thailand. It couldn't be any nearer the river, shaded tables for chatting or eating abound, and motorcycle rental and other tourist amenities are available.

Try to score one of the two upstairs rooms in the main structure that feature vast balconies overlooking Mae Wang, or the huge two-room suite.

Eating & Drinking

Aroy One Baht
Thai $

(cnr Th Suandawg & Th Thipchang; mains 15-80B; 4pm-midnight) Some nights it can seem like everybody in Lampang is here, and understandably so: the food is tasty and embarrassingly cheap, and the setting in a wooden house is heaps of fun.

Niyom Sen
Northern Thai $

(125 Th Talad Gao; mains 30-40B; 9am-7pm Tue-Sun) The house speciality is kà·nŏm jeen nám ngée·o, a northern-style broth of pork and tomato.

Khun Manee

Lampang is known for its addictive kôw dǎan, deep-fried rice cakes seasoned with watermelon juice and drizzled with palm sugar. You can pick up a few bags or even watch the sweets being made at a homey **factory** (35 Th Ratsada; daylight hours) just off Th Ratsada – look for the yellow arrow.

Mae Hae
Northern Thai $

(1017 Th Upparaj, no Roman-script sign; mains 20-50B; ⏰11am-7pm) Boost your Lampang foodie street cred by eating at this unassuming and long-standing northern-Thai-style restaurant. There's no menu, so simply point to the soup, curry, dip or salad that looks tastiest.

Phat Thai Yay Fong
Thai $

(Th Boonyawat, no Roman-script sign; mains 35-60B; ⏰5-10pm) How do northern Thais take their *pàt tai*? With minced pork and pork rinds, of course. This popular stall is located just east of Wat Suan Dok.

Vegetarian Food
Vegetarian, Thai $

(Th Talad Gao; mains 25-35B; ⏰8am-6pm Mon-Sat; 🖉) A wide selection of Thai-style vegie dishes is served at this shophouse restaurant.

Riverside
International-Thai $$

(328 Th Thipchang; mains 80-210B; ⏰10am-10pm) This wooden shack that appears to be on the verge of tumbling into Mae Wang is extremely popular with both visiting and resident foreigners. Live music, a full bar and an expansive menu of local and Western dishes bring in the crowds.

🛈 Getting There & Away

Lampang's airport is about 1.5km south of the centre of town, at the east end of Th Phahonyothin (Asia 1 Hwy). At research time, **Bangkok Airways** (📞0 5482 1522, nationwide 1771; www.bangkokair.com; Lampang Airport; ⏰7.30-11.30am & 12.30-6.30pm), with flights to/from Bangkok, was the only airline operating out of Lampang. *Sǎwng·tǎa·ou* from the airport to downtown cost 50B, taxis charge 200B.

Lampang's bus and minivan terminal is nearly 2km south of the centre of town, at the corner of Th Phahonyothin (Asia 1 Hwy) and Th Chantarasurin – frequent *sǎwng·tǎa·ou* run between the station and town from 3am to 9pm (20B, 15 minutes).

Lampang's historic **train station** (📞0 5421 7024, nationwide 1690; www.railway.co.th; Th Phahonyothin) dates back to 1916 and is a fair hike from most accommodation; a túk-túk between here and the centre of town should be about 80B.

🛈 Getting Around

Getting around central Lampang is possible on foot. The Tourism Authority of Thailand office has free bicycle rental from 10am to 4pm; bring your passport. Both bicycles (per day 60B) and motorcycles (per day 200B) are available for rent at **Ozone** (395 Th Thipchang; ⏰9am-8pm). For

Transport to/from Lampang

DESTINATION	AIR	BUS	MINIVAN	TRAIN
Bangkok	2340B; 1½hr; 2 daily (to Suvarnabhumi International Airport)	378-756B; 9hr; frequent 7.30-11.30am & 6.30-9pm	–	256-1872B; 12hr; 6 daily
Chiang Mai	–	53-140B; 2hr; half-hourly 2am-8.30pm	70B; 1½hr; hourly 6.30am-5.30pm	23-413B; 3hr; 6 daily
Chiang Rai	–	111-153B; 4hr; frequent 6.30am-3pm	–	–
Mae Sai	–	138B; 6hr; 10.30am & 12.30pm	–	–
Mae Sot	–	199-265B; 4hr; 1pm & 2.30pm	–	–
Phitsanulok	–	171-256B; 4½hr; hourly 5am-10.30pm	–	48-1542B; 5hr; 6 daily
Sukhothai	–	178B; 3½hr; hourly 5am-7pm	–	–

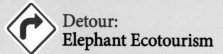

Detour:
Elephant Ecotourism

These two elephant-care facilities can be reached by Chiang Mai-bound minivan bus or *sŏrng·tăa·ou* (30B to 70B, 40 minutes) from Lampang's bus station. Let the driver know where you are headed and get off at the Km 37 marker. TECC is 1.5km from the highway, and shuttle buses will take you inside. Alternatively, you can charter a blue *sŏrng·tăa·ou* for 600B at Lampang's bus station or a taxi for about 1000B.

Thai Elephant Conservation Center (TECC; ☏ 0 5482 9333; www.thailandelephant. org; Rte 11; adult/child 170/110B; ☉ elephant bathing 9.45am & 1.15pm, public shows 10am, 11am & 1.30pm) This popular centre promotes the role of the Asian elephant in ecotourism. In addition to elephant shows, there is an exhibit on the history and culture of elephants, an elephant art gallery, an elephant graveyard, and **elephant rides** (10/30/60min 200/500/1000B; ☉ 8am-3.30pm) through the surrounding forest.

For those keen on delving deeper into pachyderm culture, the TECC's **Mahout Training School** (☏ 0 5424 7875; www.thailandelephant.org; 1–30 days 3500–100,000B) offers an array of programs ranging from one day to one month.

All proceeds from the entrance fee and souvenir shops go to the elephant hospital on-site, which cares for old, abandoned and sick elephants from all over Thailand, as well as working for the preservation of elephants through various research and breeding programs.

FAE's Elephant Hospital (Friends of the Asian Elephant; ☏ 08 1914 6113; www.elephant-soraida.com; off Rte 11; admission by donation; ☉ 8am-5pm) Located next door to the TECC (but not affiliated) is this hospital, which claims to be the first of its kind in the world. Although visitors are appreciated and provided for, keep in mind that this is a functioning medical facility: there are no guided tours and certainly no elephant art. Donations are greatly appreciated.

destinations outside of town, there is a taxi stall (☏ 0 5421 7233; Th Suandawg; ☉ 6.30am-5pm) near the Pin Hotel.

CHIANG RAI PROVINCE

Chiang Rai เชียงราย
POP 68,000

Founded by Phaya Mengrai in 1262 as part of the Lao-Thai Lanna kingdom, Chiang Rai didn't become a Siamese territory until 1786 and a province until 1910. The small delightful city of Chiang Rai is worth getting to know, with its relaxed atmosphere, good-value accommodation and great local food. It's also the logical base from which to plan excursions to the more remote corners of the province.

◎ Sights

Oub Kham Museum   Museum
(พิพิธภัณฑ์อูบคำ; www.oubkhammuseum.com; Th Nakhai; adult/child 300/100B; ☉ 8am-5pm) This slightly zany museum houses an impressive collection of paraphernalia from virtually every corner of the former Lanna kingdom. The items, some of which truly are one of a kind, range from a monkey-bone food taster used by Lanna royalty to an impressive carved throne from Chiang Tung, Myanmar.

The Oub Kham Museum is 2km west of the town centre and can be a bit tricky to find; túk-túk will go here for about 50B.

Chiang Rai

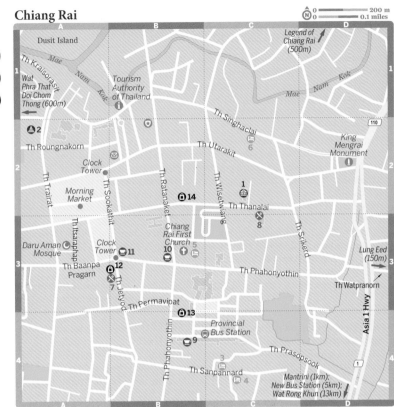

Chiang Rai

⊙ Sights
1 Hilltribe Museum & Education
   Center... C2
2 Wat Phra Kaew...................................... A2

⊕ Activities, Courses & Tours
PDA Tours & Travel .... (see 1)

🛏 Sleeping
3 Baan Warabordee................................. C4
4 Diamond Park Inn C4
5 Golden Triangle Inn B3
6 Moon & Sun Hotel................................. C2

⊗ Eating
7 Khao Soi Phor Jai B3
8 Phu-Lae.. C3

⊙ Drinking & Nightlife
9 BaanChivitMai Bakery B4
10 Doi Chaang... B3
11 Pangkhon Coffee................................... B3

⊕ Shopping
12 Fair Trade Shop B3
13 Night Bazaar.. B4
14 Walking Street B2

Mae Fah Luang
Art & Culture Park   Museum

(ไร่แม่ฟ้าหลวง; www.maefahluang.org/rmfl; 313
Mu 7, Ban Pa Ngiw; admission 200B; ⊙8.30am-
4.30pm Tue-Sun) In addition to a museum
that houses one of Thailand's biggest col-
lections of Lanna artefacts, this meticu-
lously landscaped compound includes
antique and contemporary Buddhist
temples, art and other structures.

Mae Fah Luang Art & Culture Park is
located about 4km west of the centre of

Chiang Rai; a túk-túk or taxi here will run around 100B.

Hilltribe Museum & Education Center
Museum

(พิพิธภัณฑ์และศูนย์การศึกษาชาวเขา; www.pdacr. org; 3rd fl, 620/25 Th Thanalai; admission 50B; ⊙9am-6pm Mon-Fri, 10am-6pm Sat & Sun) This museum and cultural centre is a good place to visit before undertaking any hill-tribe trek. Run by the nonprofit Population & Community Development Association (PDA), the displays are underwhelming in their visual presentation, but contain a wealth of information on Thailand's various tribes and the issues that surround them.

Wat Phra Kaew
Buddhist Temple

(วัดพระแก้ว; Th Trairat; ⊙temple 7am-7pm, museum 9am-5pm) **FREE** Originally called Wat Pa Yia (Bamboo Forest Monastery) in the local dialect, this is the city's most revered Buddhist temple. The main prayer hall is a medium-sized, well-preserved wooden structure. The octagonal *chedi* behind it dates from the late 14th century and is in typical Lanna style. The adjacent two-storey wooden building is a **museum** housing various Lanna artefacts.

Legend has it that in 1434 lightning struck the temple's *chedi*, which fell apart to reveal the Phra Kaew Morakot, or Emerald Buddha (actually made of jade). After a long journey that included a long stopover in Vientiane, Laos, this national talisman is now ensconced in the temple of the same name in Bangkok.

🏃 Activities

Nearly every guest-house and hotel in Chiang Rai offers trek-king excursions in hill tribe country.

Trek pricing depends on the type of activities and the number of days and participants. Rates, per person, for two people for a two-night trek range from 2500B to 6500B.

Mirror Foundation
Trekking

(☎0 5373 7616; www.thailandecotour.org) Although its rates are higher, trekking with this nonprofit NGO helps support the training of its local guides. Treks range from one to three days and traverse the Akha, Karen and Lahu villages of Mae Yao District, north of Chiang Rai.

PDA Tours & Travel
Trekking

(☎0 5374 0088; www.pda.or.th/chiangrai/pack age_tour.htm; 3rd fl, Hilltribe Museum & Education Center, 620/25 Th Thanalai; ⊙9am-6pm Mon-Fri, 10am-6pm Sat & Sun) One- to three-day treks are available through this NGO. Profits go back into community projects that include HIV/AIDS education, mobile health clinics, education scholarships and the establishment of village-owned banks.

The museum at Wat Phra Kaew
KYLIE MCLAUGHLIN/GETTY IMAGES ©

Rai Pian Karuna Trekking
(☏08 7186 7858, 08 2195 5645; www.facebook.
com/raipiankaruna) This new, community-
based social enterprise conducts one-
and multi-day treks and homestays at
Akha, Lahu and Lua villages in Mae Chan,
north of Chiang Rai.

🛏 Sleeping

IN TOWN

Baan Warabordee Hotel $
(☏0 5375 4488; baanwarabordee@hotmail.
com; 59/1 Th Sanpannard; r 500-600B; ❄ 🛜)
A delightful small hotel has been made
from this modern three-storey Thai villa.
Rooms come decked out in dark woods
and light cloths, and are equipped with
air-con, fridge and hot water.

Moon & Sun Hotel Hotel $
(☏0 5371 9279; www.moonandsun-hotel.com;
632 Th Singhaclai; r incl breakfast 500-600B; ste
incl breakfast 800B; ❄ 🛜) Bright and sparkling clean, this little hotel offers large
modern rooms. Some feature four-poster

beds, while all come with desk, cable TV
and refrigerator. Suites have a separate,
spacious sitting area.

Diamond Park Inn Hotel $$
(☏0 5375 4960; www.diamondparkinn.com;
74/6 Th Sanpannard; r incl breakfast 1100B; ste
incl breakfast 1400-1500B; ❄ @ 🛜 ⛆) Ag-
gressive marketing strategy aside ('When
ever you are at Chiang Rai. Stay at The
Diamond Park Inn'), this vast hotel is a
safe midrange choice. Rooms are attrac-
tive, with modern furniture and beds on
an elevated platform. The more expensive
rooms have tubs and wide balconies, and
are big enough to feel slightly empty.

Golden Triangle Inn Hotel $$
(☏0 5371 1339; www.goldentriangleinn.com; 590
Th Phahonyothin; s/d incl breakfast 700/800B;
❄ 🛜) Resembling an expansive Thai
home (including the occasional lived-in
untidiness this can entail), the 31 rooms
here have tile or wood floors, wooden
furniture and twin beds. The compound
includes a restaurant, a Budget car-rental
office and an efficient travel agency.

OUTSIDE OF TOWN

**Bamboo Nest de
Chiang Rai** Guesthouse $$
(☏08 9953 2330, 08 1531 6897; www.
bamboonest-chiangrai.com; bungalows incl
breakfast 650-1300B) The Lahu vil-
lage that's home to this unique
accommodation is only 23km
from Chiang Rai but feels a
world away. Bamboo Nest
takes the form of simple
but spacious bamboo
huts perched on a hill
overlooking tiered rice
fields. The only electric-
ity is provided by solar
panels, so leave your
laptops in the city and
instead take part in ac-
tivities that range from
birdwatching to hiking.

Đôm yam, a hot and sour Thai soup
RACHEL LEWIS/GETTY IMAGES ©

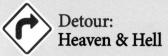

Detour: Heaven & Hell

Lying just outside Chiang Rai are two of the province's most touted – and bizarre – destinations.

Whereas most of Thailand's Buddhist temples have centuries of history, the construction of **Wat Rong Khun** (White Temple, วัดร่องขุ่น; off Asia 1 Hwy; ⏰8am-5pm Mon-Fri, 8am-5.30pm Sat & Sun) **FREE** began in 1997 by noted Thai painter-turned-architect Chalermchai Kositpipat. Seen from a distance, the temple appears to be made of glittering porcelain; a closer look reveals that the appearance is due to a combination of whitewash and clear-mirrored chips.

Wat Rong Khun is about 13km south of Chiang Rai. To get to the temple, hop on one of the regular buses that run from Chiang Rai to Chiang Mai or Phayao (20B). The temple was severely damaged by an earthquake in May 2014.

The bizarre brainchild of Thai National Artist Thawan Duchanee, and a rather sinister counterpoint to Wat Rong Khun, **Baan Dum** (บ้านดำ; Black House; off Asia 1 Hwy; ⏰9am-noon & 1-5pm) **FREE** unites several quasi-traditional structures, most of which are stained black and decked out with animal pelts and bones.

Baan Dum is located 13km north of Chiang Rai in Nang Lae; any Mae Sai-bound bus will drop you off here for around 20B.

Free transport to/from Chiang Rai is available for those staying two nights or more.

Ben Guesthouse
Guesthouse **$$**
(☎0 5371 6775; www.benguesthousechiangrai. com; 351/10 Soi 4, Th Sankhongnoi; r 350-850B, ste 1500-3000B; 🌬@🛜🏊) Ben is one of the best budget-to-midrange places we've encountered in the north. The absolutely spotless compound has a bit of everything, from fan-cooled cheapies to immense suites, not to mention a pool. It's 1.2km from the centre of town, at the end of Soi 4 on Th Sankhongnoi (the street is called Th Sathanpayabarn where it intersects with Th Phahonyothin) – a 60B túk-túk ride.

Legend of Chiang Rai
Hotel **$$$**
(☎0 5391 0400; www.thelegend-chiangrai. com; 124/15 Th Kohloy; r incl breakfast 3900-5900B, bungalow incl breakfast 8100-12,900B; 🌬@🛜🏊) One of the few hotels in town to boast a riverside location, this upscale resort feels like a traditional Lanna village. Rooms feel romantic and luxuriously understated with furniture in calming creams and rattan. The riverside infinity pool and spa are the icing on the comfort-filled cake. The resort is about 500m north of Th Singhaclai.

Le Meridien Chiang Rai Resort
Hotel **$$$**
(☎0 5360 3333; www.lemeridien.com; 221/2 Th Kwaewai; r incl breakfast 3800-4300B, ste incl breakfast 5300-16,000B; 🌬@🛜🏊) Chiang Rai's newest upscale resort is about 2km outside of the city centre on a beautiful stretch of Mae Nam Kok. Rooms are immense and decked out in greys, whites and blacks, and the compound includes two restaurants and an infinity pool, in addition to the usual amenities of a hotel of this price range.

🍴 Eating

Come mealtime, you'll almost certainly be pointed in the direction of Chiang Rai's night bazaar, but the food there is generally pretty dire – don't say we didn't warn you! Instead, if you're in town on a weekend, hit the vendors at Chiang Rai's open-air markets, Thanon Khon Muan and the walking street, which feature a good selection of local dishes.

KEVIN LANDWER-JOHAN/GETTY IMAGES ©

⭐ Don't Miss
Cafe Culture, Chiang Rai Style

For a relatively small town, Chiang Rai has an enviable spread of high-quality, Western-style cafes. This is largely due to the fact that many of Thailand's best coffee beans are grown in the more remote corners of the province.

BaanChivitMai Bakery (www.baanchivitmai.com; Th Prasopsook; ☺8am-9pm Mon-Sat; @ 🛜) In addition to a proper cup of joe made from local beans, you can snack on amazingly authentic Swedish-style sweets and Western-style meals and sandwiches at this popular bakery. Profits go to BaanChivitMai, an organisation that runs homes and education projects for vulnerable, orphaned or AIDS-affected children.

Doi Chaang (542/2 Th Ratanaket; ☺7am-10pm; 🛜) Doi Chaang is the leading brand among Chiang Rai coffees, and its beans are now sold as far abroad as Canada and Europe.

Pangkhon Coffee (Th Sookathit; ☺7am-10pm; 🛜) Combine coffee brewed from local beans with views of Chiang Rai's gilded clock tower.

Lung Eed
Northern Thai $

(Th Watpranorn; mains 40-100B; ☺11.30am-9pm Mon-Sat) One of Chiang Rai's most delicious dishes is available at this rustic but delicious northern-style food shack. There's an English-language menu on the wall, but don't miss the sublime *lâhp gài,* minced chicken fried with herbs and topped with crispy deep-fried chicken skin, shallots and garlic. The restaurant is on Th Watpranorn about 100m from the intersection with the Superhighway.

Paa Suk
Northern Thai $

(Th Sankhongnoi, no Roman-script sign; mains 10-25B; ☺8am-3pm) Paa Suk does rich bowls of *kà·nŏm jeen nám ngée·o,* a broth of pork or beef and tomatoes served over fresh rice noodles. The restaurant is between Soi 4 and Soi 5 of Th Sankhongnoi (the street is called Th Sathanpayabarn where it intersects with the southern end Th Phahonyothin); look for the yellow sign.

Phu-Lae
Northern Thai **$$**

(673/1 Th Thanalai; mains 80-320B; ⏱11.30am-3pm & 5.30-11pm) This air-conditioned restaurant is exceedingly popular with Thai tourists for its tasty, but somewhat gentrified northern Thai fare. Recommended local dishes include the *gaang hang·lair*, pork belly in a rich Burmese-style curry, here served with pickled garlic, and *sâi òo·a*, herb-packed pork sausages.

🔒 Shopping

Walking Street
Market

(Th Thanalai; ⏱4-10pm Sat) If you're around on a Saturday evening be sure not to miss the open-air Walking Street, an expansive street market focusing on all things Chiang Rai, from handicrafts to local dishes. The market spans Th Thanalai from the Hilltribe Museum to the morning market.

Thanon Khon Muan
Market

(Th Sankhongnoi; ⏱6-9pm Sun) Come Sunday evening, the stretch of Th Sankhongnoi from Soi 2 heading west is closed to traffic, and in its place are vendors selling clothes, handicrafts and local food. Th Sankhongnoi is called Th Sathanpayabarn where it intersects with the southern end Th Phahonyothin.

Fair Trade Shop
Handicrafts

(www.ttcrafts.co.th; Th Jetyod; ⏱9am-5pm Mon-Sat) Bright hill-tribe cloths and knick-knacks are available at this shop, the profits of which go to various development projects.

Night Bazaar
Market

(off Th Phahonyothin; ⏱6-11pm) Adjacent to the bus station off Th Phahonyothin is Chiang Rai's night market. On a much smaller scale than the one in Chiang Mai, it is nevertheless an OK place to find an assortment of handicrafts and touristy souvenirs.

ℹ️ Getting There & Away

Chiang Rai International Airport, also known as Mae Fah Luang, is approximately 8km north of the city. Air Asia (☎0 5379 3543, nationwide 0 2515 9999; www.airasia.com; ⏱8am-9pm) and Nok Air (☎0 5379 3000, nationwide 1318; www.nokair.co.th; ⏱8am-7pm) fly to Bangkok's Don Muang Airport, while THAI (THAI; ☎0 5379 8202, nationwide 0 2356 1111; www.thaiair.com; ⏱8am-8pm) fly to Suvarnabhumi. Taxis run into town from the airport for 200B.

Buses bound for destinations within Chiang Rai Province, as well as a couple of minivans and mostly slow fan-cooled buses bound for a handful of destinations in northern Thailand, depart from the inter-provincial bus station (Th Prasopsook) in the centre of town. If you're heading beyond

Coffee-maker, Chiang Rai
DAVID HANNAH/GETTY IMAGES ©

Chiang Rai (or are in a hurry), you'll have to go to the **new bus station** (☎ 0 5377 3989), 5km south of town on Asia 1 Hwy; frequent *sŏrng·tăa·ou* linking it and the inter-provincial station run from 6am to 6.30pm (15B, 15 minutes).

ℹ Getting Around

Chiang Rai Taxi (☎ 0 5377 3477) operates inexpensive metred taxis in and around town.

A túk-túk ride anywhere within central Chiang Rai should cost around 60B.

Mae Salong (Santikhiri)
แม่สลอง (สันติคีรี)

POP 20,000

For a taste of China without crossing any international borders, head to this atmospheric village perched on the back hills of Chiang Rai.

Mae Salong was originally settled by the 93rd Regiment of the Kuomintang (KMT), who had fled to Myanmar

Transport to/from Chiang Rai

DESTINATION	AIR	BUS	MINIVAN
Ban Pasang (for Doi Mae Salong)	–	25B; 30min; frequent 6am-8pm (inter-provincial bus station)	–
Bangkok	2135-3590B; 1¼hr; 2 daily (to Don Muang Airport); 2600B; 1¼hr; 3 daily (to Suvarnabhumi International Airport)	487-980B; 11-12hr; hourly 7-9.40am & 5-7.30pm (new bus station)	–
Chiang Mai	–	144-288B; 3-7hr; hourly 6.30am-7.30pm (new bus station); 144-288B; 7hr; frequent 6.30am-noon (inter-provincial bus station)	–
Chiang Saen	–	39B; 1½hr; frequent 6.20am-7pm (inter-provincial bus station)	45B; 1½hr; hourly 6.20am-5.40pm (inter-provincial bus station)
Lampang	–	112-157B; 4-5hr; hourly 9.30am-4.30pm (new bus station); 102-157B; 5hr; frequent 6.30am-noon (inter-provincial bus station)	–
Mae Sai	–	39B; 1½hr; frequent 6am-8pm (inter-provincial bus station)	46B; 1½hr; frequent 6.30am-6pm (inter-provincial bus station)
Phitsanulok	–	273-410B; 6-7hr; hourly 6.30am-10.30pm (new bus station)	–
Sob Ruak (Golden Triangle)	–	–	50B; 2hr; hourly 6.20am-5.40pm (inter-provincial bus station)
Sukhothai	–	300B; 8hr; hourly 7.30am-2.30pm (new bus station)	–

from China after the establishment of communist rule in 1949. The renegades were forced to leave Myanmar in 1961 when the then Rangoon-based government decided it wouldn't allow the KMT to legally remain in northern Myanmar. Crossing into northern Thailand with their pony caravans, the ex-soldiers and their families settled into mountain villages and re-created a society like the one they'd left behind in Yunnan.

A generation later, this unique community persists, and today the Yunnanese dialect of Chinese still remains the lingua franca, residents tend to watch Chinese, rather than Thai, TV, and you'll find more Chinese than Thai food.

🏃 Activities

Shin Sane Guest House and Little Home Guesthouse have free maps showing approximate trekking routes to Akha, Lisu, Mien, Lahu and Shan villages in the area. Nearby Akha and Lisu villages are less than half a day's walk away.

Shin Sane Guest House leads **horseback treks** to four nearby villages for 500B for about three or four hours.

🛏 Sleeping

IN TOWN

Shin Sane Guest House
Guesthouse $
(📞 0 5376 5026; www.
maesalong-shinsane.blogspot.
com; r 100B, bungalows
300B; @ 🛜) The rooms
at Mae Salong's oldest
hotel are bare but
spacious with shared
bathrooms, while the
bungalows are much
more comfortable
and have bathrooms
and TV. Located near
the morning market
intersection.

**Little Home
Guesthouse** Guesthouse $$
(📞 0 5376 5389; www.maesalonglittlehome.
com; bungalows 800B; @ 🛜) Located
behind a wooden house near the market
intersection is this handful of attractive,
great-value bungalows. Rooms are tidy
and sunny, and the owners are extremely
friendly. They have put together one of
the more accurate maps of the area.

OUTSIDE OF TOWN

**Maesalong
Mountain Home** Hotel $$
(📞 08 4611 9508; www.maesalongmountain
home.com; bungalows 1000-2500B; 🛜) Down
a dirt road 1km east of Mae Salong's town
centre (look for the orange sign), this
boutique-feeling place is a great choice
if you've got your own wheels or don't
mind walking. The 10 bungalows are in the
middle of a working farm and are bright
and airy, with wide balconies and huge
bathrooms.

Mountain road, Mae Salong
JOHN ELK/GETTY IMAGES ©

Phu Chaisai Resort & Spa
Resort $$$

(☎ 0 5391 0500; www.phu-chaisai.com; bungalows incl breakfast 4708-25,894B; ❄ ⛏ ✈)
Approximately 7km from Ban Pasang (the turn-off for Doi Mae Salong) on a remote bamboo-covered hilltop, this resort is the most unique place to stay in the area. The decidedly rustic adobe/bamboo bungalows fittingly lack TV, but have amazing views of the surrounding mountains and include access to a host of activities (including spa treatment, massage, yoga, day hikes and swimming) to keep you occupied.

Transport from Chiang Rai is available for 900B.

✖ Eating

The very Chinese breakfast of *bah·tôrng·gŏh* (deep-fried dough sticks) and hot soybean milk at the morning market is a great way to start the day.

In fact, many Thai tourists come to Mae Salong simply to eat Yunnanese dishes such as *màn·tŏh* (steamed Chinese buns) served with braised pork leg and pickled vegetables, or black chicken braised with Chinese-style herbs. Homemade wheat and egg noodles are another speciality of Mae Salong, and are served with a local broth that combines pork and a spicy chilli paste. They're available at several places in town.

Countless teahouses sell locally grown teas (mostly oolong and jasmine) and offer complimentary tastings.

Sweet Maesalong
Cafe $

(mains 45-155B; ⏰ 8.30am-5pm; 📶) If you require more caffeine than the local tea leaves can provide, stop by this modern cafe with an extensive menu of coffee drinks using local beans.

Sue Hai
Chinese $

(mains 40-250B; ⏰ 7am-9pm) This simple family-run teashop-cum-Yunnanese place has an English-language menu of local specialities including local mushroom fried with soy sauce, or the delicious air-

Left: Tea plantation, Mae Salong; **Below:** Market stall, Mae Sai

(LEFT) PETER STUCKINGS/GETTY IMAGES ©; (BELOW) JEAN-PIERRE LESCOURRET/GETTY IMAGES ©

dried pork fried with fresh chilli. It's roughly in the middle of town.

Salema Restaurant
Muslim-Chinese $$

(mains 30-250B; ⊙7am-8pm) Salema does tasty Muslim-Chinese dishes including a rich 'Beef curry Yunnan style' or a deliciously tart 'Tuna & tea leaves spicy salad'. The noodle dishes are equally worthwhile, and include a beef *kôw soy*.

ℹ️ Getting There & Away

Mae Salong is accessible via two routes. The original road, Rte 1130, winds west from Ban Pasang. Newer Rte 1234 approaches from the south, allowing easier access from Chiang Mai. The older route is more spectacular.

To get to Mae Salong, take a *sŏrng·tăa·ou* or Mae Sai–bound bus from Chiang Rai to Ban Pasang (20B to 25B, 30 minutes, every 20 minutes from 6am to 8pm). From Ban Pasang, blue *sŏrng·tăa·ou* head up the mountain to Mae Salong when full (60B, one hour, from 6am to 5pm). To get back to Ban Pasang, *sŏrng·tăa·ou*

park near Mae Salong's 7-Eleven. *Sŏrng·tăa·ou* stop running at around 5pm but you can charter one in either direction for about 500B.

Mae Sai   แม่สาย

POP 22,000

At first glance, Thailand's northernmost town appears to be little more than a large open-air market. But Mae Sai serves as a convenient base for exploring the Golden Triangle, Doi Tung and Mae Salong, and its position across from Myanmar also makes it a jumping-off point for those wishing to explore some of the more remote parts of Shan State.

🛏️ Sleeping

S-House Hotel
Hotel $

(📞0 5373 3811; www.s-house-hotel-maesai.com; 384 Th Sailomjoy; r with fan/air-con 500/600B; ❄️) At the end of the covered part of Th

Sailomjoy, a short walk from the border crossing, this budget place has spacious rooms with balconies overlooking the hills.

Afterglow
Hotel $$

(☏ 0 5373 4188; www.afterglowhostel.com; 139/5 Th Phahonyothin; r incl breakfast 600-800B, bungalows incl breakfast 600B; ❄ 🛜) Boasting a ground-floor cafe and rooms with a minimalist feel, Afterglow is probably the hippest place to stay in Mae Sai. A new addition sees a few equally stylish bungalows out back. Inconveniently located about 4km from the border.

Eating

An expansive **night market** (Th Phahonyothin; mains 30-60B; ⏲5-11pm) unfolds every evening along Th Phahonyothin. During the day, several **snack and drink vendors** (Th Phahonyothin; ⏲8am-5pm) can be found in front of the police station.

Bismillah Halal Food
Muslim-Thai $

(Soi 4, Th Phahonyothin; mains 30-60B; ⏲5am-5pm) This tiny restaurant does an excellent biryani, not to mention virtually everything else Muslim, from roti to samosa.

🛍 Shopping

Commerce is ubiquitous in Mae Sai, although most of the offerings are of little interest to Western travellers. One particularly popular commodity is gems, and a walk down Soi 4 will reveal several open-air **gem dealers** (Soi 4, Th Phahonyothin) diligently counting hundreds of tiny semiprecious stones on the side of the street.

ℹ Getting There & Away

Mae Sai's **bus station** (☏ 0 5371 1224; Rte 110) is 1.5km from the border; shared *sŏrng·tăa·ou* ply the route between the bus station and a stop on Soi 2, Th Phahonyothin (15B, five minutes, from 6am to 9pm). Alternatively, it's a 50B motorcycle taxi ride to/from the stand at the corner of Th Phahonyothin and Soi 4.

On Th Phahonyothin road, by Soi 8, is a sign saying 'bus stop'; this is where you'll find the stop for *sŏrng·tăa·ou* bound for Sop Ruak and Chiang Saen.

ℹ Getting Around

Sŏrng·tăa·ou around town cost 15B. Motorcycle taxis cost 20B to 40B.

Motorcycles can be rented at **Pornchai** (☏ 0 5373 1136; 4/7 Th Phahonyothin, no Roman-script sign; per day 250B; ⏲8am-5pm), located near Soi 9, Th Phahonyothin.

Transport to/from Mae Sai

DESTINATION	BUS	MINIVAN	SŎRNG·TĂA·OU
Bangkok	673-943B;12hr; frequent 4-5.45pm	–	–
Chiang Mai	182-364B; 5hr; 9 daily 6.15am-4.30pm	–	–
Chiang Rai	39-69B; 1½hr; frequent 5.45am-6pm	46B; 1hr; frequent 6am-5.30pm	–
Chiang Saen	–	–	50B; 1hr; frequent 8am-1pm
Phitsanulok	398-464B; 8hr; 6 daily 5.15am-6pm	–	–
Sop Ruak (Golden Triangle)	–	–	40B; 45min; frequent 8am-1pm

Chiang Saen

POP 11,000

The dictionary definition of a sleepy river town, Chiang Saen is the site of a former Thai kingdom thought to date back to as early as the 7th century. Scattered throughout the modern town are the ruins of this empire – surviving architecture includes several *chedi*, Buddha images, *wí·hăhn* pillars and earthen city ramparts.

Today huge river barges from China moor at Chiang Saen, carrying fruit, engine parts and all manner of other imports, keeping the old China-Siam trade route open. Despite this trade, the town hasn't changed too much over the last decade, and because of this is a pleasanter base than nearby Sop Ruak.

◉ Sights & Activities

Wat Phra That Pha Ngao Buddhist Temple
(วัดพระธาตุผาเงา; off Rte 1129; ☾daylight hours) **FREE** Located 3km south of town in the village of Sop Kham, this Buddhist temple complex contains a large prayer hall built to cover a partially excavated Chiang Saen–era Buddha statue. There is a beautiful golden teak *hŏr drai* (manuscript depository) and a steep road leads to a hilltop pagoda and temple with views over the area and the Mekong River.

Wat Chedi Luang Buddhist Temple
(วัดเจดีย์หลวง; Th Phahon-yothin; ☾daylight hours) **FREE** The ruins of the Buddhist Wat Chedi Luang feature an 18m octagonal *chedi* in the classic Chiang Saen or Lanna style. Archaeologists argue about its exact construction date but agree it was built some time between the 12th and 14th centuries.

Wat Pa Sak Historical Site
(วัดป่าสัก; off Rte 1290; historical park admission 50B; ☾8.30am-4.30pm Wed-Sun) **FREE** About 200m from the **Pratu Chiang Saen** (the historic main gateway to the town's western flank) are the remains of Wat Pa Sak, where the ruins of seven monuments are visible in a **historical park**. The main mid-14th-century *chedi* combines elements of the Hariphunchai and Sukhothai styles with a possible Bagan influence, and still holds a great deal of attractive stucco relief work.

Chiang Saen National Museum Museum
(พิพิธภัณฑสถานแห่งชาติเชียงแสน; 702 Th Phahonyothin; admission 100B; ☾8.30am-4.30pm Wed-Sun) This museum is a great source of local information considering its relatively small size.

Buddha statues, Chiang Saen
JOHN ELK/GETTY IMAGES ©

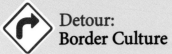

Detour:
Border Culture

Thailand, Laos and Myanmar (Burma) converge in a triangular border in northern Chiang Rai province. This geo-political anomaly was once dubbed the Golden Triangle because the region used to be the world's leading producer of opium poppies. All that is antique history, and the story of the illicit trade and how the frontier was won are now the primary draw.

Flag Peak used to host **Doi Tung Villa** (☏ 0 5376 7011; www.doitung.org; admission 90B; ⏱ 7-11.40am & 12.30-5.30pm), a royal summer palace that is now open to the public as a museum. **Mae Fah Luang Arboretum** (admission 90B; ⏱ 7am-5.30pm) is a royal initiative to educate the local hilltribe farmers in new agricultural methods to stop slash-and-burn practices and to replace opium production with cash crops, such as coffee, macadamia nuts and various fruits. But **Doi Tung**'s main attraction is the journey via Rte 1149.

Sop Ruak, in the so-called Golden Triangle, was once famous for its role in opium production. It now hosts several worthwhile history museums, including **House of Opium** (บ้านฝิ่น; www.houseofopium.com; Rte 1290; admission 50B; ⏱ 7am-7pm) and **Hall of Opium** (หอฝิ่น; Rte 1290; admission 200B; ⏱ 8.30am-4pm Tue-Sun). There are frequent *sŏrng·tăa·ou* to Chiang Saen (20B, from 7am to noon) and Mae Sai (45B, every 40 minutes from 8am to 1pm).

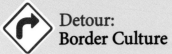

Mekong River Trips River Cruise
(Th Rimkhong; ⏱ 8am-3pm) Five-passenger speedboats leave from the waterfront jetty to Sop Ruak (per boat one way/ return 500/600B, one hour), or all the way to Chiang Khong (per boat one way/ return 2500/3000B, 1½ hours).

🛏 Sleeping

Gin's Maekhong View
Resort & Spa Hotel $$
(☏ 08 4485 1376; Th Rimkhong; r & bungalows incl breakfast 1500B; ❋ 🛜 🏊) Here you can choose between rather tight riverside bungalows or spacious rooms in a two-storey structure. There's a pool, a vast sunflower field and, by the time you read this, a spa. The same folks run the budget-oriented **Gin's Guest House** (☏ 0 5365 0847; 71 Th Rimkhong; r 300-800B, bungalows 500B; ❋ 🛜), just across the road. Gin's is located about 1km north of the centre of Chiang Saen, near the reconstructed city walls.

🍴 Eating

Every Saturday evening, a section of Th Rimkhong is closed to vehicle traffic for the busy **Walking Street** (Th Rimkhong; mains 20-60B; ⏱ 4-9pm Sat), which has lots of food.

Riverside Food Vendors Thai $
(Th Rimkhong; mains 30-60B; ⏱ 4-11pm) During the dry months, riverside vendors set up mats and sell rustic food such as fish or chicken barbecued inside thick joints of bamboo, along with sticky rice and *sôm·đam* (green papaya salad).

Kiaw Siang Hai Chinese $$
(44 Th Rimkhong; no Roman-script sign; mains 50-200B; ⏱ 8am-8pm) Serving the workers of Chinese boats that dock at Chiang Saen, this authentic Chinese restaurant prepares a huge menu of dishes in addition to the namesake noodles. Try the spicy Sichuan-style fried tofu or one of the Chinese herbal soups. The restaurant can be identified by the giant ceramic jars out the front.

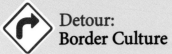

ⓘ Getting There & Away

Blue *sŏrng·tăa·ou* bound for Sop Ruak (20B) and Mae Sai (50B) wait at a **stall** (Th Phahonyothin) at the eastern end of Th Phahonyothin from 7.20am to noon.

Chiang Saen has no proper bus terminal; instead, there is a covered **bus shelter** (Th Phahonyothin) at the eastern end of Th Phahonyothin where buses pick up and drop off passengers. From this stop there are frequent buses to Chiang Rai (37B, 1½ hours, from 5.30am to 5.30pm) and a daily bus to Chiang Mai (232B, five hours, 9am).

PHITSANULOK พิษณุโลก

POP 83,000

Phitsanulok sees relatively few independent travellers but a fair amount of package tourists, probably because the city is a convenient base from which to explore the attractions of historical Sukhothai, Si Satchanalai and Kamphaeng Phet. The vibrant and extremely friendly city also boasts some interesting sites and museums, chief of which is Wat Phra Si Ratana Mahathat, which contains one of the country's most revered Buddha images.

⊙ Sights

Wat Ratburana   Buddhist Temple

(วัดราชบูรณะ; Th Phutta Bucha; ⊙daylight hours) **FREE** Across the street from Wat Phra Si Ratana Mahathat (p210), Wat Ratburana draws fewer visitors but in some ways is more interesting than its famous neighbour. In addition to a *wí·hăhn* with a 700-year-old gold Buddha, there's an *ùbohsòt* (chapel) with beautiful murals thought to date back to the mid-19th century and two wooden *hŏr đrai* (manuscript libraries).

🛏 Sleeping

Kraisaeng Place   Hotel $

(📞 0 5521 0509; www.facebook.com/kraisaeng-place45; 45 Th Thammabucha; r incl breakfast 400-450B; ❄ ✱ 🛜) Having more in common with a small apartment building than a hotel, the well-equipped rooms here are a bargain, although traffic noise can be an issue.

Yodia Heritage Hotel   Boutique Hotel $$$

(📞 0 5521 4677; www.yodiaheritage.com; 89/1 Th Phutta Bucha; r incl breakfast 3200-4200B, ste

Wat Ratburana

AUSTIN BUSH/GETTY IMAGES ©

GLENN BEANLAND/GETTY IMAGES ©

★ Don't Miss
Wat Phra Si Ratana Mahathat

The main *wí·hǎhn* (sanctuary) at this temple, known by locals as Wat Yai, appears small from the outside, but houses the Phra Phuttha Chinnarat, one of Thailand's most revered and copied Buddha images. This famous bronze statue is probably second in importance only to the Emerald Buddha in Bangkok's Wat Phra Kaew.

NEED TO KNOW

วัดพระศรีรัตนมหาธาตุ; Th Phutta Bucha, Phitsanulok; ⏱6am-9pm, museum 9am-5.30pm Wed-Sun

incl breakfast 8900B; ❄@⊠) This boutique hotel takes the crown as Phitsanulok's most upscale accommodation. Located along a quiet stretch of the Mae Nam Nan, suites are huge and feature similarly large tubs and a semi-private swimming pool.

✗ Eating

The city is particularly obsessive about night markets, and there are no fewer than three dotted in various locations around town. The most touted, Phit-sanulok's **night bazaar** (Th Phutta Bucha; ⏱7pm-midnight), focuses mainly on cloth-ing, but the southernmost restaurant

along the strip specialises in *pàk bûng loy fáh* (literally 'floating-in-the-sky morning glory vine'), in which the cook fires up a batch of *pàk bûng* in the wok and then flings it through the air to a waiting server who catches it on a plate. Another **night market** (Th Phra Ong Dam; mains 30-60B; ⏱5pm-midnight) lines either side of Th Phra Ong Dam north of Th Authong, and there's a very busy **night market** (off Th Akatossaroth; mains 30-60B; ⏱4-8pm) just south of the train station that features mostly takeaway items including *kôw něe·o hòr,* tiny banana-leaf parcels of sticky rice with various toppings.

Another dish associated with Phitsanulok is *gŏoay·dĕe·o hôy kăh* (literally, 'legs-hanging' noodles). The name comes from the way customers sit on the floor facing the river, with their legs dangling below. **Rim Nan (5/4 Th Phutta Bucha, no Roman-script sign; mains 20-35B; ⊙9am-4pm)**, north of Wat Phra Si Ratana Mahathat, is one of a few similar restaurants along Th Phutta Bucha that offer noodles and 'alternative' seating.

Paknang
Chinese-Thai $

(Th Sairuthai; mains 40-280B; ⊙10am-10pm) This corner of old Phitsanulok has a distinctly old-world Chinese feel – an excellent pairing with the tasty Chinese-style dishes at this longstanding restaurant.

Ban Mai
Thai $$

(93/30 Th Authong, no Roman-script sign; mains 100-200B; ⊙11am-10pm) Dinner at this local favourite is like a meal at your grandparents' place: opinionated conversation resounds, frumpy furniture abounds and an overfed cat appears to rule the dining room. The likewise homey dishes include *gaang pèt bèt yâhng*, a curry of grilled duck, and *yam dà·krái*, a herbal lemongrass 'salad'. Look for the yellow compound across from Ayara Grand Palace Hotel.

ⓘ Getting There & Away

Air Asia (🕿0 2515 9999; www.airasia.com; Phitsanulok Airport) and **Nok Air (**🕿0 5530 1051, nationwide 1318; www.nokair.co.th; Phitsanulok Airport; ⊙8am-5pm) operate out of Phitsanulok, with flights to/from Bangkok. The **airport (**🕿0 5530 1002) is about 5km south of town; **Golden House Tour (**🕿0 5525 9973; 55/37-38 Th Baromtrilokanart; ⊙7am-7pm Mon-Sat) provides car/minivan service from the airport to hotels (300B to 500B).

Phitsanulok's **bus station (**🕿0 5521 2090; Rte 12) is 2km east of town on Hwy 12; túk-túk and motorcycle taxis to/from town cost 60B.

Transport to/from Phitsanulok

DESTINATION	AIR	BUS	MINIVAN	TRAIN
Bangkok	520-2699B; 55min; 6 daily (to Don Muang Airport)	304-416B; 5-6hr; hourly 6.20am-12.30am	–	69-1664B; 5-7hr; 10 daily
Chiang Mai	–	299-349B; 6hr; hourly 5.40am-1.30am	–	65-1645B; 7-9hr; 6 daily
Chiang Rai	–	273-410B; 7-8hr; hourly 8am-12.40am	–	–
Kamphaeng Phet	–	59-83B; 3hr; hourly 5am-6pm	–	
Lampang	–	220-265B; 4hr; hourly 8am-midnight	–	158-1042B; 5hr; 5 daily
Mae Sai	–	398-464B; 7hr; hourly 11.30am-11.55pm	–	
Sukhothai	–	43-56B; 1hr; hourly 7.20am-6.15pm	60B; 1hr; half-hourly 5am-6pm	–
Sukhothai Historical Park	–	–	70B; 1½hr; half-hourly 5am-6pm	–

Detour:
Folk Museum, Buddha-Casting Foundry & Bird Garden

A nationally acclaimed expert on Thai folkways, former military cartographer, Buddha statue caster and apparent bird aficionado, Sergeant Major Thawee Buranakhet has drawn from his diverse experiences and interests to create three very worthwhile attractions in Phitsanulok.

The **Sergeant Major Thawee Folk Museum** (พิพิธภัณฑ์พื้นบ้านจ่าทวี; 26/43 Th Wisut Kasat; adult/child 50/25B; ☉8.30am-4.30pm) displays a remarkable collection of tools, textiles and photographs from Phitsanulok Province.

Across the street and also belonging to Sergeant Major Thawee is the small **Buranathai Buddha Image Foundry** (โรงหล่อพระบูรณะไทย; Th Wisut Kasat; ☉8am-5pm) FREE, where bronze Buddha images of all sizes are cast.

In addition to the Buddha foundry, there is also a display of fighting cocks, which are bred and sold all over the country. (The official English name for this part of the facility is The Centre of Conservative Folk Cock.)

The museums are on Th Wisut Kasat, about 1km south of Phitsanulok's train station; a túk-túk here should cost about 80B.

Transport options out of Phitsanulok are good as it's a junction for several bus and minivan routes.

Phitsanulok's **train station** (☏0 5525 8005, nationwide 1690; www.railway.co.th; Th Akatossaroth) is within walking distance of accommodation and offers a left-luggage service.

ℹ️ Getting Around

Rides on the town's Darth Vader-like sǎhm·lór start at about 60B.

Phitsanulok has a small **taxi** (☏0 5533 8888) fleet.

SUKHOTHAI PROVINCE

Sukhothai   สุโขทัย

POP 37,000

The Sukhothai (Rising of Happiness) Kingdom flourished from the mid-13th century to the late 14th century. This period is often viewed as the golden age of Thai civilisation, and the religious art and architecture of the era are considered to be the most classic of Thai styles. The remains of the kingdom, today known as *meuang gòw* (old city), feature around 45 sq km of partially rebuilt ruins, which are one of the most visited ancient sites in Thailand.

Located 12km east of the historical park on the Mae Nam Yom, the market town of New Sukhothai is not particularly interesting. Yet its friendly and relaxed atmosphere, good transport links and excellent-value accommodation make it a logical base from which to explore the old city ruins.

HISTORY

Sukhothai is typically regarded as the first capital of Siam, although this is not entirely accurate. The area was previously the site of a Khmer empire until 1238, when two Thai rulers, Pho Khun Pha Muang and Pho Khun Bang Klang Hao, decided to unite and form a new Thai kingdom.

Sukhothai's dynasty lasted 200 years and spanned nine kings. The most famous was King Ramkhamhaeng, who reigned from 1275 to 1317 and is credited with developing the first Thai script – his inscriptions are also considered the first Thai literature. Ramkhamhaeng eventually expanded his kingdom to include an area even larger than that of present-day Thailand. But a few kings later in 1438, Sukhothai was absorbed by Ayuthaya.

◎ Sights

The **Sukhothai Historical Park** (อุทยาน ประวัติศาสตร์สุโขทัย) ruins are one of Thailand's most impressive World Heritage Sites. The park includes the remains of 21 historical sites and four large ponds within the old walls, with an additional 70 sites within a 5km radius.

The architecture of Sukhothai temples is most typified by the classic lotus-bud *chedi*, featuring a conical spire topping a square-sided structure on a three-tiered base. Some sites exhibit other rich architectural forms introduced and modified during the period, such as bell-shaped Sinhalese and double-tiered Srivijaya *chedi*.

Despite the popularity of the park, it's quite expansive and solitary exploration is generally possible. Some of the most impressive ruins are well outside the city walls, so a bicycle or motorcycle is essential.

The ruins are divided into five zones. The central, northern and western zones each have a separate 100B admission fee.

CENTRAL ZONE

This is the historical park's main **zone** (admission 100B, plus per bicycle/motorcycle/car 10/30/50B; ⏱6.30am-7pm Sun-Fri, to 9pm Sat) and is home to what are arguably some of the park's most well-preserved and impressive ruins. An audio tour, available in English, Japanese or Thai, can be rented at the ticket booth for 150B.

Wat Mahathat   Buddhist Temple
(วัดมหาธาตุ; **Map p214**) Completed in the 13th century, the largest *wát* in Sukhothai is surrounded by brick walls (206m long and 200m wide) and a moat that is believed to represent the outer wall of the universe and the cosmic ocean.

The *chedi* spires feature the famous lotus-bud motif, and some of the original

---

Local Knowledge

Sukhothai

PATTAMA (MEM) HANQUART, TOUR GUIDE, CYCLING SUKHOTHAI (P216)

1 SUKHOTHAI HISTORICAL PARK
Evening is the best time to visit the historic ruins in the central area. The sun sets behind the hills, ideal for a romantic moment or a good photo shoot. Wat Sa Si is beautifully reflected in the lake at this time of day.

2 SI SATCHANALAI-CHALIANG HISTORICAL PARK
This lovely ancient city stretches along the Yom river. There are nice ruins on the hills and interesting excavation sites, such as human skeletons that are about 1500 years old.

3 NAM TOK SAI RUNG
This waterfall, 40km from Sukhothai, is a popular place where mostly locals go for a swim. There is a trail that leads to the top level of the falls where water particles refract in the sunlight (hence the name Rainbow Falls). The falls are best towards the end of the rainy season (October to November) or at the beginning of the cool season (December and January).

4 THAM CHA RAM
Get to this cave just before sunset to see hundreds of thousands of bats fly out to collect their supper. It is an amazing moment. It isn't a popular destination (50km from New Sukhothai in Lan Hoi district) but worth the trouble.

5 SUKHOTHAI COUNTRYSIDE
Sukhothai is really rural. It is a must to go and see the countryside of Sukhothai with its rice fields, network of canals and dirt roads going from farming village to farming village. It is beautiful throughout the year and is a good excuse to take a bicycle tour.

stately Buddha figures still sit among the ruined columns of the old *wí·hăhn* (sanctuary). There are 198 *chedi* within

Sukhothai Historical Park

the monastery walls – a lot to explore in what is believed to be the former spiritual and administrative centre of the old capital.

Ramkhamhaeng National Museum
Museum

(พิพิธภัณฑสถานแห่งชาติรามคำแหง; ; Map p214; admission 150B; ⊙9am-4pm) A good starting point for exploring the historical park ruins is this museum. A replica of the famous Ramkhamhaeng inscription, said to be the earliest example of Thai writing, is kept here among an impressive collection of Sukhothai artefacts. Admission to the museum is not included in the ticket to the central zone.

Wat Si Sawai
Buddhist Temple

(วัดศรีสวาย; Map p214) Just south of Wat Mahathat, this Buddhist shrine (dating from the 12th and 13th centuries) features three Khmer-style towers and a picturesque moat. It was originally built by the Khmers as a Hindu temple.

Wat Sa Si
Buddhist Temple

(วัดสระศรี; Map p214) Also known as 'Sacred Pond Monastery', Wat Sa Si sits on an island west of the bronze monument of King Ramkhamhaeng (the third Sukhothai king). It's a simple, classic Sukhothai-style wát containing a large Buddha, one chedi and the columns of the ruined wí·hăhn.

Wat Trapang Thong
Buddhist Temple

(วัดตระพังทอง; Map p214) Next to the museum, this small, still-inhabited wát with its fine stucco reliefs is reached by a footbridge across the large lotus-filled pond that surrounds it. This reservoir, the original site of Thailand's Loi Krathong festival, supplies the Sukhothai community with most of its water.

NORTHERN ZONE

This **zone** (admission 100B, plus per bicycle/motorcycle/car 10/30/50B; ⏰7.30am-5.30pm), 500m north of the old city walls, is easily reached by bicycle.

Wat Si Chum   Buddhist Temple
(วัดศรีชุม; Map p214) This wát is northwest of the old city and contains an impressive *mon·dòp* with a 15m, brick-and-stucco seated Buddha. This Buddha's elegant, tapered fingers are much photographed. Archaeologists theorise that this image is the 'Phra Atchana' mentioned in the famous Ramkhamhaeng inscription. A passage in the *mon·dòp* wall that leads to the top has been blocked so that it's no longer possible to view the jataka inscriptions that line the tunnel ceiling.

**Wat Phra
Phai Luang**   Buddhist Temple
(วัดพระพายหลวง; Map p214) Outside the city walls in the northern zone, this somewhat isolated wát features three 12th-century Khmer-style towers, bigger than those at Wat Si Sawai. This may have been the centre of Sukhothai when it was ruled by the Khmers of Angkor prior to the 13th century.

WESTERN ZONE

This **zone** (admission 100B, plus per bicycle/motorcycle/car 10/30/50B; ⏰8am-4.30pm), at its furthest extent 2km west of the old city walls, is the most expansive. In addition to Wat Saphan Hin, several mostly featureless ruins can be found. A bicycle or motorcycle is necessary to explore this zone.

Wat Saphan Hin   Buddhist Temple
(วัดสะพานหิน) Located on the crest of a hill that rises about 200m above the plain, the name of the wát, which means 'stone bridge', is a reference to the slate path and staircase that leads up to the temple, which are still in place.

All that remains of the original temple are a few chedi and the ruined *wí·hǎhn*, consisting of two rows of laterite columns flanking a 12.5m-high standing Buddha image on a brick terrace. The site is 3km west of the former city wall and gives a good view of the Sukhothai ruins to the southeast and the mountains to the north and south.

OTHER SITES

A few more worthwhile destinations lie outside the more popular paid zones.

Sangkhalok Museum   Museum
(พิพิธภัณฑ์สังคโลก; Rte 1293; adult/child 100/50B; ⏰8am-5pm) This small but comprehensive museum is an excellent introduction to ancient Sukhothai's most famous product and export, its ceramics.

Wat Trapang Thong
ANDREW WATSON/GETTY IMAGES ©

The ground floor displays an impressive collection of original Thai pottery found in the area, plus some pieces traded from Vietnam, Burma and China. The 2nd floor features examples of non-utilitarian pottery made as art, including some beautiful and rare ceramic Buddha statues.

The museum is about 2.5km east of the centre of New Sukhothai; a túk-túk here will run about 100B.

Wat Chang Lom
Historical Site

(วัดช้างล้อม; ; Map p214; off Rte 12) **FREE** Off Rte 12 in the east zone, Wat Chang Lom (Elephant Circled Monastery) is about 1km east of the main park entrance. A large bell-shaped *chedi* is supported by 36 elephants sculpted into its base.

Wat Chetupon
Historical Site

(วัดเชตุพน) **FREE** Located 1.4km south of the old city walls, this temple once held a four-sided *mon·dòp* featuring the four classic poses of the Buddha (sitting, reclining, standing and walking). The graceful lines of the walking Buddha can still be made out today.

Wat Chedi Si Hong
Historical Site

(วัดเจดีย์สี่ห้อง) **FREE** Directly across from Wat Chetupon, the main *chedi* here has retained much of its original stucco relief work, which shows still vivid depictions of elephants, lions and humans.

🤸 Activities

Cycling Sukhothai
Bicycle Tours

(☎ 0 5561 2519, 08 5083 1864; www.cycling-sukhothai.com; off Th Jarot Withithong; half-/full day 650/750B, sunset tour 350B) A resident of Sukhothai for nearly 20 years, Belgian cycling enthusiast Ronny Hanquart's rides follow themed itineraries such as the Historical Park Tour, which includes stops at lesser-seen *wát* and villages.

Cycling Sukhothai is based about 1.2km west of Mae Nam Yom, in New Sukhothai, and free transport can be arranged.

🛏 Sleeping

Most accommodation is in New Sukhothai, which is home to some of the best-value budget-level accommodation in northern Thailand.

There are an increasing number of options near the park, many of them in the upscale bracket. Prices tend to go up during the Loi Krathong festival.

NEW SUKHOTHAI

Sabaidee House
Hotel $

(☎ 0 5561 6303; www.sabaideehouse.com; 81/7 Th Jarot Withithong; r 200-600B; ❄ 🛜) This cheery guesthouse in a semi-rural setting spans seven attractive bungalows and rooms in the main structure. Sabaidee is off Th Jarot Withithong

Cycling in Sukhothai
MATTHEW MICAH WRIGHT/GETTY IMAGES ©

New Sukhothai

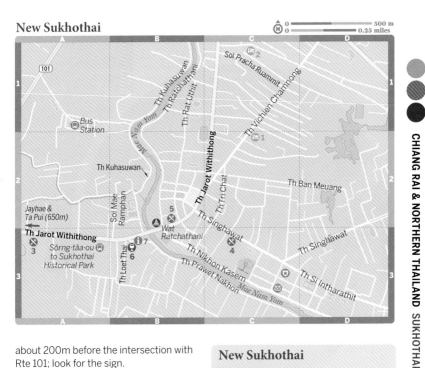

about 200m before the intersection with Rte 101; look for the sign.

At Home Sukhothai
Guesthouse **$$**

(Map p217; ☏ 0 5561 0172; www.athome sukhothai.com; 184/1 Th Vichien Chamnong; r incl breakfast 400-800B; ❊ @ ⏏) Located in the 50-year-old childhood home of the proprietor, the simple but comfortable rooms – both those fan-cooled in the original structure and the newer air-con ones – here really do feel like home. The only downside is the relative distance from 'downtown' Sukhothai.

Ruean Thai Hotel
Hotel **$$$**

(Map p217; ☏ 0 5561 2444; www.rueanthaihotel. com; 181/20 Soi Pracha Ruammit; r incl breakfast 1480-4200B; ❊ @ ⏏ ⛱) At first glance, you may mistake this eye-catching complex for a Buddhist temple or a traditional Thai house. The rooms on the upper level follow a distinct Thai theme, while the poolside rooms are slightly more modern, and there's a concrete building with simple air-con rooms out the back.

Call for free pick-up from the bus station.

New Sukhothai

SUKHOTHAI HISTORICAL PARK

Wake Up @ Muang Kao
Guesthouse **$$**

(Map p214; ☏ 0 5569 7153; 1/1 Rte 12; r incl breakfast 1000-1500B; ❊ @ ⏏) If there's a homestay equivalent to flashpacker, Wake Up has nailed it. The five rooms here are spacious and tasteful, come decked out with local touches and are looked after by a friendly local couple. A breath of fresh air in Old Sukhothai.

Thai Thai   Hotel $$

(Map p214; ☎08 4932 1006; www.thaithai
sukhothai.com; 95/8 Rte 1272; r incl breakfast
800-2400, bungalows incl breakfast 1200-1800B;
❄🛜) As the name brings home, Thai
Thai takes the form of an indigenously
inspired compound. There's a string of
10 wooden bungalows in an attractive
garden and 10 rooms in a few larger structures out back. All come fully outfitted
with TV, fridge, hot water and air-con.

✖ Eating & Drinking

Sukhothai's signature dish is *gŏo·ay đĕe·o
sù·kŏh·tai* (Sukhothai-style noodles),
which features a slightly sweet broth with
different types of pork, ground peanuts
and thinly sliced green beans. The dish
is available at **Jayhae** (Th Jarot Withithong;
dishes 25-40B; ⏲8am-4pm) and **Ta Pui** (Th
Jarot Withithong, no Roman-script sign; dishes
25-35B; ⏲7am-3pm), located across from

each other on Th Jarot
Withithong, about 1.3km west
of Mae Nam Yom.

A wise choice for cheap eats is New
Sukhothai's tiny **night market** (Map p217;
Th Jarot Withithong; mains 30-60B; ⏲6-11pm).
Most vendors here are accustomed to
accommodating foreigners and even
provide bilingual menus.

Chula   Chinese-Thai $

(Map p217; Th Jarot Withithong; dishes 30-120B;
⏲10am-11pm) It has all the charm of an
airport hangar, but the food at this local
favourite is solid. Pick and choose from
prepared dishes, or do the same with the
raw ingredients displayed out front.

Dream Café   Thai $$

(Map p217; 86/1 Th Singhawat; mains 120-250B;
⏲5-11pm; ✏) A meal at Dream Café is like
dining in an antique shop. Try one of the
well-executed *yam* (Thai-style 'salads'), or
one of the dishes that feature freshwater
fish, a local speciality.

Chopper Bar — Bar

(Map p217; Th Prawet Nakhon; mains 30-150B; ⏱10am-12.30am; 📶) Both travellers and locals congregate at this restaurant/bar from morning till hangover for food, drinks and live music.

ℹ Getting There & Away

Sukhothai's airport is located a whopping 27km from town off Rte 1195. **Bangkok Airways** (📞0 5564 7224, nationwide 1771; www.bangkokair. com; Sukhothai Airport; ⏱7.30am-5.30pm) is the only airline operating here, with flights to Bangkok. There is a **minivan service** (📞0 5564 7220; Sukhothai Airport; 180B) between the airport and New Sukhothai.

Sukhothai's minivan and **bus station** (📞0 5561 4529; Rte 101) is almost 1km northwest of the centre of New Sukhothai; a motorcycle taxi between here and central New Sukhothai should cost around 50B, or you can hop on any *sŏrng·tăa·ou* bound for Sukhothai Historical Park, which make a stop at the bus station on their way out of town (30B, 10 minutes, frequent from 6am to 5.30pm).

Alternatively, if you're staying near the historical park, **Win Tour** (Rte 12; ⏱6am-9.40pm) has an office roughly opposite Wat Trapang Thong, where you can board buses to Bangkok (356B, six hours, 8.20pm, 12.30pm and 9.40pm) and Chiang Mai (239B, five hours, hourly from 6.30am to 1.40pm).

ℹ Getting Around

A *săhm·lór* ride within New Sukhothai should cost no more than 40B.

Relatively frequent *sŏrng·tăa·ou* run between New Sukhothai and Sukhothai Historical Park (30B, 30 minutes, from 6am to 5.30pm), leaving from a stop on Th Jarot Withithong just west of Poo Restaurant. Motorcycle taxis go between the town or bus station and the Historical Park for 120B.

The best way to get around the historical park is by bicycle, which can be rented at shops outside the park entrance for 30B per day (6am to 6pm).

Transport to/from Sukhothai

DESTINATION	AIR	BUS	MINIVAN	SŎRNG·TĂA·OU
Bangkok	2490B; 1hr; 2 daily (to Suvarnabhumi International Airport)	279-416B; 6-7hr; half-hourly 7.50am-10.40pm	–	–
Chiang Mai	–	239-308B; 5-6hr; half-hourly 6.15am-5.30pm	–	–
Chiang Rai	–	266B; 9hr; 4 departures 6.40-11.30am	–	–
Kamphaeng Phet	–	60-77B; 1½hr; frequent 7.50am-11pm	–	43B; 2hr; frequent 7am-4.30pm
Lampang	–	178-229B; 3hr; half-hourly 7.15am-4.30pm	–	–
Phitsanulok	–	43B; 1hr; hourly 6am-6pm	43B; 1hr; hourly 8am-6pm	–
Sawankhalok	–	29-38B; 1hr; hourly 6.40am-6pm	85B; 2hr; half-hourly 7.10am-4.30pm	–
Si Satchanalai	–	50B; 1½hr; 11am	–	–

Si Satchanalai-Chaliang Historical Park

อุทยานประวัติศาสตร์ศรีสัชนาลัย

Set among hills, the 13th- to 15th-century ruins of the old cities of Si Satchanalai and Chaliang, 50km north of Sukhothai, are in the same basic style as those in the Sukhothai Historical Park, but the setting is more rural and arguably more peaceful. The park covers roughly 720 hectares and is surrounded by a 12m-wide moat. Chaliang, 1km southeast, is an older city site (dating to the 11th century), though its two temples date to the 14th century.

SI SATCHANALAI

This **zone** (admission 100B, plus car 50B; ◷8am-5pm) contains the majority of ruins. An **information centre** (◷8.30am-5pm) at the park distributes free maps and has a small exhibit outlining the history and at-tractions. Bikes can be **hired** (per day 30B; ◷8am-5pm) near the entrance gate.

Wat Chang Lom   Historical Site
(วัดช้างล้อม) This fine temple, marking the centre of the old city of Si Satchanalai, has elephants surrounding a bell-shaped *chedi* that is somewhat better preserved than its counterpart in Sukhothai. An inscription states that the temple was built by King Ramkhamhaeng between 1285 and 1291.

Wat Khao Phanom Phloeng   Historical Site
(วัดเขาพนมเพลิง) On the hill overlooking Wat Chang Lom are the remains of Wat Khao Phanom Phloeng, including a *chedi,* a large seated Buddha and stone columns that once supported the roof of the *wí·hăhn.*

From this hill you can make out the general design of the once-great city.

Wat Chedi Jet Thaew
Historical Site

(วัดเจดีย์เจ็ดแถว) Next to Wat Chang Lom, these ruins contain seven rows of *chedi*, the largest of which is a copy of one at Wat Mahathat in Sukhothai. An interesting brick-and-plaster *wí·hǎhn* features barred windows designed to look like lathed wood (an ancient Indian technique used all over Southeast Asia).

Wat Nang Phaya
Historical Site

(วัดนางพญา) South of Wat Chedi Jet Thaew, this *chedi* is Sinhalese in style and was built in the 15th or 16th century, a bit later than the other monuments at Si Satchanalai. Stucco reliefs on the large laterite *wí·hǎhn* in front of the *chedi* – now sheltered by a tin roof – date from the Ayuthaya period when Si Satchanalai was known as Sawankhalok. Goldsmiths in the district still craft a design known as *nahng pá·yah*, modelled after these reliefs.

CHALIANG

This older site, a short bike ride from Si Satchanalai, has two temples of note.

Good Deal

An admission fee of 220B allows entry to Si Satchanalai (p220), Wat Chao Chan (p221; at Chaliang) and the Si Satchanalai Centre for Study & Preservation of Sangkalok Kilns (p222).

Wat Phra Si Ratana Mahathat
Historical Site

(วัดพระศรีรัตนมหาธาตุ; admission 20B; ☉8am-4.30pm) These ruins consist of a large laterite *chedi* (dating back to 1448–88) between two *wí·hǎhn*. One of the *wí·hǎhn* holds a large seated Sukhothai Buddha image, a smaller standing image and a bas-relief of the famous walking Buddha, exemplary of the flowing, boneless Sukhothai style. The other *wí·hǎhn* contains some less distinguished images.

Wat Chao Chan
Historical Site

(วัดเจ้าจันทร์; admission 100B; ☉8am-5pm) The central attraction here is a large

Wat Chang Lom

VISIONSOFAMERICA/JOE SOHM/GETTY IMAGES ©

221

Speaking Northern

Northerners used to take offence when outsiders tried speaking *găm méuang* (the colloquial name for the northern dialect) to them, an attitude that dates back to a time when central Thais considered northerners to be very backward and made fun of their dialect. Nowadays, most northerners are proud of their native language, and speaking a few words of the local lingo will go a long way in getting them to open up. The following are a few words and phrases that will help you talk to, flirt with, or perhaps just win some smiles from the locals.

- *Ôo găm méuang bòr jâhng* I can't speak northern Thai

- *An nêe tôw dai?* How much is this?

- *Mee kôw nêung bòr?* Do you have sticky rice?

- *Lám đáa đáa* Delicious

- *Mâan lâ* Yes/That's right

- *Bòr mâan* No

- *Jôw* (A polite word used by women; equivalent to the central Thai *ka*)

Khmer-style tower similar to later towers built in Lopburi and probably constructed during the reign of Khmer King Jayavarman VII (1181–1217). The tower has been restored and is in fairly good shape. The roofless *wí·hǎhn* on the right contains the laterite outlines of a large standing Buddha that has all but melted away from exposure and weathering.

SAWANKHALOK KILNS

At one time, more than 200 huge pottery **kilns** FREE lined the banks of Mae Nam Yom in the area around Si Satchanalai. In China – the biggest importer of Thai pottery during the Sukhothai and Ayuthaya periods – the pieces produced here came to be called 'Sangkalok', a mispronunciation of Sawankhalok. Today, several barely recognisable kiln sites can be found along the road that runs north of Si Satchanalai. Ceramics are still made in the area, and at least one local ceramic artist even continues to fire his pieces in an underground wood-burning oven.

Si Satchanalai Centre for Study & Preservation of Sangkalok Kilns   Museum

(ศูนย์ศึกษาและอนุรักษ์เตาสังคโลก; admission 100B; ☺8.30am-5pm) Located 5km northwest of the Si Satchanalai ruins, this centre has large excavated kilns and many intact pottery samples. The exhibits are interesting despite the lack of English labels.

SAWANKHALOK

Sawanworanayok National Museum   Museum

(พิพิธภัณฑสถานแห่งชาติสวรรควรนายก; 69 Th Phracharat; admission 50B; ☺9am-4pm) In Sawankhalok town, near Wat Sawankhalam on the western river bank, this state-sponsored museum houses a very impressive collection of 12th- to 15th-century artefacts. The ground floor focuses on the area's ceramic legacy, while the 2nd floor features several beautiful bronze and stone Sukhothai-era Buddha statues.

ℹ️ Getting There & Away

Bus

Si Satchanalai-Chaliang Historical Park is off Rte 101 between Sawankhalok and Ban Hat Siaw. From New Sukhothai, take a Si Satchanalai bus (46B, 1½ hours, 11am) or one of three buses to Chiang Rai at 6.40am, 9am and 11.30am (46B), and ask to get off at 'meuang gòw' (old city). The last bus back to New Sukhothai leaves at 4.30pm.

To get to the park from Sawankhalok, you can hop on just about any north-bound line from the town's roadside bus terminal (24B to 50B, 30 minutes, frequent from 7am to 5pm).

Train

Sawankhalok's original train station is one of the local sights. King Rama VI built a 60km railway spur from Ban Dara (a small town on the main northern trunk) to Sawankhalok just so that he could visit the ruins. Amazingly, there's a daily special express from Bangkok to Sawankhalok (482B, seven hours, 10.50am). The train heads back to Bangkok at 7.40pm, arriving in the city at 3.30am. You can also take this train to Phitsanulok (328B, 3½ hours, 5.55pm). It's a 'Sprinter' – 2nd class air-con and no sleepers. The fare includes dinner and breakfast.

ℹ️ Getting Around

You can hire bicycles (p220) from near the food stalls at the entrance to the historical park.

KAMPHAENG PHET

กำแพงเพชร

POP 30,000

Located halfway between Bangkok and Chiang Mai, Kamphaeng Phet translates as 'Diamond Wall', a reference to the apparent strength of this formerly walled city's protective barrier. This level of security was necessary, as the city helped to protect the Sukhothai and later Ayuthaya kingdoms against attacks from Burma or Lanna. Parts of the wall can still be seen today, as well as impressive ruins of several religious structures. The modern city stretches along a shallow section of Mae Nam Ping and is one of Thailand's nicer provincial capitals.

◎ Sights & Activities

A Unesco World Heritage Site, the **Kamphaeng Phet Historical Park** (อุทยาน ประวัติศาสตร์กำแพงเพชร; ⊘8am-6pm)

Wat Phra Kaeo, Kamphaeng Phet Historical Park

IGOR PRAHIN/GETTY IMAGES ©

Good Deal

An admission fee of 150B allows entry to both the former walled city of Kamphaeng Phet and the larger compound outside of town.

features the ruins of structures dating back to the 14th century, roughly the same time as the better-known kingdom of Sukhothai. Kamphaeng Phet's Buddhist monuments continued to be built up until the Ayuthaya period, nearly 200 years later, and thus possess elements of both Sukhothai and Ayuthaya styles, resulting in a school of Buddhist art quite unlike anywhere else in Thailand. In general, the ruins are not nearly as well restored as those of Sukhothai, but they are smaller, more intimate and less visited.

The park consists of two distinct sections: a formerly walled city just north of modern Kamphaeng Phet, and a larger compound about 1.5km farther north.

WALLED CITY

Just north of modern Kamphaeng Phet, this walled **zone** (admission 100B; ⊙8am-4pm) is the origin of the city's name, and was formerly inhabited by *gamavasi* ('living in the community') monks.

It's a long walk or an approximately 40B motorcycle taxi ride from the centre of town.

OUTSIDE OF TOWN

The majority of Kamphaeng Phet's ruins are found in this expansive **zone** (admission 100B; ⊙8am-6pm), located about 1.5km north of the city walls. The area was previously home to *aranyavasi* ('living in forests') monks and, in addition to the two temple compounds mentioned here, contains more than 40 other former compounds. However, most of these former compounds are not much more than flat brick foundations with the occasional weather-worn Buddha image.

There is an excellent **visitor centre** (⊙8am-4.30pm) at the entrance where **bicycle hire** (per day 30B) can be arranged.

A motorcycle taxi from central Kamphaeng Phet to the entrance will cost about 80B.

OTHER SIGHTS

Kamphaeng Phet National Museum
Museum

(พิพิธภัณฑสถานแห่งชาติ กำแพงเพชร; Th Pindamri; admission 100B; ⊙9am-noon & 1-4.30pm Wed-Sun) Kamphaeng Phet's visit-worthy museum was being renovated when we stopped by. Previously, the museum has been home to an

Merit-makers, Kamphaeng Phet
AUSTIN BUSH/GETTY IMAGES ©

Northern Nosh

Much like the language, Thailand's food seems to take a slightly different form every time you cross a provincial border. The cuisine of Thailand's northern provinces is no exception and is indicative of the region's seasonal and relatively cool climate, not to mention a love for pork, vegies and all things deep-fried. Traditionally, the residents of Thailand's north ate almost exclusively *kôw něe·o*, sticky rice, known locally as *kôw nêung* ('steamed rice'). Coconut milk rarely makes its way into the northern kitchen, and northern Thai cuisine is probably the most seasonal and least spicy of Thailand's regional schools of cooking, often relying on bitter or other dried spice flavours.

○ *Gaang hang·lair* – Burmese in origin (*hang* is a corruption of the Burmese *hin*, meaning curry), this rich pork curry is often seen at festivals and ceremonies. Try a bowl at Mae Si Bua (p237) in Mae Hong Son.

○ *Kâap mǒo* – Deep-fried pork crackling is a common, delicious side dish in northern Thailand.

○ *Kôw gân jin* – Banana leaf packets of rice mixed with blood, steamed and served with garlic oil. A popular snack in Mae Hong Son.

○ *Kôw soy* – This popular curry-based noodle dish is possibly Burmese in origin and was probably introduced to northern Thailand by travelling Chinese merchants. A mild but tasty version is available at **Khao Soi Phor Jai** (Th Jetyod, no Roman-script sign; mains 30-60B; ☺7.30am-5pm) in Chiang Rai.

○ *Kà·nǒm jeen nám ngée·o* – Fresh rice noodles served with a meaty and tart pork- and tomato-based broth. An excellent bowl can be had at Paa Suk (p200), in Chiang Rai.

○ *Lâhp kôo·a* – Literally 'fried *lâhp*', this dish takes the famous Thai minced-meat 'salad' and fries it with a mixture of unique dried spices.

○ *Nǎam* – Fermented raw pork, a sour delicacy that tastes much better than it sounds.

○ *Nám prík nùm* – Green chillies, shallots and garlic are grilled then mashed into a stringy and spicy paste served with sticky rice, parboiled veggies and deep-fried pork crackling. Try it at Phu-Lae (p201), in Chiang Rai.

○ *Nám prík òrng* – A chilli dip of Shan origin made from tomatoes and minced pork – a northern Thai bolognese of sorts. Available at Banpleng (p236), in Mae Hong Son.

○ *Sâi òo·a* – A grilled pork sausage seasoned with copious fresh herbs.

○ *Đam sôm oh* – The northern Thai version of *sôm·đam* substitutes pomelo for green papaya.

expansive collection of artefacts from the Kamphaeng Phet area, including an immense Shiva statue that is the largest bronze Hindu sculpture in the country.

The image was formerly located at the nearby **Shiva Shrine** FREE until a German missionary stole the idol's hands and head in 1886 (they were later returned). Today a replica stands in its place.

Kamphaeng Phet Regional Museum   Museum

(พิพิธภัณฑ์เฉลิมพระเกียรติกำแพงเพชร; Th Pindamri; admission 10B; ⏰9am-4.30pm) The regional museum is a series of Thai-style wooden structures on stilts set among nicely landscaped grounds. There are three main buildings in the museum featuring displays ranging from history and prehistory to the various ethnic groups that inhabit the province.

🛌 Sleeping

Three J Guest House   Guesthouse $

(📞0 5571 3129, 08 1887 4189; www.three jguesthouse.com; 79 Th Rachavitee; r 250-800B; ❄@🛜) The cheapest bungalows at this welcoming guesthouse are fan-cooled and share a clean bathroom while the more expensive have air-con. There's heaps of local information, and bicycles and motorcycles are available for hire.

Grand View Resort   Hotel $

(📞0 5572 1104; 34/4 Moo 2, Nakhon Chum; r & bungalows incl breakfast 290-590B; ❄🛜) One of a handful of semi-rural 'resorts'

on the west bank of Mae Nam Ping, the highlight here are the six floating raft bungalows.

Chakungrao Riverview   Hotel $$

(📞0 5571 4900; www.chakungraoriverview.com; 149 Th Thesa 1; r incl breakfast 1000-1300B; ste incl breakfast 3500B; ❄@🛜) At Kamphaeng Phet's poshest digs, rooms are tastefully decked out in dark woods and forest green and feature balconies with river or city views. Suites are huge and are generally available at a considerable discount.

🍴 Eating & Drinking

Bamee Chakangrao   Thai $

(Th Ratchadamnoen 1, no Roman-script sign; mains 25-30B; ⏰8.30am-3pm) Thin wheat and egg noodles (bà·mèe) are a speciality of Kamphaeng Phet, and this famous restaurant is one of the best places to try them. The noodles are made fresh every day behind the restaurant, and pork satay is also available. There's no English-language sign; look for the green banners on the corner.

Fruit stall, Kamphaeng Phet

Mae Ping Riverside
Thai $

(50/1 Moo 2, Nakhon Chum, no Roman-script sign; mains 40-120B; ⏱lunch & dinner) Decent eats, draught beer and live music can be found here, on the west bank of Mae Nam Ping. There are a few other similar riverside places along this strip.

Kitti
Chinese-Thai $$

(cnr Th Vijit 2 & Th Bamrungrat, no Roman-script sign; mains 50-350B; ⏱10am-2pm & 4-10pm) Long-standing Kitti excels at Chinese-style dining. Try the unusual but delicious fried chicken with cashew nut, which also includes pickled garlic and slices of sweet pork.

ℹ Getting There & Away

Kamphaeng Phet's bus station (📞0 5579 9844; Rte 101) is about 1km west of Mae Nam Ping. Motorcycles (50B) and sŏrng·tǎa·ou (20B, frequent from 7.30am to 5pm) run between the station and town. If coming from Sukhothai or Phitsanulok, get off in the old city or at the roundabout on Th Thesa 1 to save yourself the trouble of having to get a sŏrng·tǎa·ou back into town.

Alternatively, if you're bound for Bangkok you can circumvent the bus station altogether by buying tickets and boarding a bus at Win Tour (📞0 5571 3971; Th Kamphaeng Phet) (295B, five hours, frequent from 9am-11pm), near the roundabout.

ℹ Getting Around

There are very few motorcycle taxis or túk-túk in Kamphaeng Phet. As such it's wise to consider hiring a bicycle or motorbike – Three J Guest

House has both (per day bicycle/motorcycle 50/200B).

MAE HONG SON PROVINCE

Accessible only by incredibly windy mountain roads or a dodgy flight to the provincial capital, Mae Hong Son is arguably Thailand's remotest province. Thickly forested and mountainous, and far from the influence of sea winds, the temperature seldom rises above 40°C, while in January the temperature can drop to 2°C. Mae Hong Son's location along the border with Myanmar means that it is also a crossroads for ethnic minorities (mostly Karen, with some Hmong, Lisu and Lahu), Shan and Burmese immigrants.

Pai
ปาย
POP 2000

Spend enough time in northern Thailand and eventually you'll hear the comparisons between Pai and Bangkok's Khao San Road.

However, unlike Khao San or the islands, Pai (pronounced more like the English 'bye', not 'pie') is just as popular among Thais as foreigners. During the peak of the cool season (December and January), thousands of Thais from Bangkok crowd into the town, making parts of it feel more like the Chatuchak Weekend Market than a remote village in Mae Hong Son.

Buses to/from Kamphaeng Phet

DESTINATION	PRICE (B)	DURATION (HR)	DEPARTURES
Bangkok	230-344	5	frequent 8.30am-1.30am
Chiang Mai	228-342	5	8 departures 11.30am-1am
Chiang Rai	305-773	7	frequent noon-10.30pm
Lampang	168	4	8 departures 11.30am-1am
Mae Hong Son	509-905	11	10pm & 11pm
Phitsanulok	59-83	2½	hourly 6am-6pm
Sukhothai	77	1	hourly 10.50am-8.30pm

Despite all this, the town's popularity has yet to negatively impact its nearly picture-perfect setting in a mountain valley. There's heaps of quiet accommodation outside the main drag, a host of natural, lazy activities to keep visitors entertained, a vibrant art and music scene, and the town's Shan roots can still be seen in its temples, quiet back streets and fun afternoon market.

◉ Sights

Wat Phra That Mae Yen
Buddhist Temple

(วัดพระธาตุแม่เย็น; ⏰ daylight hours) FREE This temple sits atop a hill and has good views overlooking the valley. To get there, walk 1km east from the main intersection in town to get to the stairs (353 steps) that lead to the top. Or, if you've got wheels, take the 400m sealed road that follows a different route.

WATERFALLS

There are a few waterfalls around Pai that are worth visiting, particularly after the rainy season (October to early December). The closest and the most popular, **Nam Tok Mo Paeng**, has a couple of pools that are suitable for swimming. The waterfall is about 8km from Pai along the road that also leads to Wat Nam Hoo – a long walk indeed, but suitable for a bike ride or short motorcycle trip. Roughly the same distance in the opposite direction is **Nam Tok Pembok**, just off the road to Chiang Mai. The most remote is **Nam Tok Mae Yen**, a couple of hours' walk down the rough road east of Pai, just before the turn-off to Fluid.

OTHER SIGHTS

Tha Pai Hot Springs
Hot Springs

(บ่อน้ำร้อนท่าปาย; adult/child 200/100B; ⏰ 7am-6pm) Across the Mae Nam Pai and 7km southeast of town via a paved road is this well-kept local park. A scenic stream flows through the park; the stream mixes with the hot springs in places to make pleasant bathing areas. The water is also diverted to a couple of nearby spas.

Pai Canyon
Nature Reserve

(กองแลนปาย) FREE Located 8km from Pai along the road to Chiang Mai, a paved stairway here culminates in an elevated lookout over high rock cliffs and the Pai valley. The latter can be followed by a dirt trail, but lacking shade, is best tackled in the morning or afternoon.

Memorial Bridge
Landmark

(สะพานประวัติศาสตร์ท่าปาย; Rte 1095) FREE It may look like no more than an antiquated bridge to foreigners, but to thousands of Thai tourists who stop here during the tourist season it's one of several crucial photo ops along the '762 curves' to Pai. Located 9km from Pai

Hiker, Pai Canyon
SOREN EGEBERG/ZEAMONKEY IMAGES/GETTY IMAGES ©

History of Northern Thailand

Northern Thailand's history has been characterised by the shifting powers of various independent principalities. One of the most significant early cultural influences in the north was the Mon kingdom of Hariphunchai (based in contemporary Lamphun), which held sway from the late 8th century until the 13th century. Hariphunchai art and Buddha images are particularly distinctive, and many good examples can be found at the Hariphunchai National Museum in Lamphun.

The Thais, who are thought to have migrated south from China around the 7th century, united various principalities in the 13th century – this resulted in the creation of Sukhothai and the taking of Hariphunchai from the Mon. In 1238 Sukhothai declared itself an independent kingdom under King Si Intharathit and quickly expanded its sphere of influence. Because of this, and the significant influence the kingdom had on Thai art and culture, Sukhothai is considered by Thais to be the first true Thai kingdom.

In 1296 King Mengrai established Chiang Mai after conquering Hariphunchai. Later, in the 14th and 15th centuries, Chiang Mai, in an alliance with Sukhothai, became part of the larger kingdom of Lan Na Thai (Million Thai Rice Fields), popularly referred to as Lanna. This empire extended as far south as Kamphaeng Phet and as far north as Luang Prabang in Laos. However, during the 16th century, many of Lan Na Thai's important alliances weakened or fell apart, ultimately leading to the Burmese capturing Chiang Mai in 1556. Burmese control of Lanna lasted for the next two centuries. The northern Thais ultimately regrouped after the Burmese took Ayuthaya in 1767, and under King Kawila, Chiang Mai was recaptured in 1774 and the Burmese were pushed north.

In the late 19th century, Rama V of Bangkok made efforts to integrate the northern region with the centre to ward off the colonial threat. The completion of the northern railway to Chiang Mai in 1921 strengthened those links until the northern provinces finally became part of the kingdom of Siam in the early part of the 20th century.

along the road to Chiang Mai, the bridge was originally built by Japanese soldiers during WWII.

🏃 Activities

MASSAGE & SPA TREATMENTS

Pai Traditional Thai Massage *Massage*

(PTTM; ☎ 0 5369 9121; www.pttm1989.com; 68/3 Soi 1, Th Wiang Tai; massage per 1/1½/2hr 180/270/350B, sauna per visit 100B, 3-day massage course 2500B; ⊙9am-9pm) This longstanding and locally owned outfit offers very good northern Thai massage, as well as a sauna (cool season only) where you can steam yourself in sà·mŭn·prai (medicinal herbs).

Spa Exotic *Spa*

(☎ 08 1917 9351; www.spaexotic.com; 86 Moo 2, Ban Mae Hi; thermal water soak 80B; ⊙7am-10pm) This resort channels the hot water into its bungalow bathrooms and an open-air pool.

RAFTING & KAYAKING

Rafting along Mae Nam Pai during the wet season (approximately June to February) is also a popular activity. Rates are all-inclusive (rafting equipment, camping gear, dry bags, insurance and food) and run from 1200B to 1500B per person for a one-day trip and from 1800B to 2700B per person for two days.

Pai Adventure Rafting
(0 5369 9385; www.thailandpai.net; 28 Th Chaisongkhram; 8am-10pm) The one- to two-day white-water rafting trips offered by this recommended outfit can be combined with trekking and other activities. Also offers a jungle survival course upon request.

Thai Adventure Rafting Rafting
(0 5369 9111; www.thairafting.com; Th Chaisongkhram; 8am-5pm) This French-run outfit leads one- and two-day rafting excursions. On the way, rafters visit a waterfall, a fossil reef and hot springs; one night is spent at the company's permanent riverside camp.

Back-Trax Rafting
(0 5369 9739; backtraxinpai@yahoo.com; Th Chaisongkhram; 8am-10pm) With more than a decade of experience, this company offers multiday rafting excursions, inner tubing trips and, of course, reiki lessons.

TREKKING

Guided treks range in cost from about 800B to 1000B per person per day, in groups of two or more, and are all-inclusive. Most treks focus on the Lisu, Lahu and Karen villages in and around neighbouring Soppong (Pangmapha). Treks can be booked through guesthouse-based agencies such as the long-standing **Duang Trekking** (0 5369 9101; http://sites. google.com/site/lungtangtrekking; Duang Guest House, Th Chaisongkhram; 8am-8pm), or through specific outfitters, including all of the rafting outfits listed above.

OTHER ACTIVITIES

Thom's Pai Elephant Camp Elephant Rides
(0 5369 9286; www.thomelephant.com; Th Rangsiyanon; elephant rides per person 500-2000B; 9am-6pm) Pai's most established elephant outfitter has an office in town. You can choose between riding bareback or in a seat, and some rides include

swimming with the elephants – a barrel of laughs on a bouncing elephant in the river. Rides include a soak in the hot-spring-fed tubs afterwards.

🎓 Courses

Pai Cookery School Cooking
(08 1706 3799; Th Wanchalerm; lessons 600-750B; lessons 11am-1.30pm & 2-6.30pm) With a decade of experience, this outfit offers a variety of courses spanning three to five dishes. The afternoon course involves a trip to the market for ingredients.

Mam Yoga House Yoga
(08 9954 4981; www.mamyoga.paiexplorer. com; 27 Th Rangsiyanon; lessons 200-550B; 10am-noon & 3-5pm) Just north of the police station, Mam offers Hatha Yoga classes and courses in small groups.

🛏 Sleeping

Despite several years of growth, Pai's accommodation boom continues, and the rumour during our visit was that there were more than 500 hotels, guesthouses and resorts. Yet despite the glut of accommodation, during the height of the Thai tourist season (December and January), accommodation in Pai can be nearly impossible to come by, although tents are available for about 100B.

Keep in mind that prices fluctuate significantly in Pai, and nearly all the midrange and top-end accommodation cut their prices, sometimes by as much as 60%, during the off season.

IN TOWN

Breeze of Pai Guesthouse Hotel $$
(08 1998 4597; suthasinee.svp@gmail.com; Soi Wat Pa Kham; r 400B, bungalows 800B; ❄ 🛜) This well-groomed compound near the river consists of nine attractive and spacious rooms and six large A-frame bungalows. It's close to the action without the noise pollution. A loyal customer base means you'll probably have to book ahead.

KYLIE MCLAUGHLIN/GETTY IMAGES ©

⭐ Don't Miss
Ban Santichon

Foodies make the pilgrimage to Ban Santichon, about 4km outside of Pai, for its authentic assortment of Yunnanese food. There's also a small market, tea tastings, pony rides, a tacky recreation of the Great Wall of China and a **mountaintop viewpoint** (Ban Santichon; admission 20B; ⊙4.30am-6pm) that make this former KMT village not unlike a Chinese-themed Disneyland.

NEED TO KNOW
บ้านสันติชน

Rim Pai Cottage   Hotel $$$
(✆0 5369 9133; www.rimpaicottage.com; Th Chaisongkhram; bungalows 1200-4000B; ❄️📶) The home-like bungalows (incl breakfast only from October to February) here are spread out along a secluded and beautifully wooded section of the Nam Pai. There are countless cosy riverside corners to relax in and a palpable village-like feel about the whole place.

Pai River Villa   Hotel $$$
(✆0 5369 9796; pairivervilla@gmail.com; 7 Th Wiang Tai; bungalows incl breakfast 1200-2500B; ❄️📶) This place boasts some of the more attractive riverside bungalows in town. The air-con bungalows are spacious and stylish, and have wide balconies that encourage lazy riverside relaxing and mountain viewing, while the fan bungalows are a significantly tighter fit.

OUTSIDE OF TOWN

Bueng Pai Farm   Guesthouse $$
(✆08 9265 4768; www.paifarm.com; Ban Mae Hi; bungalows 500-2000B; 📶🏊) Uniting yoga enthusiasts and fisherfolk, the 12 simple bungalows here are strategically and attractively positioned between a functioning farm and a vast pond stocked with freshwater fish.

Bueng Pai is 2.5km from Pai, off the road that leads to Tha Pai Hot Springs; look for the sign.

Pairadise   Hotel $$

(☎ 0 5369 8065; www.pairadise.com; Ban Mae Hi; bungalows 800-1400B; ❄🛜) This neat resort looks over the Pai Valley from atop a ridge just outside of town. The bungalows are stylish and spacious and include gold leaf lotus murals, beautiful rustic bathrooms and terraces with hammocks. All surround a spring-fed pond that is suitable for swimming. The hotel is about 750m east of Mae Nam Pai; look for the sign just after the bridge.

Bulunburi   Hotel $$$

(☎ 0 5369 8302; www.bulunburi.com; Ban Pong; bungalows incl breakfast 600-4000B; ❄@🛜⚡) Set in a tiny secluded valley of rice fields and streams, the seductively bucolic location is as much a reason to stay here as the attractive accommodation. The 11 bungalows, which range from tight fan-cooled rooms to huge two-bedroom houses, are well equipped and stylish.

Bulunburi is about 2.5km from the centre of town along the road to Mae Hong Son; look for the well-posted turn-off, about 1km from Pai.

Pai Treehouse   Hotel $$$

(☎08 1911 3640; www.paitreehouse.com; Mae Hi; bungalows incl breakfast 1000-6500B; ❄🛜) Even if you can't score one of the three treehouse rooms here (they're popular), there are several other attractive bungalows, many near the river. On the vast grounds you'll also find elephants and floating decks on the Mae Nam Pai, all culminating in a family-friendly atmosphere. The resort is 6km east of Pai, just before Tha Pai Hot Springs.

Eating

Larp Khom Huay Poo   Northern Thai $

(Ban Huay Pu; mains 30-70B; ⊙9am-8pm) The house special (and the dish you must order) is *làhp kôo·a,* minced meat (beef or pork) fried with local herbs and spices.

Accompanied by a basket of sticky rice, a plate of bitter herbs and an ice-cold Singha, it's the best meal in Pai.

The restaurant is on the road to Mae Hong Son, about 1km north of town, just past the well-posted turn-off to Sipsongpanna.

Yunnanese Restaurant   Chinese $

(no Roman-script sign; mains 30-180B; ⊙8am-8pm) This open-air place in the Chinese village of Ban Santichon serves the traditional dishes of the town's Yunnanese residents. Standouts include *màntŏ* (steamed buns), here served with pork leg stewed with Chinese herbs.

Or you could always go for the excellent noodles, made by hand and topped with a delicious mixture of minced pork, garlic and sesame. The restaurant is in an open-air adobe building behind the giant rock in Ban Santichon, about 4km west of Pai.

Witching Well   International $

(www.witchingwellrestaurant.com; Th Wiang Tai; mains 75-140B; ⊙7am-11pm; 🛜⚡) This buzzy foreigner-run place is where to come if you're looking for authentic sandwiches, pasta, cakes and pastries. They also do good coffee and the kind of sophisticated breakfasts you're not going to find elsewhere in Pai.

Good Life   International $

(Th Wiang Tai; mains 40-170B; 🛜⚡) Trays of wheat grass and secondhand books (sample title: *The Aloe Answer*) function as interior design at this eclectic and popular cafe.

Charlie & Lek Health Restaurant   Thai $

(Th Rangsiyanon; mains 35-180B; ⊙11am-10pm; ⚡) This popular place does central Thai-style fare for foreigners: lots of veggie options and light on the flavours.

🍷 Drinking & Entertainment

Edible Jazz   Live Music

(www.ediblejazz.com; Soi Wat Pa Kham; ⊙8.30-11pm) Probably Pai's cosiest place for live music. Stroke a cat and nurse a beer while listening to acoustic guitar performances. Depending on who's in town, the open-mic nights on Thursdays and Sundays can be surprisingly good.

Bebop
Live Music

(Th Rangsiyanon; ☺8pm-1am) This legendary box is popular with both locals and travellers and has live music nightly (from about 10pm), emphasising blues, R&B and rock.

ⓘ Getting There & Away

Pai's airport is around 1.5km north of town along Rte 1095. At research time, **Kan Air** (☏0 5369 9955, nationwide 0 2551 6111; www.kanairlines. com; Pai Airport; ☺8.30am-5pm) was the only airline operating out of the town, with a daily connection to Chiang Mai.

Pai's tiny **bus station** (Th Chaisongkhram) is the place to catch slow, fan-cooled buses and more efficient minivans to Chiang Mai and destinations in Mae Hong Son.

Aya Service also runs air-con minivan buses to Chiang Mai (150B, three hours, hourly from 8am to 4.30pm) as well as destinations in Chiang Rai province including Chiang Rai (550B, six hours, 5.30am), Mae Sai (600B, six hours, 5.30am) and Chiang Khong (650B, seven hours, 6pm).

TRANSPORT TO/FROM PAI

Destination	Air	Bus	Minivan
Chiang Mai	1990B; 20min; daily	80B; 3-4hr; noon	150B; 3hr; hourly 7am-4.30pm
Mae Hong Son	–	75B; 3-4hr; 11am	150B; 2½hr; 8.30am

ⓘ Getting Around

Most of Pai is accessible on foot. Motorcycle taxis wait at the taxi stand across from the bus station. Sample fares are 50B to Ban Santichon and 80B to Nam Tok Mo Paeng.

For local excursions you can hire bicycles or motorcycles at several locations around town.

Aya Service (☏0 5369 9888; www.ayaservice. com; 22/1 Th Chaisongkhram; bikes per 24hr 100-400B; ☺8am-9pm) This busy outfit has more than 100 bikes. There are a couple of similar places in the immediate vicinity.

North Wheels (☏0 5369 8066; www. northwheels.com; Th Khetkelang; motorcycle/ car per 24hr 140/1500B; ☺8am-6pm) Both motorcycles and cars can be hired here.

A Pai restaurant

Mae Hong Son แม่ฮ่องสอน

POP 7000

With its remote setting and surrounding mountains, Mae Hong Son fits many travellers' preconceived notion of how a northern Thai city should be. A palpable Burmese influence and a border-town feel don't clash with this image, and best of all, there's hardly a túk-túk or tout to be seen. This doesn't mean Mae Hong Son is uncharted territory – tour groups have been coming here for years – but the city's potential as a base for activities, from spa treatment to trekking, ensures that your visit can be quite unlike anyone else's.

Mae Hong Son is best visited between November and February when the town is at its coolest and most beautiful. During the hot season (approximately February to May), the Mae Nam Pai valley fills with smoke from swidden agriculture. The only problem with going in the cool season is that the nights are downright cold – you'll need at least one sweater and a thick pair of socks for mornings and evenings.

HISTORY

The city was founded as an elephant training outpost in the early 19th century, and remained little more than this until 1856, when fighting in Burma caused thousands of Shan to pour into the area. In the years that followed, Mae Hong Son prospered as a centre for logging and remained an independent kingdom until 1900, when King Rama V incorporated the area into the Thai kingdom.

◉ Sights

With their bright colours, whitewashed stupas and glittering zinc fretwork, Mae Hong Son's Burmese- and Shan-style temples will have you scratching your head wondering which country you're in.

Wat Jong Kham & Wat Jong Klang   Buddhist Temple

(วัดจองคำ/วัดจองกลาง; Th Charm-naan Satit; museum admission by donation; ⊙temple daylight hours, museum 8am-6pm) FREE Wat Jong Kham was built nearly 200 years ago by Thai Yai (Shan) people, who make up about half of the population of Mae Hong Son Province.

Next door, Wat Jong Klang houses 100-year-old glass *jataka* paintings and a **museum** with 150-year-old wooden dolls from Mandalay that depict some of the more gruesome aspects of the wheel of life.

Both temples are lit at night and reflected in Nong Jong Kham – a popular photo op for visitors.

Wat Hua Wiang   Buddhist Temple

(วัดหัวเวียง; Th Phanit Wattana; ⊙daylight hours) FREE This wát, just east of Mae

Wat Jong Kham
AUSTIN BUSH/GETTY IMAGES ©

Hong Son's main street, is recognised for its *bòht* (chapel) boasting an elaborate tiered wooden roof and a revered bronze Buddha statue from Mandalay.

🏃 Activities

TREKKING

Mae Hong Son's location at the edge of mountainous jungle makes it an excellent base for treks into the countryside. Trekking here is not quite the large-scale industry it is elsewhere, and visitors willing to get their boots muddy can expect to find relatively untouched nature and isolated villages. Trekking excursions can be arranged at several guesthouses and travel agencies.

Multiday treks in groups of two people range from 1200B to 3000B per person, per day. As is the case elsewhere in Thailand, the per-day rates drop significantly with a larger group and a longer trek.

Nature Walks   Trekking
(📞 08 9552 6899, 0 5361 1040; www.trekking thailand.com) Although the treks here cost more than elsewhere, John, a native of Mae Hong Son, is the best guide in town.

John has no office; email and phone are the only ways to get in touch with him.

Friend Tour   Trekking
(📞 0 5361 1647; PA Motor, 21 Th Pradit Jong Kham; ⏰ 7.30am-7.30pm) With nearly 20 years' experience, this recommended outfit offers trekking, elephant riding and rafting, as well as day tours. Located at PA Motor.

Namrin Tour   Trekking
(📞 0 5361 4454; 21 Th Pradit Jong Kham; ⏰ 9am-7pm) Mr Dam advertises 'Bad sleep, bad jokes', but his treks get good reports.

BOAT TRIPS

Long-tail boat trips on the nearby Mae Nam Pai are popular, and the same guesthouses and trekking agencies that organise treks from Mae Hong Son can arrange river excursions.

Detour:
Wat Phra That Doi Kong Mu

Climb the hill west of town, Doi Kong Mu (1500m), to visit this **temple compound** (วัดพระธาตุดอย กองมู; ⏰ daylight hours), also known as Wat Plai Doi. Two Shan *chedi*, erected in 1860 and 1874, enshrine the ashes of monks from Myanmar's Shan State. Around the back of the wát you can see a tall, slender, standing Buddha and catch views west of the ridge. There's also a cafe and a small tourist market. The view of the sea of fog that collects in the valley each morning is impressive; at other times you get wonderful views of the town and surrounding valleys.

On Th Pha Doong Muay Do is a long stairway leading to the top of Wat Phra That Doi Kong Mu. An alternative is a motorcycle taxi for 120B return.

MUD SPA

Pooklon Country Club   Spa
(📞 0 5328 2579; www.pooklon.com; mud treatments from 60B, massage per hr 200-400B; ⏰ 8am-6.30pm) This self-professed country club is touted as Thailand's only mud treatment spa.

Pooklon is 16km north of Mae Hong Son in Mok Champae. If you haven't got your own wheels, you can take the daily Ban Ruam Thai– or Mae Aw–bound *sŏrng·tăa·ou* (25B), but this means you might have to find your own way back.

Discovered by a team of geologists in 1995, the mud here is pasteurised and blended with herbs before being employed in various treatments (facial 60B). There's thermal mineral water for soaking (60B), and on weekends, massage (per hour 200B to 400B).

🕐 Tours

Rosegarden Tours   Tours
(📞 0 5361 1681; www.rosegarden-tours.com; 86/4 Th Khunlumprapas; tours from 600B; ⏰ 8.30am-10pm) The English- and French-speaking guides at this longstanding agency focus on cultural and sightseeing tours.

🛏 Sleeping

Mae Hong Son generally lacks inspiring accommodation, although there are a couple of standout midrange options. Because it's a tourist town, accommodation prices fluctuate with the seasons, and outside of the high season (November to January) it's worth pursuing a discount.

Jongkham Place   Guesthouse $$
(📞 0 5361 4294; 4/2 Th Udom Chao Ni-Thet; bungalows/ste 800/1500B; ❄ 🛜) This family-run place by the lake has four attractive wooden bungalows and two penthouse-like suites. All accommodation includes TV, fridge and air-con.

Fern Resort   Resort $$$
(📞 0 5368 6110; www.fernresort.info; off Rte 108; bungalows incl breakfast 2500-3500B; ❄ @ 🛜 ≋) This longstanding ecofriendly resort is one of the pleasanter places to stay in northern Thailand. The 40 wooden bungalows are set among tiered rice paddies and streams and feature stylishly decorated interiors. Nearby nature trails lead to the adjacent Mae Surin National Park.

The downside is that the resort is 7km south of town, but free pick-up is available from the airport and bus terminal, and regular shuttles run to/from town, stopping at Fern Restaurant.

Residence
@MaeHongSon   Hotel $$$
(📞 0 5361 4100; www.theresidence-mhs.com; 41/4 Th Ni-wet Pi-sarn; r 1300-1900B; ❄ 🛜) A cheery yellow building with 10 inviting rooms that boast TV, air-con, fridge, teak

furnishings and lots of windows ensuring ample natural light. There's also a sunny communal rooftop area, a friendly English-speaking owner and bicycles provided free of charge.

🍴 Eating & Drinking

Mae Hong Son's **morning market** (off Th Phanit Wattana; mains 10-30B; ⏰ 6-9am) is a fun place to have breakfast. Several vendors at the north end of the market sell unusual dishes such as *tòo·a òon*, a Burmese noodle dish supplemented with thick chickpea porridge and deep-fried chickpea flour cakes and tofu. Other vendors along the same strip sell a local version of *kà·nŏm jeen nám ngée·o* (thin rice noodles served with a pork-and-tomato-based broth) often topped with *kàhng pòrng,* a Shan snack of battered-and-deep-fried vegetables.

The city also has two good night markets: the **night market** (Th Phanit Wattana; mains 20-60B; ⏰ 4-8pm) near the airport offers mostly takeaway northern Thai–style food, while the **night market** (mains 10-60B; ⏰ 4-9pm) at the southern end of Th Khunlumprapas has more generic Thai food. Several vendors at Mae Hong Song's Walking Street market (p237) also sell a variety of dishes, some local.

Chom Mai Restaurant   Thai $
(www.sesamebar.com; off Rte 108, no Roman-script sign; mains 35-180B; ⏰ 8.30am-3.30pm; 🛜 🍴) The English-language menu here is limited, but don't miss the deliciously rich *kôw soy* or the *kôw mòk gài,* the latter the Thai version of biryani. Chom Mai is located about 4km south of Mae Hong Son along the road that leads to Tha Pong Daeng – look for the Doi Chaang coffee sign.

Banpleng
Restaurant   Northern Thai $
(108 Th Khunlumprapas; mains 30-150B; ⏰ 8am-10pm Mon-Sat) This popular open-air restaurant does a handful of tasty local dishes – you're safe going with anything that says 'Maehongson style' on the English-language menu.

Mae Si Bua
Northern Thai **$**

(cnr Th Pradit Jong Kham & Th Singha-nat Barm Rung, no Roman-script sign; mains 20-30B; ⊙lunch) Like the Shan grandma you never had, Auntie Bua prepares a huge variety of curries, soups and dips on a daily basis.

Salween River Restaurant & Bar
International **$**

(www.salweenriver.com; 23 Th Pradit Jong Kham; mains 40-240B; ⊙8am-10pm; 🛜🍴) Salween is your typical traveller's cafe: a few old guidebooks, free wi-fi and a menu ranging from burgers to Burmese. Yet unlike most traveller's cafes, the food here is good; don't miss the Burmese green tea salad.

Fern Restaurant
International-Thai **$$**

(Th Khunlumprapas; mains 65-285B; ⊙10.30am-10pm; 🛜🍴) The Fern is almost certainly Mae Hong Son's most upscale restaurant, but remember, this is Mae Hong Son. Nonetheless, service is professional and the food is decent. The expansive menu covers Thai, local and even European dishes. There is live lounge music some nights.

Crossroads
Bar

(61 Th Khunlumprapas; ⊙8am-1am) This friendly bar-restaurant is a crossroads in every sense, from its location at one of Mae Hong Son's main intersections to its clientele that ranges from wet-behind-the-ears backpackers to hardened locals. And there's steak.

🔒 Shopping

From October to February the roads around the Jong Kham Lake become a lively **Walking Street** (Th Pradit Jong Kham; ⊙5-10pm Oct-Feb) market, with handicrafts and food vendors.

A few well-stocked souvenir shops can be found near the southern end of Th Khunlumprapas, including **Maneerat** (80 Th Khunlumprapas, no Roman-script sign; ⊙8am-9pm), which features an extensive array of Shan and Burmese clothing, as well as Burmese lacquerware boxes.

🛈 Getting There & Away

For many people the time saved flying from Chiang Mai to Mae Hong Son versus bus travel is worth the extra baht. At research time, **Nok Air** (📞0 5361 2057, nationwide 1318; www.nokair.co.th; Mae Hong Son Airport; ⊙9am-5pm) was the only airline operating out of Mae Hong Song's **airport** (📞08 5361 2057). A túk-túk into town costs about 80B.

Mae Hong Son's bus and minivan station is 1km south of the city; a túk-túk or motorcycle ride to/from here costs 60B. **Prempracha Tour** (📞0 5368 4100; Mae Hong Son Bus Station) runs bus services within the province; **Sombat Tour** (📞0 5361 3211; Mae Hong Son Bus Station) operates connections between Mae Hong Son and Bangkok.

🛈 Getting Around

Because most of Mae Hong Son's attractions are outside of town, renting a motorcycle or bicycle is a wise move.

PA Motor (📞0 5361 1647; 21 Th Pradit Jong Kham; ⊙8am-6.30pm) Next to Friend House, rents motorbikes (150B to 250B per day) and trucks (2500B to 3000B per day).

Transport to/from Mae Hong Son

DESTINATION	AIR	BUS	MINIVAN
Bangkok	–	796-905B; 15hr; 3 departures 2-4pm	–
Chiang Mai	1590B; 35min; 3 daily	145B; 8hr; 8.30am & 12.30pm (northern route); 178-319B; 9hr; frequent 6am-9pm (southern route)	250B; 6hr; hourly 7am-3pm
Pai	–	80B; 4½hr; 8.30am & 4pm	150B; 2½hr; hourly 7am-4pm

Ko Samui & the Gulf Coast

The Gulf Coast mixes convenience with coastal getaways, ranging from international beach resorts to coral-fringed islands.

Known as the 'royal' coast, the Upper Gulf has long been the favoured retreat of the Bangkok monarchy and elite. Every Thai king, dating from Rama IV, has found an agreeable spot to build a royal getaway. Today domestic tourists flock to Hua Hin in the same pursuit of leisure, as well as to pay homage to the revered kings. Indeed this is the country's surf-and-turf destination, offering historic sites, pleasant provincial life and long sandy beaches, all within an easy commute from Bangkok.

The Lower Gulf features Thailand's ultimate island trifecta: Ko Samui, Ko Pha-Ngan and Ko Tao. This family of spectacular islands lures millions of tourists every year with powder-soft sands, emerald waters, pumping parties and diving and snorkelling.

Hat Lamai (p261), Ko Samui

WELCOME
Oil massage 300
THAI massage 300
FACIALS massage 300
FOOT massage 250
HEEL SCRUB 250

Hat Chaweng (p260), Ko Samui
SHAUN EGAN/GETTY IMAGES ©

Ko Samui & the Gulf Coast

Khao Yai
(1204m)

*Kheuan
Pran Buri*

Hua Hin ❷

Phetchaburi ❹
(25km)

Ko Singtoh
Khao Takiap
Khao Tao
Pranburi

4

Khao Sam Roi Yot
National Park

Dolphin Bay

Bang Pu

Kuiburi
National Park

Kuiburi

**PRACHUAP
KHIRI KHAN**

*Ao Khan
Kradai*

M Y A N M A R
(B U R M A)

**Prachuap
Khiri Khan**

Ao Noi
Ao Prachuap
Ao Manao

Dan Singkhon

Ko Raet

Ko Phing

Thap
Sakae

Ko Phang

*GULF OF
THAILAND*

0   50 km
0   25 miles

Khao Thwe
(891m)

4

Bang
Saphan Yai

Ao Bang Saphan

Khao Daen Noi
(582m)

Bang
Saphan
Noi

Ko Thalu

Ko Sing

Ko Sang

Ko Wiang

Tha Sae

CHUMPHON

Chumphon

Ko Jarakhe

Ko Ngam Yai &
Ko Ngam Noi

4

Pak Nam

Ku Poh
National Park

*Ao
Sawi*

Ko Samet

Ko Mattara

Ko Maphrao

Ko Rang Kachiu

Sawi

4139

Tako Estuary

Laem Riu

Ko Tao

Isthmus
of Kra

4006

Lang Suan

Chong Tao

Lamae

41

Ang Thong
Marine
National Park

Ko Pha-Ngan

❺

❸

Chong Pha-Ngan

Laem
Sui

Ko
Phaluai

❶ Ko Samui

Chaiya

*Ao Ban
Don*

Don Sak

Chong Samui

Phun Phin

**Surat
Thani**

401

Khanom

Ao Khanom

Hin Lat Falls

401

❶ Ko Samui

❷ Hua Hin

❸ Ang Thong National
Marine Park

❹ Phetchaburi

❺ Ko Pha-Ngan

Ko Samui & the Gulf Coast's Highlights

Ko Samui

Ko Samui (p257) is a tropical paradise with convenient air links to Bangkok. The island has beautiful beaches, amazing jungle and a sleepy island lifestyle tucked under the palm trees. At the popular beaches there's fine dining, modern conveniences, raucous recreation and lots of people-watching. But quiet corners for coastal castaways still survive. Below: Hat Chaweng (p260)

Hua Hin

A favourite weekend getaway for Bangkok's high society (including the royal family), Hua Hin (p250) is a friend indeed if beach time is short and the need for comfort is high. It is the closest to the capital with long, sandy beaches, fantastic seafood and classy city accoutrements. The only trade-off is it lacks that island vibe. Left: Mrigadayavan Palace, the Thai royal family's former Hua Hin retreat

NEAL MCCLIMON/GETTY IMAGES ©

Ang Thong National Marine Park **3**

Float between the mysterious and uninhabited islands of Ang Thong National Marine Park (p269). Blonde beaches skirt the statuesque islands that stretch from cerulean seas into the milky sky. Their limestone cliffs are dimpled and carved by millennia of crashing waves. Paddle up close to view the cliff-clinging creatures and plants that survive the sea's diurnal tides.

Phetchaburi **4**

An easy day trip from Hua Hin, this former royal retreat (p248) boasts a hilltop palace, curious cave temples and a huge dose of provincial ambience. It is a popular stop for school groups, eager to work up the courage to say 'hello' to foreigners, and for you to feel off-the-path without being far-flung. Above: Tham Khao Luang (p248)

Ko Pha-Ngan **5**

Ko Pha-Ngan (p268) has mythic status as a getaway for youthful pursuits from excessive beach raves to intense chill-laxin'. Sloppy drunk Full Moon parties bring in a tide of bodies and every other day requires doing nothing or recovering from doing too much the night before. Though creeping ever-closer to civilisation, the island is still blissfully under-developed. Above: Nightlife, Hat Rin (p274)

Ko Samui & the Gulf Coast's Best…

Diving & Snorkelling Spots

○ **Ko Tao** First stop for beginners to get dive certified; snorkel spots are steps from shore. (p279)

○ **Ko Pha-Ngan** Fun dives, fewer divers. (p268)

○ **Ang Thong National Marine Park** Underwater sightseeing tours to a surreal landscape of craggy limestone islands and cerulean seas. (p269)

Seafood

○ **Hua Hin** Mingle with holidaying Thais in al fresco night markets or antique shophouses at this seafood capital. (p252)

○ **Ko Samui** Destination dining for superb gastronomy and seaside settings. (p263)

○ **Ko Tao** The island that plays hard eats well, with kitchens that are more sophisticated than the rustic island suggests. (p278)

Party Places

○ **Ko Pha-Ngan** The poster-child of beach revelry, Ko Pha-Ngan's monthly raves are a smear of day-glo body paint, fire-twirlers, chest-thumping beats and drunken abandon. (p274)

○ **Castle** Ko Tao's rave party abode. (p279)

○ **Chaweng** Ko Samui's most popular beach reigns day and night with beachside bars, raucous discos and an assortment of party people. (p267)

Need to Know

Spas & Health Resorts

○ **Spa Resort** Ko Samui's first health retreat delivers health and wellness in a seaside setting. (p259)

○ **Tamarind Retreat** Spa among the trees and the boulders at this top-notch retreat. (p259)

○ **Sanctuary** Release your inner hippie at Ko Pha-Ngan's homage to all things New Age. (p272)

Left: Day spa, Ko Samui (p257);
Above: Ko Tao (p275)

(LEFT) MATTHEW WAKEM/GETTY IMAGES ©;
(ABOVE) GONZALO AZUMENDI/GETTY IMAGES ©

Ko Samui & the Gulf Coast Itineraries

Take a long weekend or a five-day escape to the Gulf Coast's prime attractions. Next time you can come back and be a beach hermit.

3 DAYS

HUA HIN TO PHETCHABURI
Quick Beach Break

❶ **Hua Hin** (p250) is one of the quickest and easiest beach escapes from Bangkok, an ideal road commute without the hassle of a ferry transfer. The beachfront hotels meet international standards and the nightly food market specialises in unbeatable seafood. For many Thais, the night market is the sole reason for a visit.

The mainland beach is another powerful contender, with its expanse of powder-soft sand punctuated by a rocky headland. Atop the cliff is a giant golden Buddha and temple, while sprinkled against sea and sky are colourful kites attached to wave-jumping kite boarders. It is an unbeatable convergence of city conveniences, modern attractions and coastal backdrop.

Take a break from the beach and head to ❷ **Phetchaburi** (p248) for a bit of culture – this nearby provincial town boasts a hilltop palace and a Gaudi-esque cave temple. Or day trip to ❸ **Khao Sam Roi Yot National Park** (p255), a nature preserve filled with limestone caves, the country's largest freshwater marsh and migrating birds.

Top Left: Khao Sam Roi Yot National Park (p255);
Top Right: Ko Tao (p275)

5 DAYS

KO SAMUI TO CHUMPHON

Toast the Samui Sisters

The Gulf Coast's premier island, ❶ **Ko Samui** (p257) appeals to every kind of traveller and is easily accessible from Bangkok by air. Base yourself in lovely but raucous Chaweng to be close to the action, or retreat to the laid-back northern beaches of Mae Nam and Bo Phut. Consider dabbling in the island's various health treatments, from beachside yoga to three-day fasts. Rent a motorcycle and tour the sleepy backwater villages in the southern part of the island.

Swim among the craggy and curiously shaped limestone islands of ❷ **Ang Thong National Marine Park** (p269), a popular day trip from Samui. If your timing is right, you can ferry to ❸ **Ko Pha-Ngan** (p268) for the monthly beachside raves. Welcome the rising sun and hop back to Samui for some well-earned sleep.

Devote a few days to a snorkelling or diving tour of ❹ **Ko Tao** (p275), a small island sheltering colourful coral gardens. The west coast is monopolised by the diving scene, while the rocky coves of the east coast are for solitude seekers. Then ferry to the mainland port of ❺ **Chumphon** (p255) to catch an overnight train back to Bangkok.

Discover Ko Samui & the Gulf Coast

At a Glance

- **Phetchaburi** (p248) Culture stop for royal palaces and cave temples.
- **Hua Hin** (p250) Classy seaside town with great seafood.
- **Chumphon** (p255) Northernmost mainland transfer to Samui islands.
- **Ko Tao** (p275) Dive-centric island.
- **Ko Pha-Ngan** (p268) Mellow bohemian island, unless there's a full moon.
- **Ko Samui** (p257) Well-rounded resort island.
- **Surat Thani** (p256) Southernmost transfer point to Samui islands.

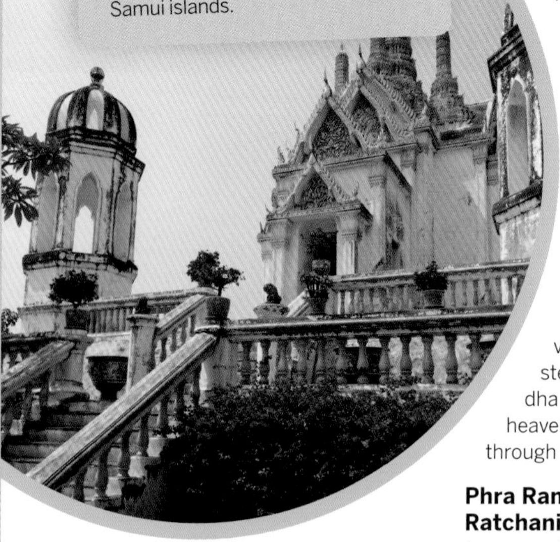

Phra Nakhon Khiri Historical Park

THOMAS KOKTA/GETTY IMAGES ©

MAINLAND GULF COAST

Phetchaburi (Phetburi)

เพชรบุรี

POP 46,600

An easy escape from Bangkok, Phetchaburi should be on every cultural traveller's itinerary. It has temples and palaces, outlying jungles and cave shrines, as well as easy access to the coast.

Historically, Phetchaburi is a visible timeline of kingdoms that have migrated across Southeast Asia. The town is often referred to as a 'Living Ayuthaya', since the equivalent of the many relics that were destroyed in the former kingdom's capital are still intact here.

Sights & Activities

Tham Khao Luang Cave

(ถ้ำเขาหลวง; 8am-6pm) FREE About 4km north of town is Tham Khao Luang, a dramatic stalactite-stuffed chamber that is one of Thailand's most impressive cave shrines and a favourite of Rama IV. Accessed via a steep set of stairs, its central Buddha figure is often illuminated with a heavenly glow when sunlight filters in through the heart-shaped skylight.

Phra Ram Ratchaniwet Historical Site

(พระรามราชนิเวศน์; 0 3242 8083; Ban Peun Palace; admission 50B; 8.30am-4.30pm Mon-Fri) Construction of this elegant summer palace began in 1910 at the behest of Rama V (who

Don't Miss
Phra Nakhon Khiri Historical Park

This national historical park sits regally atop Khao Wang (Palace Hill) surveying the city of Phetchaburi with subdued opulence. Rama IV (King Mongkut) built the palace, in a mix of European and Chinese styles, and surrounding temples in 1859 as a retreat from Bangkok. The hilltop location allowed the king to pursue his interest in astronomy and stargazing. There are two entrances to the site. The front entrance is across from Th Ratwithi and involves a strenuous footpath. The back entrance is on the opposite side of the hill and has a tram that glides up and down the summit.

NEED TO KNOW

อุทยานประวัติศาสตร์พระนครคีรี; ☏0 3240 1006; admission 150B, tram return adult/child 40B/free; ⊗park & tram 8.30am-4.30pm

died just after the project was started). The incredible art nouveau creation was designed by German architects, who used the opportunity to showcase contemporary design innovations. Inside there are spacious sun-drenched rooms decorated with exquisite glazed tiles, stained glass, parquet floors and plenty of wrought-iron details.

The palace is on a military base 1km south of town; you may be required to show your passport.

Sleeping

2N Guesthouse Guesthouse **$**
(☏0 3240 1309; two_nguesthouse@hotmail.com; 98/3 Mu 2, Tambol Bankoom; d & tw 580B; ❄⊚) There are only six big and bright rooms, all with small balconies, here. The friendly staff are a solid source of information and they offer free pick-ups and bicycles.

Monkey Business

Phetchaburi is full of macaque monkeys who know no shame or fear. They lurk by food stands, or eye up passing pedestrians as potential mugging victims. Keep a tight hold on camera bags too. Above all, don't feed or bait the monkeys. They do bite.

Sun Hotel
Hotel $$
(📞 0 3240 1000; www.sunhotelthailand.com; 43/33 Soi Phetkasem; r 900-1150B; ❄@🛜) The only realistic midrange option in town, the Sun Hotel sits opposite the back entrance to Phra Nakhon Khiri. It has large, modern but uninspired rooms with professional staff.

 Eating

Rabieng Rim Nam
International-Thai $
(📞 0 3242 5707; 1 Th Chisa-In; dishes 45-80B; ⏰7am-10pm; @🛜) This riverside restaurant serves up terrific food and the English-speaking owner is a fount of tourist information.

Night Market
Thai $
(Th Ratwithi; ⏰4pm-10pm) Big and bustling from the late afternoon, this is the place to head for all the standard Thai fast food favourites and decent barbecue.

ℹ Getting There & Away

The stop for buses to Bangkok is at the back of the night market. Across the street is a minivan stop with services to Bangkok.

Most southbound air-conditioned buses and minivans stop out of town on Th Phetkasem in front of the Big C department store. Motorcycle taxis await and can take you into town for around 50B.

Frequent rail services run to/from Bangkok's Hua Lamphong station.

ℹ Getting Around

Motorcycle taxis go anywhere in the town centre for 40B to 50B. *Sŏrng·tăa·ou* (pick-up trucks) cost about the same. It's a 20-minute walk (1km) from the train station to the town centre.

Rabieng Rim Nam restaurant hires out bicycles (100B per day) and motorbikes (200B to 300B per day).

Hua Hin   หัวหิน

POP 98,896

Thailand's original beach resort is no palm-fringed castaway island and arguably is the better for it. Instead, it is a delightful mix of city and sea with a cosmopolitan ambience, lively markets, tasty street eats, long beaches and fully functional city services (meaning no septic streams bisect the beach like those *other* places).

Hua Hin traces its aristocratic roots to the 1920s when Rama VI (King Vajiravudh) and Rama VII (King Prajadhipok) built summer residences

Transport to/from Phetchaburi

DESTINATION	BUS	MINIVAN	TRAIN
Bangkok Hua Lamphong	–	–	84-388B; 3-4hr; 12 daily 1.53am-4.47pm
Bangkok southern bus terminal	120B; 2-3hr; 8.30am & 10.30am	100B; 2hr; hourly 7am-6pm	–
Bangkok Victory Monument	–	100B; 2hr; every 45min 5am-6pm	–
Hua Hin from Th Matayawong	40B; 1½ hours; frequent	–	12 daily

here to escape Bangkok's stifling climate. The most famous of the two is **Phra Ratchawang Klai Kangwon** (Far from Worries Palace), 3km north of town. It's still a royal residence today and so poetically named that Thais often invoke it as a city slogan.

Sights

The city's beaches are numerous, wide and long; swimming is safe, and Hua Hin continues to enjoy some of the peninsula's driest weather. During stormy weather, watch out for jellyfish.

HUA HIN TOWN เมืองหัวหิน

A former fishing village, Hua Hin town retains its roots with an old teak shophouse district bisected by narrow soi, pier houses that have been converted into restaurants or guesthouses and a busy fishing pier still in use today. South of the harbour is a rocky headland that inspired the name 'Hua Hin', meaning 'Stone Head'.

KHAO TAKIAB เขาตะเกียบ

About 7km south of Hua Hin, Khao Takiab (Takiab Mountain) guards the southern end of Hua Hin beach and is adorned with a giant standing Buddha. Atop the 272m mountain is a Thai-Chinese temple (**Wat Khao Lat**) and many resident monkeys who are not to be trusted – but the views are great. Green *sŏrng·tăa·ou* go all the way from Hua Hin to Khao Takiab village, where you'll find loads of simple Thai eateries serving fish straight off the fishing boats that dock here.

Activities

Kiteboarding Asia   Kiteboarding
(📞08 1591 4593; www.kiteboardingasia.com; South Hua Hin; beginner courses

11,000B) This long-established company operates three beachside shops that rent kite-boarding equipment and offer lessons.

Hua Hin Golf Centre   Golf
(📞0 3253 0476; www.huahingolf.com; Th Selakam; ⏰noon-9pm) The friendly staff at this pro shop can steer you to the most affordable, well-maintained courses where the monkeys won't try to run off with your balls. The company also organises golf tours and rents sets of clubs (500B to 700B per day).

👉 Tours

Hua Hin Bike Tours   Cycling Tours
(📞08 1173 4469; www.huahinbiketours.com; 15/120 Th Phetkasem btwn Soi 27 & 29; tours 1500-2750B) Pedal to the Hua Hin Hills Vineyard for some well-earned refreshment, tour the coastal byways south of Hua Hin, or ride among the limestone mountains of Khao Sam Roi Yot National Park.

Playing golf, Hua Hin
ENVIROMANTIC/GETTY IMAGES ©

Sleeping

HUA HIN TOWN

Fulay Guesthouse Guesthouse **$**
(📞0 3251 3145; www.fulayhuahin.net; 110/1
Th Naresdamri; r 550-900B; ❄️ 🛜) With the
waves crashing underneath and the
floorboards creaking, this is a fine old-
school pier guesthouse. Good beds, OK
bathrooms and flowering plants in the
common area.

Tai Tai Guest House Guesthouse **$$**
(📞0 3251 2891; 1/8 Th Chomsin; r 800B;
❄️ @ 🛜) Formerly known as the Supasu-
da, the large rooms come with excellent
beds, mermaid murals and hot showers.
The more expensive ones have verandahs
and a bit of road noise. There's a cosy
communal roof terrace.

Hotel Alley Hotel **$$**
(📞0 3251 1787; www.hotelalleyhuahin.com; 13/5
Soi Hua Hin 63, Th Phetkasem; r 1200-1400B;
😀 ❄️ 🛜) New hotel in a quiet soi with
spacious rooms decorated in pastel col-

ours. Most have balconies and breakfast
is included.

HUA HIN BEACHES

Rahmahyah Hotel Guesthouse **$$**
(📞0 3253 2106; Rahmahyah@yahoo.co.uk;
113/10 Soi Hua Hin 67, Th Phetkasem, South Hua
Hin; r 800-1200B; ❄️ 🛜 🏊) Across the street
from Market Village, about 1km south
of town, is a small guesthouse enclave
tucked between the high-end resorts,
with beach access. The Rahmahyah is the
best of the bunch with clean, functional
rooms. Guests can use the communal
swimming pool opposite.

Baan Bayan Hotel **$$$**
(📞0 3253 3540; www.baanbayan.com; 119
Th Phetkasem, South Hua Hin; r 3300-9000B;
❄️ 🛜 🏊 🚹) A colonial beach house built
in the early 20th century, Baan Bayan
is perfect for travellers seeking a luxury
experience without the overkill of a big
resort. Airy, high-ceilinged rooms, at-
tentive staff and the location is absolute
beachfront.

Baan Laksasubha Hotel **$$$**
(📞0 3251 4525; www.baanlaksasubha.com; Th
53/7 Naresdamri; r 2999-13,275B; ❄️ 🛜 🏊)
Sixteen much-in-demand cottages are
on offer at this petite resort, owned by
a Bangkok aristocrat. The decor is
crisp and subdued, meandering
garden paths lead to the beach
and there's a dedicated kid's
room with toys and books.
The taxi drivers will under-
stand you better if you say
'baan lak-su-pah'.

Eating

**Night
Market** Thai **$**
(Th Dechanuchit btwn Th
Phetkasem & Th Sasong;
dishes from 50B; ⏰5pm-
midnight) An attraction
that rivals the beach, Hua
Hin's night market tops

Hua Hin
IGOR PRAHIN/GETTY IMAGES ©

Weekend Eating with Bangkok's Thais

On weekends, a different kind of tidal system occurs in Hua Hin. Bangkok professionals flow in, filling hotels and restaurants on Th Naebkehardt, washing over the night market and crowding into nightclubs. Come Sunday they clog the roadways heading north, obeying the pull of the upcoming work week.

And because of restaurant features on Thai TV or food magazines, everyone goes to the same places. To join the flow, don your designer sunglasses and elbow your way to a table at one of these popular spots in North Hua Hin:

Sôm·đam Stand (Th Naebkehardt; dishes 25-70B; ⏱10am-2pm) Across from Iammeuang Hotel is a *sôm·đam* stand that easily wipes out the country's supply of green papayas in one weekend.

Eighteen Below Ice Cream (Th Naebkehardt; ice cream from 69B; ⏱11am-5pm, closed Tue) At the end of the road behind Baan Talay Chine Hotel, this gourmet ice-cream shop is run by a trained chef and specialises in rich and creamy flavours.

Ratama (12/10 Th Naebkehardt; dishes 50-390B; ⏱10am-10pm) New spot for visiting hipsters with a menu that runs from simple noodle dishes to great, spicy seafood curries.

Jae Siam (Th Naebkehardt; dishes 35-60B; ⏱9am-10pm) The shop is famous for *gŏo·ay đĕe·o mŏo đŭn* (stewed pork noodles) and *gŏo·ay đĕe·o gài đŭn* (stewed chicken noodles).

locals' lists of favourite spots to eat. ITry *pàt pŏng gà·rèe ƀoo* (crab curry), *gûng tôrt* (fried shrimp) and *hŏy tôrt* (fried mussel omelette).

Jek Pia Coffeeshop Thai $
(51/6 Th Dechanuchit; dishes 80-160B; ⏱9am-1pm & 5.30-8.30pm) More than just a coffee shop, this 50-year-old restaurant is a culinary destination specialising in an extensive array of stir-fried seafood dishes. It's wildly popular with the locals and they stick rigidly to their serving hours; get here after 7.30pm and you won't be able to order.

Hua Hin Koti Thai $$
(☎0 3251 1252; 16/1 Th Dechanuchit; dishes 120-300B; ⏱11am-10pm) Across from the night market, this Thai-Chinese restaurant is a national culinary luminary. Thais adore the fried crab balls, while foreigners swoon over *đôm yam gûng* (shrimp soup with lemon grass).

Sang Thai Restaurant Seafood $$
(Th Naresdamri; dishes 100-300B; ⏱10am-11pm) One of many beloved pier-side restaurants, Sang Thai is a Hua Hin institution and a massive operation. There's a vast choice of seafood housed in giant tanks awaiting your decision.

🍷 Drinking & Entertainment

No Name Bar Bar
(Th Naresdamri) Past the Chinese shrine that sits on the rocky headland is this cliff-side bar. It feels miles away from the lurid and loud hostess bars and is perfect for a chilled beer; sit and listen to the waves slapping against the rocks below.

Mai Tai Cocktail & Beer Garden Bar
(33/12 Th Naresdamri) Recession-era prices are on tap at this convivial, always crowded outdoor terrace made for people-watching and beer-drinking.

Kite Crazy

From here down to Pranburi, the winds blow from the northeast from October to December, and then from the southeast from January to May: perfect for kitesurfing. Even during the May to October rainy season, there are plenty of days when the wind is fine for taking to the waves. In fact, this stretch of coast is so good for kiteboarding that Hua Hin hosted the Kiteboarding World Cup in 2010.

ⓘ Getting There & Away

Hua Hin's long-distance bus station (Th Phetkasem btwn Soi Hua Hin 94 & 98) is south of town and goes to Chiang Mai, Prachuap Khiri Khan, Phuket, Surat Thani and Ubon Ratchathani. Buses to Bangkok leave from a bus company's in-town office (Th Sasong), near the night market. Buses to Bangkok Suvarnabhumi International Airport leave from the long-distance bus station.

Lomprayah offers a bus-boat combination from Hua Hin to Ko Tao (1000B, 8½ hours, one morning and one night departure).

Minivans go to Bangkok's Sai Tai Mai (southern) bus terminal and Victory Monument. A direct service to Victory Monument leaves from an office on the corner of Th Phetkasem and Th Chomsin.

There are frequent trains running to/from Bangkok's Hua Lamphong station and other stations on the southern railway line.

ⓘ Getting Around

Green sŏrng·tăa·ou depart from the corner of Th Sasong and Th Dechanuchit, near the night market and travel south on Th Phetkasem to Khao Takiab (20B). Pranburi-bound buses (20B) depart from the same stop.

Túk-túk fares in Hua Hin are outrageous and start at a whopping 100B and barely budge from there. Motorcycle taxis are much more reasonable (40B to 50B) for short hops.

Motorcycles (250B to 500B per day) can be hired from shops on Th Damnoen Kasem and Th Chomsin. Thai Rent A Car (☏ 0 2737 8888; www.thairentacar.com) is a professional car-rental agency with competitive prices, a well-maintained fleet and hotel drop-offs.

Transport to/from Hua Hin

DESTINATION	AIR	BUS	MINIVAN	TRAIN
Bangkok Don Muang Airport	from 1500B Nok Air; 1hr; 3 weekly	–	–	–
Bangkok Hua Lamphong		–	–	44-421B; 5-6hr; 13 daily 12.45am-4.01pm
Bangkok southern bus terminal		175B; 4½hr; 8 daily 3am-9pm	–	
Bangkok Suvarnabhumi Airport		305B; 5hr; 6 daily 7am-6pm	–	
Bangkok Victory Monument		–	180B; 4hr; every 30min 6am-7pm	–
Ko Tao		1000B; 8½hr; 1 daily	–	–
Phetchaburi		40B; 1½hr; frequent	–	30-40B; 12 daily

Chumphon ชุมพร

POP 55,835

A transit town funnelling travellers to and from Ko Tao or westwards to Ranong or Phuket, Chumphon is also where the south of Thailand starts proper; Muslim headscarves are a common sight here.

Travel agencies and guesthouses can book tickets, provide timetables and point you to the right bus stop; fortunately agents in Chumphon are a dedicated lot.

🛏 Sleeping

Suda Guest House   Guesthouse $

(📞 08 0144 2079; 8 Soi Sala Daeng 3; r 250-650B; ❄ @ 🛜) Suda, the friendly English-speaking owner, maintains her impeccable standards with six rooms, all with wooden floors and a few nice touches that you wouldn't expect for the price. It's very popular so phone ahead.

Fame Guest House   Guesthouse $

(📞 0 7757 1077; 188/20-21 Th Sala Daeng; r 200-300B; @ 🛜) A fa·ràng (Westerner) depot, Fame does a little bit of everything, from providing basic but OK rooms, to booking tickets and renting motorbikes.

Chumphon Cabana Resort & Diving Centre   Hotel $$$

(📞 0 7756 0245; www.cabana.co.th; Hat Thung Wua Laen; r 1650-3000B; ❄ 🛜 ⊠) 🍃 The most pleasant resort on the beach, despite the rather plain bungalows, Chumphon Cabana has done a great job upgrading its environmental profile.

Now, the grounds are devoted to raising the resort's own food with rice fields, hydroponic vegetable gardens and a chicken farm. Waste water is recycled through water-hyacinth ponds. And their efforts are used to instruct others. If you don't stay here, at least try the homegrown food at Rabieng Talay, the resort's affiliated restaurant.

🍴 Eating & Drinking

Chumphon's **night market** (Th Krom Luang Chumphon) is excellent, with a huge

Detour:
Khao Sam Roi Yot National Park

Towering limestone outcrops form a rocky jigsaw-puzzle landscape at this 98-sq-km **park** (📞 0 3282 1568; www.dnp.go.th; adult/child 200/100B), the name of which means Three Hundred Mountain Peaks. There are also caves, beaches and coastal marshlands to explore for outdoor enthusiasts and bird-watchers.

With its proximity to Hua Hin, the park is well travelled by day-trippers and contains a mix of public conservation land and private shrimp farms, so don't come expecting remote virgin territory.

Travel agencies in Hua Hin run day trips to the park. Hua Hin Bike Tours (p251) offers cycling and hiking tours.

variety of tempting food options and good people-watching. There are **day markets** along Th Tha Taphao and Th Pracha Uthit. Th Sala Daeng and Th Pracha Uthit are both lined with hole-in-the-wall noodle joints.

Prikhorm   Southern Thai $$

(32 Th Tha Taphao; dishes from 80B; ⏰ 10.30am-11pm) The place where the locals come for genuine, fiery and delicious southern Thai cuisine. The gaang sôm is a superbly spicy and flavoursome fish curry, and all the other dishes are delicious.

Ocean Shopping Mall   International $$

(off Th Sala Daeng; dishes 150-250B; ⏰ 9am-8pm) It isn't exactly a culinary destination but Chumphon's shopping mall has air-con and chain restaurants for cool and convenient layover noshing.

ⓘ Getting There & Away

Boat

You have many boat options for getting to Ko Tao, though departure times are limited to mainly morning and night.

Bus

The main bus terminal is on the highway, an inconvenient 16km from Chumphon. To get there you can catch a *sŏrng·tăa·ou* (50B) from Th Nawamin Ruamjai. You'll have to haggle with the opportunistic taxi drivers for night transit to/from the station; no matter what they tell you, it shouldn't cost more than 200B.

There are several in-town bus stops to save you a trip out to the main bus station.

Train

There are frequent services to/from Bangkok (2nd class 292B to 382B, 3rd class 235B, 7½ hours). Overnight sleepers range from 440B to 770B.

ⓘ Getting Around

Sŏrng·tăa·ou and motorcycle taxis around town cost 40B and 20B respectively per trip. *Sŏrng·tăa·ou* to Hat Thung Wua Laen cost 30B.

Motorcycles can be rented at travel agencies and guesthouses for 200B to 350B per day.

Surat Thani อำเภอเมืองสุราษฎร์ธานี

POP 128,990

Travellers rarely linger here as they make their way to the popular islands of Ko Samui, Ko Pha-Ngan and Ko Tao, but it's a great stop if you enjoy real Thai working cities and good southern style street food.

🛏 Sleeping & Eating

My Place @ Surat Hotel   Hotel $

(☏0 7727 2288; www.myplacesurat.com; 247/5 Na Meuang Rd; fan r with/without bathroom 260/199B, air-con r with bathroom 490B; ❄ 🛜) This spiffed-up Chinese hotel has surprising touches like bright paint, colourful throw cushions and modern art on the walls. It's clean, very central and the best bargain in town.

Night Market   Market $

(Sarn Chao Ma; Th Ton Pho; dishes from 35B; ⏱6-11pm) A truly fantastic smorgasbord of food including lots of melt-in-your-mouth marinated meats on sticks, fresh fruit juices, noodle dishes and desserts.

Transport to/from Chumphon

DESTINATION	AIR	BOAT	BUS	TRAIN
Bangkok Don Muang Airport	from 1674B; 2 flights daily on Nok Air	–	–	–
Bangkok Hua Lamphong		–	–	192-1162B; 8hr; 11 daily
Bangkok southern bus terminal		–	380-590B; 8hr; 11 daily	–
Ko Tao via car ferry		400B; 6hr; 1 daily (11pm Mon-Sat)	–	–
Ko Tao via Lomprayah		600B; 1½hr; 2 daily (7am & 1pm)	–	–
Ko Tao via slow boat		250B; 6hr; 1 daily (midnight)	–	–
Ko Tao via Songserm		500B; 3hr; 1 daily (7am)	–	–
Phetchaburi		–	210B; 5 daily; 6hr	11 daily
Phuket		–	350B; 4 daily; 3½hr	–

ℹ️ Getting There & Away

In general, if you are departing Bangkok or Hua Hin for Ko Pha-Ngan or Ko Tao, consider taking the train or a bus-boat package that goes through Chumphon rather than Surat. You'll save time, and the journey will be more comfortable. Travellers heading to/from Ko Samui will most likely pass through. If you require travel services, try **Pranthip Co** (Th Talat Mai) – it is reliable and English is spoken.

Air

There are daily shuttles to Bangkok on **Thai Airways International** (THAI; ☎ 0 7727 2610; 3/27-28 Th Karunarat), **Air Asia** (www.airasia. com) and **Nok Air** (www.nokair.com).

Boat

Various ferry companies offer services to the islands. Try **Lomprayah** (☎ 077 4277 656; www. lomprayah.com), **Seatran Discovery** (☎ 0 2240 2582; www.seatrandiscovery.com) or **Songserm** (☎ 0 7737 7704; www.songserm-expressboat. com).

From the centre of Surat there are nightly ferries to Ko Tao (eight hours, departs at 10pm), Ko Pha-Ngan (seven hours, departs at 10pm) and Ko Samui (six hours, departs at 11pm). These are cargo ships, not luxury boats, so bring food and water and watch your bags.

Bus & Minivan

The most convenient way to travel around the south, frequent buses and minivans depart from two main locations in town known as Talat Kaset 1 and Talat Kaset 2.

The 'new' bus terminal (which is actually a few years old now, but still referred to as new by the locals) is 7km south of town on the way to Phun Phin. This hub services traffic to and from Bangkok (380B to 800B, 11 to 14 hours).

BUSES & MINIVANS FROM SURAT THANI

Destination	Fare (B)	Duration
Bangkok	421-856	10hr
Hat Yai	160-240	5hr
Khanom	100	1hr
Krabi	150	2½hr
Phuket	200	6hr
Trang	190	2hr 10min

Train

When arriving by train you'll actually pull into Phun Phin, a nondescript town 14km west of

Detour:
Wine Tasting

Part of the New Latitudes wine movement, the **Hua Hin Hills Vineyard** (ไร่องุ่นหัวหินฮิลล์ วินยาร์ด; ☎ 08 1701 0222; www.huahinhillsvineyard. com; Th Hua Hin-Pa Lu-U; vineyard tour 1500-2100B, wine tasting 3 glasses 290B; ⏰ 9am-7pm) is nestled in a scenic mountain valley 45km west of Hua Hin. The loamy sand and slate soil feeds several Rhone grape varieties that are used in its Monsoon Valley wine label. Daily vineyard tours include return transport, wine and a three-course meal. Or you can just do the wine tasting.

Surat. The trip to Bangkok takes over 8½ hours and costs 107B to 1379B depending on class.

ℹ️ Getting Around

Air-conditioned vans to/from Surat Thani airport cost around 100B per person and they'll drop you off at your hotel.

To travel around town, *sŏrng·tăa·ou* cost 10B to 30B (it's 15B to reach Tesco-Lotus from the city centre).

GULF ISLANDS

Ko Samui   เกาะสมุย
POP 50,000

Ko Samui is like a well-established Hollywood celebrity: she's outrageously manicured, has lovely blond tresses and has gracefully removed all of her wrinkles without more than a peep in the tabloids.

Behind the glossy veneer there's still a glimmer of the girl from the country. Look for steaming street-side food stalls beyond the beach, backpacker shanties plunked down on quiet stretches of sand

Ko Samui

and secreted Buddhist temples along the backstreets.

⊙ Sights

Hin-Ta & Hin-Yai   Landmark
At the south end of **Hat Lamai**, the second-largest beach, you'll find these infamous stone formations (also known as Grandfather and Grandmother Rocks). These rocks, shaped like genitalia, provide endless mirth for giggling Thai tourists.

Ban Hua Thanon   Neighbourhood
Just beyond Hat Lamai, Hua Thanon is home to a vibrant Muslim community, and its anchorage of high-bowed fishing vessels is a veritable gallery of intricate designs.

Nam Tok Na Muang   Waterfall
At 30m, this is the tallest waterfall on Samui and lies in the centre of the island about 12km from Na Thon. The water cascades over ethereal purple rocks, and there's a great pool for swimming at the base. This is the most scenic – and somewhat less frequented – of Samui's falls.

Nam Tok Hin Lat   Waterfall
Near Na Thon, this is worth visiting if you have an afternoon to kill before taking a boat back to the mainland. After a mildly strenuous hike over streams and boulders, reward yourself with a dip in the pool at the bottom of the falls. Keep an eye out for the Buddhist temple that posts signs with spiritual words of moral guidance and enlightenment. Sturdy shoes are recommended.

Wat Khunaram
Temple

Several temples have the mummified remains of pious monks, including Wat Khunaram, which is south of Rte 4169 between Th Ban Thurian and Th Ban Hua. Its monk, Luang Phaw Daeng, has been dead for over two decades but his corpse is preserved sitting in a meditative pose and sporting a pair of sunglasses.

Activities

For top-notch pampering, try the spa at Anantara (p262) in Bo Phut, or the Hideaway Spa at the **Six Senses Samui** (☎ 0 7724 5678; www.sixsenses.com/hideaway-samui/index.php; Samrong; bungalows from 13,000B; ❄ @ 🔊 ☷). The **Spa Resort** (☎ 0 7723 0855; www.spasamui.com; Lamai North; bungalows 1000-3500B; ❄ 🔊) in Lamai is the island's original health destination, and is still known for its effective 'clean me out' fasting regime. Nonguests are welcome to dine at Radiance (p264), the resort's excellent (and healthy) restaurant.

Yoga Thailand
Yoga, Spa

(☎ 0 7792 0090; www.yoga-thailand.com; Phang Ka; retreats around €840; @ 🔊) Secreted

away along the southern shores, Yoga Thailand is ushering in a new era of therapeutic holidaying with its state-of-the-art facilities and dedicated team of trainers.

Tamarind Retreat
Thai Massage

(☎ 0 7723 0571; www.tamarindretreat.com) Tucked far away from the beach within a silent coconut-palm plantation, Tamarind's small collection of villas and massage studios is seamlessly incorporated into nature: some have granite boulders built into walls and floors, while others offer private ponds or creative outdoor baths.

Absolute Sanctuary
Yoga, Spa

(☎ 0 7760 1190; www.absolutesanctuary.com) What was once a friendly yoga studio has blossomed into a gargantuan wellness complex featuring plenty of accommodation and an exhaustive menu of detox and wellness programs. Located a few kilometres north of Chaweng.

Blue Stars
Kayaking, Snorkelling

(☎ 0 7741 3231; www.bluestars.info; Hat Chaweng; kayak & snorkelling tours 2200B) There are many choices for snorkelling and

Day spa, Ko Samui

kayak tours to Ang Thong Marine National Park, but Blue Stars has the best reputation and the coolest boat.

🛏 Sleeping

HAT CHAWENG

Busy, bodaciously flaxen Chaweng is packed wall-to-wall with every level of accommodation from cheap backpacker pads advertised with cardboard signs (some as low as 300B for a double) to futuristic villas with private swimming pools – and these might be just across the street from each other. If you're hoping for early nights, pick a resort near the southern half of the beach or bring earplugs.

Jungle Club   Bungalow **$$**
(📞08 1894 2327; www.jungleclubsamui. com; huts 800-1800B, houses 2700-4500B; ❄@🛜🏊) The perilous drive up the slithering road is totally worthwhile once you take in the incredible views from the top. This isolated mountain getaway is a huge hit among locals and tourists alike. There's a relaxed back-to-nature vibe – guests chill around the stunning horizon

pool or catnap under the canopied roofs of an open-air *sǎh·lah* (often spelt sala).

Call ahead for a pick-up – you don't want to spend your precious jungle vacation in a body cast.

**Pandora
Boutique Hotel**   Resort **$$**
(📞0 7741 3801; www.pandora-samui.com; r 2940-4470B; ❄🛜🏊) As adorable as it is memorable, Pandora looks like it just fell out of a comic book – maybe *Tintin & the Mystery of Surprisingly Cheap Accommodation in Chaweng*? Rooms are outfitted with cheerful pastels, wooden mouldings and the occasional stone feature. It's about a five-minute walk to the beach.

Library   Resort **$$$**
(📞0 7742 2767; www.thelibrary.name; r from 9140B; ❄@🛜🏊) This library is too cool for school. The entire resort is a sparkling white mirage accented with black trimming and slatted curtains. Besides the swish iMac computer in each page (rooms are 'pages' here), our favourite feature is the large monochromatic wall art – it glows brightly in the evening and you can adjust the colour to your mood.

Library resort, Hat Chaweng

Baan Chaweng Beach Resort
Resort $$$

(☎ 0 7742 2403; www.baanchawengbeachresort.com; bungalows 4500-13,600B; ❄@🛜🐊) A bit of luxury without the hefty bill, Baan Chaweng draws in families and retiree bargain-seekers who roast themselves on loungers along the lovely beach. The immaculate rooms are painted in various shades of peach and pear, with teak furnishings that feel both modern and traditional.

HAT LAMAI

Beer's House
Bungalow $

(☎ 0 7723 0467; 161/4 Moo 4, Lamai North; bungalows 600-700B, r 1000B) One of the last of a dying breed on Ko Samui, this old-school-backpacker, low-key village of coconut bark huts sits right on a beautiful, sandy beach.

If the huts are too basic for you, check out the plain air-con rooms at Beer & Wine's Hut, across the road and away from the beach.

Amarina Residence
Hotel $

(www.amarinaresidence.com; r 900-1200B; ❄🛜) A two-minute walk to the beach, this excellent-value small hotel has two storeys of big, tastefully furnished, tiled rooms encircling the lobby and an incongruous dipping pool.

Rocky Resort
Resort $$$

(☎ 0 7741 8367; www.rockyresort.com; Hua Thanon; r 6800-11,800B; ❄🛜🐊) Our favourite spot in Lamai (well, actually just south of Lamai), Rocky finds the right balance between an upmarket ambience and unpretentious, sociable atmosphere. During the quieter months the prices are a steal, since ocean views abound, and each room has been furnished with beautiful Thai-inspired furniture that seamlessly incorporates a modern twist.

CHOENG MON

Those with mortal budgets tend to stay on the beach at Choeng Mon proper whose perfect (although busy) half-moon

1 NAM TOK HIN LAT
Samui isn't all white-sand beaches and clear seas. There are still patches of interior jungle where waterfalls cascade and pool through rugged terrain. Nam Tok Hin Lat (p258) is accessible by a pleasant walking trail. It takes about an hour from the road to reach the waterfall and there's a refreshing swimming hole to cool you down.

2 BO PHUT & FISHERMAN'S VILLAGE
The northern beach of Bo Phut and its atmospheric Fisherman's Village (so named because of the village's traditional profession) has to be one of the most romantic places on Samui. There are plenty of cosy restaurants for candlelit dinners and evening sunset drinks. Despite tourism, there are still many locals and many are extended families who have lived in the village for generations. Many of the elderly residents refuse to have loud noises from pubs and bars so it also stays quiet and peaceful. The village is very interesting and charming in the way that the residents have integrated modern tourism with a traditional lifestyle.

3 BAN HUA THANON
Ban Hua Thanon (p258) retains much of its local multicultural appeal: Chinese, Muslim and Buddhist communities live together in this fishing village. The old-fashioned fishing boats dock in the shallow harbour and a market sells local specialities.

4 CHOENG MON
Choeng Mon has been my secret beach for all these years. I especially like the beach just behind Imperial Boat House hotel. There is a small restaurant owned by a local who goes out to catch fresh fish for his guests. Sometimes when the tide is low you can walk to a small island nearby called Ko Fan.

If You Like…
Beach Getaways

Continuing along the highway south from Hua Hin leads to **Pranburi**, the 'country cousin' alternative to Hua Hin.

1 AWAY HUA HIN
(☎08 9144 6833; www.away-huahin.com; south of Khao Kalok; r 3500-4500B; ❄️🖥️) A boutique resort with seven antique teak houses napping on a coastal patch of paradise.

2 BRASSIERE BEACH
(☎0 3263 0554; www.brassierebeach.com; Dolphin Bay; r 4000-5000B; ❄️🖥️🏊) Privacy and personality combine at these 12 stucco villas abutting the mountains of a national park.

3 DOLPHIN BAY RESORT
(☎0 3255 9333; www.dolphinbayresort.com; Dolphin Bay; r 1790-14,300B; ❄️@🖥️🏊) This low-key holiday camp has adequate bungalows and apartments on a great sandy beach; ideal for families.

of sand is considered by many to be the most beautiful beach on the island.

Ô Soleil
Bungalow **$**
(☎0 7742 5232; osoleilbungalow@yahoo.fr; Choeng Mon; r with fan/air-con from 500/700B; ❄️🖥️) Located in a sea of luxury resorts, Thai-Belgian family-run stalwart Ô Soleil offers a welcome scatter of budget concrete bungalows and semidetached rooms extending inland from a gorgeous stretch of sand.

Sala Samui
Resort **$$$**
(☎0 7724 5888; www.salasamui.com; Choeng Mon; r 6200B, villas 8400-20,100B; ❄️@🖥️🏊) Is the hefty price tag worth it? Definitely. The dreamy, modern design scheme is exquisite – clean whites and lacquered teaks are lavish throughout, while subtle turquoise accents draw on the colour of each villa's private plunge pool. It feels like a surreal dream of a futuristic Asia.

BO PHUT

Bo Phut's Fisherman's Village is a collection of narrow Chinese shophouses that have been transformed into some of the island's best trendy (and often midrange) boutique hotels and eateries. The beach along most of this stretch, particularly the eastern part, is slim and coarse but it becomes whiter and lusher further west.

Samui-Ley
Guesthouse **$$**
(☎0 7724 5647; samuileyhouse@gmail.com; r 2300-2500B; ❄️🖥️) This tiny boutique guesthouse is shabby chic at its finest. It's very laid-back and not a top choice for luxury hounds, but we love it.

Eden
Bungalow **$$**
(☎0 7742 7645; www.edenbungalows.com; bungalows 1500-1900B; ❄️🖥️🏊) Eden is an exceptional find. The 10 bungalows and five rooms are all tucked away in a gorgeous tangle of garden with a small pool at its centre. It's about a two-minute walk to the beach.

Cocooning
Hotel **$$**
(☎08 5781 4107; cocooning.samui@hotmail.com; r/ste 1000/1800B; ❄️🖥️🏊) New owners have spiffed up this small hotel with teak windows aplenty, which let in lovely muted light. Service is exceptionally friendly and you'll find yourself making friends around the little green plunge pool. The beach is but a skip away.

Anantara
Resort **$$$**
(☎0 7742 8300; samui.anantara.com; r 5300-18,600B; ❄️@🖥️🏊) Anantara's stunning palanquin entrance satisfies fantasies of a far-flung oriental kingdom. Clay and copper statues of grimacing jungle creatures abound on the property's wild acreage, while guests savour wild teas in an open-air pagoda, swim in the lagoonlike infinity-edged swimming pool or indulge in a relaxing spa treatment.

Zazen
Resort **$$$**
(☎0 7742 5085; www.samuizazen.com; r 6160-17,200B; ❄️@🖥️🏊) Welcome to one of the boutique-iest boutique resorts on Samui – every inch of this charming geta-

way has been thoughtfully and creatively designed. It's 'Asian minimalism meets modern rococo' with a scarlet accent wall, terracotta goddesses, a dash of feng shui and a generous smattering of good taste.

MAE NAM & BANG PO

Mae Nam's slim stretch of white that slopes down to a calm, swimmable aqua sea is one of the island's prettiest. It's popular with families and older couples, that give it a quiet yet still vibrant ambience perfect for reading under the shade of a palm tree, sleeping and indulging in beach massages. Bang Po, just around the tiny peninsula, is even quieter.

Shangri-la
Bungalow $

(📞 0 7742 5189; Mae Nam; bungalows fan/air-con from 500/1300B; ❄) A backpacker's Shangri La indeed – these are some of the cheapest huts around and they're on a sublime part of the beach.

Coco Palm Resort
Bungalow $$

(📞 0 7742 5095; www.cocopalmbeachresort.com; Mae Nam; bungalows 2500-9000B; ❄ 🛜 🏊 👶) The huge array of bungalows at Coco Palm have been crafted with hard wood, bamboo and rattan touches. A rectangular pool is the centrepiece along the beach, and the price is right for a resortlike atmosphere.

✗ Eating

HAT CHAWENG

Laem Din Market
Market $

(dishes from 35B; ⏰ 4am-6pm, night market 6pm-2am) A busy day market, Laem Din is packed with stalls that sell fresh fruits, vegetables and meats and stock local Thai kitchens. For dinner, come to the adjacent night market and sample

the tasty southern-style fried chicken and curries.

Ninja Crepes
Thai $

(dishes from 75B; ⏰ 11am-midnight) The food, from Thai seafood and classics to sweet and savoury pancakes, is a delectable bargain.

Dr Frogs
Steakhouse $$$

(mains 220-1350B; ⏰ lunch & dinner) Perched atop a rocky overlook, Dr Frogs combines incredible ocean vistas with delicious international flavours (namely Italian and Thai favourites). Delectable steaks and crab cakes, and friendly owners, put this spot near the top of our dining list.

Prego
Italian $$$

(www.prego-samui.com; mains 200-700B; ⏰ dinner) This smart ministry of culinary style serves up fine Italian cuisine in a barely there dining room of cool marble and modern geometry. Reservations are accepted for seatings at 7pm and 9pm.

Ark Bar (p267), Hat Chaweng
LONELY PLANET/GETTY IMAGES ©

Detour:
Ko Tah

Tired of tours and busy beaches? For the intrepid DIY traveller there's no better way to spend a day on Ko Samui than with a trip to the white sands of Ko Tah. Hire a long-tail boat from the operators who beach their boats alongside the strip of seafood restaurants on Hat Thong Tanote on Ko Samui's south coast; a boat for up to six people should cost 1500B to 2000B for a four-hour trip. The island itself is only about 15 minutes from Ko Samui.

HAT LAMAI

Hua Thanon Market   Market $
(dishes from 30B; ⏱6am-6pm) Slip into the rhythm of this village market slightly south of Lamai; it's a window into the food ways of southern Thailand. Follow the market road to the row of food shops delivering edible Muslim culture: chicken *biryani,* fiery curries or toasted rice with coconut, bean sprouts, lemon grass and dried shrimp.

Lamai Day Market   Market $
(dishes from 30B; ⏱6am-8pm) Lamai's market is a hive of activity, selling food necessities and takeaway food. It's next door to a petrol station.

Radiance   International $$
(meals 100-400B; ⏱breakfast, lunch & dinner; 🛜🍴) Radiance is the restaurant of Spa Resort (p259); non-guests are welcome to dine here. Even if you're not a vegetarian, healthy food never tasted this good. Plus the semi-outdoor Zenlike setting is relaxing without a hint of pretension.

French Bakery   Bakery $$
(set breakfasts from 120B; ⏱breakfast & lunch) The expat's breakfast choice is away from the main zone, near Wat Lamai on Rte 4169, but it's worth the 10-minute walk.

Rocky's   International $$$
(dishes 300-950B; ⏱lunch & dinner) Easily the top dining spot on Lamai. Try the signature beef tenderloin with blue cheese – it's like sending your taste buds on a Parisian vacation. On Tuesday evenings diners enjoy a special Thai-themed evening with a prepared menu of local delicacies.

CHOENG MON & BIG BUDDHA BEACH (HAT BANG RAK)

BBC   International $$
(Big Buddha Beach; dishes 70-300B; ⏱breakfast, lunch & dinner) No, this place has nothing to do with *Dr Who* – BBC stands for Big Buddha Café. It's popular with the local expats, the international menu is large and there are exquisite ocean views from the patio.

Dining on the Rocks   Asian Fusion $$$
(📞0 7724 5678; reservations-samui@sixsenses. com; Choeng Mon; menus from 2200B; ⏱dinner) Samui's ultimate dining experience takes place on nine cantilevered verandahs of weathered teak and bamboo that yawn over the gulf. After sunset (and some wine), guests feel like they're dining on a barge set adrift on a starlit sea. Each dish on the six-course prix-fixe menu is the brainchild of the cooks who regularly experiment with taste, texture and temperature.

BO PHUT

The Fisherman's Village is the nicest setting for a meal but you'll find heaps of cheaper options on the road leading inland towards the main road.

The Hut   Thai $
(mains 80-300B; ⏱dinner) You'll find basic Thai specialities at reasonable prices (for the area) as well as more expensive fresh seafood treats. There are only about a dozen tables and they fill fast so get here early or late if you don't want to wait.

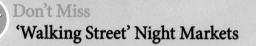

LONELY PLANET/GETTY IMAGES ©

⭐ Don't Miss
'Walking Street' Night Markets

The most fun dining experiences on Ko Samui are on 'Walking Streets', where once (or more) per week each beach village sets up a food-filled marketplace where you can sample local delicacies at hawker stalls, shop for crafts and trinkets and mingle with tourists and locals. All the markets are on or near the host village's main drag so they're hard to miss, and they all start setting up at around 4pm to 5pm and run till 11pm or midnight.

- **Ban Chaweng** Every night except Friday and Sunday.
- **Ban Lamai** Sunday
- **Ban Mae Nam** Thursday
- **Bo Phut** Friday
- **Ban Choeng Mon** Friday

69   Thai Fusion **$$**
(mains 179-550B; ⊙11am-11pm Mon-Thu, 6-11pm Fri; 🛜) Vivian is a food genius who is constantly coming up with creative twists on Thai favourites and she'll even encourage you to come up with your own ideas as you order.

The roadside setting isn't the best but the decor is as *vavoom* as the food:

a cabaret of sequined tablecloths, bouquets of feathers and hanging tassels.

Starfish & Coffee   Thai **$$**
(mains 150-280B; ⊙breakfast, lunch & dinner) This streamer-clad eatery was probably named after the Prince song, since we couldn't find any starfish on the menu (there's loads of coffee though). Evenings

Below: Thai noodle soup; **Right:** Hat Chaweng (p260)

(BELOW) OTTO STADLER/GETTY IMAGES ©; (RIGHT) OTTO STADLER/GETTY IMAGES ©

feature standard Thai fare and sunset views of rugged Ko Pha-Ngan.

Zazen
Asian Fusion **$$$**
(dishes 540-900B, set menu from 1300B; ☺lunch & dinner) The chef describes the food as 'organic and orgasmic', and the ambient 'yums' from elated diners confirm the latter. This romantic dining experience comes complete with ocean views, dim candle lighting and soft music.

MAE NAM & BANG PO

Bang Po Seafood
Seafood **$$**
(Bang Po; dishes from 100B; ☺dinner) A meal at Bang Po Seafood is a test for the taste buds. It's one of the only restaurants that serves traditional Ko Samui fare: recipes call for ingredients such as raw sea urchin roe, baby octopus, sea water, coconut and local turmeric.

Farmer
International **$$$**
(☎0 7744 7222; Mae Nam; mains 350-1000B; ☺lunch & dinner) Magically set in a rice field, the Farmer is a refreshing change of setting and a romantic one at that, especially when the candlelight flickers on a clear starry night. The mostly European-inspired food is tasty and well-presented and there's a free pick-up for nearby beaches since this place is far from the main tourist areas.

WEST & SOUTH COASTS

Ging Pagarang
Seafood **$**
(Thong Tanote; meals from 50B; ☺11.30am-8pm) Locals know this is one of the island's best beachside places to sample authentic Samui-style seafood. It's simple and family-run, but the food and views are extraordinary.

About Art & Craft Café
Vegetarian $$

(Na Thon; dishes 80-180B; ☺breakfast & lunch)
An artistic oasis in the midst of hurried Na Thon, this cafe serves an eclectic assortment of healthy and wholesome food, gourmet coffee and, as the name states, art and craft, made by the owner and her friends.

🍷 Drinking & Nightlife

Samui's biggest party spot is, without a doubt, noisy Hat Chaweng. Lamai and Bo Phut come in second and third respectively, while the rest of the island is generally quiet, as the drinking is usually focused around self-contained resort bars.

Making merry in Chaweng is a piece of cake. Most places are open until 2am and there are a few places that go strong all night long.

Beach Republic
Bar

(www.beachrepublic.com; 176/34 Mu 4, Hat Lamai) Recognised by its yawning thatch-patched awnings, Beach Republic could be the poster child of a made-for-TV, beachside, booze swilling holiday. There's a wading pool, comfy lounge chairs, an endless cocktail list and even a hotel if you never, ever want to leave the party. The Sunday brunches here are legendary.

Ark Bar
Bar

(www.ark-bar.com; Hat Chaweng) Drinks are dispensed from the multicoloured bar draped in paper lanterns, guests recline on loungers on the beach, and the party is on day and night.

Green Mango
Bar

(Hat Chaweng) Samui's favourite power drinking house is very big, very loud and very *fa·ràng*. Green Mango has blazing lights, expensive drinks and masses of sweaty bodies swaying to dance music.

Reggae Pub
Bar

(Hat Chaweng) This fortress of fun sports an open-air dance floor with music spun by foreign DJs. The whole place doubles as a shrine to Bob Marley.

ℹ Getting There & Away

Air

Ko Samui's airport is in the northeast of the island near Big Buddha Beach. **Bangkok Airways** (www.bangkokair.com) operates flights roughly every 30 minutes between Samui and Bangkok's Suvarnabhumi International Airport (50 minutes). **Firefly** (www.fireflyz.com.my) operates direct flights from Ko Samui to Kuala Lumpur's Subang airport.

Boat

To the Mainland

There are frequent boat departures between Samui and the mainland. Two options are the high-speed Lomprayah (p257; 450B), which departs from Na Thon and the slower, stinkier **Raja** (☏0 2276 8211-2; www.rajaferryport.com) car ferry (150B), which departs from Thong Yang. A couple of these departures can connect with the train station in Phun Phin (for a nominal extra fee).

To Ko Pha-Ngan & Ko Tao

There are almost a dozen daily departures between Ko Samui and Thong Sala on the west coast of Ko Pha-Ngan and many of these continue on to Ko Tao. These leave from the Na Thon, Mae Nam or Big Buddha Beach pier, take from 20 minutes to one hour and cost 200B to 300B to Ko Pha-Ngan, depending on the boat.

To go directly to Hat Rin, the *Haad Rin Queen* goes back and forth between Hat Rin and Big Buddha Beach four times a day. The voyage takes 50 minutes and costs 200B.

Bus & Train

Several services offer these bus-boat combo tickets, the fastest and most comfortable being the Lomprayah which has two daily departures from Bangkok at 6am and 9pm and two from Samui to Bangkok at 8am and 12.30pm. The total voyage takes about 13½ hours and costs 1450B.

ℹ Getting Around

Drivers of *sŏrng·tăa·ou* (pick-up trucks) love to try to overcharge you, so it's always best to ask a third party for current rates, as they can change with the season. These vehicles run regularly during daylight hours. It's about 50B to travel between beaches, and no more than 100B to travel halfway across the island.

Taxi service is quite chaotic due to the plethora of cabs. Taxis typically charge around 500B for an airport transfer.

··

Ko Pha-Ngan เกาะพะงัน

POP 12,500

Slacker, hippie-at-heart Ko Pha-Ngan has become so synonymous with the wild and massive Full Moon Party on Hat Rin that the rest of the island – and even Hat Rin outside of full moon week – gets forgotten. This will probably change quickly with the imminent opening of the island's airport in late 2014, but for now this exceptionally gorgeous island is in a sleepy sweet spot where you can even find a solid bungalow on Hat Rin for around 1000B outside of full moon mania.

🤿 Activities

With Ko Tao, the high-energy diving behemoth, just a few kilometres away, Ko Pha-Ngan enjoys a much quieter, more laid-back diving scene focused on fun diving rather than certifications. A recent drop in Open Water certification prices has made local prices competitive with Ko Tao. Group sizes tend to be smaller on Ko Pha-Ngan since the island has fewer divers in general.

The most popular trips departing from Ko Pha-Ngan are three-site day trips which stop at **Chumphon Pinnacle**, **Sail Rock** and one of the other premier sites in the area. These three-stop trips cost from around 3650B to 4000B and include a full lunch. Two-dive trips to Sail Rock will set you back around 2500B to 2800B.

Chaloklum Diving
Diving

(☏0 7737 4025; www.chaloklum-diving.com) One of the more established dive shops on the island, these guys (based on the main drag in Ban Chalok Lam) have quality equipment and high standards in all that they do.

LUIS CAGIAO PHOTOGRAPHY/GETTY IMAGES ©

★ Don't Miss
Ang Thong National Marine Park

The 40-some jagged jungle islands of Ang Thong Marine National Park stretch across the cerulean sea like a shattered emerald necklace – each piece a virgin realm featuring sheer limestone cliffs, hidden lagoons and perfect peach-coloured sands.

February, March and April are the best months to visit this ethereal preserve of greens and blues; crashing monsoon waves mean that the park is almost always closed during November and December.

The best way to reach the park is to take a private day tour from Ko Samui or Ko Pha-Ngan (28km and 32km away, respectively). The park officially has an admission fee (adult/child 400/200B), although it should be included in the price of every tour (ask your operator if you are unsure).

NEED TO KNOW
อุทยานแห่งชาติหมู่เกาะอ่างทอง; ☏ 0 7728 0222

Reefers   Diving
(☏ 08 6471 4045; www.reefersdiving.com) Vic, the owner, and his gaggle of instructors are chilled and professional. Has a solid reputation. Recommended.

Haad Yao Divers   Diving
(☏ 08 6279 3085; www.haadyaodivers.com; Hat Yao; ☏) Established in 1997, this dive operator has garnered a strong reputa-

tion by maintaining European standards of safety and customer service.

Tours

Eco Nature Tour   Eco Tour
(☏ 08 4850 6273) This exceedingly popular oufit offers a 'best of' island trip, which includes elephant trekking, snorkelling and a visit to the Chinese temple, a stunning viewpoint and Nam Tok Phaeng. The

day trip, which costs 1500B, departs at 9am and returns around 3pm. Bookings can be made at its office in Thong Sala or at the Backpackers Information Centre. **Pha-Ngan Safari** (📞0 7737 4159, 08 1895 3783) offers a similar trip for 1900B.

🛏 Sleeping

HAT RIN

Hat Rin sees Thailand's greatest accommodation crunch during the full moon festivities. At this time, bungalow operations expect you to stay for a minimum number of days (usually five). If you plan to arrive the day of the party (or even the day before), we strongly suggest booking a room in advance, or else you'll probably have to sleep on the beach (which you might end up doing anyway).

Needless to say, the prices listed here are meaningless during periods of maximum lunar orbicularity. Expect rates to increase by 20% to 300% during full moon.

Lighthouse Bungalows
Bungalow $

(📞0 7737 5075; www.lighthousebungalows.com; Hat Seekantang; bungalows 500-1200B; ❄🛜) This hidden, low-key collection of hip huts gathers along a sloping, bouldered terrain punctuated by towering palms. The fan options are rustic but the newest, spacious air-con bungalows are terrific value. Every option has a terrace and sweeping view of the sea plus there's a cushion-clad restaurant/common area. To get there, follow the wooden boardwalk southeast from Hat Leela.

Sea Breeze Bungalow
Bungalow $$

(📞0 7737 5162; Ban Hat Rin; bungalows 1500-8000B; ❄🛜🏊) Sea Breeze gets a good report card from our readers, and we agree; the labyrinth of secluded hillside cottages is a pleasant hammocked retreat for any type of traveller. Several bungalows, poised high on stilts, deliver stunning views of Hat Rin and the sea. There's a big range of options here.

HAT YAO & HAT SON

One of the busier beaches along the west coast, Hat Yao sports a swimmable beach, numerous resorts and a few extra services such as ATMs and convenience stores. Hat Son is a quiet, much smaller beach that feels like a big secret.

High Life
Bungalow $

(📞0 7734 9114; www.highlifebungalow.com; Hat Yao; fan bungalows 500B, air-con bungalows 800-2200B; ❄🛜🏊) We can't decide what's more conspicuous: the dramatic ocean views from the infinity-edged swimming pool, or the blatant double entendre in the resort's name. True to its moniker, the 25 bungalows, of various shapes and sizes, sit on a palmed outcropping of granite soaring high above the cerulean sea.

Haad Son Resort & Restaurant
Resort $$

(📞0 7734 9104; www.haadson.info; Hat Son; bungalows 1000-8000B; ❄@🛜🏊) There's a mixed bag of rooms here from big, older wooden bungalows with terraces on the hillside to brand-new polished cement suites and rooms along the beachfront. The secluded beach setting is spectacular and is highlighted by one of the most beachy-chic restaurants on the island on a jungle- and boulder-clad peninsula overlooking the sea.

HAT SALAD

This slim, pretty beach on the northwest coast is fronted by shallow blue water – a clutch of photogenic long-tail boats tend to park at the southern end. It's slightly rustic, with local Thai fishers coming out to throw their nets out at sunset, yet with plenty of amenities and comfortable accommodation.

Cookies Salad
Resort $$

(📞0 7734 9125, 08 3181 7125; www.cookies-phangan.com; bungalows 1600-5000B; 🛜🏊) The resort with a tasty name has delicious, private Balinese-styled bungalows on a steep hill, orbiting a two-tiered lap pool tiled in various shades of blue. Shaggy thatching and dense tropical foliage give the realm a certain rustic quality, although you won't want for creature comforts. It's super friendly and books up fast.

Green Papaya
Bungalow $$$

(☏0 7737 4182; www.greenpapayaresort.com; bungalows 4300-8500B; ❄@🛜🏊) The polished wooden bungalows at Green Papaya are a clear standout along the lovely beach at Hat Salad; however, they come at quite a hefty price and you'll need a posh attitude to fit in.

AO MAE HAT

The relatively undeveloped northwest tip of the island has excellent ocean vistas, plenty of white sand and little Ko Ma is connected to Pha-Ngan by a stunning sandbar.

Mae Hat
Beach View Resort
Bungalow $

(☏08 9823 9756; bungalows 400-600B) Hidden behind the dune of the beach's southern end, this lost-in-time cluster of bungalows was empty when we passed save a few friendly Myanmar staff. The bamboo, fan-cooled bungalows with solid tiled floors are the perfect place to disappear into tropical mode with a good book for a few days.

HAT KHUAT (BOTTLE BEACH)

This isolated dune in the north of the island has garnered a reputation as a low-key getaway, and has thus become quite popular. During high season, places can fill up fast so it's best to try to arrive early. Grab a long-tail taxi boat from Chalok Lam for 100B to 150B (depending on the boat's occupancy).

Smile Bungalows
Bungalow $

(☏08 1956 3133; smilebeach@hotmail.com; Bottle Beach/Hat Khuat; bungalows 400-700B) At the far western corner of the beach, Smile features an assortment of wooden huts that climb up a forested hill. The two-storey bungalows (700B) are our favourite. Listen for the Bottle Beach song by Bottle Beach lover and musician John Nicholas, playing on the stereo in the loungable beach cafe.

Bottle Beach II
Bungalow $

(☏0 7744 5156; Bottle Beach/Hat Khuat; bungalows 300-500B; 🛜) At the far eastern corner of the beach, this double string of very basic, turquoise bungalows is the ideal place to chill out – for as long as you can – if you don't need many creature comforts.

THONG NAI PAN

The pair of rounded bays at Thong Nai Pan, in the northeast of the island, are some of the most remote yet busy beaches on the island.

Hat Rin
MATTHEW MICAH WRIGHT/GETTY IMAGES ©

Dolphin
Bungalow $

(Thong Nai Pan; bungalows 500-1800B; ❄ 🛜)
This hidden retreat gives you a chance to rough it in style. Quiet afternoons are spent lounging on the comfy cushions in one of the small pagodas hidden throughout the jungle and bungalows are quite private. Lodging is only available on a first-come, first-served basis.

THAN SADET

From Thong Sala a 4WD taxi leaves for Than Sadet on the east coast daily at 1pm for 200B per person. Otherwise catch the *Thong Nai Pan Express* boat from Ko Samui.

Mai Pen Rai
Bungalow $

(📞 0 7744 5090; www.thansadet.com; Than Sadet; bungalows 500-1200B; 🛜 🐾) This quiet, beachy bay elicits nothing but sedate smiles. Bungalows sit on the hilly headland, and sport panels of straw weaving with gabled roofs. There's a friendly on-site restaurant.

HAT THIAN & HAT YUAN

These beaches are quite secluded. You can walk between the two in under 10 minutes. Hat Yuan is the more developed beach and has the whiter, wider stretches of sand, while Hat Thian is relatively empty and is back-to-nature pretty.

To get here hire a long-tail from Hat Rin (300B to 400B for the whole boat) or organise a boat pick-up from your resort.

Sanctuary
Bungalow $$

(📞 08 1271 3614; www.thesanctuarythailand.com; Hat Thian; dm 220B, bungalows 770-6000B) A friendly forested enclave of relaxed smiles, the Sanctuary is a haven of splendid lodgings, yoga classes and detox sessions. Accommodation, in various manifestations of twigs, is scattered along a tangle of hillside jungle paths while Hat Thian is wonderfully quiet and great for swimming.

Pariya Resort & Villas
Resort $$$

(📞 08 7623 6678; www.pariyahaadyuan.com; Hat Yuan; villas 8000-17,000B; ❄ 🛜 🏊) The swankiest option on these beaches is found right in front of the softest sands of Hat Yuan in majestic burnt-yellow painted concrete. If you can find a promotion this may be worth it but, otherwise, the resort is overpriced.

Hat Yao (p270)

Eating

HAT RIN

The infamous Chicken Corner is a popular intersection stocked with several faves such as **Mr K Thai Food** (Ban Hat Rin; dishes 30-80B) and **Mama Schnitzel** (Ban Hat Rin; dishes 40-100B), which promise to cure any case of the munchies, be it noon or midnight.

Kawee   Thai, French **$$**
(dishes 100-350B) Calling itself an 'art-mosphere', this French-run place raises the bar for Hat Rin both with its jungle-y, dimly lit, bookstore-attached decor and its fantastic French- and Thai-inspired dishes. The *hòr mòk* (a savoury steamed pudding of coconut milk, curries and meat) and Kawee skewers (crispy white fish on lemon grass blades) are not to be missed.

Lazy House   International **$$**
(Hat Rin Nai; dishes 90-270B; ⊙lunch & dinner) Back in the day, this joint was the owner's apartment – everyone liked his cooking so much that he decided to turn the place into a restaurant and hang-out spot. Today, Lazy House is easily one of Hat Rin's best places to veg out in front of a movie with a scrumptious shepherd's pie.

SOUTHERN BEACHES

On Saturday evenings from 4pm to 10pm, a side street in the eastern part of Thong Sala becomes **Walking Street** – a bustling pedestrian zone mostly filled with locals hawking their wares to other islanders.

Night Market   Market **$**
(Thong Sala; dishes 25-180B; ⊙dinner) A heady mix of steam and snacking locals, Thong Sala's night market is a must for those looking for a dose of culture while nibbling on a low-priced snack.

**Fisherman's
Restaurant**   Seafood **$$**
(☎08 4454 7240; Thong Sala; dishes 50-600B; ⊙1-10pm) Lit up at night, it's one of the

---

Salt & Spice

Dishes you are likely to come across in southern Thailand include the following:

○ *Gaang đai 'blah* – An intensely spicy and salty curry that includes *đai 'blah* (salted fish stomach), which is much tastier than it sounds.

○ *Gaang sôm* – Known as *gaang lěu·ang* (yellow curry) in central Thailand, this sour/spicy soup gets its hue from the liberal use of turmeric, a root commonly used in southern Thai cooking.

○ *Gài tôrt hàht yài* – The famous deep-fried chicken from the town of Hat Yai gets its rich flavour from a marinade containing dried spices.

○ *Kà·nǒm jeen nám yah* – This dish of thin rice noodles served with a fiery currylike sauce is always accompanied by a tray of fresh vegetables and herbs.

---

island's nicest settings and the food, from the addictive yellow curry crab to the massive seafood platter to share (with all assortment of critters; 800B to 900B), is as wonderful as the ambience.

Fabio's   Italian **$$**
(☎08 3389 5732; Ban Khai; dishes 150-400B; ⊙1-10pm Mon-Sat) An intimate, authentic and truly delicious Italian place with golden walls, cream linens and bamboo furniture. There are only seven tables so reserve in advance.

OTHER BEACHES

Cucina Italiana   Italian **$$**
(Jenny's; Chalok Lam; pizzas 180-200B; ⊙dinner) If it weren't for the sand between your toes and the long-tail boats whizzing by, you might think you had been transported to the Italian countryside. The friendly Italian chef is passionate about his food,

and creates everything from his pasta to his tiramisu daily, from scratch. The rustic, thin-crust pizzas are out-of-this-world good.

🍷 Drinking & Nightlife

HAT RIN

Hat Rin is the beating heart of the legendary full moon fun. When the moon isn't lighting up the night sky, partygoers flock to other spots on the island's south side. Most party venues flank Hat Rin's Sunrise Beach from south to north.

Rock   Bar, Nightclub
There are great views of the party from the elevated terrace on the far south side of the beach. Also, Rock has the best cocktails in town.

Mellow Mountain   Bar, Nightclub
Also called 'Mushy Mountain' (you'll understand why when you get there), this trippy hang-out sits at the northern edge of Hat Rin Nok delivering stellar views of the shenanigans below. It's one of those places you need to at least see if you're on Hat Rin.

OTHER BEACHES

Pirates Bar   Bar
(Hat Chaophao) This wacky drinkery is a replica of a pirate ship built into the cliffs. When you're sitting on the deck and the tide is high (and you've had a couple of drinks), you can almost believe you're out at sea. These guys host the well-attended Moon Set parties, three days before Hat Rin gets pumpin' for the full moon fun.

Amsterdam   Bar
(Ao Plaay Laem) Near Hat Chaophao on the west coast, Amsterdam attracts tourists and locals from all over the island, who are looking for a chill spot to watch the sunset.

ℹ️ Getting There & Away

Air

Ko Pha-Ngan's new airport is scheduled to open in September 2014 with two daily flights to/from Bangkok on **Kan Air** (www.kanairlines.com).

Boat

To Ko Samui

There are around a dozen daily departures between Thong Sala on Ko Pha-Ngan and Ko

Full Moon Party, Ko Pha-Ngan (p268)

Samui. These boats leave throughout the day from 7am to 6pm, take from 20 minutes to an hour and cost 200B to 300B depending on the boat.

The Haad Rin Queen (🕿 0 7748 4668) goes back and forth between Hat Rin and Big Buddha Beach on Ko Samui four times a day. The voyage takes 50 minutes and costs 200B.

The *Thong Nai Pan Express* is a wobbly old fishing boat (not for the faint-hearted) that runs once a day from Mae Hat on Ko Samui to Hat Rin on Ko Pha-Ngan and then up the east coast, stopping at all the beaches as far as Thong Nai Pan Noi. Prices range from 200B to 400B depending on the destination. The boat won't run in bad weather.

To Ko Tao

Ko Tao–bound Lomprayah ferries (500B) depart from Thong Sala on Ko Pha-Ngan at 8.30am and 1pm and arrive at 9.45am and 2.15pm. The Seatran service (430B) departs from Thong Sala at 8.30am and 2pm daily. Taxis depart Hat Rin for Thong Sala one hour before the boat departure. The cheaper-but-slower Songserm (350B) service leaves Ko Pha-Ngan at 12.30pm and alights at 2.30pm.

To Surat Thani & the Andaman Coast

There are approximately eight daily departures between Ko Pha-Ngan and Surat Thani on the Songserm (350B, 4½ hours) or Lomprayah (550B, 2¾ hours) services, both travelling via Ko Samui. Every night, depending on the weather, a night boat runs from Surat (350B, seven hours), departing at 11pm.

Combination boat-bus tickets are available at any travel agency. Most travellers will pass through Surat Thani as they swap coasts.

ℹ Getting Around

You can rent motorcycles all over the island for 150B to 250B per day.

Pick-up trucks and *sŏrng·tăa·ou* chug along the island's major roads and the riding rates double after sunset. The trip from Thong Sala to Hat Rin is 100B; further beaches will set you back around 150B to 200B.

Long-tail boats depart from Thong Sala, Chalok Lam and Hat Rin, heading to a variety of far-flung destinations such as Hat Khuat (Bottle Beach) and Ao Thong Nai Pan. Expect to pay anywhere from 50B for a short trip, and up to 300B for a lengthier journey.

Ko Tao เกาะเต่า

POP 1500

The island is consistently gaining popularity and going more upscale, but for now this jungle-topped cutie has the busy vibe of Samui mixed with the laid-back nature of Pha-Ngan. But Tao also has its wildcard, something the others don't: easy-to-get-to, diverse diving right off its shores.

✪ Activities

DIVING

The intense competition among scuba schools means that certification prices are unbeatably low and the standards of service top-notch; dozens of dive shops vie for your baht, so be sure to shop around.

Roctopus Diving

(🕿 0 7745 6611; www.roctopusdive.com; Sairee Beach) One of the newer places on the scene, Roctopus already has a near legendary reputation for its great staff and high standards.

Big Blue Diving Diving

(🕿 0 7745 6772, 0 7745 6415; www.bigblue diving.com; Sairee Beach) If Goldilocks were picking a dive school, she'd probably pick Big Blue – this midsize operation (not too big, not too small) gets props for fostering a sociable vibe while maintaining a high standard of service.

Scuba Junction Diving

(Scuba J; 🕿 0 7745 6164; www.scuba-junction. com; Sairee Beach) A groovy new storefront and a team of outgoing instructors lure travellers looking for a more intimate dive experience. Scuba Junction guarantees a maximum of four people per diving group.

SNORKELLING

Most snorkel enthusiasts opt for the do-it-yourself approach on Ko Tao, which involves swimming out into the offshore bays or hiring a long-tail boat to putter around further out. Guided tours are also available and can be booked at any local

If You Like...
Diving

Each dive school chooses a smattering of sites for the day depending on weather and ocean conditions.

1 CHUMPHON PINNACLE
(36m maximum depth) A colourful assortment of sea anemones along the four interconnected pinnacles 13km west of Ko Tao. Whale sharks are known to pop up once in a while.

2 GREEN ROCK DIVE SITE
(25m maximum depth) An underwater jungle gym featuring caverns, caves and small swim-throughs. Rays, grouper and triggerfish are known to hang around.

3 JAPANESE GARDENS DIVE SITE
(12m maximum depth) Between Ko Tao and Ko Nang Yuan is this low-stress dive site, perfect for beginners. There's plenty of colourful coral, and turtles, stingray and pufferfish often pass by.

4 MANGO BAY
(16m maximum depth) This might be your first dive site if you are putting on a tank for the first time.

5 SAIL ROCK DIVE SITE
(34m maximum depth) Best accessed by Ko Pha-Ngan, this site features a massive rock chimney with a vertical swim-through, and large pelagics such as barracuda and kingfish.

6 SOUTHWEST PINNACLE
(33m maximum depth) A small collection of pinnacles that are home to giant groupers and barracudas.

7 WHITE ROCK DIVE SITE
(29m maximum depth) Home to colourful coral, angelfish, clown fish and territorial triggerfish.

travel agency. Tours range from 500B to 800B (usually including gear, lunch and a guide/boat captain) and stop at various snorkelling hotspots around the island.

Sleeping

SAIREE BEACH

Giant Sairee is the longest and most developed strip on the island, with a string of dive operations, bungalows, travel agencies, minimarkets and internet cafes. The northern end is the prettiest and quietest while there's more of a party scene and noise from the bars to the south.

Blue Wind   Bungalow $
(☏0 7745 6116; bluewind_wa@yahoo.com; bungalows 350-1400B; ❄️ 📶) Blue Wind offers a breath of fresh air from the high-intensity dive resorts strung along Sairee Beach. Sturdy bamboo huts are peppered along a dirt trail behind the beachside bakery. It's rustic but relaxing.

Spicytao
Backpackers   Hostel $
(☏08 1036 6683; www.spicyhostels.com; dm 200-250B; ❄️ 📶) Like your own supersocial country hang-out, Spicytao is hidden off the main drag in a rustic garden setting. Backpackers rave about the ambience and staff who are always organising activities. Book in advance!

Sairee Cottage   Bungalow $$
(☏0 7745 6126; www.saireecottage diving.com; bungalows 350-2800B; ❄️ 📶) Bungalows are connected by a sand path through a sun-splotched garden of palms and hibiscus. Even the smallest, most budget options here are of higher standard than most and very good value. The beach out front is slim and under the shade of a giant ironwood tree.

CHALOK BAN KAO

This is a slim stretch of sand in a scenic half-circle bay framed by boulders at either end.

Viewpoint Resort   Resort $$
(☏0 7745 6666; www.kohtaoviewpoint.com; bungalows 1200-14,000B; ❄️ 📶 🏊) Lush grounds of ferns and palms meander across a

276

boulder-studded hillside offering stunning views over the sea and the bay. All options, from the exquisite private suites that feel like Tarzan and Jane's love nest gone luxury to the huge, view-filled bungalows, use boulders, wood and concrete to create comfortable, naturalistic abodes.

Freedom Beach · Bungalow $$
(☎ 0 7745 6596; bungalows 700-3500B; ❄ 📶) On its own secluded beach shaded by tall, pretty bushes and connected to Ao Chalok Ban Kao by a boardwalk, Freedom feels like a classic backpacker haunt.

New Heaven Resort · Bungalow $$
(☎ 0 7745 6422; www.newheavenkohtao.com; r & bungalows 700-3800B; ❄ 📶) Just beyond the clutter of Chalok Ban Kao, New Heaven delivers colourful huts perched on a hill over impossibly clear waters.

HIN WONG

A sandy beach has been swapped for a boulder-strewn coast on the serene east side of the island, but the water is crystal clear. The road to Hin Wong is paved in parts, but sudden sand pits and steep hills can toss you off your motorbike.

Hin Wong Bungalows · Bungalow $
(☎ 0 7745 6006; Hin Wong; bungalows 350-700B; 📶) Pleasant wooden huts are scattered across vast expanses of untamed tropical terrain – it all feels a bit like *Gilligan's Island*.

View Rock · Bungalow $
(☎ 0 7745 6549, 0 7745 6548; viewrock@hotmail. com; Hin Wong; bungalows 500-2000B; ❄ 📶) View Rock is precisely that: views and rocks. The hodgepodge of wooden huts, which looks like a secluded fishing village, is built into the steep crags offering stunning views of the bay.

AO TANOT (TANOTE BAY)

Tanote Bay is more populated than some of the other eastern coves, but it's still rather quiet and picturesque. It is the only bay on the east coast that is accessible by a decent road.

Family Tanote · Bungalow $$
(☎ 0 7745 6757; Ao Tanot; bungalows 800-3500B; ❄ @ 📶) As the name suggests, this scatter of hillside bungalows is run by a local family who take pride in providing comfy digs to solitude seekers.

Ko Tao

JG TOKSVIG-STEWART/GETTY IMAGES ©

🍴 Eating

With super-sized Ko Samui lurking on the horizon, it's hard to believe that quaint little Ko Tao holds its own in the gastronomy category.

SAIREE BEACH

Su Chili   Thai $

(dishes 70-150B; ⏱lunch & dinner; 📶) Fresh and tasty Thai food served by friendly waitstaff who always ask how spicy you want your food and somehow get it right. Try the delicious northern Thai specialities or Penang curries.

ZanziBar   Cafe $

(sandwiches 90-150B; ⏱breakfast, lunch & dinner) The island's outpost of sandwich yuppie-dom slathers an array of yummy ingredients between two slices of wholegrain bread.

**Barracuda
Restaurant & Bar**   Asian Fusion $$

(📞08 0146 3267; mains 180-400B; ⏱dinner) Chef Ed Jones caters for the Thai princess when she's in town but you can sample his exquisite cuisine for mere pennies in comparison to her budget. Locally sourced ingredients are used to make creative, fresh, fusion masterpieces.

**Chopper's
Bar & Grill**   International $$

(dishes 60-200B; ⏱breakfast, lunch & dinner) So popular that it has become a local landmark, Chopper's is a two-storey hang-out where divers and travellers can widen their beer belly. There's live music, sports on the TVs, billiards and a cinema room.

MAE HAT

Pim's Guesthouse   Thai $

(curry 70B; ⏱lunch) Everyday Pim makes a daily curry (the massaman is everyone's favourite) at this humble spot, and everyday she sells out before the lunch hour is over. People from all over the island flock here.

Pranee's Kitchen   Thai $

(dishes 50-150B; ⏱breakfast, lunch & dinner; 📶) An old Mae Hat fave, Pranee's serves scrumptious curries and other Thai treats in an open-air pavilion sprinkled with lounging pillows, wooden tables and TVs.

Food Centre   Thai $

(mains from 30B; ⏱breakfast, lunch & dinner) An unceremonious gathering of hot-tin food stalls, Food Centre – as it's come to be known – lures lunching locals with veritable smoke signals rising up from the concrete parking lot abutting Mae Hat's petrol station.

Whitening
                    International $$

(dishes 150-400B; ⏱dinner; 📶) Dine amid dangling white Christmas lights while keeping your bare feet tucked into the sand.

Sairee Beach
ALVARO LEIVA/GETTY IMAGES ©

And the best part? It's comparatively easy on the wallet.

🍷 Drinking & Nightlife

Castle
Nightclub

(www.thecastlekohtao.com; Mae Hat) Located along the main road between Mae Hat and Chalok Ban Kao, the Castle has quickly positioned itself as the most-loved party venue on the island, luring an array of local and international DJs to its triad of parties each month.

Office Bar
Bar

(Sairee Beach) With graffiti proudly boasting 'No Gaga, and no Black Eyed F*^£*£ Peas', this hexagonal hut lures regulars with grunge beats and rickety wooden seats.

ⓘ Getting There & Away

Note that we highly advise purchasing your boat tickets *several* days in advance if you are accessing Ko Tao from Ko Pha-Ngan after the Full Moon Party.

Boat

To Ko Pha-Ngan

The Lomprayah catamaran offers a twice-daily service (500B), leaving Ko Tao at 9.30am and 3pm and arriving on Ko Pha-Ngan around 10.50am and 4.10pm. The Seatran Discovery Ferry (430B) offers an identical service. The Songserm express boat (350B) departs daily at 10am and arrives on Ko Pan-Ngan at 11.30am.

To Ko Samui

The Lomprayah catamaran offers a twice-daily service (600B), leaving Ko Tao at 9.30am and 3pm and arriving on Ko Samui via Ko Pha-Ngan, around 11.30am and 4.40pm. The Seatran Discovery Ferry (600B) offers an identical service. The Songserm express boat (450B) departs daily at 10am and arrives on Samui (again via Ko Pha-Ngan) at 12.45pm.

To Surat Thani & the Andaman Coast

The easiest option is to stop over on either Ko Pha-Ngan or Ko Samui to shorten the trip and lessen the number of connections.

Ko Tao Dive Schools

A **PADI** (www.padi.com) Open Water certification course costs 9800B; an **SSI** (www.ssithailand.com) Open Water certificate is slightly less (9000B) because you do not have to pay for instruction materials. Fun divers should expect to pay roughly 1000B per dive, or around 7000B for a 10-dive package.

Remember: the success of your diving experience (especially if you are learning how to dive) will largely depend on how much you like your instructor. There are other factors to consider as well, like the size of your diving group, the condition of your equipment and the condition of the dive sites, to name a few.

Expect large crowds and booked-out beds throughout December, January, June, July and August, and a monthly glut of wannabe divers after every Full Moon Party on Ko Pha-Ngan.

The second option is to take a ferry to Chumphon on the mainland and then switch to a bus or train bound for the provinces further south.

ⓘ Getting Around

Sŏrng·tǎa·ou

In Mae Hat *sŏrng·tǎa·ou*, pick-up trucks and motorbikes crowd around the pier as passengers alight. If you know where you intend to stay, we highly recommend calling ahead to arrange a pick up.

Water Taxi

Boat taxis depart from Mae Hat, Chalok Ban Kao and the northern part of Sairee Beach (near Vibe Bar). Boat rides to Ko Nang Yuan will set you back at least 100B. Long-tail boats can be chartered for around 1500B per day, depending on the number of passengers carried.

Phuket & the Andaman Coast

With the tallest karsts, the softest sands and the bluest water, the Andaman Coast is the ultimate land of superlatives.

Along the coast, boats from Khao Lak idle between the Similan and Surin Islands, dropping scuba buffs deep into the greatest dive sites around. Further south, Phuket, the biggest island, is the region's international beach resort.

The Andaman's signature pinnacles of jagged jungle-clad karst come to a stunning climax in Krabi, where rock-climbers take in the scenery of Railay as they dangle like ornaments on a giant karst Christmas tree. Ko Phi-Phi Don's unimaginable beauty exceeds even the highest expectations and its party prowess does too.

The catch is that the destination is no secret and the beaches are crowded with backpackers, package tourists and everyone else in between.

Long-tail boats, Railay (p315)

Ko Phi-Phi Don (p319)
INGOLF POMPE/GETTY IMAGES ©

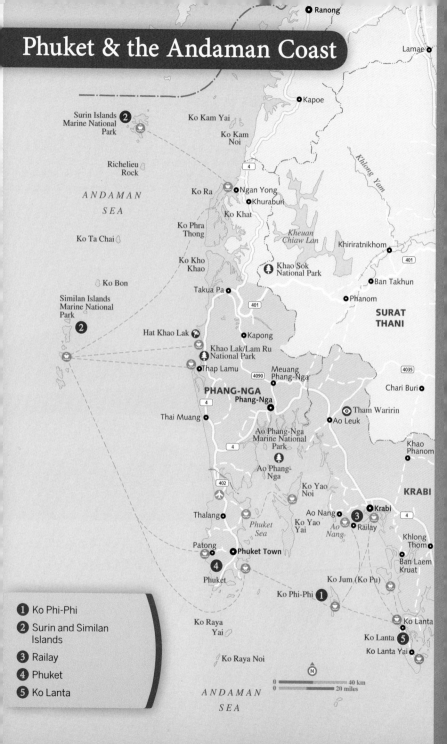

Phuket & the Andaman Coast

Ranong

Lamae

Kapoe

Ko Kam Yai

Khlong Yam

Surin Islands Marine National Park 2

Ko Kam Noi

4

Richelieu Rock

ANDAMAN SEA

Ko Ra

Ngan Yong

Khuraburi

Khiriratnikhom

401

Ko Phra Thong

Ko Khat

Kheuan Chiaw Lan

Ko Ta Chai

Ban Takhun

Ko Kho Khao

Khao Sok National Park

Ko Bon

Takua Pa

Phanom

SURAT THANI

Similan Islands Marine National Park 2

401

Hat Khao Lak

Kapong

Khao Lak/Lam Ru National Park

4035

Thap Lamu

Meuang Phang-Nga

Chari Buri

4090

PHANG-NGA

Phang-Nga

Tham Waririn

Thai Muang

Ao Leuk

Khao Phanom

4

Ao Phang-Nga Marine National Park

KRABI

Ao Phang-Nga

Ko Yao Noi

402

Ko Yao Yai

Ao Nang

Krabi

3

4

Thalang

Phuket Sea

Railay

Ao Nang

Khlong Thom

Patong

Phuket Town

Ban Laem Kruat

4

Phuket

Ko Jum (Ko Pu)

Ko Phi-Phi 1

Ko Lanta

Ko Raya Yai

Ko Lanta 5

Ko Lanta Yai

1 Ko Phi-Phi

2 Surin and Similan Islands

3 Railay

4 Phuket

5 Ko Lanta

N

ANDAMAN SEA

0 ――――― 40 km
0 ――――― 20 miles

Phuket & the Andaman Coast's Highlights

Ko Phi-Phi

Come worship upon the white-sand altar of Ko Phi-Phi (p319), one of the most beautiful beaches on planet earth. The bearded limestone cliffs, ribbons of emerald and turquoise water, and voluptuous contours of sand are a sensory feast. Soak it all in with an afternoon swim or an all-night booze fest. True to its looks, Phi-Phi is courted by crowds of beach-lovers and long ago abandoned a hermit lifestyle.

Diving the Surin & Similan Islands

The two Andaman marine parks at Surin (p293) and Similan (p294) offer some of the best diving in Thailand. The water is incredibly blue and clear, the topography is varied and the marine life is diverse and spectacular. The famous dive spots are best visited on a live-aboard trip departing the mainland; these tours cut out the commute, for more sea time.

REINHARD DIRSCHERL/GETTY IMAGES ©

Rock Climbing, Railay

The Andaman's famous limestone formations pierce sea and sky like prehistoric teeth around Krabi's scenic peninsula. The area's rock-climbing headquarters can be found on Railay (p317), a photogenic corner of tightly packed peaks, both on land and sea. These vertical challenges reward one's huffing and puffing with breathtaking ocean vistas. Even if you're not a climber, there are intimate beaches with equally rewarding views.

Phuket

Phuket (p294) is an easy-peasy beach getaway paired with fine dining and fine living. Wide swathes of sand attract herds of sun-deprived visitors. As an old port town, Phuket boasts a strong culinary tradition influenced by Chinese, Indian, Malay and Western traders. Plus there are modern dining and cooking opportunities beside the sea, loads of raucous bars and other attractions once scenery-boredom sets in.

Ko Lanta

If Ko Phi-Phi is just too pretty and popular for you, then placid Ko Lanta (p324) might be just your type. The island excels in the personality department with a laid-back island vibe and cultural insights into the Thai-Muslim fishing community. It is a marathon book-reading place popular with package tourists, families and quieter types who no longer howl at the moon.

Phuket & the Andaman Coast's Best…

Diving & Snorkelling

○ **Surin Islands Marine National Park** Famous seamount of Richelieu Rock and soft coral earn top marks from divers. Best visited on a liveaboard. (p293)

○ **Similan Islands Marine National Park** Protected park with great visibility and marine life for all diving levels. Best visited on a liveaboard. (p294)

○ **Ko Lanta** Undersea pinnacles of Hin Muang and Hin Daeng attract large pelagic fish. (p325)

Karst Scenery

○ **Ao Phang-Nga Marine National Park** Dramatic missile-shaped islands guard an aquamarine bay. (p306)

○ **Ko Phi-Phi Leh** Ko Phi-Phi Don's uninhabited sister is decorated with soaring cliffs and gem-coloured lagoons and overrun with day trippers and party-boaters. (p322)

○ **Railay** Rock-climb, kayak, snorkel or simply admire these limestone outcroppings. (p315)

Fine Dining

○ **Rum Jungle** Tropical open-air restaurant delivering top-notch seafood and Mediterranean fare. (p303)

○ **Siam Indigo** A stylish and classic Phuket Town restaurant with exceptional French cuisine. (p299)

○ **Taste** Surfside dining samples the best of Thai and Mediterranean dishes. (p310)

Beaches

○ **Hat Kata** Phuket's just-right beach has a social easygoing vibe, seasonal surfing and golden sands. (p303)

○ **Sirinat National Park** Phuket's 'castaway' beaches are where civilisation feels kilometres away even with planes passing overhead. (p310)

○ **Hat Yao** Ko Phi-Phi's pretty stretch of sand is ideal for swimming and beach frolicking. (p320)

Need to Know

ADVANCE PLANNING

○ **One month before** Book accommodation.

○ **One week before** Book your dive trip and domestic plane trip.

○ **One day before** Book a table at one of Phuket's high-end restaurants.

RESOURCES

○ **Jamie's Phuket** (www.jamie-monk.blogspot.com)

○ **One Stop Phuket** (www.1stopphuket.com)

○ **Railay.com** (www.railay.com)

○ **Phuket Wan** (phuketwan.com)

GETTING AROUND

○ **Boat** Everything that floats will take you where roads can't; less so during the rainy season (June to October).

○ **Bus** Good way to get between mainland towns or to/from Bangkok.

○ **Minivan** Faster and more flexible option than the bus.

○ **Motorcycle** Self-touring option on Phuket and Ko Lanta.

○ **Sŏrng·tăa·ou** Small pick-up trucks that act as public buses on the mainland and Phuket.

○ **Taxi & túk-túk** Chartered vehicles that charge a lot on the islands; remember to bargain.

BE FOREWARNED

○ **Dive trips** Book directly with the dive shop, not with an agent.

○ **Motorcycle travel** Always wear a helmet when riding a motorcycle and don't put valuables in the front basket.

○ **Rainy season** Except for Phuket, much of the Andaman Coast closes between June and October as seas can be too rough for transport and diving.

○ **Drownings** Common on Phuket's west coast beaches, especially during the rainy season.

○ **Sunbathing** Women, don't go topless.

Left: Marine life, Similan Islands (p294);
Above: Boat tour, Krabi Province (p313)

(LEFT)TUNART/GETTY IMAGES ©; (ABOVE) CULTURA TRAVEL/
PHILIP LEE HARVEY/GETTY IMAGES ©

Phuket & the Andaman Coast Itineraries

You can pop into Phuket in a hurry thanks to the conveniently located airport, but give yourself time to savour the dramatic coastline and peep underneath the ocean's surface on a dive trip.

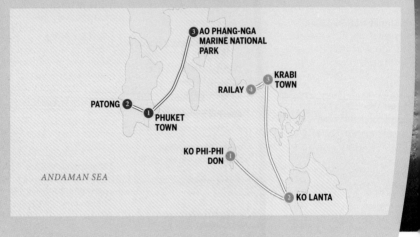

AO PHANG-NGA MARINE NATIONAL PARK

KRABI TOWN

RAILAY

PATONG

PHUKET TOWN

KO PHI-PHI DON

KO LANTA

ANDAMAN SEA

---

3 DAYS

PHUKET TO AO PHANG-NGA MARINE NATIONAL PARK

Phuket in a Nutshell

You can fly to Phuket from Bangkok for a long weekend without wasting much time in transit. Increasingly, you can even bypass Bangkok entirely with direct Phuket flights.

The largest of Thailand's islands, Phuket has lovely west-coast beaches that are lined with professional resorts and intimate boutiques, umbrella lounge-chairs and warm, clear water. All of the international standards of leisure apply and you can treat yourself to spa sessions, cooking classes and fine meals. People don't come to Phuket to 'rough it'.

Explore the old Sino-Portuguese architecture and Chinese shrines of

❶ **Phuket Town** (p296) and cool down at a local eatery or cafe to savour old Phuket, one of Thailand's few resort islands with a lengthy historical record.

Once the sun has set, the night creatures descend on ❷ **Patong** (p306), a rowdy strip of neon lights, ladyboy cabarets, screaming discos and a touch of port-town seediness.

Devote one day to ❸ **Ao Phang-Nga Marine National Park** (p306), a protected bay cluttered with more than 40 peaked karst islands. Vast mangrove forests border the bay, providing fertile fishing grounds for local villagers.

5 DAYS

KO PHI-PHI DON TO RAILAY

Go 'Ko' Hopping

South of Phuket, small islands and beaches are cradled together in a scenic coastal neighbourhood. Travellers visit them in succession as if they were all cherished family members.

From Phuket, boat to ❶**Ko Phi-Phi Don** (p319), the beauty queen of the Thai islands with just the right beach proportions of mod-cons and a heaping helping of party power.

Then hop to ❷**Ko Lanta** (p324), which has exceptional dive sites and lots of 'island' personality. Hire a motorcycle and cruise the fishing villages and roadside food shacks to get in touch with Lanta's local

population of Muslim and Buddhist Thais as well as *chow lair* (also spelt *chao leh,* sea gypsies). This kicked-back island doesn't have the flawless good looks of Ko Phi-Phi, but it has a whole lot of soul.

Another boat journey will take you to ❸**Krabi Town** (p313), where you can transfer to a long-tail boat headed for ❹**Railay** (p315). This coastal peninsula is hemmed in by limestone stacks. Rock climbers creep up the pitted vertical walls, while kayakers prefer a surface view. You're just a step away from Krabi Town for a quick air return to Bangkok.

Long-tail boat, Ko Phi-Phi Don
MIKEL BILBAO/GETTY IMAGES ©

Discover Phuket & the Andaman Coast

Khao Lak
OTTO STADLER/GETTY IMAGES ©

PHANG-NGA PROVINCE

Khao Sok National Park
อุทยานแห่งชาติเขาสก

If your leg muscles have atrophied after one too many days of beach-bumming, consider venturing inland to the wondrous **Khao Sok National Park** (☎ 0 7739 5025; www.khaosok.com; adult/child 200/100B). Many believe this lowland jungle – the wettest spot in Thailand – to be over 160 million years old, making it one of the oldest rainforests on the globe. It features dramatic limestone formations and waterfalls that cascade through juicy thickets drenched with rain. A network of dirt trails snakes through the quiet park, allowing visitors to spy on the exciting array of indigenous creatures.

The best time of year to visit is the dry season (December to April). During the wet season (June to October), trails can be extremely slippery, flash flooding is common and leeches come out in force. On the other hand, animals leave their hidden reservoirs throughout the wet months, so you're more likely to stumble across big fauna.

◎ Sights & Activities

Khao Sok's vast terrain makes it one of the last viable habitats for **large mammals**. There are more than 300 bird species, 38 bat varieties and one of the world's largest flowers, the rare *Rafflesia kerrii*, which, in Thailand, is found only in Khao Sok.

Chiaw Lan, created in 1982 by an enormous shale-clay dam called

Ratchaprapha (Kheuan Ratchaprapha or Chiaw Lan), sits about an hour's drive (65km) east of the visitors centre. The limestone outcrops protruding from the lake reach a height of 960m, over three times higher than the formations in the Phang-Nga area.

Tham Nam Thalu cave contains striking limestone formations and subterranean streams, while **Tham Si Ru** features four converging passageways used as a hideout by communist insurgents between 1975 and 1982.

Elephant trekking, kayaking and rafting are popular park activities. The hiking is also excellent, and you can arrange park tours from any guesthouse in or around the park.

🛏 Sleeping & Eating

We recommend going on a two-day, one-night trip (2500B per person) to Chiaw Lan where you sleep in floating huts on the lake and go on a variety of canoe and hiking excursions.

Art's Riverview Jungle Lodge
Guesthouse $$

(📞 09 0167 6818; http://krabidir.com/artsriverviewlodge; 54/3 Mu 6; bungalows 650-1500B) In a monkey-filled jungle bordering a river with a natural limestone cliff–framed swimming hole, this is the prettiest location in Khao Sok. Wood bungalows are simple but big; all have river views.

Tree House
Guesthouse $$

(📞 0 7739 5169; www.khaosok-treehouse.com; 233 Mu 6; r with fan/air-con 1000/2000B; ❄🛜🏊) Don't be dissuaded by the Disney-esque facade, here is a complex of rather excellent and spacious bungalows connected by raised paths and bridges. The best nests have flat screens, air-con and two terraces. Fan rooms are simpler and smaller but very clean.

Elephant Hills
Resort $$$

(📞 0 7638 1703; www.elephant-hills.com; 170 Mu 7 Tambon Klong Sok; d all-inclusive from 12,500B; 🅿🛜🚶) 🌿 Set above the Sok River, at the base of stunning limestone mountains draped in misty jungle, the

area's only tented camp offers the kind of rootsy luxury you'd most associate with the Serengeti.

It's all inclusive and the price includes average meals, guided hikes through the jungle and a canoe trip downriver to their elephant camp where 15 lovely ladies – rescues from other camps where they were forced to carry tourists around – are treated kindly. Reservations only.

ℹ Getting There & Around

Minivans to Surat Thani (250B, one hour), Krabi (300B, two hours) and a handful of other destinations leave daily from the park.

To explore Chiaw Lan lake on your own, charter a long-tail (2000B per day) at the dam's entrance.

Khao Lak & Around
เขาหลัก

Hat Khao Lak is a beach for folks who shun the glitz of Phuket's bigger resort towns, but still crave comfort, shopping and plenty of facilities. With warm waves to frolic in, long stretches of golden sand backed by forested hills, and easy day trips to the Similan and Surin Islands, Khao Sok and Khao Lak/Lam Ru National Parks, and even Phuket, the area is a central base for exploring the North Andaman – above and below the water.

🤿 Activities

Diving or snorkelling day excursions to the Similan and Surin Islands are immensely popular but, if you can, opt for a live-aboard. All dive shops offer live-aboard trips from around 17,000/29,000B for three-/five-day packages and day trips for 4900B to 6500B.

Although geared towards divers, all dive shops welcome snorkellers who can hop on selected dive excursions or live-aboards for a discount of around 40%; otherwise, tour agencies all around town offer even cheaper snorkelling trips to the Similan Islands for around 3200B.

Wicked Diving   Diving
(☎0 7648 5868; www.wickeddiving.com) An exceptionally well-run and environmentally conscious outfit that runs diving and snorkelling overnight trips offering a range of live-aboard options including Whale Sharks & Mantas, Turtle & Reefs and Sharks & Rays conservation trips, run in conjunction with **Ecocean** (www.whaleshark.org).

Sea Dragon Dive Centre   Diving
(☎0 7648 5420; www.seadragondivecenter.com; Th Phetkasem) One of the older operations in Khao Lak, Sea Dragon has maintained high standards throughout the years.

Fantastic   Snorkelling
(☎0 7648 5998; www.fantasticsimilan.com; adult/child 3200/2200B) Fantastic is a campy frolic of a Similans snorkelling tour featuring players from the local cross-dressing cabaret as guides. No booking office; meet at the pier or Fantastic can arrange pick-ups from your hotel.

🛏 Sleeping

Fasai House   Guesthouse $
(☎0 7648 5867; r 500-700B; ❄@) The best budget choice in Khao Lak, Fasai has immaculate motel-style rooms and smiling staff members.

Greenbeach   Hotel $$
(☎0 7648 5845; www.khaolakgreenbeachresort.com; bungalows 1400-2300B; ❄🐾) On an excellent stretch of Khao Lak beach and extending back into a garden, this place has a warm family-style soul. The wooden bungalows have glass doors, air-con and

fan, shady terraces and views of a towering, ancient banyan tree.

Nangthong Bay Resort   Hotel $$
(☎0 7648 5088; nangthong.com; r 1800B, bungalows 2500-3000B; ❄@🛜🏊🐾) Rooms are designed with a sparse black-and-white chic decor. The cheapest rooms are set back from the beach, but are fantastic value. Grounds are lush and service is excellent.

Monochrome   Boutique Hotel $$$
(☎0 7642 7700; www.monochromeresort.com; 67/238 Mu 5, Ban Niang; r/ste from 3900/7900B; P❄@🛜🏊) Just four months old at research time, the newest splashy address in Khao Lak is set on the road to Bang Niang, about 200m from the beach. It's modern, with a vertical louvred facade, a beer garden off the entryway and pool in the courtyard, with lots of charcoal grey and natural cherrywood to soothe the eye.

✕ Eating & Drinking

Go Pong   Thai $
(Th Phetkasem; dishes 30-100B; ⏱noon-10pm) Get off the tourist taste-bud tour at this terrific little street-side diner where they stir-fry noodles and spicy rice dishes, and simmer an aromatic noodle soup that attracts a local lunch following.

Takieng   Thai $$
(☎08 6952 7693; 26/43 Mu 5, Bang Niang; dishes 80-350B; ⏱11am-10pm) Set on the east side of the highway just before the Bang Niang turn are two open-air Thai restaurants beneath stilted tin roofs. This is the more visually appealing of the two, and the dishes are also stylish. They steam fresh fish in green curry, do a scintillating chicken and pork *lâhp,* and fry squid in chilli paste.

ℹ Getting There & Away

Khao Lak Land Discoveries runs hourly minibuses to Phuket International Airport (600B, one hour 15 minutes). Alternately, you can take **Cheaper Than Hotel** (☎08 6276 6479, 08 5786 1378), which admittedly is an odd name for a taxi and transport service. They make the run to the Phuket airport (1000B) and points south.

Surin Islands Marine National Park

อุทยานแห่งชาติหมู่เกาะสุรินทร์

The five gorgeous islands that make up the **Surin Islands Marine National Park** (www.dnp.go.th; adult/child 500/300B; ☾mid-Nov–mid-May) sit 60km offshore, just 5km from the Thailand–Myanmar marine border. Healthy rainforest, pockets of white-sand beach in sheltered bays and rocky headlands that jut into the ocean characterise these granite-outcrop islands. The clearest of water makes for great marine life, with underwater visibility often up to 35m. The islands' sheltered waters also attract *chow lair* – sea gypsies – who live in a village onshore during the monsoon season from May to November.

Ko Surin Neua (north) and Ko Surin Tai (south) are the two largest islands. Park headquarters and all visitor facilities are at Ao Chong Khad and Ao Mai Ngam on Ko Surin Neua, near the jetty.

Khuraburi is the jumping-off point for the park. The pier is about 9km north of town, as is the mainland **national park office** (☎ 0 7649 1378; ☾8am-5pm), with good information, maps and helpful staff.

Dive sites in the park include **Ko Surin Tai** and **HQ Channel** between the two main islands. **Richelieu Rock** (a seamount 14km southeast) is also technically in the park and happens to be one of the best dive sites, if not the best, on the Andaman coast. There's no dive facility in the park itself, so dive trips (four-day live-aboards around 20,000B) must be booked from the mainland. Bleaching has damaged the hard corals but you'll see plenty of fish and soft corals. Two-hour snorkelling trips (per person 100B, gear per day 40B) leave the park headquarters at 9am and 2pm daily. Expect to be in the company of mostly Thais who swim fully clothed. If you'd like a more serene snorkelling experience, charter your own long-tail from the national park (half day 1500B), or better yet, directly from the Moken (*chow lair*) themselves in **Ban Moken** (Moken Village).

Surin Islands Marine National Park

Diving Surin & Similan Islands

The Surin and Similan Islands Marine National Parks rank among the world's top dive sites. Here are just a few of the most famous spots:

North Point The huge boulder formations at this dive site are majestic. The water is often very blue and clear. The dive starts in deep water and finishes in a shallow reef where turtles are common.

West of Eden Another boulder site, this is a fun dive because you can drift along in the current (saving your strength for other dives). The colours of the soft corals and sea fans are an amazing collection of pinks and purples. It is also less crowded than other spots in the park.

Tachai Pinnacle The northern part of this pinnacle dive is beloved because of its schools of fish and soft corals. But the real deal is the challenge of the current.

Richelieu Rock Probably the most famous dive site in the Andaman Sea, Richelieu Rock has everything from soft corals to schools of fish.

Ko Bon Ridge Best known for its possible encounters with Manta rays.

Similan Islands Marine National Park

อุทยานแห่งชาติหมู่เกาะสิมิลัน

Known to divers the world over, beautiful **Similan Islands Marine National Park** (www.dnp.go.th; adult/child 400/200B; ⊗Nov-May) is 70km offshore. Its smooth granite islands are as impressive above water as below, topped with rainforest, edged with white-sand beaches and fringed with coral reefs. Unfortunately, recent coral bleaching has killed off many of the hard corals but soft corals are still intact, the fauna is there and it's still a lovely place to dive.

'Similan' comes from the Malay word *sembilan,* meaning 'nine', and while each island is named, they're more commonly known by their numbers. Relatively recently, the park was expanded to included Ko Bon and Ko Tachai, and both have remained unscathed by coral bleaching, making them some of the better diving and snorkelling areas.

Hat Khao Lak is the jumping-off point for the park. The pier is at Thap Lamu, about 10km south of town.

The Similans offer diving for all levels of experience, at depths from 2m to 30m. There are rock reefs at **Ko Payu** (Island 7) and dive-throughs at **Hin Pousar** (Elephant Head), with marine life ranging from tiny plume worms and soft corals to schooling fish and whale sharks. No facilities for divers exist in the national park itself, so you'll need to take a dive tour. Agencies in Hat Khao Lak and Phuket book dive trips (three-day live-aboards from around 15,000B, but you'll pay more to rent gear).

Plenty of tour agencies in Hat Khao Lak offer snorkelling-only day/overnight trips (from around 3000/5000B), and the beach can become positively packed. Some snorkelling outfits go so far as to feed the fish, which is a big ecological no-no.

KO PHUKET ภูเก็ต

POP 83,800

The island of Phuket has long been misunderstood. Firstly, the 'h' is silent. Ahem. And secondly, Phuket doesn't feel like an island at all. It's so huge (the biggest in Thailand) that you rarely get the sense that you're surrounded by water, which is probably the reason why the Ko (meaning 'island') was dropped from its name.

Jet-setters come through in droves, getting pummelled during swanky spa sessions and swigging sundowners at one of the many fashion-forward nightspots or on their rented yacht. But you don't have to be an heiress to tap into Phuket's trendy to-do list. With deep-sea diving, high-end dining and white beaches all within reach, it really is hard to say farewell.

ℹ Getting There & Away

Air

Phuket International Airport (☏ 0 7632 7230; www.phuketairportonline.com) is 30km northwest of Phuket Town and it takes around 45 minutes to an hour to reach the southern beaches from here.

Bangkok Airways (☏ 0 7622 5033; www.bangkokair.com; 58/2-3 Th Yaowarat, Phuket Town) and **THAI** (☏ 0 7621 1195; www.thaiairways.com; 78/1 Th Ranong, Phuket Town) have offices on Phuket.

Bus

All buses depart from the **bus terminal** (☏ 0 7621 1977; Th Thepkrasattri), to the east of Phuket Town's centre.

Destination	Bus type	Fare (B)	Duration (hr)
Bangkok	2nd class	543	15
Bangkok	air-con	680	13-14
Bangkok	VIP	1058	13
Ko Samui	air-con	430	8 (bus/boat)
Krabi	air-con	150	3½
Phang-Nga	ordinary	90	2½
Phang-Nga	air-con	270	5
Surat Thani	ordinary	195	6
Surat Thani	air-con	220	5

Ferry & Speedboat

Phuket's Tha Rasada, southeast of Phuket Town, is the main pier for boats to Ko Phi-Phi, connecting onward to Krabi, Ko Lanta, the Trang Islands, Ko Lipe and even as far as Langkawi Island in Malaysia (where there are further ferry connections to Penang). For additional services to Krabi and Ao Nang via the Ko Yao Islands, boats leave from Tha Bang Rong north of Tha Rasada.

Thai massage, Swasana Spa (p306), Hat Patong

Minivan

Phuket travel agencies all around the island sell tickets (including ferry fare) for air-con minivans down to Ko Samui and Ko Pha-Ngan.

ⓘ Getting Around

Local Phuket transport is terrible. There are *sŏrng·tǎa·ou* (passenger pick-up trucks) which run to the beaches from Phuket Town but often you'll have to go via Phuket Town to get from one beach to another (say Hat Surin to Hat Patong), which can take hours.

At research time, Phuket authorities had evicted the legions of drivers who used to gather at the doors to baggage claim and haggle for passengers. Now, just seven drivers, of metered taxis only, will be allowed in at any one time, making for a far more soothing first step on the island.

Phuket Town   เมืองภูเก็ต
POP 94,325

Attracting entrepreneurs from as far away as the Arabian Peninsula, China, India and Portugal, Phuket Town was a colourful

Flights to/from Phuket

DESTINATION	AIRLINE	FREQUENCY	PRICE (B)
Bangkok	Air Asia	several daily	around 1480
Bangkok	Bangkok Airways	daily	1725
Bangkok	Nok Air	3-4 daily	1488
Bangkok	THAI	seven daily	3000
Ko Samui	Bangkok Airways	daily	2380
Chiang Mai	Air Asia	twice daily	1600

blend of cultural influences, cobbled together by tentative compromise and cooperation. Wander down streets clogged with Sino-Portuguese architecture housing arty coffee shops, galleries, wonderful inexpensive restaurants and hip little guesthouses; peek down alleyways to find Chinese Taoist shrines shrouded in incense smoke.

⊚ Sights

Sino-Portuguese Architecture
Architecture

Stroll along Th Thalang, Dibuk, Yaowarat, Ranong, Phang-Nga, Rasada and Krabi for a glimpse of some of the best architecture on offer. Soi Romanee off Th Thalang is the most ambient area of town.

The fabulous **Phra Phitak Chyn Pracha Mansion** (www.blueelephant.com; 9 Th Krabi) has been restored and turned into a branch of the upscale Blue Elephant restaurant chain and culinary school.

Phuket Thaihua Museum
Museum

(พิพิธภัณฑ์ภูเก็ตไทยหัว; 28 Th Krabi; admission 200B; ⊙9am-5pm) This flashy museum, set in an old Sino-Portuguese home, is filled with photos and exhibits on Phuket's history. The last room is covered in photos of local dishes – if this makes you hungry, info on where to find the food stalls is listed.

🛏 Sleeping

Phuket Town is the cheapest place on the island to get some zzz's and is a treasure trove of budget lodging.

Romanee
Guesthouse **$$**

(☏08 9728 9871; Th Romanee; r standard/deluxe 890/1090B; ❄ 🛜) This place certainly has style, with its polished concrete floors and wood block reception bar. Rooms likewise have an airy modern feel with wood floors, flat screens, pastel accent walls, fine linens and tasteful lighting. Deluxe rooms are huge and worth the extra coin.

Ko Phuket

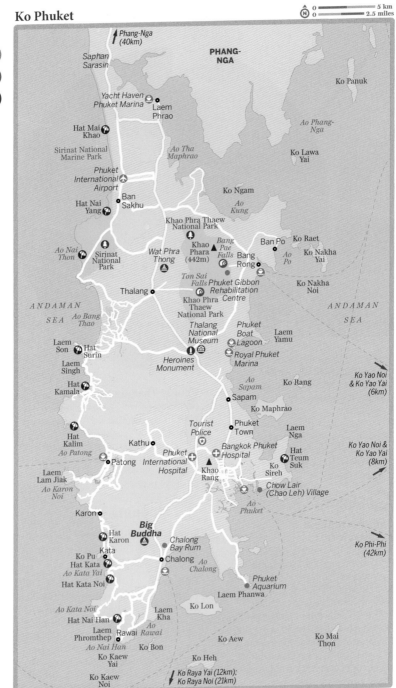

LYNN GAIL/GETTY IMAGES ©

Don't Miss
Big Buddha

Set on a hilltop just northwest of Chalong circle and visible from almost half of the island, the Big Buddha has the best view on Phuket.

NEED TO KNOW

พระใหญ่; mingmongkolphuket.com; off Hwy 402

🍴 Eating

Kopitiam by Wilai
Thai **$**

(☎ 08 3606 9776; www.facebook.com/kopitiam bywilai; 18 Th Thalang; mains 70-120B; ⏰ 11am-10pm Mon-Sat; 📶) Wilai serves Phuket soul food. It does Phuketian *pàt tai* with some kick to it, and a fantastic *mèe sua*: think noodles sautéed with egg, greens, prawns, chunks of sea bass and squid. Wash it all down with fresh chrysanthemum juice.

Suay
International-Thai **$$**

(☎ 08 1797 4135; www.suayrestaurant.com; 50/2 Th Takuapa; most dishes 90-350B; ⏰ 5-11pm) Fusion at this converted house just south of old town proper means salmon carpaccio piled with a tart and bright pomelo salad, an innovative take on *sôm·dam* featuring mangosteen that pops with flavour, a yellowfin tuna *lâhp,* smoked eggplant served with roast chilli paste and crab meat, and a massaman curry with lamb chops.

Siam Indigo
International-Thai **$$**

(☎ 0 7625 6697; www.siamindigo.com; 8 Th Phang-Nga; dishes 120-280B; ⏰ 2-11pm) One of Phuket's most stylish gems is set in an 80-year-old Sino-Portuguese relic and specialises in Thai cuisine – including classic recipes rarely seen these days – with a French-International twist. Meals are plated on gorgeous china, the room is glorious and the food is exceptional.

PAUL KENNEDY/GETTY IMAGES ©

⭐ Don't Miss
Vegetarian Festival

Loud popping sounds similar to machine-gun fire fill the streets, the air fills with grey-brown smoke and men and women traipse along blocked-off city roads, their cheeks pierced with skewers and knives or, more surprisingly, lamps and tree branches. Some have blood streaming down their fronts or open lashes across their backs. This isn't a war zone – it's one of Phuket's most important festivals, centred in Phuket Town.

The festival, which takes place during the first nine days of the ninth lunar month of the Chinese calendar – usually late September or October – celebrates the beginning of 'Taoist Lent', when devout Chinese abstain from eating meat.

In Phuket Town, the festival activities are centred around five Chinese temples, with the **Jui Tui** temple on Soi Puthon the most important, followed by **Bang Niew** and **Sui Boon Tong** temples. Other ceremonies occur throughout the festival at the temples and can include firewalking and knife-ladder climbing. Beyond the headlining gore, fabulous vegetarian food stalls line the side streets offering a perfect opportunity to sample cheap local treats and strike up interesting conversations with the locals.

NEED TO KNOW
www.phuketvegetarian.com

🍷 Drinking & Nightlife

This is where you can party like a local. Bars buzz until late, patronised almost exclusively by Thais and local expats.

Sanaeha   Bar
(📱08 1519 8937; 83, 85 Th Yaowarat, Phuket Town; ⏱6pm-late) Sanaeha is an upscale bohemian joint lit by seashell chandeliers, with plenty of dark corners where you can

sip, snuggle, snack and dig that soulful crooner on stage.

Timber Hut
Club

(☎ 0 7621 1839; 118/1 Th Yaowarat, Phuket Town; ⏰ 6pm-2am) Thai and expat locals have been filling this old clubhouse every night for nearly 20 years. They gather at long wooden tables on two floors, converge around thick timber columns, swill whiskey and sway to live bands that swing from hard rock to funk to hip-hop.

🔒 Shopping

Drawing Room
Gallery

(☎ 08 6899 4888; isara380@gmail.com; 56 Th Phang Nga; ⏰ 9am-11pm) With a vibe reminiscent of pre-boom Brooklyn or East London, this wide-open, almost reclaimed, co-operative is by far the most interesting gallery in a town full of them. Canvasses can be colourful abstract squiggles or dreamy pen-and-ink meanderings.

Ban Boran Textiles
Textiles

(☎ 0 7621 1563; 51 Th Yaowarat; ⏰ 10.30am-6.30pm Mon-Fri) Simply put, this dusty hole-in-the-wall is the best shop on the island for silk, raw silk, cotton textiles and sarongs.

Ranida
Gallery

(119 Th Thalang; ⏰ 10am-6pm) An exquisite antique gallery featuring antiquated Buddha statues and sculpture, organic textiles and interesting fashions inspired by vintage Thai garments and fabrics. The clothing is striking and ambitious, but on the right woman it can be a tasteful high fashion statement.

ℹ Getting There & Around

To/from the Airport

Despite what airport taxi touts would like you to believe, a bright-orange government airport bus (☎ 0 7623 2371; www.airportbusphuket.com; tickets 90B) runs between the airport and Phuket Town via the Heroines Monument about every hour between 6am and 7pm. There's also a minibus service at the airport that will take you into Phuket Town for 150B per person.

Local Knowledge

Phuket

TAMMASAK (NOI) CHOOTONG, CHEF, SUAY (P299)

1 SURFING
Phuket is a secret surf destination with swells arriving during the low season (July to October). Hat Kata, Hat Nai Han, Hat Nai Yang and Kamala among other beaches are all known for their breaks. Kata's break can reach 2m, while Hat Nai Han can get bigger waves (up to 3m) but both have vicious undertows that can claim lives. Talk to Phuket Surf (based in Kata at the south end of the bay near the best breaks) for more information.

2 BEACH CLUBS
Phuket has a lot of beach clubs but my favourite is Bimi Beach Club at Twin Palms (p309); it is a fun, all-day party scene and the name is short for 'bikinis and martinis'. The food and drinks are not too overpriced and it has a DJ in the afternoon.

3 PHUKET TOWN
Phuket Town is a historic district for shopping, dining and enjoying the old buildings, which were built in the Sino-Portuguese style. Hua Pan Bar (183/33 Th Phang Nga) is a local club that plays punk rock and crunch music; it is low budget but a cool setting.

4 CRUISE THE COAST
Phuket has a beautiful coastline that can be explored on a motorbike. The perfect time to ride is from 5pm to 6.30pm. Start from Hat Rawai, go along the coast to Hat Nai Han, Kata, Karon and north to Surin. It will take approximately 1½ hours and is a beautiful coastal route.

5 LUNCH
Stop at the sea gypsy village in Rawai, north of the pier; it is the place to get fresh seafood. You can pick it out yourself then take it over to the adjacent restaurants. The price is very reasonable and it makes for a fine afternoon.

Phuket for Children

There's plenty for kids to do on Phuket. And while the seedier face of the sex industry is on full show in Patong (we wouldn't take our kids there, although many people do), the rest of the island is fairly G-rated.

Elephant treks are always a big hit with kids, with the best options available on the Kata-Hat Nai Han road. **Phuket Aquarium** (☏ 0 7639 1126; www.phuketaquarium.org; adult/child 100/50B; ☉8.30am-4.30pm) and a visit to the tiny **Phuket Gibbon Rehabilitation Centre** (☏ 0 7626 0492; www.gibbonproject.org; admission 10B; ☉9am-4pm) are also terrific animal-themed activities that are sure to please.

The main family-flogged feature of Phuket is **Phuket Fantasea** (☏ 0 7638 5000; www.phuket-fantasea.com; admission with/without dinner 1900/1500B; ☉shows 7pm & 9pm Wed & Fri, 9pm only Sat-Tue), which is a pricey extravaganza of animals, costumes, song, special effects, pyrotechnics, and a lousy dinner.

The newest attractions for kids of all ages, but especially for tweeners and above, is the **Phuket Wake Park** (☏ 0 7620 2527; www.phuketwakepark.com; 86/3 Mu 6, Th Wichitsongkram, Kathu; two hours 500-650B, day pass 1200B; ☉7:30am-11pm), where you can learn to wake board by buzzing a lake nestled in the mountains of Kathu.

Car

There are cheap car-rental agencies on Th Rasada near **Pure Car Rent** (☏ 0 7621 1002; www.purecarrent.com; 75 Th Rasada), which is a good choice.

Sŏrng·tăa·ou & Túk-túk

Large bus-sized *sŏrng·tăa·ou* run regularly from Th Ranong near the market to the various Phuket beaches (25B to 40B per person). These run from around 7am to 5pm; outside these times you have to charter a túk-túk to the beaches, which will set you back 500B to Patong, Kata and Rawai, and 600B to Karon and Kamala.

For a ride around town, túk-túk drivers should charge 100B to 200B.

Motorcycle taxis around town cost 30B.

Rawai ราไวย์

Now this is a place to live, which is exactly why Phuket's rapidly developing south coast is teeming with retirees, Thai and expat entrepreneurs, and a service sector that, for the most part, moved here from somewhere else.

The region is defined not only by its beaches but also by the lush coastal hills that rise steeply and tumble into the Andaman Sea forming **Laem Promthep**, Phuket's southernmost point.

🛏 Sleeping

Ao Sane Bungalows　　　Hotel **$**
(☏ 0 7628 8306; 11/2 Mu 1, Th Viset, Hat Nai Han; bungalows 600-1200B) The rickety cold-water, fan-cooled wooden bungalows are on a secluded beach, with million-dollar views of Ao Sane and Ao Nai Han. There's a beachside restaurant, dive centre and an old-hippie vibe.

Vijitt　　　Hotel **$$$**
(☏ 0 7636 3600; www.vijittresort.com; 16 Mu 2, Th Viset; villas from 6700B; ❄) Arguably the area's most elegant property, Vijitt is sprinkled with deluxe villas that boast limestone floors, large bathtubs, outdoor showers and gorgeous sea views from private terraces. The stunning black-bottom infinity pool overlooks Friendship Beach.

✖️ Eating & Drinking

Roti House
Southern Thai $

(81/6 Soi Sameka, Rawai; mains 20-40B; ⏰7-11am) If you like French toast or croissants in the morning, you'll love roti, Thailand's Muslim morning delicacy. You'll receive a plate of savoury crepes and a bowl of sweet breakfast curry. Dunk, munch, repeat.

Rum Jungle
International $$$

(🕿 0 7638 8153; 69/8 Th Sai Yuan, Rawai; meals 300-500B; ⏰11.30am-10.30pm) The best restaurant in the area and one of the best in all of Phuket is family run and spear-headed by a terrific Aussie chef. The New Zealand lamb shank is divine, as are the steamed clams, and the pasta sauces are all made from scratch.

ℹ️ Getting There & Away

Rawai is about 18km from Phuket Town. *Sŏrng·tăa·ou* (30B) run from Phuket's fountain circle at Th Ranong – some continue to Hat Nai Han, but not all of them, so ask first. The túk-túk trip from Rawai to Nai Han is a hefty 200B.

You can hire taxis (which are actually just chartered cars) from Rawai and Hat Nai Han to

the airport (800B), Patong (700B) and Phuket Town (500B).

Hat Kata
หาดกะตะ

Travellers of all ages, styles and tastes descend on this bustling tourist enclave with its bustling restaurants, wet season surfing and luscious beach, which is without the seedy hustle endemic to Patong.

The beach is divided in two by a rocky headland, and the road between them is home to Phuket's original millionaire's row. Hat Kata Yai is on the north end, while the more secluded Hat Kata Noi unfurls to the south. Both offer soft golden sand and attract a bohemian crowd.

👁️ Sights & Activities

The small island of **Ko Pu** is just off shore, but be careful of rip tides, heed the red flags and don't go past the breakers in the wet season unless you are a strong ocean swimmer with experience. Both Hat Kata Yai and Hat Kata Noi offer decent surfing from April to November. **Surf House** (🕿08 1979 7737; www.surfhousephuket.com;

Rawai

4 Mu 2, Th Kata; ◷10am-midnight), a bar across the street from Hat Kata, has a man-made surf park (per hour 800B) that kids love.

If it's heat and sweat you crave, drop into **Kata Hot Yoga** (☏0 7660 5950; www.katahotyoga.com; 217 Th Khoktanod; per class 500B; ◷classes 9am, 5:15pm & 7:15pm).

🛏 Sleeping

Chanisara Guesthouse
Guesthouse $

(☏08 5789 5701; 48/5 Soi Casa del Sol, Hat Kata; r from 1000B; ❄🛜) One of several townhouse-style guesthouses on the Casa Del Sol cul de sac. Rooms are super-bright, tiled affairs with air-con, flat-screen TVs, recessed lighting and a little balcony. Beds are dressed in Thai linens and bottled water is delivered daily. Low season rates drop to 600B per night.

Sabai Corner
Bungalow $$

(☏0 9875 5525; www.sabaicorner.com; Th Karon Lookout; r 1950B) No room on this sweet island offers the view available from the two chalets set on the hillside above Sabai Corner. Each is an independent studio with granite tile in the baths, canopied bed, wall-mounted flat screen with satellite TV, sofa, wardrobe and security boxes. They also have wide outdoor patios that function as an outdoor living room.

Mom Tri's Boathouse
Boutique Hotel $$$

(☏0 7633 0015; www.boathousephuket.com; 2/2 Th Kata (Patak West); r from 6000B; ❄🛜🏊) For Thai politicos, pop stars, artists and celebrity authors, the intimate boutique Boathouse is still the only place to stay on Phuket. Rooms are spacious and gorgeous, some sporting large breezy verandahs. Critics complain that the Boathouse is a bit stiff-lipped and old-fashioned for this century, but no-one can deny that the main reason to stay here is for the food.

🍴 Eating

Sabai Corner
International-Thai $$

(☏0 9875 5525; www.sabaicorner.com; Th Karon Lookout, Hat Kata; mains 200-499B; ◷10am-10pm; 🛜) There is no better view on the island than the one you'll glimpse from the deck at this superlative pub.

Yet it's rare that a location like this gets the restaurant it deserves. You'll find it downhill and around a bend from the Karon Lookout, a little over halfway between Rawai and Kata.

Boathouse Wine & Grill
International $$$

(☏0 7633 0015; www.boathousephuket.com; 2/2 Th Kata (Patak West), Hat Kata; mains 450-950B; ◷11am-11pm) The perfect place to wow a fussy date, the Boathouse is the pick of the bunch for most local foodies. The atmosphere can be a little stuffy – this is the

Swimming pool. Hat Kata
INGOLF POMPE/GETTY IMAGES ©

closest that Phuket gets to old-school dining – but the Mediterranean fusion food is fabulous, the wine list expansive and the sea views sublime.

🍷 Drinking & Nightlife

Ska Bar   Bar

(186/12 Th Koktanod, Kata; ⊗noon-late) At Kata's southernmost cove, tucked into the rocks and seemingly intertwined with the trunk of a grand old banyan tree, this is our choice for oceanside sundowners. The Thai bartenders add to Ska's funky Rasta vibe, and the canopy dangles with buoys, paper lanterns and the flags of 10 countries.

ℹ Getting There & Around

Sŏrng·tǎa·ou to both Kata and Karon (per person 25B) leave frequently from the day market on Th Ranong in Phuket from 7am to 5pm. The main *sŏrng·tǎa·ou* stop in Kata is in front of Kata Beach Resort.

Taxis from Kata go to Phuket Town (600B), Patong (600B) and Karon (200B).

Hat Karon   หาดกะรน

Hat Karon is like Hat Patong and Hat Kata's love child: it's chilled-out, a touch glamorous and a tad sleazy. There are two megaresorts and package tourists aplenty, but there's still more sand space per capita than at either Patong or Kata. The further north you go the more beautiful the beach gets, culminating at the northernmost edge, accessible from a rutted road that extends past the vendors and food stalls, where the water is like turquoise glass.

🛏 Sleeping

Bazoom Haus   Guesthouse $

(☎08 9533 0241; www.bazoomhostel.com; 269/5 Karon Plaza, Hat Karon; dm 300B, r 2700B; ❄@🛜) The fabulous private rooms offer wood floors and furnishings, recessed lighting, flat screens and mosaic showers. There's a Jacuzzi and barbecue on the rooftop deck, DJ decks in the in-house

Korean restaurant (the owners are from Korea) and a dive shop, too. Dorms have six beds to a room. Discounts of up to 65% in low season.

Kangaroo Guesthouse   Guesthouse $$

(☎0 7639 6517; www.kangarooguesthouse.com; 269/6-9 Karon Plaza, Hat Karon; r 1200B; ❄🛜) Basic, but very clean and sun-filled tiled rooms with hot water, air-con, a cute breakfast nook and balconies overlooking a narrow, slightly seedy soi.

In On The Beach   Hotel $$$

(☎0 7639 8220; www.karon-inonthebeach.com; 695-697 Mu 1, Th Patak; r from 3500B; ❄@🛜🏊) This is a sweet, tasteful inn on Karon Park. The location is sublime, and the rooms feature marble floors and sea views. Other perks include wi-fi, air-con, ceiling fans and a horseshoe-shaped pool. With substantial low-season discounts, this is the perfect surf lair.

🍴 Eating & Drinking

Pad Thai Shop   Thai $

(Th Patak East, Hat Karon; dishes 50-60B; ⊗9am-8pm) On the busy main road behind Karon, just north of the tacky Ping Pong Bar, is this glorified food stand where you can find rich and savoury chicken stew (worthy of rave reviews in its own right) and the best *pàt tai* on planet earth: spicy and sweet, packed with prawns, tofu, egg and peanuts, and wrapped in a fresh banana leaf.

Mama Noi's   Thai, Italian $

(Karon Plaza, Hat Karon; mains 60-185B; ⊗8am-10pm; 🛜) A simple tiled cafe with a handful of plants out front that has been feeding the expat masses for nearly a generation. They do all the Thai dishes and some popular pasta dishes too. It's all cheap and tasty, and arrives in ample portions.

Bai Toey   Thai $$

(☎08 1691 6202; www.baitoeyrestaurant.com; 192/36 Th Patak West; meals 200-300B; ⊗11am-10pm; 🛜) This is a charming Thai bistro with shaded outdoor patio and

If You Like...
Karst Scenery

The karst-studded bay of **Ao Phang-Nga Marine National Park** (☏0 7641 1136; www.dnp.go.th; adult/child 200/100B; ☺8am-4pm) is an easy day trip from Phuket – visit on a kayak tour or stay overnight on a local island. The park protects more than 40 towering limestone islands and mangrove forests. It is often overrun by package tourists during the day so is best visited in the early morning or early evening.

1 **JOHN GRAY'S SEACANOE**
(☏0 7622 6077; www.johngray-seacanoe.com) These trips dodge the crowds and soak up the scenery.

2 **LOM LAE**
(☏0 7659 7486; www.lomlae.com; Ko Yao Noi; bungalows 2500-6000B; 🏊) The island of Ko Yao Noi has a front-row view of the bay. It hosts a small Muslim fishing community and several laid-back bungalow operations that offer a country retreat from Phuket. There's biking, rock climbing and bay exploring. Another good sleeping option is **Ko Yao Beach Bungalows** (☏0 7645 4213, 08 1693 8935; www.kohyaobeach.com; Hat Tha Khao; bungalows 1500B; ❄🖥).

3 **THIWSON BEACH RESORT**
(☏08 1737 4420; www.thiwsonbeach.com; Ko Yao Yai; bungalows 3200B; ❄🏊) The best lodging option on Ko Yao Yai, the bigger but less-developed sister island, which has a few strips of fine sand and jungle trails.

indoor seating. It has the traditional curry, stir-fry and noodle dishes, but you'd do well to sample the Thai-style grilled beef.

Hat Patong   หาดป่าตอง

Patong is a free-for-all. Anything, from a Starbucks venti latte to an, ahem, companion for the evening is available for the right price. Of course, that doesn't mean

you're going to like it. But when you arrive you'll take one look at the wide, white-sand beach and its magnificent crescent bay, and you'll understand how the whole thing started.

Diving and spa options abound, as well as upscale dining, street-side fish grills, campy cabaret, Thai boxing, dusty antique shops and one of Thailand's coolest shopping malls.

Activities & Courses

Sea Fun Divers   Diving
(☏0 7634 0480; www.seafundivers.com; 29 Soi Karon Nui, Patong; 2/3 dives per day 4100/4500B, open-water course 18,400B) This is an outstanding and very professional diving operation. Its standards are extremely high and the service is impeccable. There's an office at Le Meridien resort in Patong and a second location at the **Katathani Resort** (☏0 7633 0124; www.katathani.com; 14 Th Kata Noi; r from 7800B; ❄🖥🏊).

Swasana Spa   Spa
(Treatments from 850B; ☺10am-9pm) This four-star spa at **Impiana Phuket Cabana** (☏0 7634 0138; www.impiana.com; 41 Th Thawiwong; r from 4500-7000B; ❄🖥🏊) is right on the beach at the quiet north end of Patong. The best deal is the traditional Thai massage (850B). You'll be nestled in a cool glass cube on a cushy floor mat with ocean views.

Sleeping

It's getting pretty difficult to find anything in Patong costing less than 1000B from about November to April, but outside this time period rates drop by 40% to 60%.

Patong Backpacker Hostel   Hostel $
(☏0 7625 6680; www.phuketbackpacker.com; 140 Th Thawiwong; dm 250-450B; ❄🖥) This is a great location near the beach and the owner offers info on all the best and cheapest places to eat in town. Dorm

prices vary depending on the number of beds in the room (three to 10). The top floor is the brightest but dorm rooms on the lower floors each have their own attached bathroom. Skip the overpriced room.

Merrison Inn
Hotel **$$**

(☏ 0 7634 0383; www.merrisoninn.com; 5/35 Th Hat Patong; r 1300B; ❄ 🛜) Polished concrete floors, terrazzo bathrooms, wall-mounted flat-screen TVs, queen-sized beds and more than a little Asian kitsch make this place a real bargain.

Baipho, Baithong & Sala Dee
Guesthouse **$$**

(☏ 0 7629 2738, 0 7629 2074; www.baipho.com; 205/12-13 & 205/14-15 Th Rat Uthit 200 Pee; r 1800-3300B; ❄ 🛜) These three arty guesthouses are all on the same little soi under the same friendly, organised management. Rooms and common areas are filled with Buddha imagery and Zen-like trimmings mingling with modern art and urban touches. The dimly lit, nestlike rooms are all unique so ask to see a few if possible.

🍴 Eating & Drinking

The most glamorous restaurants are in a little huddle above the cliffs on the northern edge of town.

Bargain seafood and noodle stalls pop up across town at night – try the lanes on and around Th Bangla, or venture over to the **Patong Food Park** (Th Rat Uthit; meals 100-200B; ⏱4pm-midnight) once the sun drops.

Mengrai Seafood
Seafood **$$**

(☏ 08 7263 7070; Soi Tun; meals 120-300B) Located down a sweaty, dark soi off Th Bangla is a wonderful food court serving fresh, local food. The stalls towards the end of the soi serve daily curries that local expats swear by. This restaurant specialises in (very) fresh fish, prawns and mussels.

Shalimar
Indian **$$**

(207/7, 8 Soi Patong Lodge, 200 Pee; dishes 120-600B; buffet 300B; ⏱11am-11:30pm) This Indian kitchen offers a daily vegie lunch buffet and a half-dozen dishes off the menu, ranging from samosas and butter chicken to tandoori mixed grill and biryani. In a

Baan Rim Pa (p308)

INGOLF POMPE/GETTY IMAGES ©

town with a hefty share of Indian joints, these wood tables and leather seats are consistently packed with Indians.

Baan Rim Pa   Thai $$$

(☏0 7634 4079; Th Kalim Beach; dishes 215-475B) Stunning Thai food is served with a side order of spectacular views at this institution. Standards are high, with prices to match, but romance is in the air, with candlelight and piano music aplenty. Book ahead and tuck in your shirt.

Seduction   Nightclub

(www.facebook.com/seductiondisco; 39/1 Th Bangla, Patong; ☉10pm-4am) International DJs, professional grade sound system and the best dance party on Phuket, without question. Winner and still champion.

⭐ Entertainment

Phuket Simon Cabaret   Cabaret

(☏0 7634 2011; www.phuket-simoncabaret.com; Th Sirirach; admission 700-800B; ☉performances 6pm, 7.45pm & 9.30pm nightly) About 300m south of town, this cabaret offers entertaining transvestite shows. The 600-seat theatre is grand, the costumes are gorgeous and the ladyboys (*gà·teu·i*) are

convincing. The house is often full – book ahead.

Bangla Boxing Stadium   Thai Boxing

(☏0 7282 2348; 198/4 Th Rat Uthit; admission 1000-1500B; ☉9-11.30pm Tue, Wed, Fri & Sun) Old name, new stadium, same game: a packed line-up of competitive *moo·ay tai* (Thai boxing) bouts.

❶ Getting There & Around

Sŏrng·tăa·ou from Phuket Town to Patong leave from Th Ranong, near the day market and fountain circle; the fare is 25B. The after-hours charter fare is 500B. *Sŏrng·tăa·ou* then drop off and pick up passengers at the southern end of Patong beach. From here you can hop on a motorbike taxi (20B to 40B per ride), flag down a túk-túk (prices vary widely) or walk till your feet hurt.

Hat Kamala   หาดกมลา

A chilled-out hybrid of Hat Karon and Hat Surin, calm but fun Kamala tends to lure a mixture of longer-term, lower-key partying guests, families and young couples. The bay is magnificent, turquoise and serene with shore breakers that lull

Cabaret performers, Hat Patong

you to sleep. Palms and pines mingle on the leafy and rocky northern end where the water is a rich emerald green and the snorkelling around the rock reef is halfway decent, while new resorts are ploughed into the southern bluffs above the gathering long-tails.

Sleeping & Eating

Clear House Hotel **$$**
(☎ 0 7638 5401; www.clearhousephuket.com; 121/2, 121/10 Th Rimhaad, Hat Kamala; r 1300B; ❄️🛜) Shabby chic with a mod twist, the whitewashed rooms have pink feature walls, plush duvets, flat-screen TVs, wi-fi and huge pebbled baths. This place just feels good.

Beach Restaurants Thai, International **$**
(Hat Kamala; dishes 50-250B; ⏲11am-9pm) One of Kamala's highlights is its long stretch of eateries where you can dine in a swimsuit with your feet in the sand. There's everything from Thai to pizza, and plenty of cold beer. **Ma Ma Fati Ma**, at the far northern part of the beach, is our favourite.

ⓘ Getting There & Away

To catch a regular *sŏrng·tǎa·ou* from Kamala to Patong costs 50B per person, while a *sŏrng·tǎa·ou* charter (starting in the evenings) costs 250B.

Hat Surin หาดสุรินทร์

With a wide, blonde beach, water that blends from pale turquoise in the shallows to a deep blue on the horizon, and two lush, boulder-strewn headlands, Surin could easily attract tourists on looks alone.

Sleeping

Surin Phuket Hotel **$$$**
(☎ 0 7662 1579; www.thesurinphuket.com; 118 Mu 3, Hat Pansea; r 17,000-58,000B; ❄️🛜🏊) Almost any place located on a private beach this quiet and stunning would have to be a top pick. But the bungalows at the

Gay Pride in Phuket

Although there are big gay pride celebrations in Bangkok and Pattaya, the **Phuket Gay Pride Festival** is considered by many to be the best in Thailand, maybe even Southeast Asia. The date has changed several times, but it usually lands between February and April.

The main events of the four-day weekend are a huge beach volleyball tournament and, of course, the Grand Parade, featuring floats, cheering crowds and beautiful costumes in the streets of Patong.

Any other time of year, the network of streets that link the Royal Paradise Hotel with Th Rat Uthit in Patong is where you'll find Phuket's gay pulse. For updates on future festivals or for more information about the scene in general, go to **Gay Patong** (www.gaypatong.com).

Surin (previously known as the Chedi), with naturalistic wooden exteriors that hide beneath hillside foliage, and earthy, luxurious interiors, make the site that much better.

Twin Palms Resort **$$$**
(☎ 0 7631 6500; www.twinpalms-phuket.com; 106/46 Mu 3, Th Surin Beach; r 8100-25,850B; ❄️@🛜🏊) This is the Audrey Hepburn of Phuket's hotels: it's classic yet completely contemporary. Even the simplest rooms are extra spacious and have oversized bathrooms, sublimely comfortable beds and a supreme sense of calm.

It's a few minutes' walk to the beach. Expats from all over Phuket can be found here on Sunday at the island's most popular brunch (open noon to 2pm; buffet 1300B).

🍴 Eating & Drinking

Twin Brothers Thai **$$**
(Hat Surin; mains 150-350B; ⏰10.30am-10.30pm)
By day, one brother mans the wok, cooking up decent Thai food at local prices. At night, the other fires up a fresh seafood grill for beachside diners. It's a bit more down to earth than other Surin choices.

Taste International-Thai **$$**
(☎08 7886 6401; tapas 160-225B) The best of a new breed of urban-meets-surf eateries along the beach. Dine indoors or alfresco on meal-sized salads, perfectly cooked filet mignon or a variety of Thai-Mediterranean starters and mains.

ℹ️ Getting There & Away

A regular *sŏrng·tăa·ou* from Phuket Town's Th Ranong to Hat Surin costs 40B per person, and túk-túk or *sŏrng·tăa·ou* charters cost 600B.

Ao Bang Thao อ่าวบางเทา

Almost as large and even more beautiful than Ao Patong, the stunning, 8km-long white-sand sweep of Ao Bang Thao is the glue that binds the region's disparate elements. The southern half is home to a sprinkling of three-star bungalow resorts. Further inland you'll find an old fishing village laced with canals along with a number of upstart villa subdivisions.

The **Hideaway Day Spa** (☎08 1750 0026; www.phuket-hideaway.com; 382/33 Th Srisoontorn, Chergtalay; treatments from 1500B) has an excellent reputation. It offers traditional Thai massage, sauna and mud body wraps in a tranquil wooded setting at the edge of a lagoon.

🛏️ Sleeping

Laguna Phuket is home to five luxury resorts, including **Banyan Tree Phuket** (☎0 7632 4374; www.banyantree.com; villas from 16,200B; ❄️@🛜♿), an 18-hole golf course and 30 restaurants. Guests at any one of the resorts can use the dining and recreation facilities at all of them. Frequent shuttle buses make the rounds

of all the hotels, as do pontoon boats (via the linked lagoons).

🍴 Eating

Tawai Thai **$$$**
(☎0 7632 5381; Mu 1, Laguna Resort Entrance; mains 180-300B) Set in a lovely old house decorated with traditional art is this gem of a Thai kitchen, serving classics like roast duck curry and pork *lâhp*. A free shuttle service is available to and from the Laguna hotels.

Tatonka International **$$$**
(☎0 7632 4349; Th Srisoonthorn; dishes 180-790B; ⏰6pm-late Thu-Tue) This is the home of 'globetrotter cuisine', which owner-chef Harold Schwarz developed by taking fresh local products and combining them with cooking techniques learned in Europe, Colorado and Hawaii. The eclectic, tapas-style selection includes creative vegetarian and seafood dishes. Book ahead.

Siam Supper Club International **$$$**
(☎0 7627 0936; Hat Bang Thao; dishes 290-1290B; ⏰6pm-1am) One of the hippest spots on Phuket, this is where the 'infamous' come tó sip cocktails, listen to jazz and eat an excellent meal. The menu is predominantly Western with gourmet pizzas, seafood *cioppino* (stew) and hearty mains such as veal tenderloin with wild mushrooms on truffle mash.

ℹ️ Getting There & Away

A *sŏrng·tăa·ou* between Ao Bang Thao and Phuket Town's Th Ranong costs 40B per person. Túk-túk charters are 700B.

Sirinat National Park
อุทยานแห่งชาติสิรินาถ

Comprising the exceptional beaches of Nai Thon, Nai Yang and Mai Khao, as well as the former Nai Yang National Park and Mai Khao wildlife reserve, **Sirinat National Park** (☎0 7632 8226; www.dnp.go.th; adult/child 200/100B; ⏰8am-5pm) encompasses 22 sq km of coastal land, plus 68 sq km of sea.

The whole area is 15 minutes or less from Phuket International Airport, which makes it particularly convenient for a first stop after a long trip. This is one of the sweetest slices of the island.

◉ Sights & Activities

If you're after a lovely arc of fine golden sand away from Phuket's busyness, **Hat Nai Thon** is it. The closest ATM is in Nai Yang, so stock up on baht before you come.

Hat Nai Yang's bay is sheltered by a reef that slopes 20m below the surface – which makes for both good snorkelling in the dry season and fantastic surfing in the monsoon season.

Hat Nai Yang is also a great place to go kiteboarding. Three fine operators with offices here are **Bob's Kite School Phuket** (www.kiteschoolphuket.com; Nai Yang; 1hr discovery lesson 1000B, 3hr course 3300B), **Kiteboarding Asia** (☏08 1591 4594; www.kiteboardingasia.com; lessons from 4000B) and **Kite Zone** (☏08 3395 2005; www.kitesurfingphuket.com; 1hr beginner lessons from 1100B; half-day lesson 4400B; ⊙May-late Oct).

About 5km north of Hat Nai Yang is **Hat Mai Khao**, Phuket's longest beach. Sea turtles lay their eggs here between November and February. Take care when swimming, as there's a strong year-round undertow. Except on weekends and holidays, you'll have this place almost to yourself.

🛏 Sleeping & Eating

HAT NAI THON หาดในทอน

Phuket Naithon Resort Hotel **$$**
(☏0 7620 5233; www.phuketnaithonresort.com; 24 Mu 4; r 2500B; ❄ 🛜) A great midrange choice set across from the beach and smack in the middle of the strip. Rooms are spacious tiled affairs with floating queen beds, built-in day beds, mini fridge, desk, tub and shower. Check in at the Wiwan Restaurant.

Pullman Resort **$$$**
(☏0 7630 3299; www.pullmanphuketarcadia.com; 22/2 Mu 4, Hat Nai Thon; r from 3100B; P ❄ @ 🛜 ☎) The area's newest resort is a stunner. Set high on the cliff above Hat Nai Thon, the lobby alone will make you weak in the knees, with its soothing grey

Long-tail boats, Ao Bang Thao

Below: Roti vendor, Ko Phi-Phi Don (p319); **Right:** Night market, Krabi
(BELOW) FELIX HUG/GETTY IMAGES ©; (RIGHT) PAUL KENNEDY/GETTY IMAGES ©

and lavender colour scheme, hardwood floors and exposed rough cut limestone walls. A dreamy network of reflection pools extend out above the sea, 180 degrees to the horizon.

HAT NAI YANG & HAT MAI KHAO หาดในยาง/หาดไม้ขาว

Discovery Beach Resort
Guesthouse $

(65/17 Mu 5, Hat Nai Yang; r with fan/air-con 800/1500B; ❄ 🛜) With wooden Thai accents on the facade and lacquered timber handrails and furnishings, this spotless, budget three-star spot has enough motel kitsch to make it interesting, and its location – right on the beach – makes it a terrific value.

Dewa
Resort $$$

(📞 0 7637 2300; www.dewaphuketresort.com; 65 Tambon Sakoo; condos & villas from 7000B; 🅿 ❄ 🛜 ♿) An independently owned boutique resort that offers one- and two-bedroom condos and luscious pool villas, steps from the virgin national park beach. You'll have more space (and a full kitchen) in the condos, but the villas are secluded pods with reclaimed wood accents, vintage wrought-iron motifs and a wall-mounted flat screen.

Ban Ra Tree
Thai $$

(Hat Nai Yang; mains 90-350B; ⏰ 11am-10.30pm) The best choice on the Hat Nai Yang strip, the plastic tables are elegantly dressed in turquoise and white linen and sunk in the sand beneath parasols. The seafood is dynamite: think green curry fried rice topped with coconut milk. Ask for yours with crab, and it will be topped with a whole, meaty cracked crab for just 220B!

🛈 Getting There & Away

If you're coming from the airport, a taxi costs about 200B. There is no regular sŏrng·tăa·ou, but a túk-túk charter from Phuket Town costs about 800B.

KRABI PROVINCE

Krabi Town กระบี่

POP 27,500

Krabi Town is majestically situated among impossibly angular limestone karsts jutting from the mangroves, but when mid-city you're more likely to be awe-struck by the sheer volume of guesthouses and travel agencies packed into this compact, quirky little town.

🛏 Sleeping

Pak-up Hostel _Hostel $_

(☎0 7561 1955; www.pakuphostel.com; 87 Th Utarakit; dm 220-270B, d 500-600B; ❄@🛜) This snazzy hostel features several uberhip 10-bed dorms with big wooden bunks built into the wall, each equipped with a personal locker. Massive, modern shared bathrooms have cold-water stalls as well as a few hot-water rain showers. There are two on-site bars (p314), one with nightly live music, and a young, hip, clublike vibe.

Hometel _Hotel $_

(☎0 7562 2301; 7 Soi 2, Th Maharat ; r 750B; ❄🛜) A modern and funky boutique sleep with 10 rooms on three floors crafted entirely from polished concrete. Abstract art brings colour, there are rain showers, some rooms have two terraces and all have high ceilings.

🍴 Eating & Drinking

Night Market _Thai $_

(Th Khong Kha; meals 20-50B) The most popular and pleasant place for an evening meal is near the Khong Kha pier. Menus are in English but the food is authentic: try papaya salad, fried noodles, _đôm yam gûng_ (prawn and lemongrass soup) and sweet, creamy Thai desserts.

Relax Coffee _Cafe $_

(Th Chao Fah; mains 45-220B; ⏲7.30am-6pm; 🛜) Krabi's best coffee shop offers both

Krabi Town

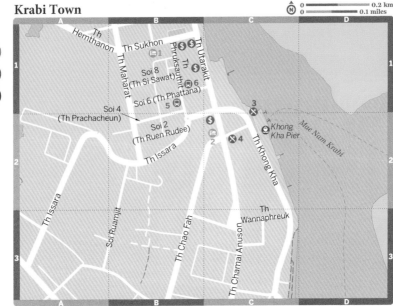

Krabi Town

Thai and Western breakfasts and ample salads, sandwiches and curries at lunch, and they do pizza too. All of it served in a charming, restored wooden storefront near the river.

Playground   Bar
(87 Th Utarakit; 🛜) Pak-up (p313)'s rollicking downstairs courtyard bar is where the fun and games gather and bloom. From beer pong and open-mic nights to live music and game nights, there is always something on and new friends to enjoy.

ⓘ Getting There & Away

Air
Most domestic carriers offer flights between Bangkok and Krabi International Airport (one-way around 4400B, 1¼ hours). **Bangkok Air (www. bangkokair.com)** has a daily service to Ko Samui for around 3800B.

Boat
Boats to Ko Phi-Phi and Ko Lanta leave from the passenger pier at Khlong Chilat, about 4km southwest of Krabi. Travel agencies will arrange free transfers when you buy a boat ticket with them.

If you want to get to Railay, long-tail boats leave from Krabi's Khong Kha pier to Hat Railay East (150B, 45 minutes) from 7.45am to 6pm. The boatmen will wait until they can fill a boat with 10 people before they leave; if you're antsy to go before then, you can charter the whole boat for 1500B. Boats to Hat Railay West leave from Ao Nang.

To get to Phuket or the Ko Yao Islands, the quickest route is with direct boats from the pier at Ao Nang. *Sŏrng·tăa·ou* run between the two piers for 50B, or a taxi costs 400B to 500B.

Bus

The **Krabi bus terminal** (📞 0 7561 1804; cnr Th Utarakit & Hwy 4) is in nearby Talat Kao, about 4km north of Krabi. Air-conditioned government buses leave for Bangkok (720B, 12 hours) at 7am, 4pm and 5.30pm. There's a very plush 24-seat VIP bus to Bangkok (1100B) departing at 5.30pm daily. From Bangkok's southern bus terminal, buses leave at 7.30am and between 7pm and 8pm.

Minivan

Dozens of travel agencies in Krabi run air-con minivans and VIP buses to popular tourist centres throughout southern Thailand, but you may end up crammed cheek to jowl with other backpackers.

Sŏrng·tăa·ou

Sŏrng·tăa·ou run from the bus station to central Krabi and on to Hat Nopphrat Thara (50B), Ao Nang (50B) and the Shell Cemetery at Ao Nam Mao (50B). There are services from 6am to 6.30pm. In the high season there are more frequent services until 10pm for a 10B surcharge. For Ao Luk (80B, one hour) there are frequent *sŏrng·tăa·ou* from the corner of Th Phattana and Th Phruksauthit; the last service leaves around 3pm.

ℹ️ Getting Around

A taxi from the airport to town will cost 400B. Agencies in town can arrange seats on the airport bus for 100B. *Sŏrng·tăa·ou* between the bus terminal and central Krabi cost 50B.

Railay ไร่เล

Krabi's fairy-tale limestone crags come to a dramatic climax at Railay (also spelt Rai Leh), the ultimate jungle gym for rock-climbing fanatics. This quiet slice of paradise fills in the sandy gaps between each craggy flourish, and although it's just around the bend from the chaotic tourist hustle in Ao Nang, the atmosphere here is nothing short of laid-back, Rasta-Thai heaven.

◎ Sights

Tham Phra Nang   Cave
(Princess Cave) At the eastern end of Hat Phra Nang is Tham Phra Nang, an important shrine for local fishermen. Legend has it that a royal barge carrying an Indian princess foundered in a storm here during the 3rd century BC. The

Long-tail boats, Railay

spirit of the drowned princess came to inhabit the cave, granting favours to all who came to pay respect.

Tham Phra Nang Nai   Cave
(Inner Princess Cave; adult/child 40/20B; ⏰5am-8pm) Above Hat Railay East is another large cave called Tham Phra Nang Nai, also known as Diamond Cave. A wooden boardwalk leads through a series of caverns full of beautiful limestone formations but, with shifting rain patterns, the water is now gone and with it the illuminated effects that won the cave its diamond moniker.

🤸 Activities

Dive operations in Railay run trips out to Ko Poda and other dive sites. Two local dives at outlying islands costs about 2000B while a three- or four-day PADI Open Water dive course is 12,000B to 15,000B.

Full-day, multi-island **snorkelling** trips to Ko Poda, Chicken Island and beyond can be arranged through any of the resorts for about 2000B (maximum six people) or you can charter a long-tail (half-/full-day 1800/2500B) from Hat Railay West beach. If you just want to snorkel off Railay, most resorts can rent you a mask set and fins for 100B to 150B each.

Flame Tree Restaurant (Hat Rai Leh West) rents out **sea kayaks** for 200B per hour or 800B per day.

🛏 Sleeping & Eating

HAT RAILAY WEST

Sand Sea Resort   Hotel $$
(☎ 0 7562 2608; www.krabisandsea.com; Hat Railay West; bungalows 1950-5950B; ❄@☎) The lowest-priced resort on this beach offers everything from ageing fan-only bungalows to newly remodelled cottages with every amenity.

Railei Beach Club   Villa Rental $$$
(☎08 6685 9359; www.raileibeachclub.com; houses from 3000B; 🛜) At the northern end of the beach is this collection of Thai-style homes, each unique in size and design, rented out on behalf of absentee owners. They come with patios, kitchens and amenities, and some have pools to make extended stays very comfortable.

Rock-climbers, Railay

INGOLF POMPE/GETTY IMAGES ©

Rock Climbing

With nearly 500 bolted routes, ranging from beginner to advanced, and all with unparalleled clifftop vistas, it's no surprise that Railay is among the top climbing spots in the world. Deep-water soloing offers the biggest thrill. That's where free-climbers scramble up ledges over deep water sans rope – if you fall you will most likely just get wet, so even daring beginners can give this a try.

The going rate for climbing courses is 800B to 1000B for a half-day and 1500B to 2000B for a full day. If you're planning to climb independently, you're best off bringing your own gear from home; be sure to bring plenty of slings and quickdraws, chalk (sweaty palms are inevitable in the tropics) and a small selection of nuts and cams as backup for thinly protected routes. A woven rattan mat (available locally for 100B to 150B) will help keep the sand out of your gear.

Several locally published books detail climbs in the area, but *Rock Climbing in Thailand*, by Elke Schmitz and Wee Changrua, is one of the more complete guides.

Base Camp Ton Sai (☏ 08 1149 9745; www.tonsaibasecamp.com; Hat Ton Sai; ⊗ 8am-9:30pm) Arguably the most professional outfit in the area.

Highland Rock Climbing (☏ 08 0693 0374; highlandrockclimbingthailand.weebly.com; Hat Railay East) If you're bunking on the mountain, the owner of this outfit is the man to climb with.

It's a superb deal and a romantic location, so book well in advance for the high season.

HAT RAILAY EAST

Railay Garden View   Bungalow **$$**
(☏ 08 5888 5143; www.railaygardenview.com; Hat Railay East; bungalows 1300B) A collection of tin-roof, woven-bamboo bungalows, stilted high above the mangroves on the east beach. They look weather beaten from the outside, but are spacious and super clean. They are graced with Thai linens and creative concrete baths, and there's a cushioned seating area on the floor, too. Bring mosquito repellent, and all will be peachy.

Sunrise Tropical Resort   Hotel **$$**
(☏ 0 7562 2599; www.sunrisetropical.com; bungalows incl breakfast 2500-6750B; ❇ @ 🛜 🌊) Bungalows here rival the better ones on Hat Railay West but are priced for Hat Railay East – so we think this is one of the best deals in Railay.

Mangrove Restaurant   Thai **$**
(dishes 70-120B; ⊗ 8am-10pm) This humble, local-style place, set beneath a stilted thatched roof on the recently detoured trail between the east and west beaches, turns out all your spicy Thai faves cheaply, from beef salad and noodles to curries and *sôm dam*. Praise goes to the kitchen's matriarch.

RAILAY HIGHLANDS

Railay Cabana   Guesthouse **$**
(☏ 0 7562 1733, 08 4534 1928; Railay Highlands; bungalows 350-600B) Superbly located high in the hills in a bowl of karst cliffs, this is your hippie tropical mountain hideaway. Simple, clean thatched bungalows are surrounded by mango, mangosteen, banana and guava groves. The only sounds are birds chirping and children laughing.

Railay Phutawan Resort   Hotel **$$**
(☏ 0 7581 9479, 08 4060 0550; www.railayphutawan.com; r from 1850B, bungalows from 2150B; ❇ @) The best options here are

317

the super-spacious polished-cement bungalows highlighted with creamy yellow walls, big rain-shower bathrooms and all the trimmings of a high-end resort. Tiled rooms in an apartment-style block are a step down in luxury but very comfortable; fan-cooled bungalows with bamboo ceilings are musty but good value.

HAT PHRA NANG หาดถ้ำพระนาง

Rayavadee Hotel $$$
(☏ 0 7562 0741, 0 7562 0740; www.rayavadee .com; pavilions from 14,500B, villas from 75,000B; ❄ 🞉 🏊) This exclusive resort has sprawling banyan tree– and flower-filled grounds navigated by golf buggies. The two-storey mushroom-domed pavilions are filled with antique furniture and every mod con – as well as the occasional private Jacuzzi, swimming pool or butler service.

HAT TON SAI หาดต้นไทร

Paasook Hotel $
(☏ 08 9648 7459; Hat Ton Sai; bungalows 200-900B) Definitely the most stylish budget establishment on Ton Sai: wooden bungalows have elongated floor-to-ceiling windows and concrete floors. The gardens are lush, management is friendly and there's a rustic-chic outdoor restaurant, perfect for steamy evenings.

Mountain View Resort Hotel $$
(☏ 08 9783 4008, 0 7581 9819; www.citykrabi. com; bungalows 1300-1900B; ❄) This place is bright, cheery and immaculate with mint-green walls, tiled floors and crisp sheets in lodge-like environs. Some rooms are slightly musty, so sniff around.

Mama's Chicken Thai $
(Hat Ton Sai; 50-90B; ⏱7.30am-10pm) One of the more popular of the Ton Sai beach stalls offers Western breakfasts, fruit smoothies and a range of cheap Thai dishes, including a massaman tofu, which is a rarity. Grab a table and watch management engage in their daily battle with a thieving mob of macaques, who do love their mangoes.

🛈 Getting There & Around

Long-tail boats to Railay run from Khong Kha pier in Krabi and from the seafronts of Ao Nang and Ao Nam Mao. Boats between Krabi and Hat Railay East leave every 1½ hours from 7.45am to 6pm when they have six to 10 passengers (150B, 45 minutes). Chartering the whole boat costs 1500B.

Boats to Hat Railay West or Hat Ton Sai from Ao Nang cost 100B (15 minutes) from 7.30am to 6pm or 150B at other times; boats don't leave until eight people show up. Private charters cost 800B.

From October to May the *Ao Nang Princess* runs from Hat Noppharat Thara National Park headquarters to Ko Phi-Phi with a stop at Hat Railay West. Long-tails run out to meet the boat at around 9.15am from in front of the Sand Sea Resort in Hat Railay West. The fare to Ko Phi-Phi from Railay is 350B.

Ao Ton Sai, Ko Phi-Phi

Ko Phi-Phi Don เกาะพีพีดอน

With its flashy, curvy blonde beaches and bodacious jungles it's no wonder that Phi-Phi has become the darling of the Andaman coast. And, like any good starlet, this island can party hard all night and still look like a million bucks the next morning.

◉ Sights & Activities

DIVING

Crystal-clear Andaman water and abundant marine life make the perfect recipe for top-notch scuba. Popular sights include the **King Cruiser Wreck**, sitting a mere 12m below the surface; **Anemone Reef**, teeming with hard corals and clownfish; **Hin Bida**, a submerged pinnacle attracting turtles and large pelagic fish; and **Ko Bida Nok**, with its signature karst massif luring leopard sharks. Hin Daeng and Hin Muang, about 70km south, are expensive ventures from Ko Phi-Phi – it's cheaper to link up with a dive crew in Ko Lanta.

An Open Water certification course costs around 12,900B to 13,800B, while the standard two-dive trips cost from 2500B to 3200B. Trips out to Hin Daeng/Hin Muang will set you back 5500B.

Adventure Club   Diving
(📞08 1970 0314; www.phi-phi-adventures.com) Our favourite diving operation on the island runs an excellent assortment of educational, eco-focused diving, hiking and snorkelling tours.

SNORKELLING

A popular snorkelling destination is **Ko Mai Phai** (Bamboo Island), 5km north of Phi-Phi Don. Snorkelling trips cost between 600B to 2400B, depending on whether you travel by long-tail or motorboat. There is also good snorkelling along the eastern coast of **Ko Nok**, near Ao Ton Sai, and along the eastern coast of **Ko Nai**.

ROCK CLIMBING

Yes, there are good limestone cliffs to climb on Ko Phi-Phi, and the views are spectacular. Climbing shops on the island charge around 1200B for a half-day of climbing or 2000B for a full day, including instruction and gear. **Spider Monkey** (📞0 7581 9384; www.spidermonkeyphiphi.com) is run by Soley, one of the most impressive climbers on Phi-Phi. **Ibex Climbing & Tours** (📞0 7560 1423, 08 4309 0445; www.ibexclimbingandtours.com) is one of the newest and best outfitters in the Village.

✊ Tours

Aside from long-tail boat tours to Phi-Phi Leh and Ko Mai Phai (Bamboo Island), tour agencies can arrange sunset tours to Monkey Bay and the beach at Wang Long, both on Phi-Phi Leh, for 600B. Adventure Club (p319) is a good choice. **U-Rip** (📞0 7560 1075; per person 600B) offers the same trip and is also highly recommended.

You can no longer camp on Maya Beach, but you can join the **Plankton Sunset Cruise** (www.mayabaytours.com; per person 1200B) and sleep aboard the boat just offshore. They only take online bookings.

Captain Bob's Booze Cruise (📞08 4848 6970; www.phiphiboozecruise.com; men/women 3000/2500B; ⊙departs at 1pm, returns at 7pm) is the latest buzz-worthy excursion and is exactly what it sounds like. You're cruising the waters around Phi Phi Don and Phi Phi Leh, on a sailboat, adult beverage in hand.

Another unique choice is the **Watersports Experience** (www.facebook.com/watersportsexperience; per person with/without sports 1500/2500B), where guests can stand-up paddle (SUP), wake board, water ski and snorkel the waters around Phi Phi Don and Phi Phi Leh.

🛏 Sleeping

Finding accommodation on this ever-popular island has never been easy and you can expect serious room shortages at peak holiday times. Masses of touts meet incoming boats and, while often annoying, can make your life easier.

Be sure you lock the door while you sleep and close all the windows when you go out. Break-ins can be a problem.

TONSAI VILLAGE บ้านต้นไทร

The flat, hourglass-shaped land between Ao Ton Sai and Ao Lo Dalam is crowded with loads of lodging options.

Tee Guesthouse　Guesthouse **$**
(☑ 08 4851 5721; Tonsai Village; r with fan/air-con 800/1200B; ❄) A fun and funky choice tucked down a side road. Rooms are simple with graceful touches like exposed brick and lavender walls, queen beds, mosaic-tiled baths, and a welcome blast of graffiti on the exterior. They have a darling little **cafe** (�time 8am-4pm) here too.

JJ Residence　Inn **$$**
(☑ 0 7560 1098; d 1900-2500B; ❄ ☎ ✉) Expect spacious tiled rooms with funky wood panelling, beamed ceilings, duvee, mini fridge, flat screen, built-in desk and wardrobe and private terrace. Those on

the first floor spill right onto the pool. One of the nicer choices in Ton Sai.

HAT HIN KHOM หาดหินคม

This area has a few small white-sand beaches in rocky coves that are relatively quiet. It's about a 15-minute jungle walk from both Hat Yao and the Ao Ton Sai bustle.

Viking Natures Resort　Hotel **$$**
(☑ 0 7581 9399; www.vikingnaturesresort.com; bungalows 1500-12,000B; ☎) OK, it's funky (in all senses of the word), but the wood, thatch and bamboo bungalows here are dreamily creative and stylish with lots of driftwood, shell mobiles and hammock-decked lounging spaces with outrageous views of Ko Phi-Phi Leh. All bungalows have mosquito nets and balconies, but the cheaper rooms don't have their own bathrooms.

HAT YAO หาดยาว

You can either walk here in about 30 minutes from Ton Sai via Hat Hin Khom or take a long-tail (100B to 150B) from Ton Sai pier. This long stretch of pure-white beach is perfect for swimming and well worth the walk but don't expect to have it to yourself – it's popular with families and sporty types playing volleyball.

Paradise Resort Phi Phi　Hotel **$$$**
(☑ 08 1968 3982; www.paradiseresort.co.th; bungalows from 3000B; ❄ ☎) Rooms in the uber-white lodge have South Beach echoes and are plush with granite-tiled floors, wood-panelled walls, floating beds, flat screens and desks. They also have stand-alone beach cottages with similar furnishings in older bones. Low season deals are superb.

Boat cruise, Ko Phi-Phi
JOHN HARPER/GETTY IMAGES ©

PHUKET & THE ANDAMAN COAST KO PHI-PHI DON

Sleeping (or Trying to) on Ko Phi-Phi

Noise pollution on Phi-Phi is bad and is centred on central Ao Ton Sai and Ao Lo Dalam – although don't expect an early night on Hat Hin Khom either. At the time of writing, bars had a 2am curfew in Ao Lo Dalam and 1.30am in Ton Sai, but that doesn't stop inebriated revellers from making plenty of other noises (door slamming seems to be a late-night island pastime).

The most peaceful accommodation can be found in these areas:

o Phi-Phi's east coast

o The back road that connects the southeast end of Ao Ton Sai with Ao Lo Dalam (and passes Chunut House)

o The hill near the road up to the viewpoint

o The far western section of Ao Ton Sai

o Hat Yao

Of course, the best option may simply be to grab a bucket and join the scrum.

HAT RANTEE & AO TOH KO

Still fairly low-key, this series of small, remote grey-gold beaches has good snorkelling. You can either get here by long-tail from Ao Ton Sai pier (300B – although most resorts provide free pick-up if you reserve; the return trip is 150B) or by making the strenuous 45-minute hike over the viewpoint.

PP Rantee — Bungalows **$$**
(📞08 1597 7708; Hat Rantee; bungalow with fan 1200-1600B, air-con 2000B; ⏱restaurant 7am-10pm; ❄ 🛜) Here are basic but acceptable woven-bamboo bungalows and newer tiled bungalows with wide porches overlooking a trim garden path that leads to the sand. They also have the best restaurant on the beach and a big wooden swing on the tree out front.

HAT PHAK NAM & AO LO BAKAO

Hat Phak Nam is a gorgeous white-sand beach sharing the same bay as a small fishing hamlet. To get here, either charter a long-tail from Ao Ton Sai for around 500B (150B by shared taxi boat upon your return) or make the very sweaty one-hour hike over the viewpoint.

Ao Lo Bakao's fine stretch of palm-backed sand, ringed by dramatic hills, is one of Phi-Phi's most lovely beaches, with offshore views over aqua bliss to Bamboo and Mosquito Islands. Phi-Phi Island Village arranges transfers for guests; on your own a charter from Ao Ton Sai will cost 800B.

Relax Beach Resort — Hotel **$$**
(📞08 9475 6536, 08 1083 0194; www.phiphi relaxresort.com; bungalows 1800-4900B; @ 🏊) There are 47 unpretentious but pretty Thai-style bungalows with wood floors, two-tiered terraces with lounging cushions, and mosaic bathrooms in the newest nests. All are rimmed by lush jungle – there's a good restaurant and breezy bar, and it's run by incredibly charming staff who greet and treat you like family.

🍴 Eating

Local Food Market — Thai **$**
(Ao Ton Sai; meals 30-60B; ⏱8am-8pm) The cheapest and most authentic eats are at the market. A handful of local stalls huddle on the narrowest sliver of the isthmus and serve up scrumptious pàt tai, fried rice, sôm·dam (spicy green papaya salad) and smoked catfish.

MELISSA TSE/GETTY IMAGES ©

⭐ Don't Miss
Ko Phi-Phi Leh   เกาะพีพีเล

Rugged Phi-Phi Leh is the smaller of the two islands and is protected on all sides by soaring cliffs. Coral reefs crawling with marine life lie beneath the crystal-clear waters and are hugely popular with day-tripping snorkellers. Two gorgeous lagoons await in the island's interior – **Pilah** on the eastern coast and **Ao Maya** on the western coast.

At the northeastern tip of the island, **Viking Cave** (Tham Phaya Naak) is a big collection point for swifts' nests. Nimble collectors scamper up bamboo scaffolding to gather the nests. Before ascending, they pray and make offerings of tobacco, incense and liquor to the cavern spirits.

There are no places to stay on Phi-Phi Leh and most people come here on one of the ludicrously popular day trips out of Phi-Phi Don. Tours last about half a day and include snorkelling stops at various points around the island, with detours to Viking Cave and Ao Maya. Long-tail trips cost 800B; by speedboat you'll pay around 2400B. Expect to pay a national park day-use fee (adult/child 400/200B) upon landing.

Papaya Restaurant Thai $
(📞08 7280 1719; dishes 80-300B; 🕐11am-11pm)
Here's some real-deal Thai food served in heaping portions that's cheap, tasty and spicy. It has your basil and chilli, all the curries and *dôm yam,* too. They're so popular they decided to open a second,

smaller **cafe** (📞08 7280 1719; Ton Sai Village; dishes 80-300B) a block away.

Unni's International $$
(mains 200-320B; 🕐8am-10pm) Come here for lunch to dine on homemade bagels topped with everything from smoked salmon to meatballs. There are also mas-

sive salads, Mexican food, tapas, cocktails and more.

🍷 Drinking & Nightlife

A rowdy nightlife saturates Phi-Phi. Sticky-sweet cocktails and buckets of cheap whiskey and Red Bull make this the domain for spring-break wannabes and really bad hangovers. The truth is that if you're nesting within earshot of the partying, you may as well enjoy the chaos.

Sunflower Bar   Bar
(Ao Lo Dalam) Poetically ramshackle, this driftwood gem is still the chillest bar in Phi-Phi. Destroyed in the tsunami, the owner rebuilt it with reclaimed wood. The long-tail booths are named for the four loved ones he lost in the flood.

Slinky Bar   Nightclub
(Ao Lo Dalam) This was the beach dance floor of the moment when we visited. Expect the standard fire show, buckets of candy juice and throngs of people mingling, flirting and flailing to throbbing bass on the sand.

Chukit Bar & Karaoke   Bar
(⏱11am-2am) Part of the otherwise forgettable Chukit Resort complex, this fine bar extends over a long-tail harbour on the lip of Ao Ton Sai. In addition to bar stools with a supreme view, they have a pool table, live bands and a happy hour crowd. Don't worry, it's not that kind of karaoke joint.

ℹ Getting There & Away

Ko Phi-Phi can be reached from Krabi, Phuket, Ao Nang, Railay and Ko Lanta. Most boats moor at Ao Ton Sai, though a few from Phuket use the isolated northern pier at Laem Thong. The Phuket and Krabi boats operate year-round,

while the Ko Lanta and Ao Nang boats only run in the October-to-April high season.

Krabi Boats depart from Krabi for Ko Phi-Phi (300B, 1½ hours) at 9am, 10.30am, 1.30pm and 3.30pm, and return at 7.30am, 10.30am, 1.30pm, 3.30pm.

Ao Nang Boats leave Ao Nang for Ko Phi-Phi (350B, 1½ hours) at 3.30pm and leave Ko Phi-Phi for Ao Nang at the same time.

Phuket From Phuket (250B to 350B, 1¾ to two hours), boats leave at 9am, 2pm, and 2.30pm, and return from Ko Phi-Phi at 10am, 3.30pm and 4pm.

Ko Lanta From Ko Lanta (350B, 1½ hours), boats leave at 1pm, 3.30pm and 4.30pm, and return from Ko Phi-Phi at 11.30am, 2pm and 3pm.

Railay For Railay (350B, 1¼ hours), take the Ao Nang–bound ferry.

ℹ Getting Around

There are no roads on Phi-Phi Don so transport on the island is mostly by foot, although long-tails can be chartered at Ao Ton Sai for short hops around Ko Phi-Phi Don and Ko Phi-Phi Leh.

Ao Maya, Ko Phi-Phi Leh
MATTEO COLOMBO/GETTY IMAGES ©

Long-tails leave from the Ao Ton Sai pier to Hat Yao (100B to 150B), Laem Thong (800B), Hat Rantee (500B) and Viking Cave (on Ko Phi-Phi Leh; 500B). Chartering speedboats for six hours costs around 6500B, while chartering a long-tail boat costs 1500B for three hours or 3000B for the whole day.

Ko Lanta   เกาะลันตา

POP 20,000

Once the domain of backpackers and sea gypsies, Lanta hasn't just gentrified, it's morphed almost completely from a luscious southern Thai backwater into a midrange getaway for French, German and Swedish package tourists who come for divine beaches (though the northern coast is eroding rapidly) and the nearby dive spots of Hin Daeng, Hin Muang and Ko Ha. Within eyeshot of Phi Phi, Lanta remains far more calm and real, however, and caters to all budget types. It's also flat compared to the karst formations of its neighbours and laced with good roads.

Ko Lanta is technically called Ko Lanta Yai, the largest of 52 islands in an archipelago protected by the Mu Ko Lanta Marine National Park. Almost all boats pull into Ban Sala Dan, a dusty two-street town at the northern tip of the island.

◉ Sights

Ban Ko Lanta   Town

Halfway down the eastern coast, Ban Ko Lanta (Lanta Old Town) was the original port and commercial centre for the island, and provided a safe harbour for Arabic and Chinese trading vessels sailing between Phuket, Penang and Singapore. Some of the gracious and well-kept wooden stilt houses and shopfronts here are over 100 years old.

Pier restaurants offer a fresh catch and have views over the sea.

Ko Lanta Marine National Park   National Park

(อุทยานแห่งชาติเกาะลันตา; www.dnp.go.th; adult/child 200/100B) Established in 1990, this marine national park protects 15 islands in the Ko Lanta group, including the southern tip of Ko Lanta Yai. The park is increasingly threatened by the runaway development on the western coast of Ko Lanta Yai. The other islands in the group have fared slightly better – **Ko Rok Nai** is

Restaurant, Ko Lanta

GARDEL BERTRAND/GETTY IMAGES ©

still very beautiful, with a crescent-shaped bay backed by cliffs, fine coral reefs and a sparkling white-sand beach.

🏃 Activities

Some of Thailand's top diving spots are within arm's reach of Ko Lanta. The best diving can be found at the undersea pinnacles called **Hin Muang** and **Hin Daeng**, about 45 minutes away by speedboat.

Trips out to Hin Daeng and Hin Muang cost around 4500B to 5500B, while trips to Ko Ha tend to be around 3300B to 4000B. PADI Open Water courses will set you back around 14,000B to 17,000B.

Numerous tour agencies in the main tourist areas can organise snorkelling trips out to Ko Rok Nok, Ko Phi-Phi and other nearby islands.

Scubafish Diving
(☏0 7566 5095; www.scuba-fish.com; Ban Sala Dan) One of the best dive operations on the island is located at **Baan Laanta Resort** (☏0 7566 5091; www.baanlaanta. com; Ao Kantiang; bungalow pool/seaview from 2000/3000B; ✳@☏☝) on Ao Kantiang; there's also a small second office at the Narima resort.

🛌 Sleeping

Some resorts close down for the May-to-October low season, others drop their rates by 50% or more.

Reservations are a must in high season.

HAT PHRA AE หาดพระแอ

The beach at Hat Phra Ae (Long Beach) is only mediocre, but the ambience is lively. A large travellers' village has set up camp and there are loads of *fa·ràng*-oriented restaurants, beach bars, internet cafes and tour offices.

Sanctuary Guesthouse $
(☏08 1891 3055; sanctuary_93@yahoo.com; Hat Phra Ae; bungalows 600-1200B) The original Phra Ae resort is still a delightful place to stay. There are artistically designed wood-and-thatch bungalows with lots of grass and a hippie-ish atmosphere that's low-key and friendly. The restaurant

Detour:
Caves & Caverns

Monsoon rains pounding away at limestone cracks and crevices for millions of years have created **Tham Khao Maikaeo** (ถ้ำเขาไม้แก้ว), a complex of forest caverns and tunnels. There are chambers as large as cathedrals that are dripping with stalactites, and tiny passages you have to squeeze through on hands and knees. There's even a subterranean pool you can take a chilly swim in. Sensible shoes are essential and getting totally covered in mud is almost guaranteed.

Most resorts can arrange transport and a local family can provide guided tours.

offers Indian and vegetarian eats and the Thai usuals. Sanctuary also holds yoga classes.

Andaman Sunflower Bungalow $
(☏0 7568 4668; Hat Phra Ae; bungalows 850B; ☾Oct-Apr; ☏) A terrific collection of wood and bamboo bungalows with built-in platform beds, high palm-leaf ceilings, polished wood floors and glass bowl sinks in the bath. Set back from the beach, these are some of the best budget bunga-lows around.

HAT KHLONG KHONG หาดคลองโขง

This is thatched-roof, Rasta-bar bliss with plenty of beach volleyball games, moon parties and the occasional well-advertised mushroom shake (imbibe at your own risk). Still, it's all pretty low-key and all ages are present. The beach goes on forever in either direction.

Bee Bee Bungalows Bungalow $
(☏08 1537 9932; www.beebeebungalows; Hat Khlong Khong; bungalows 900B; @☏) One

of the best budget spots on the island, Bee Bee's super friendly staff care for a dozen creative bamboo cabins – every one is unique and a few are up on stilts in the trees.

HAT KHLONG NIN หาดคลองนิน

The first beach here is lovely, white Hat Khlong Nin. There are lots of small inexpensive guesthouses at the north end of the beach that are usually attached to restaurants – it's easy to get dropped off here then shop around for a budget place to stay.

Round House   Guesthouse $

(☎ 08 1606 0550; www.lantaroundhouse. com; Hat Khlong Nin; r/bungalow/house 800/1000/2400B; ✴ 🛜) A cute little find on the north end of this beach with three options. The wooden and bamboo bungalows are closest to the beach, just behind the breezy restaurant. They also have a cool adobe round house (hence the name) off the road and a nearby beach house that's perfect for families.

Sri Lanta   Hotel $$

(☎ 0 7566 2688; www.srilanta.com; Hat Khlong Nin; cottages from 1800-6200B; ✴ @ 🛜 ⊠) 🖉 At the southern end of the beach, this decadent resort consists of minimalist wooden villas in wild gardens stretching from the beach to a landscaped jungle hillside. The resort strives for low environmental impact by using biodegradable products and minimising energy use and waste.

AO KANTIANG อ่าวกันเตียง

This superb sweep of sand backed by mountains is also its own self-contained little village complete with minimarts, internet cafes, motorbike rental and restaurants. It's far from everything; if you land here don't expect to move much.

Phra Nang Lanta   Inn $$$

(☎ 0 7566 5025; Ao Kantiang; studios 2500-8500B; ✴ @ 🛜 ⊠) The gorgeous Mexican-style adobe concrete studios are huge and straight off the pages of an architectural mag. Interiors are decorated with clean lines, hardwoods and whites accented with bright colours.

Seafood, Ko Lanta

OTTO STADLER/GETTY IMAGES ©

AO KHLONG JAAK & LAEM TANOD อ่าวคลองจาก/แหลมโตนด

The splendid beach at Ao Khlong Jaak is named after the inland waterfall.

Baan Phu Lae
Bungalows $

(☑0 7566 5100, 08 5474 0265; www.baanphulae.com; Ao Mai Pai; bungalows 800-1000B) Set on the rocks at the end of this tiny beach, the last before the cape, are a collection of romantic, canary-yellow concrete bungalows with thatched roofs, bamboo beds and private porches.

La Laanta
Boutique Hotel $$$

(☑0 7566 5066; www.lalaanta.com; Ao Mai Pai; bungalows 2800-6200B; ❄ @ 🛜 ✖ 🛖) Owned and operated by a young English-speaking Thai-Vietnamese couple, this is the grooviest spot on the entire island. Thatched bungalows have polished-concrete floors, platform beds, floral-design motifs and decks overlooking a pitch of sand, which blends into a rocky fishermen's beach.

BAN KO LANTA บ้านเกาะลันตา

There are a handful of inns open for business on Lanta's oft-ignored, wonderfully dated and incredibly rich Old Town.

Mango House
Guesthouse $$

(☑0 7569 7181; www.mangohouses.com; Ban Ko Lanta; suites 1500-3000B; ☉Oct-April) These 100-year-old Chinese teak pole houses and a former opium den are stilted over the harbour. The original time-worn wooden floors are still intact, ceilings soar and the house-sized rooms are decked out with satellite TVs, DVD players and ceiling fans. The restaurant is just as sea-shanty chic and serves Thai and Western dishes with panache.

Eating

Lanta Seafood
Seafood $$

(☑0 7566 8411; Ban Sala Dan; mains 80-300B) The best option of the seafood-by-weight choices. Order the *blah tôrt kà mîn* – it's white snapper rubbed with fresh, hand-ground turmeric and garlic, then deep fried.

Lym's Rice Bowl
Thai $$

(Hat Phra Ae; mains 80-180, seafood dinners 450B; ☉8am-10pm Oct-Apr; 🛜) Authentic curries, noodles, soups and stir-fries are served under the casuarinas, right on the beach. At dinner time they also do fresh fish, steamed, grilled and fried. If you eat and drink here you are welcome to their beach lounges all day long.

ℹ Getting There & Away

Boat

There is one passenger ferry connecting Krabi's Khlong Chilat pier with Ko Lanta departing from Ko Lanta at 8am (400B, two hours) and returning from Krabi at 11am. It also stops at Ko Jum (for the full 400B fare).

Boats between Ko Lanta and Ko Phi-Phi technically run year-round, although service can peter out in the low season if there are too few passengers. Ferries usually leave Ko Lanta at 8am and 1pm (300B, 1½ hours); in the opposite direction boats leave Ko Phi-Phi at 11.30am and 2pm. From here you can transfer to ferries to Phuket.

Minivan

Minivans run year-round and are your best option from the mainland. Daily minivans to Krabi airport (300B, 1½ hours) and Krabi Town (250B, 1½ hours) leave hourly between 7am and 3.30pm. From Krabi, minivans depart hourly from 8am till 4pm.

Minivans to Phuket (500B, four hours) leave Ko Lanta every two hours or so, but are more frequent in the high season.

ℹ Getting Around

Most resorts send vehicles to meet the ferries – a free ride *to* your resort. In the opposite direction expect to pay 80B to 350B.

Motorcycles (250B per day) can be rented all over the island. Unfortunately, very few places provide helmets and none provide insurance, so take extra care on the bumpy roads.

Thailand
In Focus

Young monks, Sukhothai (p212)

ANTHONY CASSIDY/GETTY IMAGES ©

Thailand Today

There is no doubt Thailand is getting richer. But the country continues to grapple with political instability.

Pedestrian overpass, Bangkok (p51)

belief systems
(% of population)

94
Buddhist

5
Muslim

1
Christian

if Thailand were 100 people

75 would be Thai

14 would be Chinese

11 would be Other

population per sq km

 = 30 people

Thailand   USA   UK

Thailand continues to ride a wave of prosperity. The standard and cost of living has increased, the coming ASEAN Economic Community promises increased business opportunities and tourism has discovered a new supply of visitors from China. But the country continues to grapple with political instability.

The Post Coup Years

Although former prime minister Thaksin Shinawatra was removed from office by a military coup in 2006, and subsequently fled the country to avoid prosecution on corruption charges, he still exerts a strong influence on Thailand's political process. His politically allied party, Puea Thai, won a majority of parliamentary seats in 2011, and his sister Yingluck Shinawatra was elected prime minister. She is often viewed as a proxy for her brother.

Meanwhile, the legislature has spent two years debating the details of the so-called amnesty bill that would allow Thaksin to return to the country by absolving him of criminal

TONY BURNS/GETTY IMAGES ©

an ill-fated government scheme to boost rice revenues by buying the domestic product at 50% above market value, hoping that market prices would follow. Instead India and Vietnam supplied the missing inventory at lower prices, leaving Thailand with stockpiles of an overvalued product and down billions of dollars in subsidies. The scheme was designed to boost incomes for rural rice farmers, a strong political base for the Puea Thai party.

Hello Neighbour

At the end of 2015, the ASEAN Economic Community (AEC) will unite 10 Southeast Asian countries into a liberalised marketplace where goods, services, capital and labour are shared across borders with little or no country-specific impediments.

charges, which he is now evading through self-imposed exile. The Senate ultimately rejected the bill but it is unclear if amnesty is dead or just resting. There was also a related political manoeuvre to ensure a more supportive legislature for Thaksin and his allies by changing the make-up of the Senate to a fully elected body, but the charter amendment was rejected by the constitutional court. Pro- and anti-government groups (sporting bells and whistles, respectively) have once again flooded the streets of Bangkok. After occasionally violent clashes that led to the death of more than 20 people and a nullified election, in May 2014 Thailand's Constitutional Court found Yingluck and nine members of her cabinet guilty of abuse of power, forcing them to stand down. At press time, a caretaker prime minister had been named and a general election was slated for July.

Thailand has also lost ground as the world's largest rice exporter thanks to

Riding the Wealth Wave

Smartphones everywhere, cars instead of motorcycles and the need for immigrant labour – there's no doubt Thailand is getting richer. In 2011 the World Bank upgraded the country's category from a lower-middle-income economy to an upper-middle-income economy, a designation based on gross national income (GNI) per capita. Thailand's GNI is US$4210, almost double what it was a decade ago.

In recent years the government passed a minimum wage hike to 300B per day. Though the increase hurt small and mid-sized labour-intensive factories, the unemployment rate remains extremely low (it was 0.7% in 2012), and economic growth remains strong at 5% for 2013. Thai workers might earn more, but costs have also risen: the prices of cooking gas, fuel, utilities and food items have all increased.

History

HM the King's Birthday celebrations (p45)

TOM COCKREM/GETTY IMAGES

Thai history has all the dramatic elements to inspire the imagination: palace intrigue, wars waged with spears and elephants, popular protest movements and a penchant for 'smooth-as-silk' coups.

From the Beginning

Though there is evidence of prehistoric peoples, most scholars start the story of Thai nationhood at the arrival of the 'Tai' people during the first millennium AD. The Tai people migrated from southern China and spoke Tai-Kadai, a family of tonal languages said to be the most significant ethno-linguistic group in Southeast Asia. The language group branched off into Laos (the Lao people) and Myanmar (the Shan). Most of these

4000–2500 BC
Prehistoric inhabitants of northeastern Thailand develop agriculture and tool-making.

new arrivals were farmers and hunters who lived in loosely organised villages, usually near a river source, with no central government or organised military.

The indigenous Mon people are often recognised as assembling an early confederation (often referred to as Mon Dvaravati) in central and northeastern Thailand from the 6th to 9th centuries. Little is known about this period, but scholars believe that the Mon Dvaravati had a centre in Nakhon Pathom, outside of Bangkok, with outposts in parts of northern Thailand.

The ancient superpower of the region was the Khmer empire, based in Angkor (in present-day Cambodia), which expanded across the western frontier into present-day northeastern and central Thailand starting in the 11th century. Sukhothai and Phimai were regional administrative centres connected by roads with way-station temples that made travel easier and were a visible symbol of imperial power. The Khmer monuments started out as Hindu but were later converted into Buddhist temples after the regime converted. Though their power would eventually decline, the Khmer imparted to the evolving Thai nation an artistic, bureaucratic and even monarchical legacy.

Thai history is usually told from the perspective of the central region, where the current capital is. But the southern region has a separate historical narrative that didn't merge with the centre until the modern era. Between the 8th and 13th centuries, southern Thailand was controlled by the maritime empire of Srivijaya, based in southern Sumatra (Indonesia), and controlled trade between the Straits of Malacca.

**The Best...
Historical
Sights**

1 Sukhothai (p213)

2 Ayuthaya (p106)

3 Phimai (p135)

4 Phanom Rung (p136)

The Rise of Thai Kingdoms

While the regional empires were declining in the 12th to 16th centuries, Tai peoples in the hinterlands established new states that would eventually unite the country.

Lanna Kingdom

In the northern region, the Lanna kingdom, founded by King Mengrai, built Chiang Mai (meaning 'new city') in 1292 and proceeded to unify the northern communities into one cultural identity. For a time Chiang Mai was something of a religious centre for the region. However, Lanna was plagued by dynastic intrigues, fell to the Burmese in 1556

6th–11th centuries AD
The Mon Dvaravati thrive in central Thailand.

10th century
Tai peoples arrive in Thailand.

1351
The legendary kingdom of Ayuthaya is founded.

and was later eclipsed by Sukhothai and Ayuthaya as the progenitor of the modern Thai state.

Sukhothai Kingdom

Then just a frontier town on the westernmost edge of the ailing Khmer empire, Sukhothai expelled the distant power in the mid-13th century and crowned the local chief as the first king. But it was his son Ramkhamhaeng who led the city-state to become a regional power with dependencies in modern-day Laos and southern Thailand. The city-state's local dialect (known as Siamese Tai) became the language of the ruling elite and the king is credited for inventing an early version of the script used today. Sukhothai replaced Chiang Mai as a centre of Theravada Buddhism on mainland Southeast Asia. The monuments built during this era helped define a distinctive architectural style. After his death, Ramkhamhaeng's empire disintegrated. In 1378 Sukhothai became a tributary of Ayuthaya.

Ayuthaya Kingdom

Close to the Gulf of Thailand, the city-state of Ayuthaya grew rich and powerful from the international sea trade. The legendary founder was King U Thong, one of 36 kings and five dynasties that steered Ayuthaya through a 416-year lifespan.

Ayuthaya presided over an age of commerce in Southeast Asia. Its main exports were rice and forest products, and many commercial and diplomatic foreign missions set up headquarters outside the royal city.

Ayuthaya adopted Khmer court customs, honorific language and ideas of kingship. The monarch styled himself as a Khmer *devaraja* (divine king) instead of the Sukhothai ideal of *dhammaraja* (righteous king). Ayuthaya paid tribute to the Chinese emperor, who rewarded this ritualistic submission with generous gifts and commercial privileges.

Ayuthaya's reign was constantly under threat from expansionist Burma. The city was occupied in 1569 but later liberated by King Naresuan. In 1767 Burmese troops successfully sacked the capital and dispersed the Thai leadership into the hinterlands. The destruction of Ayuthaya remains a vivid historical event in the nation, and the tales of court life are as evocative as the stories of King Arthur.

Name Changes

The country known today as Thailand has had several monikers. The Khmers are credited for naming this area 'Siam'. In 1939 the name of the country was changed from Siam (Prathet Syam) to Thailand (Prathet Thai).

1767
Ayuthaya falls at the hands of the Burmese.

1768–82
King Taksin rules from the new capital of Thonburi.

1782
King Taksin dies, Chakri dynasty is founded, and Bangkok becomes the new capital.

The Bangkok Era

The Revival

With Ayuthaya in ruins and the dynasty destroyed, a general named Taksin filled the power vacuum and established a new capital in 1768 in Thonburi, across the river from modern-day Bangkok. King Taksin was deposed and executed in 1782 by subordinate generals. One of the leaders of the coup, Chao Phraya Chakri, was crowned King Buddha Yot Fa (Rama I), the founder of the current Chakri dynasty. He moved the capital across the river to the Ko Ratanakosin district of present-day Bangkok.

The new kingdom was viewed as a revival of Ayuthaya and its leaders attempted to replicate the former kingdom's laws, government practices and cultural achievements. They also built a powerful military that avenged Burmese aggression, kicking them out of Chiang Mai and charging into Laos and Cambodia. The Bangkok rulers continued courting Chinese commercial trade and cultural exchange.

The Best...
Landmarks of the Bangkok Era

1 Wat Arun (p60)

2 Wat Phra Kaew & Grand Palace (p60)

3 Dusit Palace Park (p67)

The Reform Era

The Siamese elite had long admired China, but by the 1800s the West dominated international trade and geopolitics.

King Mongkut (Rama IV; r 1851–68), often credited with modernising the kingdom, spent 27 years prior to assuming the crown as a monk in the Thammayut sect, a reform movement he founded to restore scholarship to the faith. During his reign the country was integrated into the prevailing market system that broke up royal monopolies and granted more rights to foreign powers.

Mongkut's son, King Chulalongkorn (Rama V; r 1873–1910) took greater steps in replacing the old political order. He abolished slavery and introduced the creation of a salaried bureaucracy, a police force and a standing army. His reforms brought uniformity to the legal code, law courts and revenue offices. Schools were established along European models. Universal conscription and poll taxes made all men the king's men. Many of the king's advisors were British, and they ushered in a remodelling of the old Ayuthaya-based system.

Distant subregions were brought under central command and railways were built to link them to population centres. Pressured by French and British colonies on all sides, the modern boundaries of Siam came into shape, partly from ceding territory.

Successive kings continued to adopt European procedures and models to better survive in the new world order.

1868–1910
King Chulalongkorn (Rama V) reigns; it's a time of modernisation and European imperialism.

1932
A bloodless revolution ends absolute monarchy.
Left: Withunthatsana Hall, Bang Pa In Palace (p123)

TOM COCKREM/GETTY IMAGES ©

Democracy Versus Dictator

The 1932 Revolution

During a period of growing independence movements in the region, a group of foreign-educated military officers and bureaucrats led a successful (and bloodless) coup against absolute monarchy in 1932. But democracy did not (and still doesn't) have a smooth road ahead.

The pro-democracy party soon splintered and, by 1938, General Phibul Songkhram, one of the original democracy supporters, had seized control of the country. Japanese aggression during WWII changed the regional political landscape and Phibul (pronounced 'pee-boon'), who was staunchly anti-royalist, strongly nationalistic and pro-Japanese, allowed that country to occupy Thailand as a base for assaults on British colonies in Southeast Asia. In the post-WWII era, Phibul positioned Thailand as an ally of the US with staunch anti-communist policies.

The Cold War

During the Cold War and the US conflict in Vietnam, the military leaders of Thailand gained legitimacy and economic support from the US in exchange for the use of military installations in Thailand.

By the 1970s a new era of political consciousness bubbled up from the universities, marking a period of cultural turmoil. In 1973 more than half a million people – intellectuals, students, peasants and workers – demonstrated in Bangkok and major provincial towns, demanding a constitution from the military government. The bloody dispersal of the Bangkok demonstration on 14 October led to the collapse of the regime and the creation of an elected constitutional government. This lasted only three years until another protest movement was brutally squashed and the military returned in the name of civil order.

By the 1980s the so-called political soldier General Prem Tinsulanonda forged a period of political and economic stability that led to the 1988 election of a civilian government. Prem is still involved in politics today as the president of the palace's privy council, a powerful position that joins the interests of the monarchy with the military.

The Business Era

The new civilian government was composed of former business executives, many of whom represented provincial commercial interests, instead of Bangkok-based military officials, signalling a shift in the country's political dynamics. Though the country was doing well economically, the government was accused of corruption and vote-buying and the military moved to protect its privileged position with a 1991 coup.

Elected leadership was restored shortly after the coup, and the Democrat Party, with the support of business and the urban middle class, dominated the parliament.

1939
The country's English name is officially changed from Siam to Thailand.

1941
Japanese forces enter Thailand.

1946
King Bhumibol Adulyadej (Rama IX) accedes; Thailand joins the UN.

The 1997 Asian currency crisis derailed the surging economy and the government was criticised for its ineffective response. That same year, the parliament passed the watershed 'people's constitution', which enshrined human rights and freedom of expression and granted more power to a civil society to counter corruption. (The 1997 constitution was thrown out during the 2006 coup.)

By the turn of the millennium, the economy had recovered and business interests had succeeded the military as the dominant force in politics. The telecommunications billionaire and former police officer Thaksin Shinawatra ushered in the era of the elected CEO. He was a capitalist with a populist message and garnered support from the rural and urban poor and the working class. From 2001 to 2005 Thaksin and his Thai Rak Thai party transformed national politics into one-party rule.

The Ongoing Crisis

Though Thaksin enjoyed massive popular support, his regime was viewed by urban intellectuals as a kleptocracy, with the most egregious example of corruption being the tax-free sale of his family's Shin Corporation stock to the Singaporean government in 2006, a windfall of 73 billion baht (US$1.88 billion) that was engineered by special

Wat Arun (p60), Bangkok
EDUCATION IMAGES/UIG/GETTY IMAGES ©

1957
A successful coup by Sarit Thanarat starts a period of military rule that lasts until 1973.

1968
Thailand is a founding member state of the Association of Southeast Asian Nations.

1973
Civilian demonstrators overthrow the military dictatorship; a democratic government is installed.

The Best... Historic Museums

1 National Museum (p61)

2 Chiang Mai City Arts & Cultural Centre (p148)

3 Hilltribe Museum & Education Center (p197)

legislation. This enraged the upper and middle classes and led to street protests in Bangkok. Meanwhile behind the scenes, Thaksin had been working to replace key military figures with his loyalists, strategic moves that would realign the military's long-standing allegiance to the Bangkok aristocracy.

On 19 September 2006 the military staged a bloodless coup, the first in 15 years, which brought an end to the country's longest stretch of democratic rule. The military dissolved the constitution that had sought to ensure a civilian government and introduced a new constitution that limited the resurgence of one-party rule by interests unsympathetic to the military and the elites.

Since the coup, political stability has yet to be achieved. The reinstatement of elections restored Thaksin's political friends to power, a victory that was unacceptable to Bangkok's aristocracy who, with the implicit support of the military, staged huge protests that closed down Bangkok's two airports for a week in 2008. The most recent round of protests in 2014 signals more trouble ahead.

The Modern Monarchy

The country's last absolute monarch was King Prajadhipok (Rama VII), who accepted the 1932 constitution, abdicated the throne and went into exile. By 1935 the new democratic government had reinstated the monarchy, appointing the abdicated king's 10-year-old nephew, Ananda Mahidol (Rama VIII), who was living in Europe at the time. In 1946, after the king came of age, he was shot dead under mysterious circumstances. His younger brother was crowned King Bhumibol (Rama IX) and remains monarch today.

At the beginning of his reign King Bhumibol was primarily a figurehead promoted by various factions to appeal to the public's imagination of national unity. The military dictator General Sarit, who controlled the government from 1958 to 1963, supported the expansion of the king's role as a symbol of modern Thailand. The attractive royal couple, King Bhumibol and Queen Sirikit, made state visits abroad, met Elvis and were portrayed in photographs in much the same way as the US president John F Kennedy and his wife: young and fashionable models of the postwar generation.

Through rural development projects the king became regarded as the champion of the poor. The Royal Project Foundation was created in 1969 and is credited with helping to eradicate opium cultivation among the northern hill tribes. During the violence of the 1970s protest movements, the king came to be regarded as a mediating

1997
The Asian economic crisis hits; 'people's constitution' is passed in parliament.

2004
A Boxing Day tsunami kills 5000 people and damages tourism and fishing on the Andaman Coast. Right: Memorial plaques for tsunami victims, Khao Lak

ANDREW BAIN/GETTY IMAGES ©

voice in tumultuous times and called for the resignation of the military leaders. He also gave his consent to the reinstatement of military rule three years later, a symbolic gesture that helped ensure civil order. During another political crisis in 1992, the king summoned the leaders of the warring factions to the palace in an effort to quell street protests.

The king's annual birthday speech (5 December) is deeply revered for its guiding message and indicates palace sentiments towards rival political factions. In 2013, street protesters suspended their activities in honour of his birthday and the nation listened attentively to his address, which called for unity.

The king is in his 80s now and due to his failing health has receded from public life while the country's political future remains uncertain. Since the late 1950s the palace and the military have been closely aligned, a relationship that is currently cemented by General Prem Tinsulanonda, a retired military commander, former prime minister and current high-ranking palace advisor, who is believed to have instigated the 2006 coup. In previous political confrontations, the king has appeared to be above the bickering, but the palace's role in ousting the popular prime minister indicates a destabilisation of the monarch as a unifying figure. The anti-Thaksin, pro-royalist movement originally dressed in the royal colour of yellow and proclaimed to be protecting the king. Meanwhile the pro-Thaksin camp dressed in red and viewed themselves as the protectors of democracy, much like the revered anti-dictator groups of the 1970s (known as the October generation).

Though King Bhumibol has carved a unique niche for the postmodern monarch, it is uncertain whether his son, Crown Prince Vachiralongkorn, will enjoy the same public support or the traditional political allegiances. Concerns over succession is an undercurrent in the ongoing political crisis. And it is often theorised that the adoration that the average Thai once had for the king has been transferred to former prime minister Thaksin Shinawatra.

Picking Sides

The most recent round of street protests have introduced a rebranding of the fractious political camps. The anti-government group – formerly known as the 'yellow shirts' for their royally affiliated colour – has now adopted the colours of the Thai flag (red, white and blue) and don whistles to signal themselves as whistleblowers against corruption. Thaksin supporters wear red, which has been dubbed the colour of democracy. Those in between wear white as a symbol of peace; but critics claim that these are just reds in sheep's clothing.

2006
Prime Minister Thaksin Shinawatra is ousted by a military coup.

2011
Yingluck Shinawatra becomes the first female prime minister; destructive floods hit the country.

2014
Thailand's Constitutional Court find Yingluck Shinawatra and nine members of her cabinet guilty of abuse of power, forcing them from office.

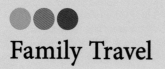

Family Travel

Songkran (p43), Chiang Mai

ALAIN EVRARD/GETTY IMAGES ©

Thais are so family focused that even grumpy taxi drivers want to pinch your baby's cheeks and play a game of peekaboo (called já ăir). On crowded buses, adults will stand so that children can sit, and hotel and restaurant staff willingly set aside chores to become a child's playmate.

Sights & Activities

Children will especially enjoy the beaches, as most are in gentle bays good for beginner swimmers. For the more experienced, some of the Gulf and Andaman islands have near-shore reefs for snorkelling.

Crocodile farms, monkey shows and tiger zoos abound in Thailand, but conditions are often below Western standards. There is a new generation of ecotour projects – in Ayuthaya, Chiang Mai and Lampang – that focus on humane conditions and animal conservation. The mahout-training schools and elephant sanctuaries are excellent places to see the revered pachyderm in a dignified setting. Older children will enjoy jungle-trekking tours that often include elephant rides and bamboo rafting. Many of the beach resorts, such as Phuket and Ko Chang, also have wildlife encounters, waterfall spotting and organised water sports.

In urban areas, kids might feel cooped up, in which case a hotel with a small garden or swimming pool will provide necessary play space. Playgrounds are neither widespread nor well maintained, though every city has an exercise park where runners and families go in the early evening. Though Bangkok is lean on green, it is still great fun for little ones in awe of construction sites and mass transit and for older ones obsessed with shopping malls.

If you're worried about long-distance journeys with a fussy passenger, opt for the train. Kids can walk around the carriage and visit the friendly locals; they are assigned the lower sleeping berths which have views of the stations, trotting dogs and dust-kicking motorcycles.

The Best... Kid-Friendly Beaches

1 Ko Samui: Bo Phut (p262) and Choeng Mon (p261)

2 Ko Lanta (p324)

3 Hua Hin (p250)

4 Ko Samet (p119)

Kid-Friendly Eats

In general, Thai children don't start eating spicy food until primary school; before then they seemingly survive on rice and junk food. Child-friendly meals include chicken in all of its nonspicy permutations – *gài yâhng* (grilled chicken), *gài tôrt* (fried chicken) and *gài pàt mét má·môo·ang* (chicken stir-fried with cashews). Some kids will even branch out to *kôw pàt* (fried rice), though the strong odour of *nám blah* (fish sauce) might be a deal breaker. Helpful restaurant staff will enthusiastically recommend *kài jee·o* (Thai-style omelette), which can be made in a jiffy.

If all else fails, tropical fruits and juices are ubiquitous and delectable and will keep the kids hydrated. Of course, most tourist centres also have Western restaurants catering to homesick eaters of any age.

Need to Know

Changing facilities Non-existent

Cots By special request at midrange and top-end hotels

Health Drink a lot of water; wash hands regularly; warn children against playing with animals

Highchairs Sometimes available in resort areas

Nappies (diapers) Minimarkets and 7-Elevens carry small sizes; try Tesco Lotus or Tops Market for size 3 or larger

Strollers Bring a compact umbrella stroller

Transport Car seats and seat belts are not widely available on public or hired transport

Culture & Customs

Vegetarian Festival (p300), Phuket Town

PAUL KENNEDY/GETTY IMAGES ©

It is easy to love Thailand: the pace of life is unhurried and the people are friendly and kind-hearted. A smile is a universal key in most social situations, a cheerful disposition will be met in kind, and friendships are spontaneous creations requiring little more than curiosity and humour. Though Thais don't expect foreigners to know much about their country, they are delighted and grateful if they do.

The Monarchy

Thailand expresses deep reverence for the reigning monarch, King Bhumibol Adulyadej (boo-mee-pone a-dun-ya-det). Pictures of the king are enshrined in nearly every household and business, and life-size billboards of the monarchs line Th Ratchadamnoen Klang, Bangkok's royal avenue. The king's image, which is printed on money and stamps, is regarded as sacred, and criticising the king or the monarchy is a prosecutable offence.

The monarch's relationship to the people is intertwined with religion; it is deeply spiritual and personal. Most Thais view the king with great reverence, as an exalted father figure (his birthday is recognised as national Father's Day) and as a protector of the good of the country.

The National Psyche

In most social situations, establishing harmony is often a priority and Thais take personal pride in making others feel at ease.

Sà·nùk

Thais place a high value on having *sà·nùk* (fun). It is the underlying measure of a worthwhile activity and the reason why the country ranks so highly as a tourist destination. Thais are always up for a party, be it of their own invention or an import. Case in point: Thais celebrate three new years – the eve of the resetting of the international calendar, the Chinese lunar New Year and Songkran (the Southeast Asian Buddhist new year).

This doesn't mean that Thais are averse to work. Most offices are typically open six, and sometimes seven, days a week, and most Thais have side jobs to provide extra income. But every chore has a social aspect that lightens the mood and keeps it from being too 'serious' (a grave insult). Whether it's the backbreaking work of rice farming, the tedium of long-distance bus driving or the dangers of a construction site, Thais often mix their work tasks with socialising.

Thais in the tourism industry extend this attitude towards their guests and will often describe foreign visitors as needing a rest after a year of hard work. This cultural mindset reflects the agricultural calendar in which a farmer works from dawn to dusk during the rice-planting and harvesting season then rests until the next year's rains. That rest period involves a lot of hanging out, going to festivals and funerals (which are more party than pity) and loading up family and friends into the back of a pick-up truck for a *têe·o* (trip).

Status

Though Thai culture is famously nonconfrontational and fun-loving, it isn't a social free-for-all. Thais are very conscious of status and the implicit rights and responsibilities. Buddhism plays a large part in defining the social strata, with the heads of the family, religion and monarchy sitting at the top of various tiers.

Gauging where you fit into this system is a convenient ice-breaker. Thais will often ask a laundry list of questions: where are you from, how old are you, are you married, do you have children? They are sizing you up in the social strata. In most cases, you'll get the best of both worlds: Thais will care for you as if you are a child and honour you as if you are a *pôo yài* (literally 'big person', or elder). When sharing a meal, don't be surprised if a Thai host puts the tastiest piece of fish on your plate.

Thais regard each other as part of an extended family and will use familial prefixes such as *pêe* (elder sibling) and *nórng* (younger sibling) when addressing friends as well as blood relations. When translated into English, this often leads foreigners to think that their Thai friends have large immediate families. Thais might also use *bâh* (aunt) or *lung* (uncle) to refer to an older person. Rarely do foreigners get embraced in this grand family reunion; *fa·ràng* is the catch-all term for foreigner. It is mostly descriptive but can sometimes express cultural frustrations.

Beloved Monarchs

Through history, there have been other monarchs who have crossed into national-hero status, including King Chulalongkorn (Rama V; r 1868–1910), whose picture often decorates residences and amulets. He travelled to Europe, built fine Victorian-style palaces and is greatly revered, especially in Bangkok and by Thais who have travelled abroad.

Saving Face

Interconnected with status is the concept of 'saving face', a common consideration in Asian cultures. In a nutshell, 'face' means you strive for social harmony by avoiding firm or confrontational opinions and displays of anger. Thais regard outbursts of emotion and discourteous social interactions as shameful, whereas Westerners might shrug them off.

Social Conventions & Etiquette

Thais are generally tolerant of most social faux pas as they assume that foreign visitors know very little about their culture. Their graciousness should be returned with a concerted effort of respect.

Greetings

The traditional Thai greeting is with a prayer-like palms-together gesture known as a *wâi*. If someone shows you a *wâi*, you should return the gesture, unless the greeting comes from a child or a service person. A *wâi* can also express gratitude or an apology. Foreigners are continually baffled by when and how to use the *wâi* and such cultural confusion makes great conversation fodder.

The all-purpose greeting is a cheery '*sà·wàt·dee kráp*' if you're male or '*sà·wàt·dee kâ*' if you're female. A smile usually accompanies this and goes a long way to diffuse a tense social situation. Also, Thais are great connoisseurs of beauty and a smile improves one's countenance.

Visiting Temples

When visiting a temple, it is important to dress modestly (cover yourself to the elbows and the ankles) and to take your shoes off when you enter any building that contains a Buddha image. Buddha images are sacred objects, so don't pose in front of them for pictures and definitely do not clamber on them. When visiting a religious building, act like a worshipper by finding a discreet place to sit in the 'mermaid' position (with your feet tucked behind you so that they point away from the Buddha images). Temples are maintained from the donations received and contributions from visitors are appreciated.

Touching

In the traditional parts of the country, it is not proper for members of the opposite sex to touch one another. Same-sex touching is quite common and is typically a sign of friendship, not sexual attraction. Older Thai men might grab a younger man's thigh in the same way that buddies slap each other on the back. Thai women are especially affectionate, often sitting close to female friends or linking arms. Women should not touch monks or their belongings; they should not sit next to them on public transport or accidentally brush against them on the street.

Dos & Don'ts

- Stand for the royal and national anthems.
- Don't show anger or frustration.
- Remove shoes before entering homes or temples; step over the threshold.
- Keep your feet off furniture.
- In temples, sit in the mermaid position (with your feet tucked behind you).
- If invited to someone's house, bring a gift of fruit or drinks.
- Pass and receive things with your right hand.
- Use your spoon like a fork and fork like a knife.

Religion

Reclining Buddha, Ayuthaya (p106)

STEVE ALLEN/GETTY IMAGES ©

Religion is a fundamental component of Thai society and culture, and colourful examples of daily worship can be found on nearly every corner. Walk the streets early in the morning and you'll see the solemn progression of Buddhist monks engaged in bin·da·bàht, the daily house-to-house alms-/food gathering. Small household shrines decorate the humblest abodes, and protective amulets, ranging from discreet to overt, are common pieces of jewellery.

Buddhism

Approximately 95% of Thai people are Theravada Buddhists. This form of Buddhism is often called the Southern School because it travelled from the Indian subcontinent to Southeast Asia.

Religious Principles

Buddhism was born in India in the 6th century. A prince named Siddhartha Gautama left his life of privilege, seeking religious fulfilment. According to the practices of the time, he became an ascetic and subjected himself to many years of severe austerity before he realised that this was not the way to reach the end of suffering. Adopting a more measured Middle Way, his practice became more balanced until, on the night of the full moon of the fifth month (nowadays celebrated as Visakha Bucha), he became enlightened under the Bodhi tree. He became known as Buddha, 'the enlightened' or 'the awakened', and spoke of four noble truths that had the power to liberate any human being who could realise them.

The four noble truths deal with the nature and origin of suffering and the path to the cessation of suffering. Loosely explained, this includes *dukkha* (all forms of existence are subject to suffering, disease, imperfection), *samudaya* (the origin of suffering is desire), *nirodha* (cessation of suffering is the giving up of desire) and *magga* (the path to cessation of suffering is the eightfold path).

The eightfold path is often described as the middle path: a route between extreme asceticism and indulgence. Following the path will lead to *nibbana* ('nirvana' in Sanskrit), which literally means the 'blowing out' or extinction of all grasping and thus of all suffering. Effectively, *nibbana* is also an end to the cycle of rebirths (both moment-to-moment and life-to-life) that is existence.

Religious Practice

In reality, most Thai Buddhists aim for rebirth in a 'better' existence rather than the supramundane goal of *nibbana*. By feeding monks, giving donations to temples and worshipping regularly at their local temple they hope to improve their lot, acquiring enough merit (*bun* in Thai) to prevent rebirths (or at least reduce their number). The concept of rebirth is almost universally accepted in Thailand, even by non-Buddhists.

Thai Buddhists look to the Triple Gems for guidance in their faith: the Buddha, the *dhamma* and the *sangha*. The Buddha, in myriad sculptural forms, is usually the centrepiece of devotional activity inside a temple and many of the most famous Thai Buddha images have supernatural tales associated with them. The *dhamma* is chanted morning and evening in every temple and taught to every Thai citizen in primary school. There are two *sangha* sects in Thailand: the Mahanikai and Thammayut. The former is more mainstream, while the latter is aligned more with the monarchy and sees itself as slightly stricter in its practice of the teachings.

Hinduism & Animism

There are many enduring legacies of Hinduism and animism in Thai culture and in the practice of Thai Buddhism today. Hinduism was the religious parent of Buddhism, imparting lasting components of mythology, cosmology and symbolism. Thais recognise the contributions of Hinduism and treat its deities with reverence. Bangkok is especially rich in Hindu shrines. Many of the royally associated ceremonies stem from Brahmanism.

Spirit worship and Buddhism have commingled to the point that it is difficult to filter the two. Monks often perform obviously animistic rituals, and Thais believe that making merit (Buddhist religious rituals) benefits deceased relatives. In fact, many of the religious rituals of Thai Buddhists, apart from meditation, appear to be deeply rooted in the spirit world. Trees are wrapped in sacred cloth to honour the spirits of the natural world. Altars are erected on the dashboards of taxis to ensure immunity from traffic laws and accidents. Thais

Houses of the Holy

Many dwellings in Thailand have a 'spirit house' for the property's *prá poom* (guardian spirits). Based on pre-Buddhist animistic beliefs, guardian spirits live in rivers, trees and other natural features and need to be honoured (and placated) like a respected but sometimes troublesome family member. Elaborate doll-house-like structures, where the spirits can 'live' comfortably separated from human affairs, are consecrated by a Brahman priest and receive daily offerings of rice, fruit, flowers and water.

often wear amulets embossed with a Buddha figure or containing sacred soil from a revered temple to protect the wearer from misfortune.

Monks & Monasteries

Every Thai male is expected to become a monk (*prá* or *prá pík·sù* in Thai) for a short period, optimally between the time he finishes school and the time he starts a career or marries. A family earns great merit when one of its sons 'takes robe and bowl' and many young men enter the monastery to make merit for a deceased patriarch or matriarch. Traditionally, Buddhist Lent (*pan·săh*), which begins in July and coincides with the three-month period of the rainy season, is when most temporary monks enter the monastery. Nowadays, though, men may spend as little as a week there.

Historically the temple provided a necessary social safety net for families in need. The monastery was a de facto orphanage, caring for and educating children whose parents couldn't provide for them, and also acted as a retirement home for older rural men. Though these charitable roles are not as sought after today, the temples still give refuge and sanctuary to all living creatures. This might mean that they help feed families in need, adopt orphaned or injured animals and give shelter to overnight travellers (usually impoverished Thai university students).

In Thai Buddhism, women who seek a monastic life are given a minor role in the temple that is not equal to full monkhood. A Buddhist nun is known as *mâa chee* (mother priest) and lives as an *atthasila* nun (following eight precepts of Buddhism's code of ethics as opposed to the five for lay people and 227 for ordained monks), a position traditionally occupied by women who had no other place in society. Thai nuns shave their heads, wear white robes and take care of temple chores. Generally speaking, *mâa chee* aren't considered as prestigious as monks and don't have a function in the laypeople's merit-making rituals, although there are *mâa chee* who have become revered teachers in their own right, with large followings.

Temple Visits

Thai Buddhism has no particular sabbath day when the faithful are supposed to congregate at the temple. Instead, Thai Buddhists visit whenever they feel like it, most often on *wan prá* (holy days), which occur every seventh or eighth day, depending on phases of the moon.

A temple visit is usually a social affair involving groups of friends, families or office workers. Thais will also make special pilgrimages to famous temples in other regions as sightseeing and merit-making outings.

Most merit-makers visit the *wí·hăhn* (the central sanctuary), which houses the primary Buddha figure. Worshippers will offer lotus buds (a symbol of enlightenment) or flower garlands, light three joss sticks and raise their hands to their forehead in a prayerlike gesture.

Other merit-making activities include offering food to the temple *sangha* (community), meditating (individually or in groups), listening to monks chanting *suttas* (Buddhist discourse) and attending a *têht* or *dhamma* (teachings) talk by the abbot or some other respected teacher.

Thai Buddhists will also visit the temple to consult with monks in order to pick an auspicious time to get married, start a business or perform child-naming rituals. Funeral rites are also held at the temple.

Islam & Other Religions

Although Thailand is predominantly Buddhist, its minority religions often practise alongside one another.

About 4.6% of the population are followers of Islam. The remainder are Christian, including missionary-converted hill tribes and Vietnamese immigrants, as well as Confucians, Taoists, Mahayana Buddhists and Hindus.

The majority of Muslims in Thailand live in the southern provinces, though there are pockets in Bangkok and central and northern Thailand. In the southernmost provinces the Muslims are ethnic Malays, while northern Thailand's Muslims are Yunnanese descendants. The form of Islam found in southern Thailand is mixed with elements of Malay culture and animism, creating a more culturally relaxed religion than that of Arab nations. The southernmost provinces of Yala, Pattani and Narathiwat contain the country's largest Muslim majority and have long been geographically isolated and culturally alien to the mainstream society. Historically, parts of these provinces were independent sultanates that were conquered by the Bangkok-based kings. During the ultranationalist era in the 1940s, this region responded with separatist resistance, later becoming a sanctuary for communist and insurgent activities in the 1980s. Violence flared again in the early 2000s and has persisted, with no end in sight. Most observers classify the conflict as an ethno-nationalist struggle.

Thai Muslim women function in the society as actively as their Buddhist sisters. Headscarves are prevalent but not mandatory: sometimes a visitor only realises that someone is a Muslim when they decline an offering of pork at the dinner table.

Devout Thai Muslims often encounter spiritual incompatibilities with their identities as Thai citizens, which is largely defined by the Buddhist majority. The popular view of the Thai monarch as godlike is heresy for a monotheistic religion like Islam, though many Thai Muslims respect and even love the king and do not voice open criticism of his veneration. Muslims also avoid alcohol and gambling (in varying degrees) – two pursuits that define much of rural life for Buddhist Thais. In this way, religious precepts keep the two cultures distinct and slightly distrustful of each other.

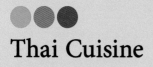

Thai Cuisine

Gaang kĕe·o wăhn (Thai green curry)

SHUTTERWORX/GETTY IMAGES ©

Thai food — one of the country's most famous exports — balances spicy, sweet, sour and salty flavours in complex and zesty combinations. Ingredients are fresh, flavours are assertive and the sting of the beloved chilli triggers an adrenalin rush.

Rice

In the morning Thais rise with two fundamental smells: rice being cooked and the burning joss sticks that are offered in household shrines. The start of the new day means another opportunity to eat, and eating in Thailand means eating rice (the Thai word 'to eat' is *gin kôw*, literally 'to eat rice').

Rice can be steamed, fried, boiled in a soup, formed into noodles or made into a dessert. In its steamed form it is eaten with a spoon or, in the case of *kôw nĕe·o* (sticky rice), eaten with the fingers. The classic morning meal is a watery rice soup (either *jóhk* or *kôw đôm*) that is the ultimate comfort food, the equivalent of oatmeal on a cold day. The next meal of the day will probably be a stir-fry or curry, typically served over rice, bought from a street stall or shopfront canteen. In the evening in provincial towns, everyone heads to the night market to see and be seen and to eat more rice.

Noodles

When rice just won't do there is another, albeit rice-derived, alternative: *gŏo·ay đĕe·o* (rice noodles). Day or night, city or village, *gŏo·ay đĕe·o* is the original Thai fast food, served by itinerant vendors or from humble shopfronts. It demonstrates Thais' penchant for micromanaging flavours. You choose the kind of noodle and the kind of meat and you flavour it yourself with a little fish sauce, sugar, vinegar and chillies; don't shy away from the sugar, it works wonders.

There are three basic kinds of rice noodles – *sên yài* (wide), *sên lék* (thin) and *sên mèe* (thinner than thin) – as well as *bà·mèe,* which is a curly noodle made from wheat flour and egg. Most of these only appear in noodle soups but a few are used in various stir-fries, such as *pàt tai* (thin rice noodles stir-fried with dried or fresh shrimp, tofu and egg).

Head to the morning market for a bowl of *kà·nŏm jeen* (rice noodles doused in a thin curry). This dish is piled high with strange pickled and fresh vegetables that will make you feel as if you've grazed on the savannah and swum through the swamp. *Kà·nŏm jeen* is usually served at rickety wooden tables shared with working-class women dressed in polyester market clothes.

Curries

The overseas celebrity of Thai cuisine, curry (*gaang*) is a humble dish on home turf. At roadside stands, especially in southern Thailand, big metal pots contain various curry concoctions of radioactive colours. When you ask vendors what they have, they'll lift the lids and name the type of meat in each: for example *gaang gài* (curry with chicken) or *gaang blah* (shorthand for sour fish curry). In Bangkok, street-side vendors and small shops will display their curry-in-a-hurry in buffet-style trays. In either case, you point to one and it will be ladled over rice. Use a spoon to scoop it up and push the lime leaves to the side – they aren't edible.

All curries start with a basic paste that includes ground coriander seed, cumin seed, garlic, lemongrass, kaffir lime, galangal, shrimp paste and chillies (either dried or fresh). Thai cooks used to make these from scratch but these days they go to the market and buy them in bulk. The curry paste recipe varies from region to region; for example, one that is known in the West, *gaang mát·sà·màn* (Muslim curry), uses star anise, which is considered a Thai-Muslim spice. Most visitors know their curries by their colour, mainly red (from dried red chillies) and green (from fresh green chillies). Green curry is a classic central-Thailand dish.

Tips on Tipples

o Thai beers, such as Singha (pronounced 'sing'), are hoppy lagers which are often mixed with ice to keep them cool and palatable.

o Fruit shakes are refreshing on a hot day and are served with a pinch of salt to help regulate body temperature.

o Sweet iced coffee and tea are popular street stall drinks.

o Thais get their drink on with rice whisky mixed with ice, soda water and a splash of Coke.

Regional Cuisines

Over the past 20 years there has been so much migration within Thailand that many of the once region-specific dishes have been incorporated into the national cuisine.

Northern Thai

True to its Lanna character, northern Thai cuisine is more laid-back – the flavours are mellow and the influences have migrated over the mountains from Myanmar (Burma) and China. Thanks to the travelling Chinese caravans and settlers, northern cuisine is enamoured with pork, which features in almost every dish including *sâi òo·a* (local-style sausages), *kâap mŏo* (crackling) and the popular street food *mŏo bîng* (grilled pork skewers). The Burmese influence has imparted the use of turmeric and ginger (though some could argue that northern Burmese food was influenced by Chinese) into the curry pastes used in *gaang hang·lair* (rich pork stew).

Northern flavours favour sour notes. Pickled vegetables are loaded on top of the signature noodle dishes of *kôw soy* (wheat-and-egg noodles with a thick coconut red curry) and *kà·nŏm jeen nám ngée·o* (rice noodles served with thin curry broth made with pork and tomatoes); shallots and lime wedges are common seasoning garnishes.

Northern Thailand shares Isan's love of *kôw nĕe·o*, which is often served in rounded wicker baskets and accompanies such standard dishes as *nám prík òrng* (a chilli paste made with ground pork and tomato).

Southern Thai

Southern Thai food draws from the traditions of seafaring traders, many of whom were Muslims from India, or ethnic Malays. Indian-style flat bread (known as roti) often competes with rice as a curry companion or is drizzled with sugar and sweetened condensed milk as a market dessert. Turmeric imparts its telltale yellow hue to *kôw mòk gài* (chicken biryani) and southern-style fried chicken.

The curries here are flamboyant, with dry-roasted spice bases prepared in the Indian fashion and featuring lots of locally produced coconut milk. Shaved, milked, strained and fresh, the coconut is a kitchen mainstay.

Seafood is plentiful and fresh in southern cuisine. Plump squid is grilled and served on a stick with an accompanying sweet-and-spicy sauce. Whole fish are often stuffed with lemongrass and limes and barbecued over a coconut-husk fire.

Northeastern Thai

Northeasterners are known for their triumvirate dishes: *sôm·đam* (green papaya salad), *kôw nĕe·o* and *gài yâhng* (grilled chicken).

In the morning, open-coal grills are loaded up with marinated chicken. Alongside the grill is a large mortar and pestle in which *sôm·đam* is prepared. In go strips of green papaya, sugar, chillies, fish sauce, green beans, tomatoes, dried shrimps and a few special requests: peanuts to make it *sôm·đam Thai,* or field crabs and *blah ráh* (fermented fish sauce) to make it *sôm·đam Lao* (referring to the ethnic Lao who live in northeastern Thailand).

The vendor pounds the ingredients together with the pestle to make a musical 'pow-pow-pow' sound that is sometimes used as an onomatopoetic nickname. Isan girls are often told that they'll make good wives if they are adept at handling the pestle when making *sôm·đam* – the obvious sexual connotations are intended.

The Best... Street-Vendor Meals

1 *kôw pàt* – fried rice

2 *gŏo·ay đĕe·o pàt kêe mow* – stir-fried noodles with basil, chillies and a choice of meat (usually chicken)

3 *pàt gá·prow* – freshly sliced chillies, holy basil and a choice of chicken or pork stir-fry served over rice

4 *pàt pàk ká·náh* – stir-fried Chinese kale, often matched with *mŏo gròrp* (fried pork)

Arts & Architecture

Detail of mural, Wat Phra Kaew (p60), Bangkok

Thais have a refined sense of beauty that is reflected in their artistic traditions, from Buddhist sculpture to temple architecture. Monarchs were the country's great artistic patrons; their funeral monuments were ornate stupas, and handicrafts were developed specifically for royal use. Today religious artwork continues to dominate the artistic imagination but has been adapted to the modern context with museum multimedia installations and contemporary canvas works.

Religious Art

Temples are the country's artistic repositories, where you'll find ornate murals depicting Hindu-Buddhist mythology and Buddha sculptures, which define Thailand's most famous contribution to the world of religious art.

Always instructional in intent, temple murals often show depictions of the *jataka* (stories of the Buddha's past lives) and the Thai version of the Hindu epic *Ramayana*. Reading the murals requires both knowledge of these religious tales and an understanding of the murals' spatial relationship and chronology. Most murals are divided into scenes, in which the main theme is depicted in the centre with resulting events taking place above and below the central action. Usually in the corner of a dramatic tableau featuring the story's leading characters are independent scenes of Thai village life: women carrying bamboo baskets, men fishing, or a festive get-together.

Alongside the vivid murals are revered Buddha images that trace Thailand's sculptural evolution. The country is most famous for its graceful and serene Buddhas that emerged during the Sukhothai era.

Contemporary Art

Adapting traditional themes and aesthetics to the secular canvas began around the turn of the 20th century, as Western influence surged in the region. In general, Thai painting favours abstraction over realism and continues to preserve the one-dimensional perspective of traditional mural paintings.

Italian artist Corrado Feroci is often credited with being the father of modern Thai art. He was first invited to Thailand by Rama VI in 1924 and built Bangkok's Democracy Monument, among other European-style statues. Feroci founded the country's first fine arts institute in 1933, a school that eventually developed into Silpakorn University, Thailand's premier training ground for artists. In gratitude, the Thai government made Feroci a Thai citizen, with the Thai name Silpa Bhirasri.

The Modern Buddha

In the 1970s Thai artists began to tackle the modernisation of Buddhist themes through abstract expressionism. Leading works in this genre include the mystical pen-and-ink drawings of Thawan Duchanee. Montien Boonma used the ingredients of Buddhist merit-making, such as gold leaf, bells and candle wax, to create abstract temple spaces within museum galleries.

Protest & Satire

In Thailand's quickly industrialising society, many artists watched as rice fields became factories, forests became asphalt and the spoils went to the politically connected. During the student activist days of the 1970s the Art for Life Movement was the banner under which creative discontents – including musicians, intellectuals and painters – rallied against the military dictatorship and embraced certain aspects of communism and workers' rights. Sompote Upa-In and Chang Saetang are two important artists from that period.

An anti-authority attitude continues today. Photographer Manit Sriwanichpoom is best known for his Pink Man on Tour series, in which he depicted artist Sompong Thawee in a pink suit and with a pink shopping cart amid Thailand's most iconic attractions, suggesting that Thailand's cultural and natural spaces were for sale. He's

Handicrafts

Thailand's handicrafts live on for the tourist markets, and some have been updated by chic Bangkok designers.

Ceramics The best-known ceramics are the greenish Thai-style celadon, and central Thailand's *ben·jà·rong* (five colour).

Lacquerware Northern Thailand is known for this handicraft inherited from Burma.

Textiles The northeast is famous for *mát·mèe* cloth – a thick cotton or silk fabric woven from tie-dyed threads. Each hill tribe has a tradition of embroidery; Chiang Mai and Chiang Rai are popular handicraft centres.

Thailand's Artistic Periods

The development of Thai religious art and architecture is broken into different periods or schools defined by the patronage of the ruling capital. A period's characteristics are seen in the depiction of the Buddha's facial features, the top flourish on the head, the dress, and the position of the feet in meditation. Another signature of each period is the size and shape of the temples' *chedi* (stupas) – telltale characteristics are shown in the pedestal and the central bell before it begins to taper into the uppermost tower.

PERIOD	TEMPLE & CHEDI STYLES	BUDDHA STYLES	EXAMPLES
Dvaravati period (7th-11th centuries)	Rectangular-based *chedi* with stepped tiers	Indian-influenced with a thick torso, large hair curls, arched eyebrows to represent a flying bird, protruding eyes, thick lips and a flat nose	Phra Pathom Chedi, Nakhon Pathom; Lopburi Museum, Lopburi; Wat Chama Thawi, Lamphun
Srivijaya Period (7th-13th centuries)	Mahayana-Buddhist-style temples; Javanese-style *chedi* with elaborate arches	Indian influenced: heavily ornamented, humanlike features and slightly twisted at the waist	Wat Phra Boromathat, Chaiya; Wat Phra Mahathat Woramahawihaan and National Museum, Nakhon Si Thammarat
Khmer period (9th-11th centuries)	Hindu-Buddhist temples; corn-cob-shaped *prang*	Buddha meditating under a canopy of the seven-headed *naga* and atop a lotus pedestal	Phimai, Nakhon Ratchasima; Phanom Rung, Surin
Chiang Saen-Lanna period (11th-13th centuries)	Teak temples; square-based *chedi* topped by gilded umbrella; also octagonal-base *chedi*	Burmese influences with plump figure, round, smiling face and footpads facing upwards in meditation pose	Wat Phra Singh, Chiang Mai; Chiang Saen National Museum
Sukhothai period (13th-15th centuries)	Khmer-inspired temples; slim-spired *chedi* topped by a lotus bud	Graceful poses, often depicted 'walking', no anatomical human detail	Sukhothai Historical Park
Ayuthaya period (14th-18th centuries)	Classical Thai temple with three-tiered roof and gable flourishes; bell-shaped *chedi* with tapering spire	Ayuthaya-era king, wearing a gem-studded crown and royal regalia	Ayuthaya Historical Park
Bangkok-Ratanakosin period (19th century)	Colourful and gilded temple with Western-Thai styles; mosaic-covered *chedi*	Reviving Ayuthaya style	Wat Phra Kaew, Wat Pho and Wat Arun, Bangkok

since followed up this series with other socially evocative photographs poking fun at ideas of patriotism and nationalism.

Finding a Home for Art

In this hierarchical society, artistic innovation is often stifled by the older generation who holds prestige and power. In the 1990s there was a push to move art out of the dead zones of the museums and into the public spaces, beyond the reach of the cultural authoritarians. An artist and art organiser, Navin Rawanchaikul, started his 'in-the-streets' collaborations in his home town of Chiang Mai and then moved his big ideas to Bangkok, where he filled the city's taxi cabs with art installations, a show that literally went on the road. His other works have had a way with words, such as the mixed-media piece *We Are the Children of Rice (Wine)* in 2002 and his rage against the commercialisation of museums in his epic painting entitled *Super (M)art Bangkok Survivors* (2004), which depicts famous artists, curators and decision-makers in a crowded Paolo Veronese setting. The piece was inspired by the struggles the Thai art community had in getting the new contemporary Bangkok art museum to open without it becoming a shopping mall in disguise.

Pop Fun

True to the Thai nature, some art is just fun. The works of Thaweesak Srithongdee are pure pop. He paints flamboyantly cartoonish human figures woven with elements of traditional Thai handicrafts or imagery. In a similar vein, Jirapat Tasanasomboon depicts traditional Thai figures in comic-book-style fights or in sensual embraces with Western icons. In *Hanuman Is Upset!* the monkey king chews up the geometric lines of Mondrian's famous gridlike painting. Thai-Japanese artist Yuree Kensaku creates cartoon-like paintings with pop-culture references.

Sculpture

Although lacking in commercial attention, Thai sculpture is often considered to be the strongest of the contemporary arts: not surprising considering the country's relationship with Buddha figures. Moving into nonreligious arenas, Khien Yimsiri is the modern master creating elegant human and mythical forms out of bronze. Kamin Lertchaiprasert explores the subject of spirituality and daily life in his sculptural installations, which often include a small army of papier-mâché figures. His exhibit *Ngern Nang* (Sitting Money) included a series of figures made of discarded paper bills from the national bank and embellished with poetic instructions on life and love.

Theatre & Dance

Traditional Thai theatre consists of dance-dramas, in which stories are acted out by masked or costumed actors. Traditional theatre was reserved for royal or religious events but, with the modernisation of the monarchy, the once-cloistered art forms have lost their patrons and gone into decline. Classical Thai dance, on the other hand, has survived quite well in the modern era and is still widely taught in schools and universities.

Kŏhn & Lí·gair

Kŏhn is a masked dance-drama depicting scenes from the *Ramakian* (the Thai version of India's *Ramayana*). The central story revolves around Prince Rama's search for his beloved Princess Sita, who has been abducted by the evil 10-headed demon Ravana and taken to the island of Lanka.

Most often performed at Buddhist festivals by troupes of travelling performers, *lí·gair* is a gaudy, raucous theatrical art form thought to have descended from drama rituals brought to southern Thailand by Arab and Malay traders. It contains a colourful mixture of folk and classical music, outrageous costumes, melodrama, slapstick comedy, sexual innuendo and up-to-date commentary.

Classical & Folk Dance

Inherited from the Khmer, classical dance was a holy offering performed by the earthly version of *apsara* (heavenly maidens blessed with beauty and skilled in dance, who are depicted in graceful positions in temple murals and bas reliefs). But traditional dancing enjoyed its own expressions in the villages and defined each region. In some cases the dances describe the rice-planting season, while others tell tales of flirtations. During local festivals and street parades, especially in the northeast, troupes of dancers, ranging from elementary-school age to college age, will be swathed in traditional costumes, ornate headdresses and white-powder make-up to perform synchronised steps accompanied by a marching band.

Music

Classical Thai music features a dazzling array of textures and subtleties, hair-raising tempos and pastoral melodies. The classical orchestra is called the *bèe pâht* and can include as few as five players or more than 20. Among the more common instruments is the *bèe*, a woodwind instrument that has a reed mouthpiece; it is heard prominently at Thai-boxing matches. The *rá·nâht èhk*, a bamboo-keyed percussion instrument resembling the xylophone, carries the main melodies. The slender *sor*, a bowed instrument with a coconut-shell soundbox, is sometimes played solo by street buskers.

If you take a cab in Bangkok, you're likely to hear Thailand's version of country music: *lôok tûng* (literally 'children of the fields'). Lost love, tragic early death and the plight of the hard-working farmers are popular themes sung plaintively over a melancholy accompaniment. More upbeat is *mŏr lam,* a folk tradition from the rural northeast that has been electrified with a fast-paced beat.

Step into a shopping mall or a Thai disco and you'll hear the bouncy tunes of Thai pop (also dubbed 'T-pop'). The ageing hippies from the protest era of the 1970s and 1980s pioneered *pleng pêu·a chee·wít* (songs for life), which feature in the increasingly hard-to-find Thai country bars. The 1990s gave birth to an alternative pop scene – known as 'indie'.

The Best... Old-Fashioned Thai Houses

1 Jim Thompson House (p72)

2 Baan Sao Nak (p193)

3 Suan Pakkad Palace Museum (74)

Architecture

Traditional Homes

Traditional Thai homes were adapted to the weather, the family and artistic sensibilities. These antique specimens were humble dwellings consisting of a single-room wooden house raised on stilts. More elaborate homes, for the village chief or minor royalty for instance, might link a series of single rooms by elevated walkways. Since many Thai villages were built near rivers, the elevation provided protection from flooding during the annual monsoon. During the dry season the space beneath the house was used as a hideaway from the heat of the day, an out-door kitchen or as a barn for farm animals. Later this all-purpose space would shelter bicycles and motorcycles. Once plentiful in Thai forests, teak was always the material of choice for wooden structures and its use typically indicates that a house is at least 50 years old.

Rooflines in central, northern and southern Thailand are steeply pitched and often decorated at the corners or along the gables with motifs related to the *naga,* a mythical water serpent long believed to be a spiritual protector of Tai cultures throughout Asia.

In Thailand's southern provinces it's not unusual to come upon houses of Malay design, using high masonry pediments or foundations rather than wooden stilts. Residents of the south also sometimes use bamboo and palm thatch, which are more plentiful than wood. In the north, the homes of community leaders were often decorated with an ornate horn-shaped motif called *galare,* a decorative element that has become shorthand for old Lanna architecture. Roofs of tile or thatch tend to be less steeply pitched, and rounded gables – a feature inherited from Myanmar (Burma) – can also be found further north.

Temples

The most striking examples of Thailand's architectural heritage are the Buddhist temples (wát), which dazzle in the tropical sun with wild colours and soaring rooflines. Thai temples are compounds of different buildings serving specific religious functions. The most important structures include the *uposatha* (*bòht* in central Thai, *sĭm* in northern and northeastern Thai), which is a consecrated chapel where monastic ordinations are held, and the *wí·hǎhn,* where important Buddha images are housed.

Temple Symbols

The architectural symbolism of Thai temples relies heavily on Hindu-Buddhist iconography.

Naga, the mythical serpent that guarded Buddha during meditation, appears on handrails at temple entrances. A silhouette of the birdlike *chôr fáh* adorns the tip of the roof. Three-tiered roofs represent the triple gems of Buddhism: the Buddha, the *dhamma* and the *sangha* (the Buddhist community).

The lotus, a reminder of religious perfection, decorates temple gates and posts, verandah columns and spires of Sukhothai-era *chedi,* and often forms the pedestal for images of the meditating Buddha. Lotus buds are used solely for merit-making.

A classic component of temple architecture is the presence of one or more *chedi* (stupas), a solid mountain-shaped monument that pays tribute to the enduring stability of Buddhism. *Chedi* come in myriad styles, from simple inverted bowl-shaped designs imported from Sri Lanka to the more elaborate octagonal shapes found in northern Thailand. Many are believed to contain relics (often pieces of bone) belonging to the historical Buddha. Some *chedi* also house the ashes of important kings and royalty. A variation of the stupa inherited from the Angkor kingdom is the corn-cob-shaped *prang,* a feature in the ancient Thai temples of Sukhothai and Ayuthaya.

Contemporary Architecture

Thais began mixing traditional architecture with European forms in the late 19th and early 20th centuries, as exemplified by Bangkok's Vimanmek Teak Mansion in Dusit Palace Park and certain buildings of the Grand Palace.

The port cities of Thailand, including Bangkok and Phuket, acquired fine examples of Sino-Portuguese architecture – buildings of stuccoed brick decorated with an ornate facade – a style that followed the sea traders during the colonial era. In Bangkok this style is often referred to as 'old Bangkok' or Ratanakosin.

In the 1960s and 1970s the European Bauhaus movement shifted contemporary architecture towards a stark functionalism. During the building boom of the mid-1980s, Thai architects used high-tech designs such as ML Sumet Jumsai's famous Robot Building on Th Sathon Tai in Bangkok.

In the new millennium, shopping centres and hotels have reinterpreted the traditional Thai house through an industrial modernist perspective, creating geometric cubes defined by steel beams and glass curtains.

Environment

Hot-air balloons over Doi Inthanon National Park (p180)

COPYRIGHT ANEK/GETTY IMAGES ©

Thailand clings to a southern spur of the Himalayas in the north, cradles fertile river plains at its core and tapers between two warm, shallow seas fringed by coral reefs. Its shape is often likened to an elephant's head, with the Malay peninsula representing the trunk. Spanning 1650km and 16 latitudinal degrees from north to south, Thailand has the most diverse climate of any country in mainland Southeast Asia.

Northern Thailand

Northern Thailand is fused to Myanmar (Burma), Laos and southern China through the southeast-trending extension of the Himalayan mountain range known as the Dawna-Tenasserim. The tallest peak is Doi Inthanon (measured heights vary from 2565m to 2576m), which is topped by a mixed forest of evergreen and swamp species, including a thick carpet of moss. Monsoon forests comprise the lower elevations and are made up of deciduous trees, which are green and lush during the rainy season but dusty and leafless during the dry season. Teak is one of the most highly valued monsoon forest trees but it now exists only in limited quantities and is illegal to harvest.

The cool mountains of northern Thailand are considered to be some of the

most accessible and rewarding birding destinations in Asia and are populated by montane species and migrants with clear Himalayan affinities, such as flycatchers and thrushes.

Central Thailand

In the central region the topography mellows into a flat rice basket, fed by rivers that are as revered as the national monarchy. Thailand's most exalted river is the Chao Phraya, which is formed by the northern tributaries of the Ping, Wang, Yom and Nan – a lineage as notable as any aristocrat's. The river delta spends most of the year in cultivation, changing with the seasons from fields of emerald-green rice shoots to golden harvests. This region has been heavily sculpted by civilisation: roads, fields, cities and towns have transformed the landscape into a working core.

In the western frontier, bumping into the mountainous border with Myanmar (Burma) is a complex of forest preserves that cover 17,800 sq km – the largest protected area in Southeast Asia and a largely undisturbed habitat for endangered elephants and tigers. These parks have little in the way of tourist infrastructure or commercial development.

Northeastern Thailand

The landscape of Thailand's northeastern region is occupied by the arid Khorat Plateau rising some 300m above the central plain. This is a hardscrabble land where the rains are meagre, the soil is anaemic and the red dust stains as stubbornly as the betel nut chewed by the local grandmothers. The dominant forest is dry dipterocarp, which consists of deciduous trees that shed their leaves in the dry season to conserve water. The region's largest forest preserve is Khao Yai National Park, which, together

Khao Sok National Park (p290)

with nearby parks, has been recognised as a Unesco World Heritage Site. The park is mainly arid forest, a favourite of hornbills and more than 300 other bird species. There is a small population of wild elephants in the park but development around the perimeter has impacted important wildlife corridors.

Southern Thailand

The kingdom's eastern rivers dump their waters and sediment into the Gulf of Thailand, a shallow basin off the neighbouring South China Sea. In the joint of the fishhook-shaped gulf is Bangkok, surrounded by a thick industrial zone that has erased or polluted much of the natural environment. The extremities of the gulf, both to the east and to the south, are more characteristic of coastal environments: mangrove swamps form the transition between land and sea and act as the ocean's nursery, spawning and nurturing fish, bird and amphibian species. Thailand is home to nearly 75 species of these salt-tolerant trees that were once regarded as wastelands and were vulnerable to coastal development.

The long slender 'trunk' of land that runs between the Gulf of Thailand and the Andaman Sea is often referred to as the Malay Peninsula. This region is Thailand's most tropical: rainfall is plentiful, cultivating thick rainforests that stay green year-round. Malayan flora and fauna predominate and a scenic range of limestone mountains meanders from land to sea.

On the west coast, the Andaman Sea is an outcropping of the larger Indian Ocean and home to astonishing coral reefs that feed and shelter thousands of varieties of fish and act as breakwaters against tidal surges. Many of the coral-fringed islands are designated marine national parks, limiting – to some degree – coastal development and boat traffic. The 2010 global coral bleaching phenomenon (in which El Niño weather conditions contributed to warmer sea temperatures) killed or damaged significant portions of Thailand's reefs.

The Best... National Parks

1 Khao Yai National Park (p112)

2 Khao Sok National Park (p290)

3 Doi Inthanon National Park (p180)

4 Similan Islands Marine National Park (p294)

5 Ao Phang-Nga Marine National Park (p306)

National Parks & Protected Areas

With 15% of the kingdom's land and sea designated as park or sanctuary, Thailand has one of the highest percentages of protected areas of any Asian nation. There are more than 100 national parks, plus more than 1000 'nonhunting areas', wildlife sanctuaries, forest reserves, botanic gardens and arboretums.

Thailand began its conservation efforts in 1960 with the creation of a national system of wildlife sanctuaries under the Wild Animals Reservation and Protection Act, followed by the National Parks Act of 1961. Khao Yai National Park was the first wild area to receive this new status.

Despite promises, official designation as a national park or sanctuary does not guarantee protection from development or poaching. Local farmers, hunters and moneyed interests often circumvent conservation efforts. Enforcement of environmental regulations lacks political will and proper funding. Foreign visitors are

Environmental Trivia

- Thailand is equivalent in area to the size of France.
- Bangkok sits at about N14° latitude, level with Madras, Manila, Guatemala and Khartoum.
- The Mekong rivals the Amazon River in terms of biodiversity.
- Thailand is home to venomous snakes, including the pit viper and the king cobra.
- Thailand's limestone formations are a soft sedimentary rock created by shells and coral from an ancient sea bed 250 to 300 million years ago.

often confused by Ko Chang's, Ko Samet's and Ko Phi-Phi's development as beach resorts despite their protected status. In some cases private ownership of land pre-dated the islands' protected status, while in other cases rules are bent for powerful interests.

Mekong River

Defining the contours of Thailand's border with Laos is the Mekong River, Southeast Asia's artery. The Mekong is a workhorse, having been dammed for hydroelectric power, and a mythmaker, featuring in local people's folktales and festivals. The river winds in and out of the steep mountain ranges to the northeastern plateau where it swells and contracts according to sea-sonal rainfall. In the dry season, riverside farmers plant vegetables in the muddy floodplain, harvesting the crop before the river reclaims its territory.

Scientists have identified the Mekong River as having impressive biodiversity. As many as 1000 previously unidentified species of flora and fauna have been discovered in the last decade in the Mekong region (which includes Vietnam, Laos and Cambodia).

Environmental Issues

Thailand has put enormous pressure on its ecosystems as it has industrialised. Natu-ral forest cover now makes up about 28% of land area, compared to 70% some 50 years ago. Thailand's coastal region has experienced higher population and economic growth than the national average and these areas suffer from soil erosion, water pollu-tion and degradation of coral reef systems.

Seasonal flooding is a common natural occurrence in some parts of Thailand due to the nature of the monsoon rains. But high-level floods have increased in frequency and severity. The record-busting 2011 flooding was one of the world's costliest natural disasters. Of the country's 77 provinces, 65 were declared flood disaster zones; there were 815 deaths and an estimated US$45.7 billion worth of damage.

Survival
Guide

Coconut vendor, Phuket (p294)
HOLGER LEUE/GETTY IMAGES ©

A-Z
Directory

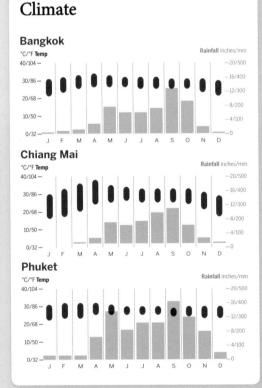

Increasingly, guesthouses can handle advance reservations, but due to inconsistent cleanliness and quality it is advisable to always look at a room in person before committing.

Note that guesthouses typically only accept cash payments.

Hotels

The new hotel norm is the 'flashpacker' hotel, which has dressed up the utilitarian options of the past with stylish decor and more creature comforts. Expect an upper budget or lower midrange price tag.

International chain hotels can be found in Bangkok, Chiang Mai, Phuket and other high-end beach resorts. Many of these upscale resorts incorporate traditional Thai architecture with modern minimalism.

Most top-end hotels and some midrange hotels add a 7% government tax (VAT) and an additional 10% service charge. The additional charges are often referred to as 'plus plus'. A

Accommodation

Thailand offers a wide variety of accommodation from cheap and basic to pricey and luxurious. Accommodation rates listed in this guide are for the high season, unless otherwise stated.

In places where spoken English might be limited, it is handy to know the following Thai phrases: *hôrng pát lom* (room with fan) and *hôrng aa* (room with air-con).

Guesthouses

Guesthouses are generally the cheapest accommodation in Thailand and can be found all along the backpacker trail.

Rates vary according to location and facilities, which range from rooms with shared bathrooms and rickety fans to rooms with private bathrooms, air-conditioning and perhaps a TV.

Many guesthouses make their bread and butter from the on-site restaurants that serve classic backpacker fare (banana pancakes and fruit shakes). Although these

Trusting the Advisors

TripAdvisor is well used by visitors to Thailand of all budget ranges and can be a helpful resource in selecting a place to stay. But be aware that criticisms of a particular place often apply to accommodations in the entire country. Check the reviews to see how the proprietor handles complaints: are they diplomatic or defensive? A proprietor willing to accept criticism and offer amends runs a good outfit.

buffet breakfast will often be included in the room rate. If the hotel offers a Western breakfast, it is usually referred to as 'ABF', meaning 'American breakfast'.

Midrange and chain hotels, especially in major tourist destinations, can be booked in advance and some offer internet discounts through their websites or online agents. They also accept most credit cards, but only a few deluxe places accept American Express.

Sleeping Price Ranges

We have used a two-tiered pricing system to determine the accommodation price ranges (budget, midrange, top end) in our reviews.

Big cities and beach resorts

$	less than 1000B
$$	1000–3000B
$$$	more than 3000B

Small towns

$	less than 600B
$$	600–1500B
$$$	more than 1500B

Customs Regulations

The **customs department** (www.customs.go.th) maintains a website with specific information about customs regulations for travellers. Thailand allows the following items to enter duty free:

o reasonable amount of personal effects (clothing and toiletries)

o professional instruments

o 200 cigarettes

o 1L of wine or spirits

Thailand prohibits the import of the following items:

o firearms and ammunition (unless registered in advance with the police department)

o illegal drugs

o pornographic media

When leaving Thailand, you must obtain an export licence for any antique reproductions or newly cast Buddha images (except for personal amulets). Submit two front-view photos of the object(s), a photocopy of your passport, the purchase receipt(s) and the object(s) in question, to the **Department of Fine Arts** (📞 0 2628

5032). Allow four days for the application and inspection process to be completed.

Electricity

Thailand uses 220V AC electricity; power outlets most commonly feature two-prong round or flat sockets.

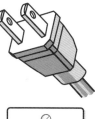

220V/50Hz

220V/50Hz

●●◐●

Embassies & Consulates

Foreign embassies are located in Bangkok; some nations also have consulates in Chiang Mai, Phuket or Pattaya.

Australia (Map p75; ✆ 0 2344 6300; www.thailand. embassy.gov.au/bkok/home. html; 37 Th Sathon Tai (South), Bangkok; ⏲ 8.30am-4.30pm Mon-Fri; Ⓜ Lumphini exit 2)

Canada Bangkok (Map p75; ✆ 0 2646 4300; www. canadainternational.gc.ca; 15th fl, Abdulrahim Pl, 990 Th Phra Ram IV, Bangkok; ⏲ 7.30am-12.15pm & 1-4.15pm Mon-Thu, to 1pm Fri; Ⓜ Si Lom exit 2, Ⓢ Sala Daeng exit 4); Chiang Mai (✆ 0 5385 0147; 151 Superhighway, Tambon Tahsala, Chiang Mai)

China Bangkok (✆ 0 2245 7044; www.fmprc.gov.cn; 57 Th Ratchadaphisek, Bangkok); Chiang Mai (Map p156; ✆ 0 5327 6125; chiangmai. chineseconsulate.org; 111 Th Chang Lor, Tambon Haiya, Chiang Mai)

Denmark (Map p75; ✆ 0 2343 1100; thailand.um.dk; 10 Soi 1, Th Sathon Tai) Consulates in Phuket and Pattaya.

France (Map p76; ✆ 0 2657 5100; www.ambafrance-th.org; 35 Soi 36, Th Charoen Krung, Bangkok; ⏲ 8.30am-noon Mon-Fri; 🚢 Tha Oriental); Bangkok Visa & Culture Services (✆ 0 2627 2150; ambafrance-th. org; 29 Th Sathon Tai); Chiang Mai (✆ 0 5328 1466; 138 Th Charoen Prathet, Chiang Mai) Consulates also in Phuket, Pattaya & Surat Thani.

Germany (Map p75; ✆ 0 2287 9000; www.bangkok.diplo. de; 9 Th Sathon Tai (South), Bangkok; ⏲ 8.30-11am Mon-Fri; Ⓜ Lumphini exit 2)

India (Map p86; ✆ 0 2258 0300-6; indianembassy.in.th; 46 Soi Prasanmit/Soi 23, Th Sukhumvit); Bangkok Visa Centre (Map p86; ✆ 0 2664 1200; www.indiavisathai.com; Th Sukhumvit, 253 Soi 21/ Asoke; ⏲ IVS Global Services, 22nd fl); Chiang Mai (✆ 0 5324 3066; 33/1 Th Thung Hotel, Wat Gate)

Ireland (Map p76; ✆ 0 2632 6720; www.irelandinthailand. com; 62 Th Silom, 4th fl, Thaniya Bldg) Consulate only; the nearest Irish embassy is in Kuala Lumpur.

Israel (Map p86; ✆ 0 2204 9200; bangkok.mfa.gov.il; 25 Soi 19, Th Sukhumvit, Ocean Tower 2, 25th fl, Bangkok)

Japan Bangkok (Map p75; ✆ 0 2207 8500; www.th.emb-japan.go.jp; 177 Th Witthayu/ Wireless Rd); Chiang Mai (✆ 0 5320 3367; 104-107 Th Mahidon, Airport Business Park)

Netherlands (Map p82; ✆ 0 2309 5200; http://thailand. nlembassy.org; 15 Soi Tonson, Bangkok; ⏲ 8.30-11.30am Mon-Wed, 8.30-11.30am & 1.30-3pm Thu (consular office); Ⓢ Chit Lom exit 4)

New Zealand (Map p82; ✆ 0 2254 2530; www.nzembassy. com/thailand; 14th fl, M Thai Tower, All Seasons Pl, 87 Th Witthayu (Wireless Rd), Bangkok; ⏲ 8am-noon & 1-2.30pm Mon-Fri; Ⓢ Phloen Chit exit 5)

Russia (Map p76; ✆ 0 2234 9824; www.thailand.mid. ru; 78 Soi Sap, Th Surawong) Consulates in Pattaya and Phuket.

Singapore (Map p76; ✆ 0 2286 2111; www.mfa.gov.sg/ bangkok; 129 Th Sathon Tai)

South Africa (Map p82; ✆ 0 2659 2900; www.dirco.gov. za; 87 Th Witthayu (Wireless Rd), 12th A fl, M Thai Tower, All Seasons Pl, Bangkok)

Spain (Map p86; ✆ 0 2661 8284; es.embassyinformation. com; 193 Th Ratchadaphisek, 23 fl, Lake Ratchada Office Complex)

Switzerland (Map p82; ✆ 0 2674 6900; www.eda.admin. ch/bangkok; 35 Th Witthayu/ Wireless Rd)

UK Bangkok (Map p82; ✆ 0 2305 8333; www.gov.

Book Your Stay Online

For more accommodation reviews by Lonely Planet authors, check out http://hotels. lonelyplanet.com. You'll find independent reviews, as well as recommendations on the best places to stay. Best of all, you can book online.

uk/government/world/
organisations/british-embassy-
bangkok; 14 Th Witthayu
(Wireless Rd), Bangkok;
⏰8am-4.30pm Mon-Thu, to
1pm Fri; Ⓢ Phloen Chit exit 5);
Chiang Mai (☎ 0 5326 3015;
www.british-consulate.net; 198
Th Bamrungrat, Chiang Mai)
Consulate also in Pattaya.

USA (Map p156; ☎ 0 5310
7700; chiangmai.usconsulate.
gov; 387 Th Wichayanon, Chiang
Mai)

Food

For in-depth information on
Thailand's glorious cuisine,
see Thai Cuisine (p349).

Eating Price Ranges

The following price ranges,
used throughout this guide,
indicate how much you should
expect to pay for a main dish
in Thailand.

$ less than 150B
$$ 150–350B
$$$ more than 350B

Gay & Lesbian Travellers

Thai culture is relatively
tolerant of both male and
female homosexuality. There
is a fairly prominent gay and
lesbian scene in Bangkok,
Pattaya and Phuket. However,
public displays of affection –
whether heterosexual or
homosexual – are frowned
upon. **Utopia** (www.utopia-
asia.com) posts lots of Thailand information for gay and

lesbian visitors and publishes
a guidebook to the kingdom
for homosexuals.

Health

Health risks and the quality of medical facilities vary
depending on where and how
you travel in Thailand. The
majority of cities and popular
tourist areas have adequate
and even excellent medical
care.

Travellers tend to worry
about contracting exotic
infectious diseases when
visiting the tropics, but these
are far less common than
problems with pre-existing
medical conditions such as
heart disease, and accidental
injury (especially as a result of
traffic accidents).

Other common illnesses
are respiratory infections,
diarrhoea and dengue fever.

Before You Go

If you take any regular
medication bring double your
needs in case of loss or theft.
In Thailand you can buy many
medications over the counter
without a doctor's prescrip-
tion, but it can be difficult to
find the exact medication you
are taking.

Contact your home
country's Department
of Foreign Affairs or the
equivalent and register
your trip; this is a helpful
precaution in the event of a
natural disaster.

Insurance

Even if you're fit and healthy,
don't travel without health
insurance – accidents *do*
happen. Inquire before

your trip about payment of
medical charges and retain
all documentation (medical
reports, invoices etc) for
claim purposes.

Recommended Vaccinations

You should arrange your
vaccines six to eight weeks
prior to departure though a
specialised travel-medicine
clinic.

The **Centers for Disease
Control and Prevention**
(CDC; www.cdc.gov) has a
traveller's health section that
contains recommendations
for vaccinations. The
only vaccine required by
international regulations is
yellow fever.

Medical Checklist

Recommended items for a
personal medical kit include
the following; most of these
medicines are available in
Thailand:

o antifungal cream, eg
Clotrimazole

o antibacterial cream, eg
Muciprocin

o antibiotic for skin infections,
eg Amoxicillin/Clavulanate or
Cephalexin

o antibiotics for diarrhoea
include Norfloxacin,
Ciprofloxacin or Azithromycin
for bacterial diarrhoea;
for giardiasis or amoebic
dysentery take Tinidazole

o antihistamine – there are
many options, eg Cetrizine for
daytime and Promethazine for
night-time

o antiseptic, eg Betadine

o antispasmodic for stomach
cramps, eg Buscopan

o contraceptives

- decongestant

- DEET-based insect repellent

- oral rehydration solution for diarrhoea (eg Gastrolyte), diarrhoea 'stopper' (eg Loperamide) and antinausea medication

- ibuprofen or another anti-inflammatory

- paracetamol

- steroid cream for allergic/itchy rashes, eg 1% to 2% hydrocortisone

- sunscreen, sunglasses and hat

- thrush (vaginal yeast infection) treatment, eg Clotrimazole pessaries or Diflucan tablet

- Ural or equivalent if prone to urine infections

In Transit

Deep Vein Thrombosis

Deep vein thrombosis (DVT) occurs when blood clots form in the legs during long trips such as flights, chiefly because of prolonged immobility. The longer the journey, the greater the risk.

The chief symptom of DVT is swelling or pain of the foot, ankle or calf, usually but not always on one side. When a blood clot travels to the lungs, it may cause chest pain and difficulty in breathing. Travellers with any of these symptoms should immediately seek medical attention.

Jet Lag & Motion Sickness

Jet lag is common when crossing more than five time zones; it results in insomnia, fatigue, malaise or nausea. To avoid jet lag drink plenty of fluids (nonalcoholic) and eat light meals. Upon arrival, seek exposure to natural sunlight and readjust your schedule.

Sedating antihistamines such as dimenhydrinate (Dramamine) or Prochlorperazine (Phenergan) are usually the first choice for treating motion sickness. Their main side effect is drowsiness. A herbal alternative is ginger. Scopolamine patches are considered the most effective prevention.

In Thailand

Availability & Cost of Health Care

Bangkok is considered a centre of medical excellence in Southeast Asia. Private hospitals are more expensive than other medical facilities but offer a superior standard of care and English-speaking staff.

Infectious Diseases

CUTANEOUS LARVA MIGRANS

This disease, caused by dog or cat hookworm, is particularly common on the beaches of Thailand. The rash starts as a small lump, and then slowly spreads like a winding line. It is intensely itchy, especially at night. It is easily treated with medications and should not be cut out or frozen.

DENGUE FEVER

This mosquito-borne disease is increasingly problematic in Thailand, especially in the cities. As there is no vaccine it can only be prevented by avoiding mosquito bites. The mosquito that carries dengue is a daytime biter, so use insect-avoidance measures at all times. Symptoms include high fever, severe headache (especially behind the eyes), nausea and body aches (dengue was previously known as 'breakbone fever'). There is no specific treatment, just rest and paracetamol – do not take aspirin or ibuprofen as they increase the risk of haemorrhaging. See a doctor to be diagnosed and monitored.

Dengue can progress to the more severe and life-threatening dengue

Further Reading

- **International Travel & Health** (www.who.int/ith) Published by the World Health Organization (WHO).

- Centers for Disease Control & Prevention (p367) Country-specific advice.

- *Healthy Travel – Asia & India* (by Lonely Planet) Pretrip planning, emergency first aid, immunisation and disease information.

- *Travelling Well* (by Dr Deborah Mills) Health guidebook and website (www.travellingwell.com.au).

haemorrhagic fever; however this is very uncommon in tourists.

HEPATITIS A

The risk in Bangkok is decreasing but there is still significant risk in most of the country. This food- and waterborne virus infects the liver, causing jaundice (yellow skin and eyes), nausea and lethargy. There is no specific treatment for hepatitis A. All travellers to Thailand should be vaccinated against hepatitis A.

HEPATITIS B

The only sexually transmitted disease (STD) that can be prevented by vaccination, hepatitis B is spread by body fluids, including sexual contact. In some parts of Thailand up to 20% of the population are carriers of hepatitis B, and usually are unaware of this. The long-term consequences can include liver cancer, cirrhosis and death.

HIV

HIV is now one of the most common causes of death in people under the age of 50 in Thailand. Always practise safe sex; avoid getting tattoos or using unclean syringes.

INFLUENZA

Present year-round in the tropics, influenza (flu) symptoms include high fever, muscle aches, runny nose, cough and sore throat. Flu is the most common vaccine-preventable disease contracted by travellers and everyone should consider vaccination.

LEPTOSPIROSIS

Leptospirosis is contracted from exposure to infected sur-

Mosquito Avoidance Tips

Travellers are advised to prevent mosquito bites by taking these steps:

o use a DEET-containing insect repellent on exposed skin

o sleep under a mosquito net, ideally impregnated with Permethrin

o choose accommodation with screens and fans

o impregnate clothing with Permethrin in high-risk areas

o wear long sleeves and trousers in light colours

o use mosquito coils

o spray your hotel room with insect repellent before going out

---

face water – most commonly after river rafting or canyoning. Early symptoms are very similar to flu and include headache and fever. It can vary from a very mild ailment to a fatal disease. Diagnosis is made through blood tests and it is easily treated with Doxycycline.

MALARIA

Malaria is caused by a parasite transmitted by the bite of an infected mosquito. The most important symptom of malaria is fever, but general symptoms such as headache, diarrhoea, cough or chills may also occur – the same symptoms as many other infections. A diagnosis can only be made by taking a blood sample.

Most parts of Thailand visited by tourists, particularly city and resort areas, have minimal to no risk of malaria, and the risk of side effects from taking antimalarial tablets is likely to outweigh the risk of getting the disease itself.

MEASLES

This highly contagious viral infection is spread through coughing and sneezing. Most people born before 1966 are immune as they had the disease in childhood. There is no specific treatment. Ensure you are fully vaccinated.

RABIES

This uniformly fatal disease is spread by the bite or lick of an infected animal – most commonly a dog or monkey. You should seek medical advice immediately after any animal bite and commence post-exposure treatment. Having a pretravel vaccination means the postbite treatment is greatly simplified.

STDS

Sexually transmitted diseases most common in Thailand include herpes, warts, syphilis, gonorrhoea and chlamydia. If after a sexual encounter you develop any rash, lumps, discharge or pain when passing urine seek immediate medical attention.

TYPHOID

This serious bacterial infection is spread through food and water. It gives a high and slowly progressive fever, severe headache, and may be accompanied by a dry cough and stomach pain. It is diagnosed by blood tests and treated with antibiotics. Vaccination is recommended for all travellers spending more than a week in Thailand, or travelling outside of the major cities.

Traveller's Diarrhoea

Traveller's diarrhoea is by far the most common problem affecting travellers. In over 80% of cases, traveller's diarrhoea is caused by a bacteria (there are numerous potential culprits), and responds promptly to treatment with antibiotics.

Here we define traveller's diarrhoea as the passage of more than three watery bowel movements within 24 hours, plus at least one other symptom such as vomiting, fever, cramps, nausea or feeling generally unwell.

Treatment consists of staying well hydrated; rehydration solutions such as Gastrolyte are the best for this. Antibiotics such as Norfloxacin, Ciprofloxacin or Azithromycin will kill the bacteria quickly. Seek medical attention if you do not respond to an appropriate antibiotic.

Loperamide is just a 'stopper' that only treats the symptoms. It can be helpful, for example if you have to go on a long bus ride.

Giardia lamblia is a parasite that is relatively common. Symptoms include nausea, bloating, excess gas, fatigue and intermittent diarrhoea. 'Eggy' burps are often attributed solely to giardiasis. The treatment of choice is Tinidazole, with Metronidazole being a second-line option.

Amoebic dysentery is very rare in travellers but may be misdiagnosed by poor-quality labs.

You should always seek reliable medical care if you have blood in your diarrhoea.

Environmental Hazards

FOOD

Eating in restaurants is the biggest risk factor for contracting traveller's diarrhoea. Ways to avoid it include eating only freshly cooked food, and avoiding food that has been sitting around in buffets. Peel all fruit and cook vegetables. Eat in busy restaurants with a high turnover of customers.

HEAT

For most people it takes at least two weeks to adapt to the hot climate. Prevent swelling of the feet and ankles as well as muscle cramps caused by excessive sweating by avoiding dehydration and excessive activity in the heat of the day.

Heat stroke requires immediate medical treatment. Symptoms come on suddenly and include weakness, nausea, a hot dry body with a body temperature of over 41°C, dizziness, confusion, loss of coordination, fits and eventually collapse and loss of consciousness.

INSECT BITES & STINGS

Bedbugs live in the cracks of furniture and walls and then migrate to the bed at night to feed on humans. You can treat the itch with an antihistamine.

Ticks are contracted when walking in rural areas. If you've been bitten by a tick and a rash develops at the site of the bite or elsewhere, along with fever or muscle aches, see a doctor. Doxycycline prevents tick-borne diseases.

Leeches are found in humid rainforests. They do not transmit disease but their bites are often itchy for weeks afterwards and can easily

Jellyfish Stings

Box jellyfish stings range from minor to deadly. It is best to presume a box jelly is dangerous until proven otherwise.

For severe life-threatening envenomations the first priority is keeping the person alive. Send someone to call for medical help, and start immediate CPR if they are unconscious. If the victim is conscious douse the stung area liberally with vinegar for 30 seconds.

Vinegar can also reduce irritation from minor stings as well. It is best to seek medical care quickly in case any other symptoms develop over the next 40 minutes.

Thanks to Dr Peter Fenner for the information on jellyfish stings.

become infected. Apply an iodine-based antiseptic to the bite to help prevent infection.

SKIN PROBLEMS

Prickly heat is a common skin rash in the tropics, caused by sweat being trapped under the skin. Treat by taking cool showers and using powders.

Cuts and scratches become easily infected in humid climates. Immediately wash all wounds in clean water and apply antiseptic. If you develop signs of infection, see a doctor.

SUNBURN

Use a strong sunscreen (at least factor 30), making sure to reapply after a swim, and always wear a wide-brimmed hat and sunglasses outdoors. If you become sunburnt stay out of the sun until you have recovered, apply cool compresses and take painkillers for the discomfort. One per cent hydrocortisone cream applied twice daily is also helpful.

Travelling with Children

Thailand is relatively safe for children. A medical kit designed specifically for children includes liquid medicines for children who can not swallow tablets. Azithromycin is an ideal paediatric formula used to treat bacterial diarrhoea, as well as ear, chest and throat infections.

Good resources are the Lonely Planet publication *Travel with Children,* and for those spending longer away Jane Wilson-Howarth's book *Your Child's Health Abroad* is excellent.

Women's Health

Pregnant women should receive specialised advice before travelling. The ideal time to travel is in the second trimester, when pregnancy-related risks are low.

Traveller's diarrhoea can quickly lead to dehydration and result in inadequate blood flow to the placenta. Azithromycin is considered one of the safest anti-diarrhoea drugs in pregnancy.

In Thailand's urban areas, supplies of sanitary products are readily available. Bring adequate supplies of your personal birth-control option. Heat, humidity and antibiotics can all contribute to thrush, which can be treated with antifungal creams and Clotrimazole. A practical alternative is one tablet of fluconazole (Diflucan). Urinary-tract infections can be precipitated by dehydration or long bus journeys without toilet stops; bring suitable antibiotics for treatment.

●●● Insurance

A travel-insurance policy to cover theft, loss and medical problems is a good idea.

Worldwide travel insurance is available at www.lonelyplanet.com/travel-insurance. You can buy, extend and claim online any time – even if you're already on the road.

●●● Internet Access

As more and more people travel with mobile devices, internet cafes have begun to disappear. Wi-fi is becoming commonplace in guesthouses, restaurants and cafes.

●●● Legal Matters

In general, Thai police don't hassle foreigners, especially tourists.

One major exception is drugs, which most Thai police view as either a social scourge against which it's their duty to enforce the letter of the law, or an opportunity to make untaxed income via bribes.

If you are arrested for any offence, the police will allow you the opportunity to make a phone call, either to your embassy or consulate in Thailand if you have one, or to a friend or relative if not.

The **tourist police** (⌨1155) can be very helpful in cases of arrest. You can call the hotline number 24 hours a day to lodge complaints or to request assistance with regards to personal safety.

●●● Money

The basic unit of Thai currency is the baht. There are 100 satang in one baht; coins include 25-satang and 50-satang pieces and baht in 1B, 2B, 5B and 10B coins. The 2B coin is similar in size to the 1B coin but it is gold in colour. The 2-satang coins are typically only issued at supermarkets where prices aren't rounded up to the nearest baht.

Paper currency is issued in the following denominations: 20B (green), 50B (blue), 100B (red), 500B (purple) and 1000B (beige).

ATMs & Credit/ Debit Cards

Debit and ATM cards issued by a bank in your own country can be used at ATMs around Thailand to withdraw cash (in Thai baht only) directly from your account back home. ATMs are widespread throughout the country and can be relied on for the bulk of your spending cash.

Thai ATMs now charge a 150B foreign-transaction fee on top of whatever currency conversion and out-of-network fees your home bank charges.

Credit cards as well as debit cards can be used for purchases at some shops, hotels and restaurants. The most commonly accepted cards are Visa and MasterCard. American Express is typically only accepted at high-end hotels and restaurants.

Contact your bank and your credit card before you leave home and notify them of your upcoming trip so that your accounts aren't suspended due to suspicious overseas activity.

To report a lost or stolen credit/debit card, call the following hotlines in Bangkok:

American Express (📞 0 2273 5544)

MasterCard (📞 001 800 11887 0663)

Visa (📞 001 800 11 535 0660)

Changing Money

Banks or private money-changers offer the best foreign-exchange rates. When buying baht, US dollars are the most accepted currency,

followed by British pounds and euros. Most banks charge a commission and duty for each travellers cheque cashed.

Tipping

Tipping is not generally expected in Thailand, though it is appreciated. At many hotel restaurants or other upmarket eateries, a 10% service charge will be added to your bill.

Opening Hours

The following are standard hours for different types of businesses in Thailand. All government offices and banks are closed on public holidays.

Banks 9.30am to 3.30pm Monday to Friday; ATMs accessible 24 hours.

Bars 6pm to midnight (officially); closing times vary due to local enforcement of curfew laws; bars close during elections and certain religious public holidays.

Clubs (discos) 8pm to 2am; closing times vary due to local enforcement of curfew laws; clubs close during elections and certain religious public holidays.

Government offices 8.30am to 4.30pm Monday to Friday; some close for lunch (noon to 1pm), while others are open Saturday (9am to 3pm).

Live-music venues 6pm to 1am; closing times vary due to local enforcement of curfew laws; clubs close during

elections and certain religious public holidays.

Restaurants 10am to 10pm; some specialise in morning meals and close by 3pm.

Stores local stores 10am to 6pm daily; department stores 10am to 10pm daily. In some small towns, local stores close on Sunday.

Post

Thailand has a very efficient postal service and local postage is inexpensive. Typical provincial post offices keep the following hours: 8.30am to 4.30pm weekdays and 9am to noon on Saturdays. Larger main post offices in provincial capitals may also be open for a half-day on Sundays.

Public Holidays

Government offices and banks close on public holidays.

1 January New Year's Day

February (date varies) Makha Bucha Day, Buddhist holy day

6 April Chakri Day, commemorating the founder of the Chakri dynasty, Rama I

13–15 April Songkran Festival; traditional Thai New Year and water festival

1 May Labour Day

5 May Coronation Day, commemorating the 1946

coronation of HM the King and HM the Queen

May/June (date varies) Visakha Bucha, Buddhist holy day

July (date varies) Asanha Bucha, Buddhist holy day

12 August Queen's Birthday

23 October Chulalongkorn Day

October/November (date varies) Ork Phansaa, the end of Buddhist 'lent'

5 December King's Birthday

10 December Constitution Day

31 December New Year's Eve

Safe Travel

Although Thailand is not a dangerous country to visit, it is smart to exercise caution, especially when it comes to dealing with strangers (both Thai and foreigners) and travelling alone.

Assault

Assault of travellers is rare in Thailand, but it does happen. Causing a Thai to 'lose face' (feel public embarrassment or humiliation) can sometimes elicit an inexplicably strong and violent reaction. Oftentimes alcohol is the number one contributor to bad choices and worse outcomes.

Women, especially solo travellers, need to be smart and somewhat sober when interacting with the opposite sex, be they Thai or *fa·ràng* (foreigners).

Practicalities

- *Bangkok Post* and the *Nation* publish English-language news daily.

- There are more than 400 AM and FM radio stations; shortwave radios can pick up BBC, VOA, Radio Australia, Deutsche Welle and Radio France International.

- Six VHF TV networks carry Thai programming, plus TrueVision cable with international programming.

- Thailand follows the international metric system. Gold and silver are weighed in *bàht* (15g).

Drug Possession

Belying Thailand's anything-goes atmosphere are severely strict punishments for possession and trafficking that are not relaxed for foreigners. It is illegal to buy, sell or possess opium, heroin, amphetamines, hallucinogenic mushrooms and marijuana in Thailand. Possession of drugs can result in at least one year or more of prison time. Drug smuggling – defined as attempting to cross a border with drugs in your possession – carries considerably higher penalties, including execution.

Scams

Thais can be so friendly and laid-back that some visitors are lulled into a false sense of security, making them vulnerable to scams of all kinds. Bangkok is especially good at long, involved frauds that dupe travellers into thinking that they've made a friend and are getting a bargain when in fact they are getting ripped off.

Follow Tourism Authority of Thailand's (TAT) number-one suggestion to tourists:

Disregard all offers of free shopping or sightseeing help from strangers.

Theft & Fraud

Exercise diligence when it comes to your personal belongings. Ensure that your room is securely locked and carry your most important effects (passport, money, credit cards) on your person.

Follow the same practice when you're travelling. A locked bag will not prevent theft on a long-haul bus.

When using a credit card, don't let vendors take your card out of your sight to run it through the machine. Unscrupulous merchants have been known to rub off three or four or more receipts with one purchase.

To avoid losing all of your travel money in an instant, use a credit card that is not directly linked to your bank account so that the operator doesn't have access to immediate funds.

Contact the **tourist police** (☏1155) if you have any problems with consumer fraud.

●●●
Shopping

Antiques

Real Thai antiques are increasingly rare. Today, most dealers sell antique reproductions or items from Myanmar. Bangkok and Chiang Mai are the two centres for the antique and reproduction trade.

Real antiques cannot be taken out of Thailand without a permit. No Buddha image, new or old, may be exported without the permission of the Department of Fine Arts.

Gems & Jewellery

Although there are a lot of gem and jewellery stores in Thailand, it has become so difficult to dodge the scammers that the country no longer represents a safe and enjoyable place to buy these goods.

Textiles

The northeast is famous for *mát·mèe* cloth – a thick cotton or silk fabric woven from tie-dyed threads, similar to Indonesia's *ikat* fabrics.

In the north, silks reflect the influence of the Lanna weaving traditions, brought to Chiang Mai and the surrounding mountains by the various Tai tribes.

Each hill tribe has a tradition of embroidery that has been translated into the modern marketplace as bags and jewellery. Chiang Mai and Chiang Rai are filled with handicraft outlets.

●●●
Telephone

The telephone country code for Thailand is 🕿66 and is used when calling the country from abroad. All Thai telephone numbers are preceded by a '0' if you're dialling domestically (the '0' is omitted when calling from overseas). After the initial '0', the next three numbers represent the provincial area code, which is now integral to the telephone number. If the initial '0' is followed by an '8' or a '9', then you're dialling a mobile phone.

Bargaining

If there isn't a sign stating the price for an item then the price is negotiable. Bargaining is common in street markets and some small shops. Prices in department stores, minimarts, 7-Elevens and so forth are fixed.

Thais respect a good haggler. Always let the vendor make the first offer, then ask 'Can you lower the price?'. This usually results in a discount. Now it's your turn to make a counteroffer; always start low, but don't bargain at all unless you're serious about buying.

It helps immeasurably to keep the negotiations relaxed and friendly, and always remember to smile. Don't lose your temper or raise your voice as drama is not a good leverage tool.

International Calls

If you want to call an international number from a telephone in Thailand, you must first dial an international access code plus the country code followed by the subscriber number.

In Thailand, there are various international access codes charging different rates per minute. Economy rates are available through different carriers; do an internet search to determine promotion codes.

The following are some common international country codes: 🕿61 Australia, 🕿44 UK and 🕿1 US.

Dial 🕿100 for operator-assisted international calls or reverse-charges (collect) calls.

Mobile Phones

The easiest phone option in Thailand is to acquire a mobile (cell) phone equipped with a local SIM card.

Thailand is on the GSM network and mobile phone providers include AIS (12 Call), DTAC and True Move.

SIM cards and refill cards (usually sold in 300B to 500B denominations) can be bought from 7-Elevens throughout the country.

Thailand finally has a 3G network and True Move is offering 4G LTE coverage in Bangkok. Coverage and quality of the different carriers varies from year to year based on network upgrades and capacity. Carriers usually sell talk-data packages based on usage amounts.

Important Numbers

Thailand's country code 📞66

Emergency 📞191

International access codes 📞001, 📞007, 📞008, 📞009

Operator-assisted international calls 📞100

Tourist police 📞1155

Time

Thailand's time zone is seven hours ahead of GMT/UTC (London). Times are expressed according to the 24-hour clock, eg 11pm is written '23.00' in most cases.

Toilets

If you encounter a squat, here's what you should know. You should straddle the two footpads and face the door. To flush use the plastic bowl to scoop water out of the adjacent basin and pour into the toilet bowl. Some places supply a small pack of toilet paper at the entrance (5B), otherwise bring your own stash or wipe the old-fashioned way with water.

Even in places where sit-down toilets are installed, the septic system may not be designed to take toilet paper. In such cases there will be a waste basket where you're supposed to place used toilet paper and feminine hygiene products. Some toilets also come with a small spray hose – Thailand's version of the bidet.

Tourist Information

The government-operated tourist information and promotion service, **Tourism Authority of Thailand** (TAT; www.tourismthailand.org), was founded in 1960 and produces excellent pamphlets on sightseeing.

Travellers with Disabilities

Thailand presents one large, ongoing obstacle course for the mobility impaired.

Counter to the prevailing trends, **Worldwide Dive & Sail** (www.sirenfleet.com) offers live-aboard diving programs for the deaf and hard of hearing.

Some organisations and publications that offer tips on international travel include the following:

Accessible Journeys (www.disabilitytravel.com)

Mobility International USA (www.miusa.org)

Society for Accessible Travel & Hospitality (SATH; www.sath.org)

Visas

The **Ministry of Foreign Affairs** (www.mfa.go.th) oversees immigration and visas issues. Check the website or the nearest Thai embassy or consulate for application procedures and costs.

Tourist Visas & Exemptions

The Thai government allows entry to 55 different nationalities, including those from Australia, New Zealand, the USA and most of Europe without prior visa arrangements for a set period of time.

For most Western nationalities arriving in the kingdom by air, a 30-day visa is issued without a fee. Some countries (including Brazil, South Korea, Argentina, Chile and Peru) receive a 90-day

Immigration Offices

The following are two immigration offices where visa extensions and other formalities can be addressed. For all types of visa extensions, bring along two passport-sized photos and one copy each of the photo and visa pages of your passport.

Bangkok immigration office (📞0 2141 9899; immigration.go.th; Th Chaeng Wattana , Bldg B, Government Centre; ⊗9am-noon & 1-4.30pm Mon-Fri, 9am-noon Sat)

Chiang Mai immigration office (📞0 5320 1755; chiangmaiimm.com; Th Mahidon; ⊗8.30am-4.30pm Mon-Fri)

free visa at all borders.

Without proof of an onward ticket and sufficient funds for one's projected stay any visitor can be denied entry, but in practice this is a formality that is rarely checked.

Visa Extensions & Renewals

If you decide you want to stay longer than the allotted time, you can extend your visa by applying at any immigration office in Thailand. The usual fee for a visa extension is 1900B.

Another visa-renewal option is to cross a land border. A new visa will be issued upon your return and some short-term visitors make a day trip out of the 'visa run'.

If you overstay your visa, the usual penalty is a fine of 500B per day, with a 20,000B limit. Fines can be paid at the airport or in advance at an immigration office. If you've overstayed only one day, you don't have to pay. Children under 14 travelling with a parent do not have to pay the penalty.

●●●

Women Travellers

Women face relatively few problems in Thailand.

Thai women, especially the younger generation, are showing more skin these days. But to be on the safe side, cover up if you're going deep into rural communities. And certainly cover up if visiting temples.

Transport

●●●

Getting There & Away

Flights and tours can be booked online at www.lonely-planet.com/bookings.

Entering the Country

Entry procedures for Thailand, by air or by land, are straightforward: you'll have to show your passport and you'll need to present completed arrival and departure cards.

You do not have to fill in a customs form on arrival unless you have imported goods to declare. In that case, you can get the proper form from Thai customs officials at your point of entry.

 Air

Airports

Bangkok is Thailand's primary international and domestic gateway. There are also smaller airports throughout the country serving domestic and sometimes regional routes.

Suvarnabhumi International Airport (BKK; ☏ 0 2132 1888; www.bangkokairportonline.com) Receives nearly all international flights and most domestic flights. It is located in Samut Prakan – 30km east of Bangkok and 110km from Pattaya. The airport name is pronounced *sù·wan·ná·poom.*

Don Muang Airport (p94) Bangkok's second airport is used by Air Asia, Nok Air and Orient Thai (formerly One-Two-Go).

Phuket International Airport (p295) International destinations include Seoul, Hong Kong, Kuala Lumpur, Singapore, Abu Dhabi, Chengdu, Shanghai and other Chinese cities. Direct charter flights from Europe are also available.

Chiang Mai International Airport (www.chiangmai airportonline.com) International destinations include Kunming, Seoul, Hong Kong, Macau, Kuala Lumpur and Singapore.

Airlines

The following airlines fly to and from Bangkok and international destinations.

Air Asia (☏ 0 2515 9999; www.airasia.com)

Air Berlin (☏ 001 800 12 0666 375; www.airberlin.com)

Air Canada (Map p76; ☏ 0 2718 1839; www.aircanada.com)

Air China (Map p76; ☏ 0 2108 1888; www.airchina.com)

Air France (📞 001 800 441 0771; www.airfrance.fr)

Bangkok Airways (📞 1771; www.bangkokair.com)

British Airways (Map p76; 📞 001 800 441 5906; www.britishairways.com)

Cathay Pacific Airways (Map p82; 📞 0 2263 0606; www.cathaypacific.com)

China Airlines (Map p82; 📞 0 2250 9898; www.china-airlines.com)

Delta Airlines (📞 001 800 658 228; www.delta.com)

Emirates (Map p86; 📞 0 2664 1040; www.emirates.com)

Eva Air (📞 0 2269 6300; www.evaair.com)

Japan Airlines (Map p82; 📞 001 800 811 0600; www.jal.co.jp)

Jetstar Airways (📞 0 2267 5125; www.jetstar.com)

KLM Royal Dutch Airlines (Map p75; 📞 001 800 441 5560; www.klm.com)

Korean Air (📞 0 2620 6900; www.koreanair.com)

Lufthansa Airlines (Map p86; 📞 0 2264 6800; www.lufthansa.com)

Myanmar Airways International (Map p86; 📞 0 2261 5060; www.maiair.com)

Philippine Airlines (📞 0 2633 5713; www.philippineairlines.com)

Qantas Airways (Map p76; 📞 0 2632 6611; www.qantas.com.au)

Royal Brunei Airlines (Map p75; 📞 0 2638 3050; www.bruneiair.com)

Scandinavian Airlines (Map p86; 📞 0 2693 7888; www.flysas.com)

Singapore Airlines (Map p76; 📞 0 2353 6000; www.singaporeair.com)

South African Airways (Map p76; 📞 0 2635 1414; www.flysaa.com)

Thai Airways International (THAI; Map p76; 📞 0 2288 7000; www.thaiair.com; 485 Th Silom; ⏱ 8am-5pm Mon-Sat; Ⓢ Chong Nonsi exit 3)

United Airlines (Map p82; 📞 0 2353 3939; www.united.com)

Tickets

The amount of commission an agent will charge varies so shop around to gauge the discrepancy in prices. Paying by credit card generally offers purchasing protection, because most card issuers provide refunds if you can prove you didn't get what you paid for. Agents who accept only cash should hand over the tickets straightaway and not tell you to 'come back to-morrow'. After you've made a booking or paid your deposit, call the airline and confirm that the booking was made.

Air fares during the high season (December to March) can be expensive.

Climate Change & Travel

Every form of transport that relies on carbon-based fuel generates CO_2, the main cause of human-induced climate change. Modern travel is dependent on aeroplanes, which might use less fuel per kilometre per person than most cars but travel much greater distances. The altitude at which aircraft emit gases (including CO_2) and particles also contributes to their climate change impact. Many websites offer 'carbon calculators' that allow people to estimate the carbon emissions generated by their journey and, for those who wish to do so, to offset the impact of the greenhouse gases emitted with contributions to portfolios of climate-friendly initiatives throughout the world. Lonely Planet offsets the carbon footprint of all staff and author travel.

Getting Around

✈ Air

Hopping around the country by air continues to be afford-able. Most routes originate from Bangkok, but Chiang Mai, Ko Samui and Phuket all have a few routes to other Thai towns.

🚢 Boat

The true Thai river transport is the *reu·a hǎhng yow* (long-tail boat), so-called because the propeller is mounted at the end of a long drive shaft extending from the engine. The long-tail boats are a

377

Road Distances (Km)

	Aranya Prathet	Ayuthaya	Bangkok	Chiang Mai	Chiang Rai	Chumphon	Hat Yai	Hua Hin	Khon Kaen	Mae Hong Son	Mae Sai	Mukdahan	Nakhon Ratchasima	Nong Khai	Phitsanulok	Phuket	Sungai Kolok	Surat Thani	Tak	Trat
Ayuthaya	246																			
Bangkok	275	79																		
Chiang Mai	844	607	685																	
Chiang Rai	1014	777	775	191																
Chumphon	727	531	452	1138	1308															
Hat Yai	1268	1072	993	1679	1849	555														
Hua Hin	458	262	183	869	1039	269	810													
Khon Kaen	432	397	440	604	774	902	1443	633												
Mae Hong Son	1013	767	800	225	406	1298	1839	1029	829											
Mae Sai	1082	845	746	259	68	1376	1917	1107	842	474										
Mukdahan	601	524	680	917	1087	1029	1570	760	313	1142	1155									
Nakhon Ratchasima	239	204	257	744	914	709	1250	440	193	969	982	320								
Nong Khai	598	563	516	720	890	1068	1609	799	166	945	958	347	359							
Phitsanulok	535	298	420	309	479	829	1370	560	295	578	547	608	435	411						
Phuket	1125	929	862	1536	1706	412	474	667	1300	1696	1774	1427	1107	1466	1227					
Sungai Kolok	1555	1359	1210	1966	2136	842	287	1097	1730	2126	2204	1857	1357	1896	1657	761				
Surat Thani	927	731	635	1338	1508	214	401	469	1102	1498	1576	1229	909	1268	1029	286	791			
Tak	581	335	435	280	460	866	1407	597	441	432	528	754	544	557	146	1264	1694	1066		
Trat	285	392	313	999	1169	765	1306	496	717	1397	1237	886	524	883	690	1163	1593	965	727	
Ubon Ratchathani	444	367	620	881	1051	872	1413	603	277	1106	1119	157	163	443	572	1270	1700	1072	707	729

staple of transport on rivers and canals in Bangkok and neighbouring provinces.

Between the mainland and small, less touristed islands, the standard craft is a wooden boat, 8m to 10m long, with an inboard engine, a wheelhouse and a simple roof to shelter passengers and cargo. But faster, more expensive hovercraft (jetfoils) and speedboats are the norm these days.

Bus & Minivan

The bus network in Thailand is prolific and reliable. The Thai government subsidises the Transport Company *(bò·rí·sàt kŏn sòng)*, usually abbreviated to Baw Khaw Saw (BKS).

By far the most reliable bus companies in Thailand are the ones that operate out of the government-run BKS stations.

We do not recommend using bus companies that operate directly out of tourist centres, like Bangkok's Th Khao San, because of repeated instances of theft and commission-seeking stops.

Minivans are increasingly becoming the middle-class option. Minivans are run by private companies and because their vehicles are smaller, they can depart from the market (instead of the out-of-town bus stations) and will deliver guests directly to their hotel.

Bus Classes

Short distances are usually covered by the basic 2nd class bus, which does not have an on-board toilet on board. For longer routes, the buses increase in comfort and amenities, ranging from 1st class to 'VIP' and 'Super VIP'. The latter two have fewer seats so that each seat reclines further; sometimes these are called *rót norn* (sleeper buses).

Bring along a jacket for long-distance bus trips as air-con keeps the cabin at arctic temperatures.

Reservations

You can book air-con BKS buses at any BKS terminal. Privately run buses can be booked through most hotels or any travel agency, but it's best to book directly through a bus office to be sure that you get what you pay for.

Car & Motorcycle

Driving Licence

In theory short-term visitors who wish to drive vehicles (including motorcycles) in Thailand need an International Driving Permit, however this isn't always enforced.

Fuel & Spare Parts

Modern petrol (gasoline) stations are plentiful. In more rural areas *ben·sin/nám·man rót yon* (petrol containing benzene) is usually available at small roadside or village stands. All fuel in Thailand is unleaded, and diesel is used by trucks and some passenger cars. Thailand also uses several alternative fuels, including gasohol (a blend of petrol and ethanol that comes in different octane levels, either 91% or 95%) and compressed natural gas, used by taxis with bifuel capabilities.

Hire & Purchase

Cars, jeeps and vans can be rented in most major cities and airports from local companies as well as international chains. Local companies tend to have cheaper rates, but the quality of their fleet varies. Check the tyre treads and general upkeep of the vehicle before committing.

Renting a motorcycle in Thailand is relatively easy and a great way to independently tour the countryside. For daily rentals, most businesses will ask that you leave your passport as a deposit. Before renting a motorcycle, check the vehicle's condition and ask for a helmet (which is required by law).

Insurance

Thailand requires a minimum of liability insurance for all registered vehicles on the road. The better hire companies include comprehensive coverage for their vehicles. Always verify that a vehicle is insured for liability before signing a rental contract; you should also ask to see the dated insurance documents. If you have an accident while driving an uninsured vehicle, you're in for some major hassles.

Road Rules & Hazards

Thais drive on the left-hand side of the road (most of the time!). Other than that, just about anything goes, in spite of road signs and speed limits.

The main rule to be aware of is that right of way goes to the bigger vehicle; this is not what it says in the Thai traffic law, but it's the reality. Maximum speed limits are 50km/h on urban roads and 80km/h to 100km/h on most highways – but on any given stretch of highway you'll see various vehicles travelling as slowly as 30km/h and as fast as 150km/h.

Road Safety

Thailand rates as one of the most dangerous places to be on the road, according to a recent World Health Organization report.

Fatal bus crashes make headlines, but more than 80% of vehicle accidents in Thailand involve motorcycles. Less than half of the motorcyclists in the country wear helmets and many tourists are injured riding motorcycles because they don't know how to handle the vehicles and are unfamiliar with local driving conventions.

If you are a novice motorcyclist, familiarise yourself with the vehicle in an uncongested area of town and stick to the smaller 100cc automatic bikes. Drive slowly, especially when roads are slick or when there is loose gravel. Remember to distribute weight as evenly as possible across the frame of the bike to improve handling. And don't expect that other vehicles will look out for you. Motorcycles are low on the traffic totem pole.

Săhm·lór & Túk-túk

Săhm·lór are three-wheeled pedicabs that are typically found in small towns where traffic is light and old-fashioned ways persist.

The modern era's version of the human-powered *săhm·lór* is the motorised túk-túk. They're small utility vehicles, powered by screaming engines (usually LPG-powered) with a lot of flash and sparkle.

With either form of transport the fare must be established by bargaining before departure. In tourist centres, túk-túk drivers often overcharge foreigners, so have a sense of how much the fare should be before soliciting a ride. Hotel staff may be able to provide reasonable fare suggestions.

Local Transport

City Bus & Sŏrng·tăa·ou

The etiquette for riding public buses is to wait at a bus stop and hail the vehicle by waving your hand palm-side downward. You typically pay the fare once you've taken a seat or, in some cases, when you disembark.

Elsewhere, public transport is provided by *sŏrng·tăa·ou* (a small pick-up truck outfitted with two facing rows of benches for passengers). They sometimes operate on fixed routes, just like buses, but they may also run a share-taxi service where they pick up passengers going in the same general direction. In tourist centres, *sŏrng·tăa·ou* can be chartered just like a regular taxi, but you'll need to negotiate the fare beforehand. You can usually hail a *sŏrng·tăa·ou* anywhere along its route and pay the fare when you disembark.

Mass Transit

Bangkok is the only city in Thailand to have an above-ground (BTS) and under-ground light-rail (MRT) public transport system.

Motorcycle Taxi

Many cities in Thailand have *mor·đeu·sai ráp jâhng* (100cc to 125cc motorcycles) that can be hired, with a driver, for short distances.

In most cities, you'll find motorcycle taxis clustered near street intersections. Usually they wear numbered jerseys. Fares tend to run from 10B to 50B, depending on distance and you'll need to establish the price beforehand.

Taxi

Bangkok has the most formal system of metered taxis. In other cities, a taxi can be a private vehicle with negotiable rates and there are a variety of shared taxis in which the fare is split among a group of passengers.

Tours

Many operators around the world can arrange guided tours of Thailand.

Asian Trails (www.asiantrails.info) Tour operator that runs programs for overseas brokers; trips include a mix of on- and off-the-beaten-path destinations.

Hands Up Holidays (www.handsupholidays.com) Volunteer tourism and village sightseeing programs.

Intrepid Travel (www.intrepidtravel.com) Specialises in small-group travel geared towards young people.

Spice Roads (www.spiceroads.com) Variety of regional cycling programs.

Tours with Kasma Loha-Unchit (www.thaifoodandtravel.com) Thai cookbook author offers personalised 'cultural immersion' tours of Thailand.

Bicycle Travel

For travelling just about anywhere outside Bangkok, bicycles are an ideal form of local transport – cheap, nonpolluting and slow moving enough to allow travellers to see everything. Bicycles can be hired from guesthouses for as little as 50B per day, though they aren't always high-quality.

🚆 Train

Thailand's train system connects the four corners of the country and is most convenient as an alternative to buses for the long journey north to Chiang Mai or south to Surat Thani.

The 4500km rail network is operated by the **State Railway of Thailand** (SRT; 📞1690; www.railway.co.th) and covers four main lines: the northern, southern, northeastern and eastern lines. All long-distance trains originate from Bangkok's Hualamphong station.

Classes

The SRT operates passenger trains in three classes – 1st, 2nd and 3rd – but each class varies considerably depending on whether you're on an ordinary, rapid or express train.

First Class – Private cabins define the 1st-class carriages, which are available only on rapid, express and special-express trains.

Second Class – The seating arrangements in a 2nd-class, non-sleeper carriage are similar to those on a bus, with pairs of padded seats, usually recliners, all facing towards the front of the train. On 2nd-class sleeper cars, pairs of seats face one another and convert into two fold-down berths. The lower berth has more headroom than the upper berth and this is reflected in a higher fare. Children are always assigned a lower berth. Second-class carriages are found only on rapid and express trains. There are air-con and fan 2nd-class carriages.

Third Class – A typical 3rd-class carriage consists of two rows of bench seats divided into facing pairs. Each bench seat is designed to seat two or three passengers, but on a crowded rural line nobody seems to care. Express trains do not carry 3rd-class carriages at all.

Costs

Fares are determined on a base price with surcharges added for distance, class and train type (special express, express, rapid, ordinary). Extra charges are added if the carriage has air-con and for sleeping berths (either upper or lower).

Reservations

Advance bookings can be made from one to 60 days before your intended date of departure. You can make bookings in person from any train station. Train tickets can also be purchased at travel agencies, which usually add a service charge to the ticket price. If you are planning long-distance train travel from outside the country, you should email SRT (passenger-ser@railway.co.th) at least two weeks before your journey. You will receive an email confirming the booking. Pick up and pay for tickets an hour before leaving at the scheduled departure train station.

It is advisable to make advanced bookings for long-distance sleeper trains between Bangkok and Chiang Mai or from Bangkok to Surat Thani as seats fill up quickly.

Partial refunds on tickets are available depending on the number of days prior to your departure you arrange for a cancellation. These arrangements can be handled at the train station booking office.

Language

There are different ways of writing Thai in the Roman alphabet – we have chosen one method below. The hyphens indicate syllable breaks within words, and some syllables are further divided with a dot to help you pronounce them. Thai is a tonal language – the accent marks on vowels represent these low, mid, falling, high and rising tones.

Note that after every sentence, men add the polite particle *káp*, and women *ká*.

To enhance your trip with a phrasebook, visit **lonelyplanet.com**. Lonely Planet iPhone phrasebooks are available through the Apple App store.

Basics

Hello.
สวัสดี   sà-wàt-dee
How are you?
สบายดีไหม   sà-bai dee măi
I'm fine.
สบายดีครับ/ค่า   sà·bai dee kráp/kâ (m/f)
Excuse me.
ขออภัย   kŏr à-pai
Yes./No.
ใช่/ไม่   châi/mâi
Thank you.
ขอบคุณ   kòrp kun
You're welcome.
ยินดี   yin dee
Do you speak English?
คุณพูดภาษา   kun pôot pah-săh
อังกฤษได้ไหม   ang-grìt dâi măi
I don't understand.
ผม/ดิฉันไม่เข้าใจ   pŏm/dì-chăn mâi kôw jai (m/f)
How much is this?
เท่าไร   tôw-rai
Can you lower the price?
ลดราคาได้ไหม   lót rah-kah dâi măi

Accommodation

Where's a hotel?
โรงแรมอยู่ที่ไหน   rohng raam yòo têe năi
Do you have a single/double room?
มีห้องเดี่ยว/   mee hôrng dèe·o/
เตียงคู่ไหม   đee·ang kôo măi

Eating & Drinking

I'd like (the menu), please.
ขอ (ว เยการ   kŏr (rai gahn
อาหาร) หน่อย   ah-hăhn) nòy
What would you recommend?
คุณแนะนำอะไรบ้าง   kun náa-nam à-rai bâhng
That was delicious.
อร่อยมาก   à-ròy mâhk
Cheers!
ไชโย   chai-yoh
Please bring the bill/check.
ขอบิลหน่อย   kŏr bin nòy
I don't eat ...
ผม/ดิฉัน ไม่กิน ...   pŏm/dì-chăn mâi gin . . .
(m/f)

eggs	ไข่	kài
fish	ปลา	ฺblah
nuts	ถั่ว	tòo·a
red meat	เนื้อแดง	néu·a daang

Emergencies

I'm ill.
ผม/ดิฉันป่วย   pŏm/dì-chăn ฺboo·ay
(m/f)
Help!
ช่วยด้วย   chôo·ay dôo·ay
Call a doctor!
เรียกหมอหน่อย   rêe·ak mŏr nòy
Call the police!
เรียกตำรวจหน่อย   rêe·ak đam-ròo·at nòy
Where are the toilets?
ห้องน้ำอยู่ที่ไหน   hôrng nám yòo têe năi

Directions

Where's (a market/restaurant)?
(ตลาดร้านอาหาร)   (đà-làht/ráhn ah-hăhn)
อยู่ที่ไหน   yòo têe năi
What's the address?
ที่อยู่คืออะไร   têe yòo keu à-rai
Could you please write it down?
เขียนลงให้ได้ไหม   kĕe·an long hâi dâi măi
Can you show me (on the map)?
ให้ดู (ในแผนที่)   hâi doo (nai păan têe)
ได้ไหม   dâi măi

Behind the Scenes

Our Readers

Many thanks to the travellers who used the last edition and wrote to us with helpful hints, useful advice and interesting anecdotes: Andrew Singer, Emmy Pang, Emmy Toonen, Gabriela Tisnado, Piotr Senator

Author Thanks

China Williams

Many thanks to my good buddy Nong, the gals at TJR, Candyhome nursery school, Pong at Libernard Café, Andrew Bond, Pim of CityLife, Aidan from Chiang Mai Mountain Bikes and Pat of Patara Elephant Farm. In Bangkok, many thanks to Ruengsang, Mai, Jane, Kanchana and Austin. Thanks to Matt and Felix for taking care of each other and to Mandy for taking care of them. Applause to the co-authors, Kirsten and the LP production staff.

Acknowledgments

Climate map data adapted from Peel MC, Finlayson BL & McMahon TA (2007) 'Updated World Map of the Köppen-Geiger Climate Classification', Hydrology and Earth System Sciences, 11, 1633-44.

Illustrations pp62-3 and pp68-9 by Michael Weldon.

Cover photographs: Front: Bang Pa In Palace, Ayuthaya Province, Jean-Pierre Lescourret/Corbis ©; Back: Railay, Krabi Province, Ingolf Pompe/Alamy ©

This Book

This 3rd edition of Lonely Planet's *Discover Thailand* guidebook was coordinated by China Williams, and researched and written by Mark Beales, Tim Bewer, Celeste Brash, Austin Bush, David Eimer and Adam Skolnick. This guidebook was commissioned in Lonely Planet's Melbourne office and produced by the following:

Commissioning Editors Ilaria Walker, Glenn van der Knijff

Coordinating Editors Kirsten Rawlings, Luna Soo

Senior Cartographer Diana Von Holdt

Book Designer Katherine Marsh

Senior Editor Karyn Noble

Assisting Editors Bruce Evans, Elizabeth Jones

Assisting Cartographer Rachel Imeson

Assisting Book Designers Lauren Egan, Jessica Rose, Wendy Wright

Cover Researcher Naomi Parker

Language Content Branislava Vladisavljevic

Thanks to Anita Banh, Sasha Baskett, Elin Berglund, Penny Cordner, Ryan Evans, Larissa Frost, Genesys India, Jouve India, Virginia Moreno, Wayne Murphy, Lorna Parkes, Martine Power, Angela Tinson

Index

INDEX S-Z

How to Use This Book

These symbols give you the vital information for each listing:

☏	Telephone Numbers	🛜	Wi-Fi Access	🚌	Bus
⊙	Opening Hours	🏊	Swimming Pool	🚢	Ferry
Ⓟ	Parking	🥗	Vegetarian Selection	Ⓜ	Metro
⊖	Nonsmoking	ⓐ	English-Language Menu	Ⓢ	Subway
❄	Air-Conditioning	👪	Family-Friendly	⊖	London Tube
@	Internet Access	🐾	Pet-Friendly	🚋	Tram

Look out for these icons:

FREE No payment required

🌿 A green or sustainable option

Our authors have nominated these places as demonstrating a strong commitment to sustainability – for example by supporting local communities and producers, operating in an environmentally friendly way, or supporting conservation projects.

All reviews are ordered in our authors' preference, starting with their most preferred option. Additionally:

Sights are arranged in the geographic order that we suggest you visit them, and within this order, by author preference.

Eating and Sleeping reviews are ordered by price range (budget, mid-range, top end) and within these ranges, by author preference.

Map Legend

Sights
- 🏖 Beach
- Buddhist
- 🏰 Castle
- ✝ Christian
- 🕉 Hindu
- ☪ Islamic
- ✡ Jewish
- ❶ Monument
- 🏛 Museum/Gallery
- Ruin
- Winery/Vineyard
- 🐾 Zoo
- ⊙ Other Sight

Activities, Courses & Tours
- Diving/Snorkelling
- Canoeing/Kayaking
- Skiing
- Surfing
- Swimming/Pool
- Walking
- Windsurfing
- Other Activity/ Course/Tour

Sleeping
- Sleeping
- Camping

Eating
- ⊗ Eating

Drinking
- Drinking
- Cafe

Entertainment
- Entertainment

Shopping
- Shopping

Information
- 🏦 Bank
- Embassy/ Consulate
- ✚ Hospital/Medical
- @ Internet
- Police
- Post Office
- Telephone
- Toilet
- Tourist Information
- ● Other Information

Transport
- ✈ Airport
- Border Crossing
- 🚌 Bus
- Cable Car/ Funicular
- Cycling
- Ferry
- Monorail
- Ⓟ Parking
- Petrol Station
- Taxi
- Train/Railway
- Tram
- Underground Train Station
- ● Other Transport

Routes
- Tollway
- Freeway
- Primary
- Secondary
- Tertiary
- Lane
- Unsealed Road
- Plaza/Mall
- Steps
- Tunnel
- Pedestrian Overpass
- Walking Tour
- Walking Tour Detour
- Path

Geographic
- Hut/Shelter
- Lighthouse
- Lookout
- ▲ Mountain/Volcano
- Oasis
- Park
-)(Pass
- Picnic Area
- Waterfall

Population
- Capital (National)
- ◉ Capital (State/Province)
- ● City/Large Town
- ○ Town/Village

Boundaries
- – – – International
- – – – State/Province
- – – Disputed
- – – Regional/Suburb
- Marine Park
- Cliff
- Wall

Hydrography
- River/Creek
- Intermittent River
- Swamp/Mangrove
- Reef
- Canal
- Water
- Dry/Salt/ Intermittent Lake
- Glacier

Areas
- Beach/Desert
- Cemetery (Christian)
- Cemetery (Other)
- Park/Forest
- Sportsground
- Sight (Building)
- Top Sight (Building)

AUSTIN BUSH

Bangkok, Chiang Rai & Northern Thailand A native of Oregon, Austin came to Thailand in 1999 as part of a language study programme hosted by Chiang Mai University. The lure of city life, employment and spicy food eventually led Austin to Bangkok. City life, employment and spicy food have managed to keep him there since. Austin is a writer and photographer who often focuses on food. Samples of his work can be seen at www.austinbushphotography.com.

DAVID EIMER

Bangkok Getaways, Ko Samui & the Gulf Coast A decade of visiting Thailand in search of beaches and fine food prompted David to relocate to Bangkok in 2012. Since then, his work as a journalist for a variety of newspapers and magazines has taken him from the far south of Thailand to its northernmost extremities, with many stops in between. Originally from London, David spent seven years living in Beijing, and another five in LA, prior to moving to Bangkok. He has contributed to 11 Lonely Planet books.

ADAM SKOLNICK

Phuket & the Andaman Coast Adam Skolnick writes about travel, culture, health, sports, human rights and the environment for Lonely Planet, *Outside*, *Travel & Leisure*, Salon.com, BBC.com and ESPN.com. He has co-authored more than 20 Lonely Planet guidebooks, and on this research trip he drove more than 3000 kilometres and hopped on more than 50 long-tails. His debut novel, *Middle of Somewhere*, is set to be published in 2014. You can read more of his work at www.adamskolnick.com. Find him on Twitter and Instagram (@adamskolnick).

Our Story

A beat-up old car, a few dollars in the pocket and a sense of adventure. In 1972 that's all Tony and Maureen Wheeler needed for the trip of a lifetime – across Europe and Asia overland to Australia. It took several months, and at the end – broke but inspired – they sat at their kitchen table writing and stapling together their first travel guide, *Across Asia on the Cheap*. Within a week they'd sold 1500 copies. Lonely Planet was born.

Today, Lonely Planet has offices in Franklin, London, Melbourne, Oakland, Beijing and Delhi, with more than 600 staff and writers. We share Tony's belief that 'a great guidebook should do three things: inform, educate and amuse'.

Our Writers

CHINA WILLIAMS

Coordinating Author, Chiang Mai Every two years, China Williams leaves her quiet suburban life for a guidebook deployment to Thailand. This time she brought along her one-year-old daughter as her research assistant and to boost her cuteness factor. It worked; the Thais were smitten. China first came to Thailand in 1997 to teach English in Surin. Since then she has shuttled across the Pacific for over a decade for various Thailand and Southeast Asia titles. Thailand gets richer and happier with every visit. China lives in Catonsville, Maryland (USA) with her husband, Matt, son, Felix, and daughter, Phoebe.

MARK BEALES

Bangkok Getaways After working as a journalist for 13 years, Mark swapped the chilly shores of England for the sunnier coasts of Thailand. Since 2004 he has lived in Thailand, where he has written several books for Lonely Planet, tried his hand at being a TV presenter and is currently Head of English at an international school in Rayong. Highlights on this trip included triumphing in a chilli-eating competition with voluntary workers in Sangkhlaburi. For more on Mark's work, visit www.markbeales.com.

TIM BEWER

Bangkok Getaways While growing up, Tim didn't travel much except for the obligatory pilgrimage to Disney World and an annual summer week at the lake. He's spent most of his adult life making up for this, and has since visited more than 80 countries, including most in Southeast Asia. After university he worked briefly as a legislative assistant before quitting capitol life to backpack around West Africa. It was during this trip that the idea of becoming a freelance travel writer and photographer was hatched, and he's been at it ever since. He has lived in Khon Kaen, Thailand, since 2007.

CELESTE BRASH

Ko Samui & the Gulf Coast Celeste first arrived in Thailand as a student of Thai language, history and culture at Chiang Mai University. She's come back countless times since and has run the gamut from wild nights on Ko Pha-Ngan to weeks of silence at a Buddhist wát. Her writing has appeared in publications ranging from *Islands* magazine to newspapers and anthologies. She's contributed to around 50 Lonely Planet guides but her heart is irrevocably stuck on *Southeast Asia*. When not in exotic places, she and her family live in Portland, Oregon. Find her on the web at www.celestebrash.com.

 More Writers ....

Published by Lonely Planet Publications Pty Ltd
ABN 36 005 607 983
3rd edition – September 2014
ISBN 978 1 74220 574 8
© Lonely Planet 2014   Photographs © as indicated 2014
10 9 8 7 6 5 4 3 2 1
Printed in China